R

# ARE THERE ALTERNATIVES?

# SOCIALIST REGISTER 1996

Edited by LEO PANITCH

D0542653

MERLIN PRESS LONDON
MONTHLY REVIEW PRESS NEW YORK
FERNWOOD PUBLISHING HALIFAX

Riverside Community College
Library
4800 Magnolia Avenue
Riverside, CA 92506
DEC '01

HX 15 .S593 1996

Socialist register (London, England)

Are there alternatives?

in 1996
ress Ltd
Road

R

© The Merlin Press 1996

Published in the US by:
Monthly Review Press
122 West 27 Street
New York
NY 10001

Published in Canada by:
Fernwood Publishing Co.
P.O. Box 9409
Station A
Halifax
Nova Scotia
B3K 5S3

*British Library Cataloguing in Publication Data*

The Socialist Register. — 1996
1. Socialism — 1996
I. Panitch, Leo
355'.005

ISBN 0-85036-455-8 (UK)
ISBN 0-85316-984-3 (US)

Typesetting by
Computerset, Harmondsworth, Middlesex

Printed in Finland by WSOY

# TABLE OF CONTENTS

# PREFACE

The ideological and material sweep encompassed by the proud capitalist assertion, 'There Is No Alternative', has been the clearest marker in our time of the contemporary crisis of socialism. How to take full measure of the power of 'TINA' (which really means treating seriously what it tells us about global capitalist economic, political and cultural power in the late 20th century) while at the same time not succumbing to the 'end of history' claim implicit within it (which means not becoming complicit with the extension of the present conjuncture into the foreseeable future) is the central political challenge of our time.

The acuteness of this challenge is compounded by the extent to which so many of those who are critical of neo-liberalism nevertheless have come to accept that any immediate alternatives to it have to be accomodated to the dynamics of the global capitalist order. Yet the material evidence continues to pile up of the growing incompatibility between such limited alternatives and real advances toward substantive democracy and social justice. In our historical context, thinking beyond TINA, rather than reconciling ourselves to it, means thinking in terms of creating the space that presently does not exist for new socialist alternatives. It means, in the wake of the failures of Communism and Social Democratic gradualism as the main 20th century expressions of socialist politics, not confining ourselves to the 'end of history' notion that socialist politics was once and for all defined within their historical ambit. It means learning from and transcending their severe limitations. But it first of all means reestablishing the relevance of a politics which would seek to put a notion of democratic and egalitarian alternatives to today's capitalism back on the political agenda, and actively building towards developing popular and institutional capacities to engage in struggles directed at achieving those goals. As Edward Thompson once put it: 'The art of the possible can only be restrained from engrossing the whole universe if the impossible can find ways of breaking back into politics, again and again.'

In posing the sober question 'Are There Alternatives?' as its theme, this 32nd issue of *The Socialist Register* seeks to take up this challenge. It does so not by canvassing the many new 'models' of (market, participatory or other) socialism which have been advanced in recent years (this will be the focus of a later volume), but by looking at alternatives that arise out of the present conjuncture. We begin in Britain where the almost two decade long sweep of Conservative rule - inaugurated by Mrs. Thatcher's stern proclamation of 'There Is No Alternative' - seems to have finally run its course. Colin Leys' detailed and acute investigation of Tony Blair's 'modernisation' of the Labour Party, through an elite centralism which has suppressed the anti-capitalist ethos of the party, reveals how Labour now runs the risk 'of achieving office - though not real power - on the basis of "realistically" accepting the market just as its ultimate unacceptability, as the motor and arbiter of social life, is once again clear.'

We follow with Patrick Bond and Mzwanele Mayekiso's sobering account of the 'engagement' with neo-liberalism that characterises South Africa's democratic transition under Mandela. This account is made all the more poignant by the authors' setting of it in a remarkably wide-ranging survey of similar constraints and disappointments encountered elsewhere around the globe. But their essay also powerfully demonstrates that South Africa's own 'most compelling lessons for the international left' lies in the 'building and maintaining [of] a class conscious civil-society in oppressed communities' as the base for a 'people-centred development'.

The search for a 'progressive competitive' strategy of engagement with neo-liberal globalisation has in fact become the leitmotif of contemporary social democracy, and it is a sad but telling sign of the limits of this approach that the emulation of Japanese productivism has displaced that of Swedish corporatism as a model. Paul Burkett and Martin Hart-Landsberg's demonstration of the empirical weakness and strategic confusion entailed in the attempt to use Japan as a progressive model concentrates on such usages on the American left, but their critique can readily be applied to such positive usage of Japan made elsewhere (for instance, in Britain, by Will Hutton's recent best-selling book, *The State We're In*). The Australian Labor Governments since 1983 have been the longest standing practictioners of the progressive competitiveness strategy, as well as highly influential exponents of this strategy internationally. John Wiseman's careful analysis of the Australian experience, building directly on the critique of progressive competitiveness offered in earlier volumes of the *Socialist Register*, is an especially useful contribution for demonstrating its severe limitations as a model for the left.

For all its insistent 'realism', such a strategy is not only ethically questionable from a socialist perspective, it is also in fact unrealistic. Jim Crotty and Gerald Epstein, in an important contribution to the development of practical alternative strategies amidst globalisation, demonstrate that the power of financial capital today is such that only a set of policies to control the international flow of money can provide the leverage to enhance the structural power of labour and secure full employment and greater income and wealth equality. Surveying the role of capital controls in the post-war era and identifying the types of controls that are practicable today, they reveal that the real impediments to their implementation are not technical but political. Enhancing the structural power of labour will also urgently require addressing, as Anna Pollert contends, the rise of 'non-standard' and 'poor' work as well as contemporary management strategies for disempowering trade unions. Focusing particularly on the form this has taken in the public service sector in Britain, she also offers an insightful account of various unions' attempts to confront this situation; and she demonstrates the vital importance of increasing the power of women in unions, defending broad-based bargaining and developing new forms of democratic participation in order effectively to change union cultures towards prioritizing organising the unorganised.

There is considerable irony in the fact that alongside the antirevolutionary slogan of TINA, fin de siecle capitalist culture is, at the same time, as Reg Whitaker notes, 'awash with prophecies of revolution . . . through the miraculous agency of that deus ex machina, technology.' Whitaker offers a stunning critique of the 'cybernauts' of the 'information revolution'. The networked computer may be constitutive of a new form of capitalism, he contends, a crucial element in a 'surveillance society' organized for competitive success. But if 'real change is to come about, it will have to be because people make it happen, by learning to use the new technologies against their owners . . .', and that will have to be accomplished by real communities, not virtual ones. Picking up the theme of the 'surveillance society', Peter Gill shows that the success of Thatcherism in appropriating popular fears amidst capitalist restructuring was used to reinforce the security apparatuses of the state in the post-Cold War era. Gill issues a strong challenge - and useful guidance - to a Labour Party, traditionally timid in this area, to undertake a programme of reform 'by asserting democratic control over domestic security apparatuses whose autonomy has been deployed on behalf of predominantly right wing causes.'

A refreshingly original example of how to broaden thinking about alternatives out of the events that define the present conjuncture is offered by Varda Burstyn. Linking the O.J. Simpson trial to the cultural practices that make sports figures 'gods in the popular pantheon', she shows the complicity of sport in the violent actions of such athletes as well as the broader role of mass sport as a central institution for 'the regeneration of anti-social and, by direct extension, anti-socialist values in contemporary society.' Renewing hope in the possibility of socialist alternatives at the end of a century of 'atrocious human cruelty', Norman Geras reminds us, must also mean confronting seriously the limits to the perfectibility of human society. Taking up Ralph Miliband's confrontation with this very question in *Socialism for a Sceptical Age*, Geras challenges traditional socialist assumptions in arriving at the conclusion that the threat of evil must be accepted as a 'permanent human possibility.' He concludes that human progress must be undertood not as some linear advance to a utopian end-point, but as an ongoing struggle which involves 'setting limits around the more harmful and menacing types of human potentiality.'

We return in our final essays to the difficult questions posed in the opening essays of the volume regarding how to fashion appropriate political vehicles for advancing this ongoing struggle for socialist alternatives. Such vehicles will have to be capable of doing more than making 'progressive competitiveness' temporarily electorally viable; yet they must still be capable of connecting with the majority of people, convincing them of the relevance of radical socialist ideas and engaging them in an open-ended process of defining, and building the political capacity to achieve, socialist alternatives. Carlos Vilas's comprehensive survey of the Latin American left reveals a widespread acceptance among parties and intellectuals of a conventional form of electoralism that rules out such a creative search for alternatives. At the same time, the impact of Chiapas on the left in Mexico, he argues, brings into clear focus the equally widespread tension between social movements and party political strategies in the context of a 'destructuring of the working classes and a new plurality of social actors'. Revealing by no means dissimilar tensions, albeit in the very different context of the immediate political situation in Britain, Barry Winter and Hilary Wainwright engage in a spirited and enlightening debate (taking off from last year's *Socialist Register*) on the advisability of still working within the Labour Party, as opposed to finally 'moving on'. Their exchange raises crucial issues concerning how to assess the appropriateness of current conditions for building new socialist parties.

Among our contributors, Colin Leys, for many years Professor of Political at Queen's University in Canada, is now researching and writing in London. Patrick Bond recently moved from the faculty of the Johns Hopkins School of Public Health in Baltimore to the National Institute for Economic Policy in Johannesburg; and Mzwanele Mayekiso is the International Representative of the South African National Civic Organization while at the Pratt Institute in New York studying urban planning. Paul Burkett and Martin Hart-Landsberg both teach economics, the former at Indiana State University in Terre Haute, the latter at Lewis & Clark College in Portland, Oregon; and John Wiseman teaches in the Department of Social Work at the Royal Melbourne Institute of Technology. James Crotty and Gerald Epstein both are in the Economics Department of the University of Massachusetts at Amherst; and Anna Pollert is in the Industrial Relations Research Unit at the University of Warwick. Reg Whitaker is Professor of Political Science at York University, Toronto; and Peter Gill is Reader in Politics and Security at Liverpool John Moors University. Varda Burstyn is an independent writer and consultant who lives in Toronto. Norman Geras is Professor of Government at Manchester University; and Carlos Vilas is in the Centro de Investigaciones Interdisciplinarias en Humanidades of the Universidad Nacional Autonoma de Mexico. Barry Winter, former Secretary of Independent Labour Publications (successor to the Independent Labour Party), teaches at Leeds Metropolitan University and the Open University; and Hilary Wainwright is the editor of *Red Pepper* magazine and Research Fellow at Manchester University's Centre for International Labour Studies.

This issue is the first produced under *The Socialist Register*'s new editorial structure. Two groups of contributing editors have been established, centered in Toronto and Manchester, who are committed not just to sustaining the role the *Register* has played for over three decades as an international locus of independent socialist thinking, debate and inquiry through its annual volume of essays, but to playing an active part, through the *Register*, in stimulating a new generation of intellectuals internationally to engage themselves in developing and advancing the ideas, analyses and strategies necessary to the project of renewing socialism at the turn of the millenium. In furthering the *Register*'s commitment to this end, corresponding editors in diverse location will work with the Manchester and Toronto collectives; and in the course of the past year, George Ross (Brandeis University, Boston), Elmar Altvater (Free University, Berlin), Michalis Spourdalakis (University of Athens) and Gerard Greenfield (Asia Monitor Research Center, Hong Kong) have joined us in that capacity.

In this context it is perhaps more necessary than ever to renew a longstanding *Register* tradition and remind our readers that neither our contributors nor the editors necessarily agree with with everything that appears in the following pages. That said, I want to thank all our contributors and editors for the work they put into this volume; and this especially applies to Paul Cammack, coordinator of the Manchester collective, for his creative planning of future volumes as well as for his hard work on this one. We have worked hard to finally put the *Register*, beginning with this volume, on a schedule that will see to its publication near the beginning of each calendar year. Thanks also to Mike Gonzalez for his translation of Carlos Vilas's essay. For the very helpful role that Martin Eve and Julie Millard of Merlin Press have played in making this possible, and for their overall support and dedication in *The Socialist Register*'s transition from the late Ralph Miliband's primary stewardship, I am particularly grateful.

January 1996 L.P.

The Socialist Register has established a 'listserv', or electronic mail discussion forum, to facilitate the exchange of ideas between readers, contributors, and the editorial board. Submission of reasoned critique, rejoinders, and other commentary are welcome from all who subscribe to this forum, with each contribution distributed to the whole membership. (The membership list itself will not be distributed.) To join the listserv, send a message containing your name and e-mail address to:
**socialist-register@yorku.ca**

# THE BRITISH LABOUR PARTY'S TRANSITION FROM SOCIALISM TO CAPITALISM

Colin Leys

> . . .each age, even each decade, has its little cant word coiled up inside real discourse like a tiny grub in the middle of an apple. Each age, even each decade, is overly impressed for a little while by half-way bright youngish men on the make who adeptly manipulate the current terminology at precisely the right moment to make precisely the right impression on those who are a little older, a little less intelligent and considerably less alert.[1]

Dennis Potter wrote these words in 1993, about the way the BBC was being denatured and commercialised in the name of 'management'. In the case of the Labour Party, the 'little cant word' is 'modernisation' (although a strong dose of 'management' comes with it).[2] In its name, a new kind of party, more and more removed from what is left of the labour movement and from its active membership in the constituencies, is being constructed. And the means used to accomplish this – an unprecedented concentration of power in the hands of the party leader – has also elevated him in relation to back-bench Labour MPs, and perhaps even, to a greater extent than in the past, his Shadow Cabinet colleagues.

The aim has been to allow the leader to determine party policy with at most the nominal approval of the party outside parliament, i.e. both its trade union wing and its constituency activists – and to be seen by the media to do so. But the process also means that for the first time in the party's history the leader is also almost completely free from the influence of the party's traditional ethos – the mix of values and practices, evolved over some 150 years of collective political effort, which has hitherto defined the priorities and principles underlying party policy.

By no means everything in this ethos was admirable – as Henry Drucker pointed out in 1979, it contained a great deal that was archaic, anti-intellectual, and so on;[3] but it also comprised the most egalitarian, humanistic, unselfish, internationalist and brave elements of progressive British culture. Previous party leaders were influenced by this ethos in different ways and to different degrees: but none has been as untouched by it as Tony Blair, either before he became leader in July 1994 or since.[4] Not only is he not someone formed by the party's ethos, or much constrained by it in his day to day work as party leader; in the Leader's Office (i.e. the official parliamentary office of the Leader of the Opposition), and in his most intimate circle of political friends, he operates in a milieu based on a different ethos, an ethos of professional politics based on higher education, management skills, and the culture of the communications industry. Some of the chief exponents of this ethos more or less openly despise that of the old labour movement, and while they may, like Blair, sometimes call themselves socialists, they no longer think of socialism as an alternative social and economic system to capitalism.

The Labour Party was, to be sure, not formed as a political party dedicated to replacing capitalism with socialism, but as a parliamentary voice for wage workers. But electoral success led to the evolution of the LRC into a mass political party which by 1944, when the 1930s depression had been followed by the social mobilisation of the second world war, led it to adopt and then implement a programme of reforms which in 1945 its leaders were happy to call socialist: including a commitment to full employment, the nationalisation of 20 percent of the economy, and the establishment of a comprehensive system of state-provided social security, health and other social services.

By 1995 all this had been abandoned as party policy, and the word 'socialism' now figured in party literature and the leader's speeches rather rarely, and always in carefully circumscribed language, usually emphasising the degree to which it is *not* socialism as it used to be understood. Socialism, for Blair in particular, refers to an ethical ideal: and for him, 'modernising' Labour policy means dropping all previous ideas about the *application* of that ideal; i.e., not just 'old Labour' ideas about public ownership or the welfare state, but also, if not even more so, all the 'new left's' thinking and practice about participative democracy in the 1970s.

In this discourse, the one thing that is clearly modern is global capitalism; fundamentally, 'modernisation' means adapting to it. As a highly public token of this, soon after his election as leader Blair set himself the task of getting rid of the party's commitment to the principle of common ownership of the means of production, embodied in Clause Four of the party constitution, and replacing it with a portmanteau commitment to a range of values (a dynamic economy, a just society, an open democracy and a healthy environment) – including, crucially for the media, an endorsement of 'the enterprise of the market and the rigour of competition' and 'a thriving private sector'.[5] After a two-month campaign of regional meetings with Labour Party members Blair secured a two-thirds majority for this change at a special party conference in April 1995. In the vote, 90 percent of the constituency parties' votes were cast in favour of the change, compared with only 54 percent of the trade union votes (though given that all that was needed was to drop a ballot paper in the letter box the constituency 'turnout' – or 'response rate' – was notably low); this reversal in the balance of forces – the constituency vote having previously been an activists' vote, and on the whole more left-leaning than the unions' – is a key measure of the change that has occurred.

Meantime the leadership also dissociated itself from almost any previous policy that the media had chosen to dub 'socialist': repudiating, for the future, increased taxation (even though Britain had become distinctly under-taxed by the standards of other European countries), all state 'intervention' in the economy, and the restoration of trade union rights (not to mention any idea of requiring companies to be as internally democratic as unions); even disavowing any idea of reducing the tax privileges of private schools.

### *The transition under Kinnock, 1983–1992*

The origins of this transformation lie in the party's divided response to the crisis of British social democracy in the 1970s, when the country's industrial weaknesses caught up with it. Chronic balance of payments difficulties forced a choice between two strategies: deflating the economy, allowing unemployment to rise, letting average real wages fall and hoping that private investment would restore competitiveness; or extending public control and forcing the pace through public investment. A majority of party activists, and the leadership of some of the biggest unions affiliated to the party, favoured the second option, while the Labour government in office from 1974 to 1979 pursued, in effect, the first. The result was a successful internal party campaign, whose most prominent champion was the former Industry minister Tony Benn, to change the party's constitution so as to make the leader and the Parliamentary Labour Party (PLP) more responsive to the views of the party outside parliament. Leaders were in future to be chosen by an electoral college drawn from the unions and constituency parties as well as the PLP; sitting Labour MPs had to submit themselves for reselection as candidates by their constituency parties before elections; and election manifestos had to be agreed between the Shadow Cabinet and the party's National Executive Committee (NEC). These changes were bitterly resisted and led to (or were the pretext for) the defection in 1981–82 of 27 MPs to form a new party, the Social Democratic Party. When Labour then proceeded to lose the 1983 election disastrously, the predominantly right-wing leadership and PLP blamed, not the defectors, but those who had spearheaded the constitutional changes, and who had also championed a strengthened public sector and other left-inclined policies which, they said, the result showed that voters did not want.

In reality, Labour's 1983 campaign was dominated by the right wing of the leadership, who conducted all the media events while the left kept a low profile. And there are several important alternative explanations for the defeat, from the continuing opinion-poll effect of the 'Falklands factor' in favour of Mrs Thatcher, to Michael Foot's vacillating and uninspiring leadership, the accelerating consumer boom (for those in work) led by Reagan's spending programmes, and so on. But faced by a tabloid press plumbing new depths of malevolence against the left, the right, supported by the unions, decided to renounce it.

The party leader, Michael Foot, resigned immediately after the election, and the new leadership electoral college overwhelmingly endorsed the so-called 'dream ticket' candidatures of Neil Kinnock as leader and Roy Hattersley as deputy.[6] Kinnock, although perceived as a 'soft' (i.e. anti-Benn) left-winger, responded to the party's predicament by establishing an altogether novel degree of personal control over it. Several circumstances allowed him to do this. First, the severity of the 1983 defeat created a mood of 'recovery at any price' in most sectors of the party. Second, 'coming from the left, he [Kinnock] did not alienate the constituency parties [which were still largely Bennite in outlook] in the way Wilson and Callaghan had'.[7] Third, Kinnock had been elected as leader by overwhelming majorities in all three sections of the new electoral college and so enjoyed a new kind of legitimacy. Fourth, the Office of the Leader of the Opposition now disposed of far more resources than ever before, thanks to a new funding policy introduced by Edward Short as Leader of the House of Commons in 1974. By 1983 the Labour front bench had at its disposal £440,000, and by 1988, £839,000, for research and assistance; and the trade unions even added a further £100,000 per annum for the free use of the Leader.[8]

Kinnock immediately set about removing effective policy-making control from where the party constitution appeared to locate it, i.e. in the National Executive Committee (NEC) and the annual party Conference. As seen by Seyd and Whiteley, academic observers not unsympathetic to Kinnock, the party had become unpopular with the electorate because its policies reflected the views of its radical activists in the constituencies and the trade unions, who were unrepresentative of the electorate. Therefore

> The party leadership's first task... was to reduce the activists' powers. It could not afford just to ignore them, because of their possession of significant constitutional powers. Yet it was electorally inexpedient for the leadership to rely on the block votes of certain trade union leaders to maintain its position at the party conference, because of the trade unions' general unpopularity, even among their own members.[9]

Kinnock's solution was to create a new system of Joint Policy Committees composed equally of NEC members and MPs. These effectively superseded the NEC's Home Policy and International Committees, with their myriad subcommittees of mainly coopted experts drawn from the party's membership; and although the joint policy committees were chaired by NEC members, and assisted by secretaries drawn from both the party headquarters and PLP staff, effective control of their agendas and outcomes passed gradually into the hands of the leader and his professional advisers. Lewis Minkin, a seasoned and meticulous researcher on the party, commented that

> . . . one must note the growing confidence, increasing resources and, at times, ruthless assertiveness of the PLP leaders, as they took full advantage of the mood change brought about by the defeat of 1983. From the first, the key Jobs and Industry Joint Committee was colonised by coopted supporters of the Shadow Chancellor and Deputy Leader. Key subcommittee chairs were taken by the Front Bench. An economic strategy emerged not only from the committee but in public speeches by Hattersley, in which the new direction was charted and new policy departures sometimes announced before they were taken into the Party's procedures. Through his political and policy advisers, the new Leader was able to exercise a selective but broad-ranging oversight. . . the Leader's assistants sat in on policy committees, formal and informal, taking initiatives, 'fighting fires', and letting others in the unions know 'what Neil wants'.[10]

The old tripartite NEC-PLP-TUC 'Liaison Committee', through which the NEC had formerly operated to secure pre-conference agreement on policy issues, was gradually sidelined. What now became dominant was the office of the Leader.

Kinnock also deployed his power directly against the party's so-called 'hard' left in other ways. He denounced the Trotskyist Militant Tendency and oversaw a series of measures to delegitimise it; he conspicuously dissociated himself from the mineworkers in their epic confrontation with the government over pit closures in 1984–85; he closed the party's mildly left-of-centre *New Socialist* magazine; and he successfully marginalised leading left-wing MPs such as Tony Benn and Eric Heffer in the party's inner councils.

Then in 1987 came the further shock of the party's third successive election defeat. A slick media-oriented campaign had failed to do more than beat back the challenge of the Liberal-SDP Alliance; the Conservatives returned with another large parliamentary majority. Now, instead of merely trying to reduce the visibility and influence of the left wing of the party, Kinnock initiated a more radical change in party policy, and a more radical loosening of the links tying the leadership to the party outside parliament.

The new overall 'Policy Review' set in motion by Kinnock after the 1987 defeat consisted of seven 'policy groups', each jointly chaired by a member of the NEC and a member of the Labour front bench. By now, what was at stake was how far the party should go in accepting the legacy of Thatcherism as a new 'settlement', as the Conservatives had once accepted that of 1945–51. In the end, the answer was mixed. 'The market' was accepted, as a potentially neutral means of allocating resources: but emphasis continued to be laid on the need to redistribute wealth for more equal opportunities in the market. The state's role in industrial policy, environmental regulation, regional policy, training, competition, and control of natural monopolies, continued to be stressed, and public ownership was not renounced, although employee share ownership schemes, cooperatives and the public ownership of individual firms rather than whole industries were endorsed. On industrial relations, a return to the pre-Thatcher system was ruled out, though trade unions were to get more rights under a new, specialised system of industrial relations courts.

The results of the Policy Review registered the balance of forces and opinions in the party's NEC down to 1989. Of perhaps greater significance in the long run were a number of organisational changes that would eventually drastically reduce the significance of the NEC and indeed the whole extra-parliamentary party. One was the creation in 1985 of a 'Communications and Campaign Directorate' (CCD), directed by Peter Mandelson, which at its peak in 1986–87 had an annual budget of £300,000 and operated in close collaboration with the leader's office and with virtually total autonomy from the administrative hierarchy in the rest of the party headquarters. Mandelson also set up a 'Shadow Communications Agency' (SCA), coordinated by a professional market research and advertising specialist, Philip Gould, and relying on a changing group of sympathetic volunteers from the same milieu to provide information about the electorate and recommend ways of appealing to it. Mandelson took the power of the media as a given and devoted himself to getting the party to present itself in ways that the media would report positively. Gould provided 'interpretations' of the opinions and attitudes of voters.

Much has been written about the influence of Mandelson and the SCA. In retrospect what seems most significant is that they were taken very seriously by Kinnock and that they reinforced three salient tendencies. First, to treat the electors primarily as consumers of party programmes, with already-given attitudes and interests, rather than as people who can be persuaded to find their needs and aspirations met in the party's project for social change. Second, to treat editors and journalists as the arbiters of what is sensible or acceptable, in a way that party members, or even national executive members, are not. Third, to treat professional interpreters of the electors' attitudes as authoritative.

The first tendency – treating voters as consumers with pre-given wishes – was noted and resisted by many in the party's senior leadership, yet it followed logically enough from defining the party's one and only task as that of winning the *next* election: even if the leader had been a thinker of vision, with a body of new philosophy and practical thinking to draw on, winning electoral support for it would have required much more time (and propitious circumstances) than was afforded by the interval between two elections. As for accepting the power of editors and journalists to define what is sound and sensible and what is not, this too is defensible if their power to damage the party's short-term electoral prospects is once taken for granted. Acceptance of the authority of opinion researchers was more problematic, especially since the methods used by the Shadow Communications Agency involved a great deal of 'interpretation' and presentational slant, the aim of which seems to have been largely to jolt senior party personnel into recognising that even Labour voters were mostly uninterested in existing Labour politics, or even opposed to them. Using the same methods a team interested in finding the bases for a new long-term socialist strategy would undoubtedly have been able to do so, and to illustrate their findings with quotations just as evocative as 'it's nice to have a social conscience but it's your family that counts' and other Thatcherite-sounding statements quoted with such effect by the SCA in one of its first presentations, 'Society and Self';[11] for, contrary to the opinion of Hughes and Wintour, two commentators very close to Mandelson, the results of opinion research are never truly 'unequivocal'.[12]

Meanwhile, as the role assigned to 'communications' expanded, the role of party members was symbolically downgraded by the curious exercise called 'Labour Listens', mounted by the party's national headquarters in 1988–89. Meetings were organised throughout the country at which members of the public were invited to tell the party what they thought. The process was barely serious. There was no concern for the representativeness of the meetings, nor were any mechanisms put in place to ensure that what people said was fed into the Policy Review.[13] The one thing that was clear was that the meetings were not for listening to Labour activists. It was clearly an effort, however misconceived or even fraudulent, to link the party to the public over the heads of its active members, and to be seen to be doing so.

The grip of the leader's office on policy-making thus became more and more detailed and exclusive, and through Mandelson's management of press relations the leader's views gradually came to be treated as party policy by the media:

> Again and again the Leader would let it be known through his private office what would and would not be Labour Party policy. The press grew accustomed to this and gave far more weight to these unattributable briefings than to the decisions of the annual Labour Party Conference. The Walworth Road [party headquarters] policy directorate became an irrelevance.[14]

In addition to keeping tight control over policy formation in the short run, Kinnock also pursued two linked strategies designed to reduce the long-term influence of both the unions and active party members. First, under the slogan 'one member one vote', all individual party members would be able to vote in elections for the party leader, the selection of candidates for parliament, and delegates to annual conferences; balloting would be done by post. Kinnock and his advisers assumed (rightly, as the 1995 Clause Four vote was to prove), that this would reduce the influence of activists who attended meetings. On the basis that this gave more power to individual members Kinnock argued that more people would want to be members, envisaging a doubling of the membership from the then level of about 250,000 (at one time Kinnock rashly set a target of one million). Second, as individual membership rose, Kinnock proposed that the weight of the trade union block vote at annual conferences should be reduced.

These proposals addressed real problems. Party activists were indeed unrepresentative of the opinions of Labour supporters and voters (in fact in pre-Thatcher days surveys regularly showed the latter supporting Conservative policy planks more than Labour ones). Party leaders had always relied on the block votes of 'affiliated' trade union members to outvote the constituency-based activists at annual conferences, so that conference policy decisions produced what they saw as potentially winning election platforms. But this was increasingly indefensible, as trade union leaders cast millions of votes for members who were less and less politically involved. Enlarging the party's individual membership was in every way desirable. On the other hand dropping the need for members to attend any meetings in order to vote on policies, combined with the leadership's espousal of policies beamed so exclusively at 'middle England', gave the change a specific political meaning. What it seemed to portend was a North American-style party of professional politicians supported by a membership who were essentially donors and election helpers, not active participants in party policy formation.

These changes were not achieved by Kinnock, but by his successor John Smith (leader from 1992 to his premature death in 1994). 'One member one vote' (or OMOV, as the new system was called) was agreed at the 1993 Conference, and in the same year the unions agreed to a reduction of their joint weight in conference votes to 70 percent, and in candidate and delegate selection at constituency level to 40 percent; and also, in principle, to a future lowering of their collective voting power at annual conferences to 50 percent once individual membership surpassed 300,000. And building on this, Smith's successor Tony Blair sought still further reductions in the influence of the trade unions, ending union sponsorship of MPs and floating the idea of a still greater reduction in the weight of the union vote at conferences; he was also thought likely to put pressure on the unions to move towards balloting their members on policy issues before conference votes, on OMOV lines.[15] And in a further centralising move Blair persuaded the PLP to let the leader select the party's Chief Whip in the House of Commons.[16]

Apart from the OMOV issue, John Smith's leadership saw a halt to the centralising process and a notable reopening of policy debate, at least within the PLP. Mandelson had already left the Communications and Campaigns Directorate in 1989 to become MP for Hartlepool; the Directorate was now wound up, while Patricia Hewitt, Kinnock's former Press Secretary and a key architect of his centralisation measures, after overseeing the Policy Review, moved to a new Labour-oriented think-tank, the Institute for Public Policy Research, and thence to a high-powered job in the private sector. A more traditional style of leadership was reestablished.

### *'New Labour': the modernisation project of Tony Blair*

With Blair's election as leader in 1994, however, the Kinnock regime was revived, with the young staffers from the Leader's Office once more omnipresent, policy documents handed to members of the NEC at the door to be signed for and returned at the end of the meeting, and shadow cabinet members required to clear all their speeches with the Leader's Office in advance. Key players in Kinnock's team also reappeared. Mandelson returned to centre stage, after a celebrated 'secret' role as Blair's campaign manager in the leadership contest, as one of the new leader's closest advisers. He was appointed a junior whip, and in July 1995 was given charge of running a by-election campaign (in Littleborough and Saddleworth) which gained instant notoriety for appealing to right-wing authoritarianism and anti-tax attitudes, and for its use of negative personal attacks on the ultimately successful Liberal Democrat candidate; in October he was appointed to the front bench in the Deputy Leader's office. Hewitt remained in the private sector but returned to the inner circle as a member of an unofficial group of policy-makers run by Mandelson for Blair.[17]

The OMOV strategy now began to show quite dramatic results. By mid-1995, according to Labour's General Secretary Tom Sawyer, 113,000 new members had joined since Blair became leader and the party's total membership had risen to 350,000. On the other hand, there was a corresponding loss of enthusiasm among activists, and in the same period 38,000 members had left. This was a serious exodus, but a price the leadership was evidently prepared to pay; an interesting example, in fact, of a government dismissing an unpopular electorate and choosing one it likes better.[18] The question was how far others in the PLP or the trade unions, whose support for the leadership remained, in spite of everything, electorally important – if only in not giving rise to displays of party disunity – would acquiesce. Signs accumulated that their toleration was wearing thin, but complaints were muted out of a desire to give the new leader the benefit of every doubt, particularly given the party's unprecedented opinion poll ratings throughout his first year. A demand from Bill Morris, the leader of the Transport and General Workers Union, that there should be a pause in the 'modernisation' process after the special Clause Four conference, was disregarded, but party agents and workers reported that constituency party General Council meetings, once the focus of rank and file participation, were increasingly inquorate. Finally three events broke the issue open: Blair's decision to accept an invitation to address a conference of Rupert Murdoch's News International group in Australia, Peter Mandelson's conduct of the Littleborough and Saddleworth by-election, and Blair's announcement that he wanted an early end to trade union sponsorship of MPs.

Murdoch's newspapers had vilified Labour throughout the Thatcher years with unremitting lack of scruple (it was of Murdoch that Dennis Potter said, in his blistering final television interview with Melvyn Bragg, 'There is no one person more responsible for the pollution of what was already a fairly polluted press');[19] and Blair's willingness to fly to Australia as his guest was of a piece with Mandelson's ruthless pursuit of votes at the Littleborough and Saddleworth by-election. Both exercises had the mark of Mandelson's famous 'unsentimentality', and both stuck in the gullets of many party activists. The issue of trade union sponsorship of MPs was a slower-burning fuse, but in the context of the impending reduction of union voting strength at party conferences, and hints that Blair would call for further reductions in future, the fact that Blair chose also to call for the end of union sponsorship was seen as further evidence of the London-based, middle-class orientation of the leader and his Office. Open resentment was eventually triggered by an article in the *New Statesman* in July 1995 by a mildly left-wing backbench MP, Richard Burden, in which he criticised the 'amorality' of the by-election campaign as a manifestation of 'New Labour's' top-down, centralised power structure, and of a party 'desperate to be elected as representative of mainstream opinion, and yet with its own inner sanctum holding a virtual monopoly on defining what such mainstream opinion consists of'.[20] This was followed by a short outburst of articles and statements also voicing what had previously been said publicly only by the party's left wing.[21]

What really united all the critics was pinpointed by Roy Hattersley, who had been deputy leader under Kinnock and a militant member of the party's right wing. 'As always', he said,

> the complaints have been directed at a series of surrogate targets – the arrogance of the young men and women in the leader's office, the increasing detachment from the trade unions, and the most wizened of old chestnuts, 'the lack of democracy in policy-making'. . .

– a formulation calculated to remind Blair that Hattersley himself had always staunchly resisted calls for democracy when these came from the party's left wing with its base in the old constituency parties. The real problem, Hattersley asserted, was a concern about policy; the present leadership had abandoned ideology so completely, and was so preoccupied with winning middle class support, that its commitment to the fundamental needs of the 'disadvantaged' was no longer clear. 'Ideology', he declared,

> is what keeps parties consistent and credible as well as honest. In the long term, the party's public esteem would be protected by a robust statement of fundamental intention. Socialism – which is proclaimed in the New Clause IV – requires the bedrock of principle to be the redistribution of power and wealth. . . When the going gets rough, it is not the new recruits from the SDP who will stay at his [Tony Blair's] side. They will jump ship as soon as they realise that he is not the reincarnation of David Owen [the former SDP leader, now Lord Owen]. The necessary support will come from members of the real Labour Party who, rightly, think he shares their basic beliefs. He ought to confirm their optimism now and bring to an end the nonsense of last week [i.e. the sudden spate of criticism].[22]

Hattersley's intervention was a good indication of how far the leadership had moved away from the the party's historic ethos. People like Hattersley had fought against the left on the basis of a counter-ideology – 'labourism' – no less powerful for being implicit in the labour movement's practices and traditions, rather than explicitly formulated in any body of doctrine. But 'New Labour' was rapidly abandoning that ideology or ethos too. Blair's response was predictable:

> [He] pledged to continue with his wide-ranging 'modernisation' of the Labour Party in order to ensure victory in the general election, making it clear that he was undeterred by criticism of his leadership style... election victory could only be gained by shaking off old-fashioned links and building up voters' trust in the new-style party... 'But [people] need to be sure of Labour, they will only be sure of Labour if we show that we have learned the lessons of the past and are a party true to our principles but applying them in the modern world'.[23]

Retreat was excluded by the logic of his sustained effort to woo 'middle England', and by his agreement with the media that his claim to be able to rid the Labour Party of its last vestiges of anti-capitalism was the acid test of his merits as a leader. Hattersley's 'real Labour' members might be alienated, but catering at all significantly to them would be pilloried by the media and could jeopardise the party's electoral prospects, which were currently strong (a Labour opinion poll lead over the Conservatives of almost 30 percent) precisely to the extent that 'old Labour' had been so publicly dethroned.[24] The new recruits (wherever they came from) might indeed prove fickle, but the party's capacity to attract them was an index of its ability to win an election with the votes of the kind of people they represented. Thereafter, perhaps with the aid of state funding for parties (advocated by Denis Healey, the former Deputy Leader, among others), party members might become as relatively unimportant as they are in the

Conservative Party or any other bourgeois political party endowed with funds sufficient to fight election campaigns, which are in any case increasingly decided in the media.

### *'New Labour' policy*

What has been described so far is primarily a change – sympathisers call it a revolution – of organisation and practice, though with obvious policy implications. Now something more needs to be said about the policy content of what Blair's team habitually call 'the project', even though this is made difficult by the project's nature: a distinctive kind of utopianism, presented as 'realism'. The 'realism' consists essentially of the assertion that global capitalism is a permanent and irremovable fact of life, not an inhuman and ultimately self-destructive system: correspondingly, politics is the art of living with it, not a vocation to overcome it. It is not clear that most 'New Labour' evangelists (a term often used on account of Blair's religious faith and zealous speaking style) are particularly concerned about the truth-value of this founding assumption; another characteristic of their writing and speeches is to proceed by denigrating any unwelcome idea as the product of 'old' Labour thinking, rather than arguing for the validity of what is offered in its place. There is perhaps also a vaguely postmodern assumption at work that no such general characterisation of something like global capitalism is really possible; 'grand narratives' are also out of date. The flavour was well summarised by Henry Porter in a very favourable survey of Blair's first year as leader: 'Nothing seems the same as it was; even the old distinctions between left and right no longer matter as much as generational differences appear to.' And what is distinctive about the new generation? Porter quotes 'a close political ally' of Blair:

> . . . Tony had been thinking along these lines long before he was made leader. In fact he was impatient under John Smith to reform the Labour Party. He understood that a whole new generation of people in their thirties and forties had arrived and that they had attitudes and a whole culture which are light years away from the old Labour Party. Intellectually *they accept the restrictions in responsible policy-making that now exist.*[25]

It is worth noting, in passing, that speaking in terms of 'whole generations', or even 'people' in general, without drawing distinctions between employed or unemployed, rich and poor — in a word, between class conditions — is a marked characteristic of 'New Labour' discourse: Seyd and Whiteley's survey of Labour members actually found the strongest left-wing views among people in their thirties and forties.[26] The thirty and forty-somethings Blair's ally had in mind no doubt exist, but they are evidently a particular social category within their age group – people like Blair himself, perhaps. Be that as it may, Blair, says Porter, 'has realised that things are not as clear as they appeared to be in the eighties and that many of the new homeowners and new parents – in his words, "the moderate middle-income majority" – are also consumers of Murdochs's various media products. They are. . . concerned with social and economic issues. . . but perhaps the emphasis is more on the good management of a society than on fairness or compassion. And this is exactly the direction Tony Blair has taken Labour, arguing that a compassionate society is firstly a competently run and prosperous society. . .' – and so on. Or as Blair put it, in the soundbite language of 'modernisation':

> What we are about is a partnership between the public and the private sectors, rather than a battle between the two. We are about reforming the welfare state, making it a platform of opportunity. Tough on crime and tough on the causes of crime. Rolling back the quango state. It is extremely important to make sure before you start getting lost in the thicket of policy that the public has really got the big picture.[27]

Perhaps what has already been said is enough to convey some of the substance as well as the flavour of 'New Labour's' Project: i.e. it offers an optimistic prospect of a more rational, somewhat fairer, more efficiently run society, in which however nothing will be done that seriously offends the sensibilities or interests of the middle classes, or invites penalties from the markets. This is consistent with Labour's perceived electoral task (i.e., to break out of its old working class base), as well as being realistic about where economic power is seen to lie.

In terms of specific policies this has meant a drastic narrowing of the gap between the Thatcher legacy and what Labour proposes. For instance, 'reforming the welfare state, making it a platform of opportunity' means cutting it, while worrying about the 'poverty trap'; 'tough on crime and tough on the causes of crime' translates roughly into not opposing the 1994 Criminal Justice Act (which drastically reduced individual rights vis a vis the police), speaking critically about single parents, and promising jail sentences for people who persistently harass their neighbours, while also implying that better government under Labour will create more jobs and provide more housing and better child care and other services that evidently have a bearing on the level of crime.

On education, Blair has retreated from the party's previous commitment to return to control by elected local authorities schools that have 'opted-out' (to be run by boards of governors responsible to the central government) under Thatcher's legislation.[28] On the economy, he has called for macro-economic policies of the strictest fiscal and monetary orthodoxy, not complemented by any firm commitment to reform the operations of the City or secure a significant increase in industrial investment. On health, he has endorsed only limited changes in the 'internal market' imposed by the Conservatives on the National Health Service, laying emphasis on the need to minimise further organisational disruption. On the constitution, he has endorsed the party's commitment to abolishing the hereditary element in the House of Lords and creating Scottish and Welsh Assemblies and – though with an unconcealed lack of enthusiasm – the commitment to hold a referendum on proportional representation; and he has retreated from the commitment to establish regional assemblies in England, proposing instead to submit the idea to regional referenda.

Except on the constitution, Porter comments, 'each statement constitutes a synthesis between the Thatcherite reforms of the early eighties and communitarian politics.'[29] And the same could really be said of the new Clause Four, which effectively ruled out any reversal of Conservative privatisations. Speaking generally, 'New Labour' policy is to accept most of Thatcher's legislative and administrative legacy in almost all spheres. The list of points on which change is promised is not long.

Lest this leave an impression of purely pragmatic adjustment to perceived electoral necessities, let us conclude this section with a quotation from one of Blair's speeches which paints the kind of broader picture that he favours (what Porter, perhaps unkindly, calls 'political cinemascope'). Celebrating the fiftieth anniversary of the 1945 Labour government, which he identified as having drawn its strength from a broad national consensus, Blair declared: 'I passionately want to lead a party which once again embodies and leads the national mood for change and renewal'. He concluded:

> Socialists have to be both moralists and empiricists. Values are fundamental. But socialism has to be made real in the world as it is and not as we would like it to be. Our commitment to a different vision of society stands intact. But the ways of achieving it must change. Those should and will cross the old boundaries between left and right, progressive and conservative. They did in 1945. What marks us out are the objectives and the sense of unity and purpose by which we are driven. Our task now is nothing less than national renewal. Rebuilding our country as a strong and active civil society. We should gain confidence from the government of 1945; confidence in our values, in our insights and in our ability to deliver change. The generation of 1945 has set us an example which it is an honour to follow.[30]

This kind of rhetoric has a forerunner, but it is the rhetoric of Ramsay MacDonald, not Clement Attlee. Of course MacDonald's style belonged to the days of platform oratory, and audiences that were still used to sermons; Blair's is attuned to the production of quotable quotes in fifteen-second soundbites. But what they have in common is the theme of class conciliation, wrapped in misty appeals to social bonds that transcend class divisions. Where MacDonald spoke of 'all practical men and women' Blair talks about 'a strong and active civil society'. Both constantly invoke 'the nation'. Both have their eyes fixed on the middle-class voter.[31]

In 1945 Attlee did not need this kind of rhetoric, for a simple reason: thanks to the slump and the war, the ideas and policies for which the party had campaigned for over a decade had already become hegemonic within a large part of the middle class, so that a spade could be called a spade.

Nationalisation, whether of the mines or the Bank of England, could be called nationalisation, and nothing could have been more specific than universal social security, a free health service, and full employment. But unlike Attlee, and like MacDonald, 'New Labour' is far from having propounded policies capable of bringing about 'national renewal', let alone made them hegemonic. This is why Blair's rhetoric has the MacDonaldite flavour it has.

*Intellectuals and 'New Labour'*

Much of what Blair has accomplished was begun by Kinnock. Their projects are separated, however, by more than John Smith's brief interregnum. There is a different rhetoric, symbolised by the 'New Labour' label adopted (in imitation of Bill Clinton's self-description as a 'New Democrat') by the Blair leadership, and it has different intellectual roots.[32] Some of these lie in Blair's own formation as a Christian socialist at Oxford, but there are other contributions that need to be taken into account, even if this can be done only in a tentative and sketchy way here.

One contribution of intellectuals to the project of the 'modernisers' is that mainstream commentators have been remarkably uncritical; whether because his interlocutors are impressed by his rhetoric, or because they tacitly yearn for a change of government, or even hope to influence it, is impossible to say. The closest Henry Porter, in the interview already cited, came to a criticism was to note Blair's unconvincing reply to the question, how he envisaged Britain after two years of a Labour government; 'it was the least fluent answer, and petered out in a series of headings.'[33] Criticism from the left of the Labour party has been dismissed (and not reported) as old-fashioned and irrelevant, though with occasional condescending acknowledgements of its 'sincerity' (or even, in the case of Tony Benn, its 'authority'); and criticism from the right, however perceptive, is seen as purely partisan.[34] One of the very few mainstream commentators to raise appropriate doubts has been the former SDP theorist David Marquand. The buzzwords of neoliberalism – 'flexibility', 'dynamism', 'enterprise' and 'competitiveness' – are now seen to be

> merely code words for harder work for longer hours, with less protection against more powerful bosses. But when we try to tell our rulers that... we face a blank wall of patronising management-speak...New Labour speaks a different dialect from the Government's, but not a different language... On the central question now facing the political economies of western Europe, new Labour and the new right are one.[35]

Television interviewers, however, have rarely confronted the Labour leader with this palpable truth. The absence of serious intellectual criticism in the mainstream media has surely played a part in the modernisers' advance.

Of course, the other side of this phenomenon has been 'New Labour's' own heavy investment in media management. Peter Mandelson, in his role as director of the Communications and Campaigns Directorate in the late 1980s, became Labour's answer to Mrs Thatcher's Press Secretary Bernard Ingham, tirelessly 'managing' news and tempting, cajoling or bullying journalists and editors to give favourable treatment to the Labour leadership. According to Bryan Gould and others, Mandelson also emulated Ingham's notorious 'black briefings', putting out unattributable negative comments on individual colleagues;[36] and he has been widely credited with doing the same, in an unofficial capacity, on behalf of Tony Blair.[37]

However Mandelson's role should not be seen in a purely practical light, nor should Blair's alleged comment that 'my project will be complete when the Labour Party learns to love Peter Mandelson' be seen as merely provocative.[38] Mandelson attracts hostility for a reason that goes deeper than his alleged deviousness: he accepts the electoral logic of social-democracy in the age of global capitalism with a consistency and wholeheartedness of which most Labour MPs, let alone rank and file members, are incapable.[39] He takes it as given that globalisation imposes very severe limits on all social and economic policies, so that the only ones worth promoting are those that capital – 'the market' – will accept; and he includes in this the power of the increasingly globally-owned media, and is determined to do whatever it takes – including getting Blair to make his highly symbolic visit to the annual meeting in Australia of Murdoch's world-wide media executives – to win whatever political leeway this situation affords (such as a less venomously hostile treatment by the one-third of British national newspaper circulation controlled by Murdoch than was given to Kinnock). In his view, to oppose this is sentimental self-indulgence which the party cannot afford; his notorious alleged remarks about the party conference or the unions being dispensable are deliberate provocations to those who resist this logic.[40] What most profoundly upsets many of his critics, one suspects, is that they do not really see a way of staying in the electoral game without adopting in practice what Mandelson makes into a point of principle, including accepting the media as they are. They know that any serious proposal to bring the media under control, to decommodify them and recreate a genuinely open medium for political debate, would attract the massed opposition of all the media, in the name – so far has the ideological pass already been sold – of the principle of 'free speech'. Mandelson's chief fault is, then, to act openly on a logic that in practice they accept, but have trouble acknowledging. It is hard to deny that in doing so he does the party the significant intellectual service of challenging hypocrisy.

But if Mandelson is the Labour Party's intellectual 'bad cop', there are others who aspire to be good ones, to equip the party with ideas and policies which on their merits will win the party a succession of elections and allow it to refashion British society. These intellectuals have operated largely, if not exclusively, through various new 'think tanks' which have proliferated in the later years of Labour's prolonged exile from office. This no doubt partly reflects the exhaustion of the Labourist tradition, embodied in the Fabian Society and discredited by the crisis of social democracy in the 1970s, although other factors are undoubtedly also involved, including the example of the role played by right-wing think tanks in the evolution of 'Thatcherism'.[41] Think-tanks also act as screening-mechanisms, putting into the public arena only work that conforms to their respective ideological orientations, for party leaders to take or leave; this may also have simplified the Blair team's task in avoiding the kind of intellectuals they felt unsympathetic towards.[42] At all events, by the end of the 1980s at least three significant left-of-centre policy study centres were in business: the Institute of Public Policy Research (IPPR), Charter 88, and Demos.

Of these only the IPPR, founded in 1988, was specifically designed to help the Labour Party. Although it was formally a non-party institution, its first director (Baroness Blackstone) and deputy director (Patricia Hewitt, fresh from supervising Labour's Policy Review) were both prominent Labour figures, and its task was to provide Labour, following its purge of old policies, with a body of solidly-researched policy documents of a calibre which the party's own 'policy directorate' did not have the resources to produce. Its publications, and most notably the much-publicised report of the Borrie Commission on Social Justice, established on the initiative of John Smith as Labour leader, have a characteristic blend of 'realistic' (in the 'modernisers'' sense) assumptions about the permanence of global capitalism, and well-documented analyses of economic and social problems and suggestions for their amelioration within the limits of the possible;[43] where the Fabians' motto was, 'When I strike, I strike hard', the IPPR's might be, 'We can't strike, but we'll try pushing'. Blair's thinking undoubtedly draws on the work of the IPPR (and David Miliband, his political adviser, was secretary to the Borrie Commission), although it is not the main source of his inspiration.

Even less central to Blair's thinking, perhaps, is Charter 88, a non-party organisation also established in 1988, which focusses on issues of democratic rights and liberties. Although its substantial work on issues like devolution and Quangos has undoubtedly contributed both to Labour thinking and to building public support for constitutional reform, its advocacy of proportional representation and a written constitution, both dear to the Liberal-Democrats and both unpopular with Blair and his team, makes it a tainted source.[44]

But the case is very different with Demos, the youngest of the three think-tanks in question, launched in early 1993. Geoff Mulgan, its founder-director, was formerly adviser to Gordon Brown, Blair's Shadow

Chancellor of the Exchequer, and felt that 'public policy and political thinking' had 'become too short-term, partisan and out of touch':

> In the past creative thinking often came from within the traditional institutions of parliament and parties, and from within the main political ideologies. But these are no longer able to keep up with the pace of change in society, the economy, technology and culture. Society has become more porous and complex, as old traditions and hierarchies have broken down. Demos is a response to this new situation. It draws on ideas from outside the political mainstream... the main focus is on long-term issues rather than the immediate programmatic needs of parties and government. In addition, Demos has two broader aims: one is to help modernise our political culture, to make it more relevant, more international and more at ease with the future. The other is to point the way to new forms of democracy and governance fit for the 21st century.[45]

There is no space here to do justice to the range and vitality of Demos's publications in the first two and a half years of its life. Mulgan's intellectual verve and energy are stamped on the whole enterprise, not only in the choice of topics and authors for research projects and publications, but also in the form of a series of impressive lead articles co-authored by him in Demos Quarterly, the organisation's theme-oriented journal: these include 'The End of Unemployment', 'Back to Greece: the Scope for Direct Democracy', and 'Well-being and Time'. These articles have distinctive merits and shortcomings; all that is possible here is to indicate certain characteristics of Mulgan's work, reflected broadly in the output of Demos generally, that are also evident in the speeches of Tony Blair.

First, there is a distinctive kind of utopianism, springing from the almost complete lack of any serious attention to political economy. Mulgan acknowledges that Demos has neglected political economy; this is deliberate, inasmuch as he thinks political economy is a 'weak' field.[47] Paradoxically, the resulting utopianism is presented as 'realism'. The question posed is predominantly one of what shall we do about various trends that are inexorably working themselves out through the dynamics of modern capitalism and the technological changes it brings – this is the 'realism' part. What is utopian is that no particular constraints accompany the options considered, and no agents of change are specified; we are often in a world of social science fiction. Mulgan seems able to envisage things which seem prima facie absurd, such as a world of totally 'flexible' employment, in which no one has a job, but only short-term contracts – casual labour in modern dress;[48] perhaps this is what 'making our political culture more relevant' (to what, exactly?) means. Sometimes, though not always, he subsequently raises doubts about these implausible futures, but by no means always feels compelled to make a final judgement between the thesis and its antithesis. For instance, on work 'flexibility', he also recognises that 'a fluid, disordered world will leave the majority miserable', so that 'alongside speed and flexibility we also need to remember the importance of balance: of mechanisms for finding useful activity for those [the majority?] left out by change; of public spaces for quiet and reflection, like parks and churches where time stands still; of home life as well as work life.'[49] But who the 'we' are, who should remember this, and what obstacles the dynamics of capitalism may place in the way of our doing anything about it, are not specified.

Second, there is a constant stress on complexity, differentiation, pluralism and choice. Partly this is code for abandoning analysis in terms of classes. Partly it seems to be a postmodern embrace of difference and particularity (which goes with a rejection of 'grand narratives', of which critical political economy is one). But whatever its sources, Mulgan's approach to the allegedly new degree of 'diversity' in contemporary capitalist societies leads him to make eclecticism into a virtue. No great effort is made to bring into any kind of systematic unity the topics, concepts, analyses and perceptions that he draws from so many diverse fields, or even to ask how far they are all compatible. There is a kaleidoscopic effect, analogous to the 'cinemascopic' character of Blair's speeches.

A third characteristic feature of Mulgan's work is a fascination with the new, especially if it comes from the USA.[50] This was well represented by Demos's sponsorship of a visit to the UK by the American 'communitarian' theorist Amitai Etzioni in March 1995, and the publication of his views on the 'parenting deficit' as a Demos pamphlet – views which accord well with the 'community oriented' Christianity that Blair adopted at Oxford; and immediately after Etzioni's visit Blair delivered a lecture in which he stressed the duties people owe to society and called for the prosecution of the parents of chronically truant schoolchildren, and action against noisy and abusive neighbours.[51] But it is not just new thinkers, so much as novelty itself, that is the key leitmotif of Mulgan's work. For him, what is wrong with past socialist thought is above all that it is 'out of touch' with the 'pace of change'; being 'in touch' is the supreme virtue. It is a virtue mainly found in the younger generation (a preoccupation with generational differences is one of Mulgan's favourite themes), but it is also something which even a middle-aged 'New Labour' standard-bearer can easily hold onto under pressure. When criticism of Blair's style of 'modernisation' finally surfaced in mid-1995, for instance, the once-radical 'old Labour' leader of Sheffield City Council, David Blunkett, now Shadow education spokesman, defended his vacationing leader in the following terms: 'The rapidity of change is such that if we don't stay ahead of the game, and are there speaking about the new world in a new situation, we will allow the election to slip away from us again.'[52]

I am not making any claim about the extent of Demos's influence on 'New Labour', in spite of Mulgan's close links to both Brown and Blair[53]. But if one were looking for the intellectual inspiration for what is most distinctive in the modernisation rhetoric of 'New Labour', this would have to be the place to start: 'realism' about (sc. acceptance of) global capitalism; a utopian approach to the discussion of responses to it, justified by the alleged incapacity of political economy to analyse it; the celebration of diversity and choice; the fetishism of change and novelty; the systematic rejection of analysis in terms of social class.

It is, as Tony Blair remarked, 'liberating' to cut free from the bonds of what he called a 'too narrow view of democratic socialism';[54] and 'New Labour's' young speechwriters, liberated from both the labour movement's past ethos and any particular intellectual discipline, may be able to deploy the buzzwords of 'modernisation' to good short-term electoral effect. But whether any serious project for social change, let alone one that can sincerely be called socialist, can be constructed on such foundations, is another question.

## *Conclusion*

This is not to say that Tony Blair and his team are not serious about social change. They were undoubtedly right to think that change in the party was called for by much more than the need – however desperate that was – to win the next election. Even if the Conservative Party and the popular press had not persuaded a majority of voters that 'nationalisation' was inefficient, and the state 'too large', it would still have been essential for Labour to 'modernise' its policies and its structures in face of the multiple changes that have occurred over the last twenty years. The question is only what kind of modernisation is called for.

The most obvious criticism to be made of 'New Labour's' version is that it accepts the market uncritically, and substitutes elite centralism for democracy within the party. Labour's historic mission has been to counterpose social need to the selfishness of the market and its socially destructive effects. Now the market's true character and destructive long-term effects are once again becoming plain for all to see – in the shape of chronic unemployment and growing job insecurity, growing inequality, social tensions and welfare dependency, a grossly neglected infrastructure and declining international competitiveness. It is by no means obvious that if the Labour Party firmly declared its opposition to a market-*driven* society (as opposed to one that accepts but seriously regulates markets) this would in the long run hurt it electorally, as the Thatcher years are exposed, week by week, as years of cruel illusion and deception. But a serious critique of the market is what 'New Labour', in its paralytic fear of seeming anti-capitalist, above all abjures. 'New Labour' runs the risk, in fact, of achieving office – though not real power – on the basis of 'realistically' accepting the market just as its ultimate *un*acceptability, as the motor and arbiter of social life, is once again becoming clear.

Labour also has a rich pool of popular democratic experience and ideas, developed in the 1970s in reaction *against* the state-socialism of the post-war years, which could be drawn upon to help build a popular consensus for a new socialist project. But this too is treated by 'New Labour' as at best an irrelevance, and at worst a contamination. Centralisation of power in the party remains the order of the day.[55] Internal party debate has been reduced to a historic minimum. Policy is now 'revealed' at the party's annual conference, not decided there. 'New Labour' has, in effect, finally broken with any idea of the party as a vehicle for the aspirations and ideas of a social movement, the expression of any kind of collective will. From now on it will frankly be run by professional politicians with at most an occasional plebiscitary relationship with its members.

NOTES

1. Dennis Potter, *Seeing the Blossom* (London: Faber and Faber, 1994) p. 47.
2. In an extraordinarily revealing interview the party's General Secretary, Tom Sawyer, said that 'he favoured management consultants to help inject new thinking into the party's targeting of new members, including judgements on whether members are best recruited in marginals or heartlands, to raise funds or to be active. Different marketing techniques will be used for different goals. . . The General Secretary has also taken members of the national executive to Cranfield Institute of Management to discuss the role of the committee.' (*Guardian* August 8 1995).
3. Henry M. Drucker, *Doctrine and Ethos in the Labour Party* (London: Allen and Unwin, 1979).
4. Part of the reason for this is that Blair joined the Labour Party in London in 1975 as it was entering into a period of bitter internal conflict, and when the labour movement was ceasing to be as representative of the whole working class as it had once felt and, in some respects, been. At the same time, in his early years in the party he seems to have been peculiarly cut off from what was still positive and morally compelling in the old party ethos; see John Rentoul, *Tony Blair* (London: Little, Brown, 1995), especially chapters 3–4.
5. The new Clause Four of the party constitution pledges the party to work for 'a just society' which 'nurtures families', but does not pledge it to make women equal with men or blacks with whites.
6. Foot had been chosen as leader by the parliamentary party in 1979 when Callaghan resigned as a means of forestalling the possible election of the left-wing Tony Benn under the new leadership election system which had been adopted at the 1979 party conference, but which was not due to come into operation until 1980.
7. Martin J. Smith, 'A Return to Revisionism? The Labour Party's Policy Review' in M.J. Smith and Joanna Spear (eds.), *The Changing Labour Party* (London: Routledge, 1992), p. 19.
8. 'There were now, for the first time in party history, resources for a sizeable advisory staff available to the PLP leadership.' Lewis Minkin, *The Contentious Alliance: Trade Unions and the Labour Party* (Edinburgh: Edinbourgh University Press, 1991), p. 400.
9. Patrick Seyd and Paul Whiteley, 'Labour's Renewal Strategy', in Smith and Spear op. cit., p. 31.
10. Minkin, op. cit., p. 409.
11. Quoted in Richard Heffernan and Mike Marqusee, *Deafeat from the Jaws of Victory;*

*Inside Kinnock's Labour Party* (London: Verso, 1992), p. 211. According to Colin Hughes and Patrick Wintour in *Labour Rebuilt: The New Model Party* (London: Fourth Estate, 1990) pp. 60–61, the crucial document of this kind was 'Labour and Britain in the 1990s', presented to the NEC and Shadow Cabinet in November 1987.

12. Hughes and Wintour, ibid., p. 153.
13. One of the points on which all commentators seem to agree is the uselessness of 'Labour Listens', however high-minded its original intentions. See, e.g., Hughes and Wintour, op. cit., pp. 98–103, and Heffernan and Marqusee, op. cit., pp. 215–16.
14. Heffernan and Marqusee, op. cit., p. 115. These authors are hostile witnesses, but the consequences of the phenomenon they correctly report in this passage were forcibly apparent following Tony Blair's election as leader in 1994. The press wanted to know from Blair's speeches what party policy would now be; the old discourse of how a new leader's personal views would sit with those of the majority in the national executive, let alone the annual conference, was completely absent. When Roland Wales, head of the party's Policy Directorate, finally resigned in October 1995, barely disguising the fact that it was because his job had become pointless, it was treated by the press as barely newsworthy.
15. This idea was widely canvassed in the aftermath of the party's special conference in April 1995, at which some big unions cast votes against the change to a new Clause Four without having balloted their members, while the votes of those which had were cast in favour of the change. The non-balloting unions cited the expense involved – estimated at over £1.5 million – as a decisive objection, although several leaders were said to agree that some further democratisation of their policy-making procedures was now needed.
16. The PLP agreed in July 1995 to allow the Chief Whip to be chosen by the leader from among the members of the Labour shadow cabinet (itself chosen by the PLP), rather than being directly elected to the post by the PLP, as the existing rules prescribed: the existing Chief Whip simultaneously agreed to stand down in October 1995 in return for a senior role in opposition and in a future Labour government, allowing Blair to appoint someone of his choice (Donald Dewar). It was also widely expected that Blair would eventually propose a name change for the party. Significantly, Blair announced at the April 1995 special conference on Clause Four that 'the name was not going to change' (i.e. from Labour to 'New Labour', as the party was now called on all its publications) – thus denying the rumour while simultaneously implying that it lay within his power to get it changed if he chose to.
17. Besides Mandelson and Hewitt the group included Roger Liddle (a former adviser to Bill Rodgers, one of the SDP's founding figures); Geoff Mulgan, the founder and director of Demos, a non-party think-tank; Derek Scott, a City-based economist amd former adviser to Denis Healey as Chancellor of the Exchequer in the 1970s; and Sir Nicholas Monck, a former permanent secretary at the Department of Employment. As the press noted, none of Blair's shadow cabinet colleagues, nor the Deputy Leader, were included in the group, which was said to meet at Westminster on alternate Fridays (Michael White in the *Guardian* July 15 1995). A spokesman for Blair's office maintained that these were merely some individuals who had offered assistance on an ad hoc basis to 'write sections of speeches and background papers' (*Guardian* July 17 1995). Patricia Hewitt said their function was to help write speeches and 'bounce ideas' (interview, August 2 1995). Given the freedom that the leader had by then acquired to make policy it would be naive to imagine that any group that had close and regular policy discussions with him was not influential.
18. This process did not originate with Blair's election as leader. Already under Kinnock, according to Heffernan and Marqusee, 'For rank and file Party members. . . attending meetings came to seem pointless since the decisions had clearly already been taken at the top' (Heffernan and Marqusee, op. cit., p. 213).
19. Dennis Potter, op. cit., p. 14.

20. *New Statesman and Society*, August 11 1995. Burden was subsequently said to have realised too late that the article would create a lot of trouble and tried unsuccessfully to withdraw it, a claim which he later denied; if so, it is an interesting example of spin-doctor disinformation.
21. For example in *Socialist Campaign News* and *Labour Briefing*. The new public critics included John Edmonds, leader of the large General Municipal and Boilermakers union, and Roy Hattersley, the former Deputy Leader under Neil Kinnock, neither of whom was left-wing. According to Patrick Wintour *(Guardian*, August 11 1995), 'Blairites argue that given the helter-skelter pace of his reform programme it is surprising that there have only been rumblings, rather than an earthquake. But much of the backstage criticism of Mr Blair is not directed at his reforms, but [sic] fears of what he may do, and the lack of consultation. Two recent deputations, one from the NEC and another from union sponsored MPs, went to complain about the threat to union sponsorship'.
22. Roy Hattersley, 'Why Labour is stumbling', *Independent* August 12 1995.
23. *Guardian* September 5 1995. In the same interview Blair was also quoted as saying that 'the party had no plans to reduce the trade unions' block vote to below 50 per cent', which the paper called 'a conciliatory gesture to the unions'. The trade unions might be forgiven for being irritated rather than conciliated by this statement, since it was not for the leader to say what plans 'the party' had on this matter (compare note 16 above, with respect to changing the party's name).
24. The 'adjusted' figure, i.e. adjusted by allocating the undecideds in the light of past voting patterns, was more like 17 percent – still a very large lead.
25. Henry Porter, 'Zealous Moderate', *Guardian*, July 18 1995 (italics added).
26. Seyd and Whiteley, op. cit., p. 37.
27. Ibid. One of the hallmarks of Blair's speaking style which may also well be a generational difference is his apparent comfort with this kind of language that the Shadow Communications Agency worked so hard to teach the Shadow Cabinet in the 1980s. Hughes and Wintour record how in 1988 Robin Cook and Harriet Harman were taught to say 'cash before care', instead of whatever they originally thought of saying in criticism of a leaked White Paper on health, and how this was worth £2m. of political advertising (op. cit. p. 59). A 'quango' is a 'quasi non-governmental organisation', appointive and largely unaccountable bodies whose number and membership (consisting largely of Conservative supporters) increased dramatically under the Thatcher years, to the point where they had many more members than the total of the country's elected councillors, and were responsible for spending roughly as much money.
28. Education policy has been an instructive example of the changed locus of policy-making. In late 1994 David Blunkett, the shadow education minister, made a speech suggesting the possibility of removing the tax privileges enjoyed by private schools. This was immediately repudiated by the leader's office in an obvious effort at 'fire-fighting' – i.e. heading off a predictable attack from the Conservatives to the effect that Labour was still a party of class envy. Subsequently, after Blair's decision to send his own son to a distinctly elitist grant-maintained school (the London Oratory School) – a decision much resented by many inside the party, which was then committed to end grant-maintained status – Blunkett announced a new policy on these schools, proposing to put them on the same financial footing as local authority-controlled schools, but to leave them free from local authority control, relabelled as 'foundation schools'. Two aspects of this decision were noteworthy, in addition to its acceptance of the new social hierarchy that the Conservatives had thus created within the state education sector. One was that the press treated the new policy document 'Diversity and Excellence', produced by Blunkett in close collaboration with Blair's office, as 'Labour's new policy'. The other was Blunkett's comment on it: 'I think I have squared the circle' (*Guardian* June 23 1995).
29. Henry Porter, 'Rampaging with Charm', *Guardian* July 17 1995.
30. Tony Blair, 'The Flavour of Success', based on a speech made on July 5 1995 to the

Fabian Society, *Guardian* July 6 1995.

31. For a discussion of MacDonald's socialism and the context that governed it see David Marquand, *Ramsay MacDonald* (London: Jonathan Cape, 1977), especially pp. 88–92, 245–56 and 279. It is sobering to note that while much of Marquand's analysis applies very closely to Blair, there is a fundamental difference: throughout the twenties MacDonald opposed the market and accorded priority to the interests of the working class and the unemployed.
32. For the visit of Tony Blair and Gordon Brown to Clinton's 'transition team' after the Presidential election of 1992 see John Rentoul, *Tony Blair* (London: Little Brown, 1995), Ch. 13. Much of the visit was arranged by the Political Secretary at the Washington embassy, Jonathan Powell; in 1995 he left the foreign service to become Blair's 'head of private office'. One of Powell's brothers, Chris, ran an advertising agency which had the Labour Party's account. Another brother, Charles, had been Thatcher's Private Secretary.
33. 'The main changes will be a strong attack on long-term unemployment, the problems of getting people back to work; a proper modern industrial policy, preparing this country for the global market; education and schools; help for small businesses; economic regeneration; science and technology. . .' ('Rampaging With Charm', op. cit.).
34. The former Conservative Minister for Defence, Alan Clark, criticising the intellectual positions of both parties in early 1995, wrote provocatively: 'Here is this great Labour movement, rooted in a noble ethic. . . Now they are quite deliberately choosing to discard the whole of that tradition. . . 'New Labour' is no more than a bunch of people who want to win an election. . . Simply an alternative cluster of suits who, marginally more "likeable", will administer virtually identical policies. . . You can anaesthetise great parties, for short periods, by the prospect of power as a reward for "good behaviour". But lobotomies are different.' (*Guardian*, March 17 1995).
35. David Marquand, 'Political babble', *Guardian* June 5 1995.
36. Bryan Gould, 'The party with no bottle', an extract from his autobiography *Goodbye To All That* (London: Macmillan, forthcoming 1995) in the *Guardian* August 19 1995.
37. According to Porter, he provided Blair with 'both manipulative expertise and certain covert services with which the leader should not be too visibly associated' ('Zealous Moderate', op. cit.). One could speculate that these services included covert help to Jack Dromney, the challenger in 1995 for the leadership of the Transport and General Workers' Union favoured by Blair, and similar interventions in candidate selection; including, perhaps, Blair's announcement in August 1995, on his own authority, that women-only shortlists, which the party had agreed to apply to candidate selection in half Labour's vacant seats and which were unpopular with many of the male members of the constituency parties concerned, would be dropped after the next election.
38. Quoted in Seumas Milne, 'The Leader's Little Helper', *Guardian* February 11, 1995.
39. One is reminded of the opprobrium heaped on Edward Bernstein for spelling out the principles of the German Social Democrats' reformist practice in his *Evolutionary Socialism*. His friend Ignaz Auer wrote protestingly: 'My dear Ede, you don't *talk* about it, you just *do* it!' (quoted in Peter Gay, *The Dilemma of Democratic Socialism* (New York: Columbia University Press, 1952, p. 267).
40. According to Heffernan and Marqusee, Mandelson once said it would be nice to abolish the party conference, but it was not worth the trouble (op. cit., p. 209), and that in private he 'made it clear that as far as he was concerned the unions were a nuisance and the sooner they were expelled from Labour headquarters the better' (p. 218).
41. Radhika Desai summarises the most commonly adduced factors as follows: 'the institutionalisation of intellectual life in the Academy, its consequent isolation from wider social currents and its attendant disciplinary specialisation; the domination of intellectual life by the media; the substitution of market-driven decisions for any independent judgement intellectuals have had in culture and politics; and the replacement of a generally educated public, interested in social and political ideas, by a plurality of more

specialised and disparate audiences' (Radhika Desai, *Intellectuals and Socialism: 'Social Democrats' and the Labour Party* (London: Lawrence and Wishart, 1994), p. 27). Whatever the mix of causes, it is striking that by 1994 it was hard to find a significant intellectual making a sustained left-wing public argument for a particular line of policy outside the framework of the think-tanks. Exceptions within the PLP would include Tony Benn and Alan Simpson in the Socialist Campaign Group of MPs, and Frank Field, an independent thinker on a wide range of social issues; outside parliament the chief exception was Will Hutton, the *Guardian's* assistant editor and columnist, arguing for a more radical set of 'social market' reforms than anything the Labour leadership was likely to countenance. Occasional commentators from the universities, such as David Marquand and Andrew Gamble at Sheffield, or John Gray at Oxford and William Wallace at the LSE, did not so much argue for a particular line of policy as comment critically on the shortcomings of current Labour and Conservative policies and ideas.

42. Numerous highly competent left intellectuals, very aware of the need for a radical rethinking of the socialist project and uninterested in Labour's shibboleths, were more than ready to work for the new leadership, but were not welcomed, let alone sought after. A study of those who were welcomed would make interesting reading. One of the striking features of Blair's immediate entourage was how many people it included who were formerly non-political or had SDP or Liberal-Democrat ties.
43. The Borrie Report, *Social Justice: Strategies for National Renewal* (London: Vintage, 1994), is actually a comprehensive programme of economic and social reform for national competitiveness.
44. The key text on Quangos is Stuart Weir and Wendy Hall (eds.), *Ego Trip: Extra-governmental organizations in the United Kingdom and their accountability* (London: The Democratic Audit of the United Kingdom and Charter 88, 1994). See also Anthony Barnett's persuasively argued *The Defining Moment* (Charter 88, 1995), setting out the constitutional issues at stake for the Labour Party in the next general election. The striking level of support for a bill of rights, proportional representation and other constitutional reforms, which have been advocated by the Liberal Democrats but not the Labour Party, must owe something to the publicity and mobilising efforts of Charter 88.
45. From the statement, 'Why Demos?', in Demos's brochure.
46. In *Demos 2*, 1994, pp. 4–14; *Demos 3* 1994, pp. 2–9; and *Demos 5* 1995, pp. 2–11.
47. Interview, August 11, 1995. Mulgan has also written that 'Marx may have had an unequalled grasp of the dynamics of capitalism but he is not much use for a world of derivatives trading' (*Guardian* January 14 1995). Demos intends to undertake work in political economy in the future.
48. Or a world of 'twin economies' in which those who can't earn incomes in the main economy operate in a separate quasi-barter economy with state support, such as free access for market stalls on derelict land and ultra-cheap building accommodation (Geoff Mulgan, 'Creating a twin economy', *Demos Quarterly* 2/1994, p. 29). Mulgan's capacity to think positively about this sort of future has something in common with Mandelson's famous 'unsentimental' approach to politics. It marks them both off decisively from the ethos of the labour movement, including its past intellectual wing.
49. Geoff Mulgan and Helen Wilkinson, 'Well-being and Time', *Demos Quarterly* 5/1995, p. 11.
50. In an interview I put it to Geoff Mulgan that his preoccupation with introducing American thinkers to the British public had a parallel with the *New Left Review's* efforts to introduce European Marxism to Britain in the late 1960s and early 1970s. He dissented to the extent that he had no specific line of thought to promote, and turned to the USA only as a major source of high-calibre and varied thought relevant to the fast-changing real world.
51. Criticism of the communitarian discourse of Blair's *Spectator* lecture was an exception to the mainstream's general tolerance of his political rhetoric; in the *Guardian* John Gray,

Will Hutton, Bea Campbell, Martin Walker and Suzanne Moore all devoted space to thoughtful critiques.

52. *Guardian* August 21 1995. Blunkett was responding specifically to the charge by Alan Simpson MP, the secretary of the Socialist Campaign group, that under Blair the party was becoming indistinguishable from the old SDP. Perhaps, if Mulgan read Blunkett's statement, he experienced the kind of feelings teachers have when they read in their students' essays unconscious and sometimes embarassingly revealing parodies of their own ideas.
53. Mulgan was a member of the previously-mentioned so-called 'secret committee of trusted moderates' set up to meet fortnightly with Blair at Westminster.
54. Tony Blair, 'The flavour of success', op. cit.
55. A further instance was the rejection by the National Executive Committee of Liz Davies as a prospective parliamentary candidate for Leeds East just before the annual Conference in October 1995. Ms Davies, a barrister, had been adopted by a substantial majority of the local party from a women-only shortlist. Her real crime, it was clear, was her advocacy of left-wing views.

# DEVELOPING RESISTANCE, RESISTING 'DEVELOPMENT': REFLECTIONS FROM THE SOUTH AFRICAN STRUGGLE

Patrick Bond and Mzwanele Mayekiso

'Never before have so many political movements of the progressive left been so close to taking power,' Ruben Zamora, a leader of the Salvadoran left, recently remarked, 'but never before has power seemed to be so strongly predetermined by external forces adverse to the interests of the majority.'[1] The disappointments are profuse, not just from the left but from other movements which had rallied under the banner of colonial, racial or ethnic liberation, human rights, anti-corruption, and other forms of the much-heralded 'transition to democracy.' Consider merely some names of leaders of contemporary movements who, riding waves of insurrectionary 'people's power,' once easily bore the mantle of change – at least in decent general direction – and in some cases, adorned with messianic status: Aquino, Arafat, Aristide, Bhutto, Manley, Mugabe, Ortega, Perez, Rawlings, Walensa (and the list could be extended still further over a period of two or three decades). And then consider the depths to which most subsequently sunk – usually not by personal choice, to be sure – in their public acceptance and indeed advocacy of neoliberal politics ('low-intensity democracy') and economics (structural adjustment).

This is also the general fate of so many social democratic and labour parties in Western Europe, Canada and Australia. Even where once-revolutionary parties remain in control of the nation-state – China, Vietnam, Angola, and Mozambique, for instance (in the latter two cases, after contesting their first, recent, elections) – ideologies have sometimes wandered over to hard, raw capitalism. And even where leaders of genuinely progressive parties remain rather far from taking power for the foreseeable future, their transitions from mass opposition mobilizer to fiscally-responsible social democrat (Lula, Cardenas) or even aspirant neoliberal manager (Villalobos) gather pace and on the basis of this momentum one is compelled to worry about yet others (Adams, Kyi) whose political movements are rich with left currents but for whom enormous dangers of ideological cooption are evident.

Movement leadership drawn from the petty bourgeoisie is notoriously and eternally unreliable, we would be quickly reminded in presenting this list. And there are, and always have been, exceptions (Castro, for instance, has kept up a left critique while forced brutally to the right; Aristide, we shall see, has relished a left flank in civil society). Moreover, the point of such a survey would certainly not be to highlight the problem of individual proclivities; it would instead assess the *social base* behind insurgent forces that were once considered natural allies by the international left.[2] Strategically, they all had or have one overriding objective: capture of the nation-state (no matter the balance of forces elsewhere). What appears universal about their experiences is that with world markets and geopolitics so inhospitable today, no amount of these state-centric movements' substantial power and vision at national-scale is sufficient to withstand global capitalism's homogenising and continually degrading leverage. It is in this very difficult context that 'There Is No Alternative' – TINA, as Margaret Thatcher remonstrated – becomes not only the final word of subjugation; in some cases it also has begun to enjoy endorsements from what were once proudly counter-hegemonic political-intellectual leaderships.

There is much to report from transitional South Africa in this vein,[3] not least Nelson Mandela's prominence on our list of comrades. In the process of such a necessarily pessimistic account, it also becomes crucial to draw attention to means by which some militants, intellectuals and ordinary people are haltingly but inexorably coming to grips with this unanticipated dilemma: their movement holding the reigns of the *state* does not mean holding *power* (as it is often phrased in Pretoria). This is not an easy realisation for many particularly from the socialist and communist wings of the nationalist movement. But political discourses and policy options for South Africa are, after all, influenced by many of the same constraints and disintegrative processes currently evident everywhere.

Indeed, an important reason that neoliberal compromises characterise South Africa's transition is that there were so many selective justifications drawn from across the world. In most socio-economic sectors, ascendant African National Congress (ANC) policy-makers were inundated with 'market-oriented' propaganda, often in the course of all-expenses paid tours funded by international financial institutions and development agencies. The three words 'international experience shows' – the preferred preface in any number of didactic briefing sessions and reports sponsored by the US Agency for International Development, the Friedrich Ebert Stiftung, the World Bank and the like – were typically followed by glowing praise for federalist constitutional frameworks (referencing the USA and Germany), export-led growth (Taiwan, South Korea), invitations to foreign financial investment (pre-crash Mexico), privatisation (Britain), low wages (China, Indonesia), high real interest rates and an independent (ie, oriented to commercial banks) central bank (Germany, the USA), tariff-reduction (India), market-oriented affirmative action (ie, building a black petty bourgeoisie) (Malaysia), social contracts (Mexico), site-and-service schemes instead of housing (Chile), pensions based on individual savings (Chile), and more generally, the demise of statism/'socialism' (Eastern Europe, Africa).

This story, hence, is not merely about 'engaging' neoliberalism (to recall the euphemistic verb so often invoked in South Africa during the course of retreat), although the futility of doing so should continually be reemphasised. Nor is it crucial here to emphasize the need for the emergence of strong working-class parties that have more consistent political trajectories than those just alluded to. Instead, South Africa's most compelling lessons for the international left are, we believe, about building and maintaining a class-conscious civil society in oppressed communities, in the spheres of both production and reproduction, and more generally against the activities of the market-oriented 'development' industry (which we contrast with 'people-centred development' for purposes of semantic clarity). In reviewing some of these throughout the following pages, particularly with respect to the township-based 'civic associations' with which we are most familiar, it is important for us to highlight the organisational instruments of poor and working people. These we term 'working-class civil society' in order to distinguish them from bourgeois non-governmental institutions (as well as from government and firms) and hence from pervasive depoliticized notions of 'civil society' (the real goal of which boils down to reducing the scope of social services provided by Third World states).

Distinctions between and within social movements, CBOs (community-based organisations) and both indigenous and international NGOs (non-governmental organisations) of various ideological predispositions are becoming as crucial, we shall see, as the practical and political distinction between market-oriented development and people-centred development. The latter – which the South African National Civic Organisation (SANCO, made up of civic associations or 'civics') took as a motto at its 1992 launch, and lobbied for during the subsequent era – is, no doubt, vulnerable to manipulation by neoliberals and populist demagogues alike. But in its strongest, most organic form, the struggle for people-centred development highlights basic needs as *entitlements*, financed and delivered in a non-commodified form, through a 'strong but slim' state capable of capturing and redistributing the social surplus, complemented with additional resources for building the organisational capacity of non-profit, community-controlled institutions.[4] To comprehend the meaning of this discourse may require a brief diversion into the politics of South Africa's progressive resistance.

*South Africa: TINA or THEMBA?*

The nationalist and class uprising within South Africa from 1973 (following a decade of defeats) to 1994 was perhaps the most closely-watched campaign for social and economic justice in history. The domestic and global anti-apartheid struggles and the African National Congress' (ANC) non-racial ideology reinforced each other symbiotically, as a broad-based internationalist movement took aim at local apartheid- and shopfloor-related grievances, at the world's financial links to Pretoria, and at many other targets inbetween. Upon growing to peak strength ten years after the Soweto uprising – through unprecedented grassroots and shopfloor protest emanating from the industrial heartland of Johannesburg and the ANC strongholds of the Eastern Cape region – the democratic movement managed to sustain the mass support of the black majority in the context of brutal repression and an enduring capital accumulation crisis.

By the time of the 1984–86 upsurge in protest, there appeared a real chance in South Africa for sustained insurgency.[5] Polls regularly showed that more than half of the black population supported 'socialism' over capitalism, and through the 1980s it was not easy to find cadres of the trade union and leading anti-apartheid social movements – and even among the progressive intelligentsia – who did not identify themselves as women and men of the left, as traditional communists, independent socialists, followers of liberation theology and the like. Apartheid and capitalism seemed so inextricably intertwined that a substantial number of theorists assumed South Africa would not witness simply nationalist liberation but that the fabled 'second stage' (in the Communists' two-stage, 'Colonialism of a Special Type' theory) was intertwined with the first.

At grassroots level heady optimism characterised the months immediately after the February 1990 unbanning of political organisations, largely because as the ANC became a political party it was enthusiastic about and respectful of its 'Mass Democratic Movement' allies: the Congress of South African Trade Unions (COSATU), the newly-unbanned SA Communist Party (SACP) (whose leaders also held extremely influential positions within the ANC), the civics, innumerable student and women's associations, progressive churches and so many other instruments of the black majority. The Mass Democratic Movement's finest hour in the post-1990 stage of struggle was undoubtedly the period immediately following the breakdown of multi-party negotiations in June 1992, when protests rocked the country for three months and forced the ruling white National Party (NP) to ditch its alliance with the Zulu-based Inkatha Freedom Party.

The hopes of left strategists then eroded steadily, as 'mass action' was instrumentally turned on and off again by the more moderate ANC leaders like the proverbial 'tap.' Throughout, radicals sensed that they could embark upon empowering strategies and tactics only up to a point, at which not just apartheid but the bourgeois rule of property was threatened. As Mandela himself put it (in a September 1992 interview just after the infamous Bisho massacre), 'We are sitting on a time-bomb. The youths in the townships have had over the decades a visible enemy, the government. Now that enemy is no longer visible, because of the transformation taking place. Their enemy now is you and me, people who drive a car and have a house. It's order, anything that relates to order, and it is a very grave situation.'[6] Rather than nurture the potentially insurrectionary forces, some ANC leaders separated themselves from the base, through negotiations with NP 'verligtes' (enlightened ones) near Johannesburg as well as in smoke-filled rooms at exclusive British, Swiss and South African lodges, culminating in the 'bosberaad' – bush-consultations – of early 1993 that set out the terms of the crucial interim constitution.[7] The most striking surrenders occurred periodically on the economic policy front, as even the ANC's mild-mannered, Keynesian-oriented MacroEconomic Research Group inexorably lost influence. And the result of the often humiliating reversals on key principles is that, since April 1994, joined in the Government of National Unity by two conservative partners (the NP and Inkatha), the ANC has been largely stymied by bickering over policies, delivery systems, day-to-day governance and friction-ridden symbols of old and new.

Thus, the denouement of the ANC/SACP 'National Democratic Revolution' has left the impoverished majority frustrated and the left divided and confused.[8] Even the ANC's 1994 progressive-populist campaign platform, a 150-page document – the *Reconstruction and Development Programme*, or RDP – which sought (quite successfully) to translate recent traditions of grassroots social struggles into social policy and programmes, has been a well-recognised failure in practice, notwithstanding its (largely rhetorical) endorsement by other partners in the Government of National Unity in the wake of the national election.

It has thus not been easy to sustain hope for social progress. As we write, eighteen months into the new order, delivery of goods and services has been negligible in most deprived rural and urban areas, and – perhaps most surprisingly – the left's hopes for transfers of resources and for shining performances from ministries once presumed friendly (Reconstruction and Development, Housing, Health, Education, Land, Water and Forestry, and Posts and Telecommunications) have been largely dashed. As the editor of a respected paper, *The Mail and Guardian*, noted a year after the 1994 elections, 'If you measure the success of the Government of National Unity in strictly numerical terms – the number of houses built, the number of people who have access to free health care or potable water – then it scores disturbingly low.'[9] How low? The late Joe Slovo had promised that in his first year as housing minister, 90,000 affordable houses would be built using a market-oriented financing system; the eight months he served plus the preceding four yielded fewer than 5,000. Failure to deliver, even at this extreme scale, was more the rule than the exception (though progress in some primary health and child nutrition services, as well as the upgrading of a handful of strife-torn communities, deserve mention).

This failure reflects a broader political problem: compromises of basic liberation movement principles have ensured an unfavourable balance of governing forces for at least the next five years. Saul's trepidation – expressed in these pages just prior to the 1994 election – was that 'the threatened foreclosure of any sense of socio-economic possibility beyond "liberal capitalist democracy" involves both a hollowing out of language and a beggaring of the historical imagination.'[10] The language of the National Democratic Revolution has indeed hollowed, it has become clear, what with the ANC's historic demands for a one-person, one-vote unitary state blurring into negotiated federalism and electoral vote-trading.[11] Crippling technical and political compromises of formal bourgeois democracy occurred at national, provincial and local scales:

- the Government of National Unity itself entails an ANC-led cabinet, but the state's economic levers remain in the hands of exceptionally conservative forces, and there are regular disruptions from the ANC's ruling partners and various degrees of sabotage by the overwhelmingly white, Afrikaner civil service (the vast majority of whose jobs are unchanged by virtue of a pre-election agreement);

- at the level of the nine provinces, similar power-sharing arrangements are in place, except that these have not worked in the crucial Inkatha-held KwaZulu-Natal province – which has not only been paralysed by ethnic nationalism but has also regularly witnessed several dozen politically-related murders on weekends – and in the Western Cape where crises have emerged over issues such as the NP provincial leadership's attempt to gerrymander the Cape Town municipality (there and in Kwazulu-Natal, the 1995 local elections had to be postponed due to unmanageable chaos); and

- at local level, though ANC-led municipalities are now nearly universal, the first democratic elections also entailed enforced power-sharing by virtue of constitutional compromises that gave whites far more municipal council representation than blacks per capita as well as – in many settings – formal veto power over redistributive budgets.

And in response, it is fair to ask this: what use is taking state 'power' under such conditions? But it is not only the extraordinary hold of the political *status quo* that 'beggars the historical imagination' of the South African left; it is the ascendance of neoliberal thinking in all aspects of development, a theme to which we will return again and again. For additional compromise constitutional provisions include a property rights clause which makes ordinary state rights of eminent domain impossible to invoke, a lock-out provision to help businesses stymie worker protest, and the insulation of the Reserve Bank from democratic input. In the sphere of social policy, the inept housing programme, for instance, is market-driven not people-driven, is coordinated by bankers not civic movement cadre, and is, hence, less about housing than about 'toilets-in-the-veld' (in the bitter words of Slovo's successor as minister, Sankie Mthembi-Nkondo).[12] With the endorsement of big business, and before anyone on the left had grasped all of this, Slovo and his aides had achieved the official erasure of the legacy of grassroots 'affordable housing for all' campaigns and policy-making sessions going back more than a decade.[13]

Similarly, the land redistribution programme was designed by the World Bank and inspired by modernisation theory – with its emphasis on markets, non-subsidized credit and individual land titles – and appeared to be not only unpopular but also unworkable in a crisis-ridden agricultural economy. Few if any experiments got underway in the form of the *decommodified* goods and social services (cooperative housing, national health insurance, consumer cooperatives, land trusts, worker-owned enterprises, people's banks, etc) envisaged by many of the left SACP/COSATU/SANCO strategists.

More worrisome still, many of the leaders and organisational instruments of poor and working people have not entirely come to grips with why this is so and what can be done about it. Indeed most of the organisational forces once associated with the Mass Democratic Movement are stuck between understandably fierce loyalties to the ANC (with gratitude that most – though certainly not all – official displays of racial repression have ended) and a grim recognition that not much has changed, or will, in socio-economic terms (aside from losing cadreship to the 'gravy train' of high-paid government work). The result is a growing tendency to 'corporatism' (by which we mean tripartite – big business, big government, big labour/community – elite deal-making, serving the respective constituency's elite fractions), sometimes misleadingly characterised as 'social contracts.'

As a result, it seems harder than ever for many organs of civil society to rearticulate the goals of an expansive welfare state, an egalitarian society and a dramatic shift in social power that were embodied in the 1955 Freedom Charter. (The Charter's more radical positions – such as nationalising the mines, banks and 'monopoly corporations' – were jettisoned by ANC leaders in 1990.) Building mass unity and maintaining the progressive vision in the course of fighting the power of a repressive state was easy, in retrospect, while fighting the power of money is intrinsically more difficult, far more divisive.

This has been the case in part for logistical reasons. Foreign donors had supported anti-apartheid organisations through the 1980s and early 1990s, and because of this many hundreds of reputable NGOs emerged, many oppositional cultural fora flourished, many excellent progressive media initiatives were undertaken, many intellectuals were given resources for progressive policy-formulation ventures, and many projects were launched that might well have established new local-level relations of production and consumption. Most of these became dependent upon external financial lubrication, however, and faced crisis when in 1995 $50 million in funding was withdrawn (reportedly leading to a 66% budget deficit in the NGO sector as a whole), and also as countless leaders and movement functionaries migrated into government. With free financial flows ebbing and government funding pledges delayed in the bureaucracy (particularly the ministry responsible for 'constitutional affairs' and local government, which was run by a key NP leader), NGOs, CBOs and social movements had to scramble desperately for crumbs. The former generally came out ahead – often on condition they adopted a rather more neoliberal character (replacing collective and politically-self-conscious decision-making with internal hierarchy and 'strategic management,' imposing cost-recovery for services, repudiating radical policy ambitions, etc.) – and even SANCO has sometimes been reduced to menial roles in partnerships with businesses and corporate-oriented service agencies (both local and foreign), merely for the sake of paying the rent and salary bill.

And yet the hunger on the ground for radical change could not – and cannot – be quenched. The confidence of oppressed people leapt to new heights in April 1994, and the subsequent period was characterised by an upsurge of often spontaneous demonstrations, marches, boycotts, highway blockades, wildcat strikes, land invasions, inner-city building squats, sit-ins and occupations of factories and government offices, disruptions of neo-apartheid education, protests against (and by) public service providers (including kidnappings), mutinies by ANC cadres in the integrated defence and police forces, and on and on. With increased crime added to the boiling pot, social tensions bubbled up to the point that Mandela (in his opening speech to the 1995 session of parliament) sternly threatened a clamp-down: 'The battle against the forces of anarchy and chaos has been joined, and no one should say they have not been warned.' Mass action 'of any kind,' he cautioned, 'would only serve to subvert the capacity of government to serve the people.'[14]

Not all (or even most) of the grassroots challenges have been progressive in content – some were the result of Inkatha turf expansion, ethnic mobilisations (for example, by 'coloured' nationalists), and internecine or personal rivalries – but many did indeed reflect the capture of democratic space opened up by the liberation process and left vacant within civil society by the rush of Mass Democratic Movement leaders into the state. Moreover, sensing the grassroots rumble has been crucial for keeping the movement's organisations attuned to the larger vision, anxious to – at minimum – maintain their own traditions of populist rhetoric and proudly take up their own hard-won space: advocacy within the variety of policy-making fora to which they at last have been given access. It is here, of course, that they run the substantial risk of allowing their ties to the base fade, and that they are sometimes even drawn into unpopular or ineffectual official initiatives.[15] On the other hand, most of these organisations' political traditions were not merely anti-apartheid in nature but also embodied a class (and sometimes gender) content, so it is natural for citizens with workplace or local-level or even household grievances to continue to seek out the organisations that served their interests consistently over the preceding fifteen or twenty years.

To cite the example we know best, SANCO affiliates (approximately 2,000 urban and rural community-based civics) have retained a strong community presence relative to other organisations and to local political parties, as well as a role in progressive advocacy at other scales. Within townships, civics continued to outnumber and outorganise even the ANC, whose branches withered quickly after April 1994. Predictions abounded that the death of the civic movement would follow the departure of thousands of leading cadres in the wake of the November 1995 local government elections, and it remains to be seen how many civics can quickly transfer leadership to the next layer of activists. But such losses would not intimidate the movement from further developing a fairly radical policy agenda, from continuing to campaign vigorously for socio-economic rights and local democracy (running into opposition from not only entrenched white interests but also, in many rural areas, from traditional tribal elders), and from joining other progressive forces in coalition around issues ranging from township ecology to international economic relations.[16]

Also on the positive side, the 1.4 million member COSATU trade union federation has shaken out some (not all) of the early 1990s devotion to corporatism which had been associated with many of its former bureaucratic staff and some leaders who have mainly since gone into government. COSATU's rhetoric remains tough, its strikes and demonstrations as militant as ever, its seriousness as a voice for all poor and working people unquestioned by even its opponents, its organisational coherence and democratic spirit still quite strong, and its international solidarity work more progressive than ever.

Elsewhere in the democratic movement, the women's struggle continues not only in decentralized settings, but in a controversial and extremely important – also unique on the African continent – national grassroots-based effort to bring to culmination the ANC's much-contested campaign promise for reproductive rights. Elsewhere there continue to be vibrant reminders of Mass Democratic Movement mobilisation in various sectors (primary health, education, church, sports, language), and although many of the alternative media went bankrupt during the recent funding crisis, there are plenty of other progressive arts and cultural groups engaged in organising, advocacy, aesthetic debate, performance and criticism. Impressive environmental activism is evolving surely and rapidly from a white middle-class base into the rest of society. Likewise gays and lesbians are racially diversifying what is already an important movement. And in addition to SANCO at least two other networks of radical community-based groups – the Trust for Christian Outreach and Education (inspired by liberation theology) and People's Dialogue (linking housing savings schemes run by township women) – are not only maintaining their grassroots base but are also thinking globally and engaging in processes of policy critique and advocacy. It is in such organisations, which are in many ways classic urban (though not entirely so) social movements and whose grassroots cadres are largely women and youth (though men do tend to dominate leadership positions), that the class-splitting forces of neoliberalism may meet their match. For it is the Mass Democratic Movement's urban and community components which are typically most insistent that the unity of poor ('outsider,' in local lingo) and working-class ('insider') interests is inviolable.

But even with strong traditions of social justice, recent memories of insurgent politics, and comrades in government offices, there is too little talk of concrete socialist principles, policies, programmes or projects in the strategic sessions of either movement activists or leftist policy-wonks. This is particularly disappointing in that the main vehicle for explicitly socialist mobilisation, the SACP, has improved immeasurably from Stalinist days past. Township branches continue to grow, total membership is in excess of 70,000 (earning the self-characterisation 'fairly mass party'), publications are consistently compelling, and most SACP leadership and cadres recognise the folly of the ANC's official turn to neoliberalism (while a few others – notably, two deputy ministers responsible for finance and defence – publicly defend and advance the new government's more backward policies). Nevertheless, even for the most committed SACP activists, winning immediate demands remains the overwhelming priority (even when these are swallowed wholesale into a market-driven policy framework). The coming period will be regenerative for the SACP only if its activists – some holding municipal office – revisit ideological debates and restore a sense of socialist purpose, begin to develop an independent working-class programme (that will often conflict with government policy), reconnect with their social base in the townships and rural areas, and confront capital and the capitalist state on a regular and sustained basis. Many hopeful signs of such directions are already appearing.

With or without ideological support from the SACP, the fragments of South Africa's left forces in civil society are beginning to come to grips with low-intensity democracy and neoliberal economics. There are the occasional moments when 'TINA,' uttered by facile bureaucrats (from both Old and New SA), is answered by a resounding cry from these social movements: 'THEMBA!' (Zulu, for hope), 'There Must Be an Alternative!' Not only in South Africa, of course, but under far less amenable conditions in many other settings, does one sense a durable passion for exploring beyond the commodification of everyday life. Frank and Fuentes have made the broader case:

> In seeking and organising to change society in smaller, immediate but doable steps, which did not require state power, the utopian socialists were perhaps much more realistic than the scientific ones – and they were more akin then to the social movements of our time than the 'scientific' socialists of the intervening century. What is more, many utopian socialists proposed and pursued social changes and particularly different gender relations, which were subsequently increasingly abandoned or forgotten by scientific socialists... The real transition to a 'socialist' alternative to the present world economy, society, and polity, much more in the hands of the social movements. Not only must they intervene for the sake of survival to save as many people as possible from any threatening abyss. We must also look to the social movements as the most active agents to forge new links, which can transform the world in new directions.[17]

If there is anything to this sentiment, South Africa has got to be one of the better sites to investigate, at both political and intellectual levels. For not only, during this extremely painful but also portentous transition process, will working-class civil society have to learn to contest the hegemony of macroeconomic neoliberalism, political low-intensity democracy, and market-oriented microeconomic development principles at home. In addition, there are a host of international lessons to digest and transcend. To do so will require both breaking through the 'impasse' that has apparently paralysed so many intellectuals in the field of international development studies, and making common cause with many other efforts – particularly arising from impoverished communities in the world's largest cities – to counter neoliberalism with diverse forms of popular resistance. These are the subjects of the rest of this chapter.

### *The impasse of development theory?*

'The current crisis in development thought,' notes Sklar, 'requires, in addition to political theories of development, political theories for development.'[18] An obvious reason is that, as Moore puts it, traditional oppositional analysis advanced by 'counter-hegemonic movements' has been 'too easily co-opted into the dominant discourse,' to the extent that 'new delineations of terms and new strategies are required.'[19] This is the case with respect to the full range of concepts – development, democracy, community, sustainability, equity, participation, empowerment, decentralization, etc. – deployed within such movements, which are now bandied about just as earnestly by neoliberal theorists as by socialists. Indeed it is precisely the easy, populist appropriation of such terms which makes it all the more crucial to locate their proponents' divergent political economic philosophies, to deconstruct particular development strategies, to explain strategic and tactical overlaps, and then to move the struggle to a higher plane.[20]

Thus while 'concern with the "impasse" of development theory is largely a concern of what used to be known as the "development industry,"' according to Munck,[21] it is nevertheless also true that the discursive impasse appears just as great to social movements in search of a theory of purposive collective action that is tough enough to withstand the co-option process. In our own research into contemporary international urban social movements, including extensive discussions with representative organisations and intellectuals of movements across the world, we have encountered a debilitating ideological vacuum when it comes to generating a breakthrough development theory and linking it to a grass-roots, people centred development practice (and this would also seem to be the case in other situations beyond the city limits). None of the main postwar intellectual choices – modernisation theory, dependency theory (and the world systems approach), a version of neo-Marxism focused on expanding the forces of production (and hence disturbingly consistent with modernisation theory), more formal neoliberal economic analysis, and 'post-Marxism' – seems adequate for explaining the combination of local and global (and all scales inbetween) socio-economic crisis conditions which radical social movements face today.

Nevertheless, the argument we would want to make is that international (and some South African) neo-Marxist development theories popular during the 1970s but out of favour today do offer perspectives very much worth revisiting – but we want to do so cognizant of some of the better post-structuralist contributions to the politics of development struggles,[22] as well through drawing heavily upon both classical and more recent Marxist theoretical insights and practical political lessons. To establish a baseline within the 'absolute general law of capitalist accumulation,' recall Marx's argument that uneven development is a necessary process of capitalism,

> . . .that in the same relations in which wealth is produced, poverty is produced also; that in the same relations in which there is a development of the forces of production, there is also the development of a repressive force; that these relations produce bourgeois wealth, i.e. the wealth of the bourgeois class, only by continually annihilating the wealth of the individual members of this class and by producing an ever growing proletariat.[23]

Hence at the international scale we would reiterate a good deal of the dependency argument, whose essence is perhaps best captured in Frank's phrase 'the development of underdevelopment' and whose inspiration for Third World (especially African) anti-imperialist thought and activism persists.[24] Where dependency theory was allegedly most flawed, in considering the relationship of a national economy to the world capitalist system as the factor most responsible for systematic underdevelopment, empirical evidence nevertheless builds in the theory's favour, though it more broadly seems to fit our understanding of 'uneven development.[25]

We might add as friendly amendments three arguments. First, in the contemporary context of neoliberal hegemony, the exceptional breakouts from dependency – the old generation of export-oriented Newly Industrialised Countries that did succeed in at least partially establishing internal articulations – appear thoroughly anachronistic to neoliberalism, what with their aggressive state industrial policy, prohibitions on the activities of foreign capital, subsidized and directed credit through a highly-regulated financial system, and thorough-going land reform (not to mention all the particularities of local/regional accumulation and unevenness on the East Asian rim).[26] The lack of space in today's world economy for potential new NICs does not bode well for turning the nation-state towards export-led growth (as is the South African elite's agenda).[27]

Perhaps, thus, semi-autarchy is a viable strategy for a robust nation-state to consider, notwithstanding the problem that today, even in Amin's mild formulation,[28] there appear no real takers among nationalist or left movements (even leaders of the admirable experiment in Eritrea, who rebuff imperialist aid, apparently harbour fantasies of a Singapore-type commercial role). As a non-starter in recent South African debates (what with all that 'engaging' of neoliberalism underway), autarchy makes sense as a strategy only when a political movement can take state power in a more decisive manner, at a time the international system is far weaker, than the ANC experienced in 1994.

Second, a several decades-long period of global overproduction and generalised capital overaccumulation overlays the structural relationship of domination between the First and Third Worlds.[29] This has at least two potential implications: first, that we are still likely to encounter a more rigorous process of devaluation of capital (taking forms including depression, financial crashes, inflation, the continuing collapse of the global social wage and/or war); and second, that limits to the success global economic managers have had to date in displacing overaccumulation crisis both through time (using credit and other financial instruments) and across space (for example, onto a Third World now apparently squeezed nearly dry) may be approaching.

Politically this could be extremely important, for it means that as contradictions intensify and ruptures appear, new counterchallenges may be feasible. These would emerge not through creatively managing the nation-state or national economies out of their crises. Instead, as Arrighi, Hopkins and Wallerstein argue, the most serious challenge occurs when 'popular movements join forces across borders (and continents) to have their respective state officials abrogate those relations of the interstate system through which the pressure is conveyed.'[30] The January 1, 1994 Zapatista attack on NAFTA and all that it implied, is instructive and inspiring. Even more so, in Haiti, the anti-privatisation campaign by the leading popular organisations begun in August 1995 – implicitly encouraged by Aristide – rose to such heights as to drive out the neoliberal prime minister by October and force a healthy confrontation with the international financial agencies. In South Africa, similarly, the capacity of democratic social forces to think globally and act locally, and in doing so to locate the vulnerabilities of the international system and develop political strategies accordingly, was conclusively demonstrated by the successful 1980s anti-apartheid sanctions campaign and by ongoing solidarity labour actions with trade unions in Europe and North America.

Third, we are concerned that *institutions* of underdevelopment (particularly corporations) remain the focus of inquiry and praxis on the left,[31] potentially leaving the *process* – 'the internationalisation of capital, not just TNCs,' as Bryan puts it – submerged. The difference here, Bryan continues, is between a) solely focusing on capital as a social relation between capital and labour (or worse, perceiving capital merely as a 'thing'), and b) highlighting 'Marx's conception of the social relation of *value in movement*. The processes which determine value accumulation involve the interactive relation of money, production and commodities to which the class relations of capitalism give rise – their interdependence and their contradictory relations.'[32] Hence, globalisation becomes an aspect of the spatial movement of value through various circuits and spaces (particularly, we argue momentarily, in an attempt to increase the productivity of capital in the urban setting).

Thus if it is true in broad-brush terms that the social surplus of the Third World has shrunk dramatically since the 1970s due to structural shifts in demand for raw materials, the rise in the interest bill on the debt, and – more generally – the terribly uneven nature of the devaluation of global capital, it is important to augment this in local terms through intermediate-level analysis of 'articulations of modes of production' and other concrete processes of capital accumulation, class formation (and class struggle), and crisis. It should, in other words, be possible to apply the immutable 'laws of motion of capitalism' identified by Marx in order to gauge the dynamics of combined and uneven development in each setting under consideration. No doubt, nuances in historical materialist analysis are required, appraisals of gender, ethnicity and environment must be unequivocally drawn aboard, and reformulations of political action – especially expanding alliances beyond the point of production – are required. But the general goals and objectives, and the analysis that undergirds much of what historical materialism has stood for, continues to have enormous integrity. In sum, getting 'beyond the impasse' perhaps means reclaiming much of the substance of the various 'political economy of . . .' articles that were once so prolific in left journals. And perhaps it also means considering whether, in this apparently globalised world of material and information flows, our theoretical conception of uneven development can move easily from the global to the national to the local scales and back again (as do capital and, increasingly we shall see, popular resistance).

At the national scale South Africa is again instructive, for successive generations of neo-Marxist development theorists also reached their own impasse, following successive commitments to the theory of 'Colonialism of a Special Type' (CST), articulations of modes of production (still in defence of the communist broad front strategy), typologising fractions of capital in the spirit of Poulantzas, the conceptualisation of 'racial capitalism,' and regulation theory.[33] By the late 1980s, there was not only an overall retreat from theory underway in key sections of the left intelligentsia, but a distinct drift rightwards.[34] Myriad newly-empowered progressive policy wonks subsequently failed (or feared) to more firmly advocate socialist-oriented policy options ('non-reformist reforms') consistent with what was, from the base, an ongoing praxis against neoliberal development. (Those options would have covered a wide field of decommodified, destratified policies and projects – in public health, beginning with national health insurance; housing, with an emphasis on cooperatives and socialised subsidies; local economic development, under worker and community control; education; pensions; and so forth – the embryos of which were to be found in the RDP.) Yet the intellectual hiatus – a diminishing dedication to revitalising socialist theory – was nevertheless overwhelming and disempowering; grassroots cries of THEMBA! often were neglected by the progressive intelligentsia; and there was, subsequently, a demise of left opportunities for, and within, the ANC.

It is not as if there were not some good reasons for progressive theorists to keep moving. Intellectuals of various stripes rejected the earlier theories one by one: CST in the 1970s because it described internal *colonialism* while SA was dominated by capitalist relations; articulations of modes of production in the 1980s because of chronological flaws in the assertion that homeland reserves were necessary for assuring industrial labour supplies; Poulantzianism in the late 1970s because of the centralisation of all fractions of capital under the hegemony of the mining finance houses and insurance companies, and the blurring of traditional white ethnic divisions; racial capitalism in the late 1980s because capital was, in fact, finally delinking from formal apartheid; and, ultimately, regulation theory in the early 1990s because of strained metaphors and questionable policy implications.[35]

Nevertheless, there was much there of great value to retain for new rounds of intermediate theorizing about the process of uneven development, particularly during times of capitalist crisis. However, that theorizing remains largely still to be done (instead, far too much reformist policy analysis has occupied the progressive intelligentsia – to some effect, perhaps, in the drafting of the ANC's RDP campaigning platform, although left policy positions which were won in late 1993 and early 1994 quickly lost ground a few months later when it came time for implementation). By all accounts, South Africa has had too few theoretical debates, Marxist reading circles and book clubs, discussion groups and left publications, with the result a generalised failure to rigorously interrogate and contest political strategies. Will there be an opportunity to restore the dramatic left cultural and intellectual advances of the 1970s and 1980s? Will sustained popular protest lend credence to reassertions of left intellectual commitments? If so, then perhaps it is in the urban sphere that we can turn for examples, beginning with critiques of uneven urban development.

*Resisting uneven urban capitalist development*

The contestation of urbanisation is a central component of the global struggle against capitalist development.[36] That struggle is becoming increasingly difficult for people of Third World cities as a result of what seems to be a shift in the scalar strategy of international capital and aid agencies. In contrast to traditional modernisationists (like Pye) who argued for, 'above all else, acceptance in the political realm of belief that the prime unit of the polity should be the nation-state,'[37] it appears now that the mega-city is becoming a new unit of analysis, control and implementation for the purpose of more efficiently imposing structural adjustment policies (especially in the wake of the destruction of many nation-state capacities). To illustrate, one senior advisor to the United Nations Conference on Human Settlements, Shlomo Angel, argues that the 1996 Habitat conference in Istanbul should be about 'creating a level playing field for competition among cities, particularly across national borders; on understanding how cities get ahead in this competition; on global capital transfers, the new economic order and the weakening of the nation state. . .' This is only one of the more vulgar articulations of an increasingly familiar theme (as expressed again by Angel): 'The city is not a community, but a conglomerate of firms, institutions, organisations and individuals with contractual agreements among them.'[38]

From such foundations, an entire neoliberal edifice is being constructed. The World Bank's efforts to do so have spanned two decades but have taken on far greater energy since the 1986 launch of the New Urban Management Programme, which was further articulated in an important

1991 policy paper.[39] Meanwhile, the UN's Development Programme and Habitat housing division have also been thoroughly co-opted, and the US Agency for International Development, British ODA, Canadian CIDA, the Japanese and other official donor agencies now strictly reinforce urban neoliberalism through cross-conditionality on grants and loans. The overall orientation is nearly identical to the austerity policies at the macro-economic scale,[40]) with US AID consultants spelling out the

> ...important change in policy thinking in the developing world closely linked to the acceptance of market-oriented economies: the growing acceptance of rapid urbanization... An emphasis on national economic growth and export-led development will usually mean that new investment resources must be directed to already successful regions and cities... Governments have considerable control over the entire cost structure of urban areas. Public policy should be directed to lowering these costs.[41]

This, perhaps, comes closest to the point. Lowering these costs – especially by lowering the social wage – is integral to a more direct insertion of 'competitive' cities into the world economy. The focus here is not merely on limiting public financing of social services to those deemed to add value (though this is one of the more obvious effects of structural adjustment, and the catalyst for many an IMF riot). Just as importantly, the New Urban Management Programme also highlights the *productivity* of urban capital as it flows through urban land markets (now enhanced by titles and registration), through housing finance systems (featuring solely private sector delivery and an end to state subsidies), through the much-celebrated (but extremely exploitative) informal economy, through (often newly-privatized) urban services such as transport, sewage, water and even primary health care services (via intensified cost-recovery), and the like.

Likewise, however, it is here that urban unevenness spawned by the rule of capital and the intensification of commodification is most vigorously contested by popular movements, which are agitating both around conjunctural social policy decisions (typically, cutbacks in subsidies for food, transport or other services) and also against the structural conditions through which the political life of cities is reproduced. The movements have, in the process, begun to transcend the traditional dichotomy between an inward-looking territorial identity and the rhetoric of a broader emancipation.[42] They have begun exploring a broader set of urban class practices, which in the Latin American case – according to Petras and Morley – entail new alliances that traverse the spheres of production and collective consumption, under conditions of persistent capitalist crisis:

> The power of these new social movements comes from the fact that they draw on the vast heterogeneous labour force that populates the main thoroughfares and the alleyways; the marketplaces and street corners; the interstices of the economy and the nerve centres of production; the exchange and finance centres; the university plazas, railway stations and the wharves – all are brought together in complex localized structures which feed into tumultuous homogenizing national movements.[43]

The main structural factor forging the unity of the urban poor and the formal working-class, Petras and Morley continue, is the capitalist crisis itself. 'The great flows of capital disintegrate the immobile isolated household units, driving millions into the vortex of production and circulation of commodities; this moment of wrenching dislocation and relocation is silently, individually experienced by the mass of people, who struggle to find their place, disciplined by the struggle for basic needs and by the absolute reign of ascending capital.' Under such conditions, the social base for urban movements is continually recreated at the point that the limits to both commodity production and consumption become evident.

With respect to production, Petras and Morley on the one hand view the rise of militant urban social movements as a consequence of the sudden increase in mass unemployment since the 1980s debt crisis began, which 'lifted the control and discipline of capital over labour – making the latter available for, and receptive to, a new kind of discipline: that associated with the structure and action of mass social movements.' On the other hand, a complementary explanation – not grounded in the formal sector labour market (unemployment) – also presents itself. 'It comes down to this. Capital transformed an inert mass of atomized producers into a concentrated army; and the market that it created could not sustain it. The impersonal ties – the cash nexus – are the only link in that anonymous urban labor market. The rupture of that tie sets the stage for the eruption of uprooted people.'[44]

By considering unevenness in both production and consumption, particularly in so many contexts characterised by market failure, this stylized theory breaks free of many of the constraints associated with previous neo-Marxist approaches to development and underdevelopment.[45] It also highlights the scope for alliance-formation between oppressed classes, and across borders. And it brings us back to the self-identity of social movements as a theoretically-relevant factor for ultimately moving beyond uneven urban capitalist development.

It is not always feasible to specify the construction of social movement identity in urban settings, where conjunctural features are legion but where overt market processes have torn asunder land relations, rural ties, indigenous culture, and many forms of pre-existing authority and social control. The identity of social movements can be traced, at least to some extent, through their implicit or explicit strategic orientations in contesting uneven capitalist development. From experiences with urban movements in Santiago, Tironi conceptualised two fields of strategic polarization: between a sense of exploitation or exclusion, and between the goals of participation within or breaking from the wider political, economic and cultural system. Four categories – and prototypical modes of political organisation – result across this matrix of characteristics (Table 1).[46]

*Table 1:* Identities of Social Movement Constituents

| *status, objectives* | *excluded* | *exploited* |
|---|---|---|
| participation | 1 | 2 |
| revolution | 4 | 3 |

First, those who feel excluded and are anxious to participate more are often supporters of traditional populism (*pobladores*). Second, those who felt both exploited and anxious to participate more in the system included traditional trade unionists. Third, those who feel exploited by the system and who are interested in its formal rupture include traditional revolutionaries. Fourth, there are those alienated social forces which are excluded from the system and which also desire its rupture – and which are also, in many cases, engaged in collective subsistence activities that aim towards the construction of an alternative life-style based, at least to some extent, on the economy of solidarity. It is in this latter category that most progress seems to be occurring by way of mass mobilising and sustained challenges to neoliberal policies.

If we accept such typologies, South African civics and their cadre can be seen to have multiple identities. They include both insiders (exploited) and outsiders (excluded), as well as revolutionaries and reformers. Civics may have had a primary identity as traditional anti-apartheid revolutionaries at one stage (Category Three). But at other times, and depending upon local conditions, there are also civics and community structures which represent a profoundly alienated social force (Four); some place today's black youth and some youth-led civics here (often out of malice).[47] In other categories, some civics and their leaderships are today vulnerable to being captured and denuded via corporatist social contracts (Two). And a good many outsiders who feel excluded are anxious to gain access to state resources, even on essentially neoliberal terms dictated by foreign (and some local) development agencies (One).

Yet at other times – particularly the mid-1980s in places like Alexandra township – the combination of advancing national anti-apartheid politics (Two) and constructing local-level 'dual power' (Three) was extraordinarily successful. Not only was the apartheid system shaken and the international progressive community conscientised and mobilised through the urban uprisings of 1984–86. In addition, local people's courts, advice offices, local media, clinics and other institutions were established. Some have compared this experience to the Paris Commune (though the lessons are tenuous),[48] and after all, as Marx understood, it was the *process* of self-emancipation from the dictates of capital, not the outcome, that was most important:

> The working class did not expect miracles from the Commune. They have no ready-made

> utopias to introduce *par decret du peuple*. They know that in order to work out their own emancipation, and along with it that higher form to which present society is irresistibly tending by its own economical agencies, they will have to pass through long struggles, through a series of historic processes, transforming circumstances and men. They have no ideals to realise, but to set free the elements of the new society with which old collapsing bourgeois society itself is pregnant.[49]

In this spirit, we might next consider the more formal challenge of characterising popular resistance to uneven, neoliberal development.

### *Developing resistance, resisting demobilisation*

Much recent resistance to uneven urban development has been defensive, ephemeral, even destructive. Peru, Bolivia, Brazil and Argentina each witnessed a dozen major anti-austerity urban protests during the 1980s; repeated uprisings were experienced in the cities of Chile, Ecuador, the Philippines, Zaire, Jamaica, Morocco, Sudan, and the Dominican Republic; in Venezuela in 1989, security forces killed more than 600 people involved in a single IMF riot; and there were isolated incidents in dozens of other countries. In the 1990s, these countries were joined by India, Albania, Nepal, Iran, Ivory Coast, Niger and Zimbabwe, where large-scale IMF riots broke out. Do or can these uprisings reflect – or perhaps stimulate – the existence of more visionary, creative, and empowering urban social movements? Are they irredeemably populist in nature? And can they avoid being captured by neoliberal conceptions of civil society, the informal economy, self-help and the like?

The leading scholars of the IMF riot, Walton and Seddon, have contemplated the transition from the chaos intrinsic in most urban uprisings to the more durable mobilisations required for movement-scale attempts at democratic transformation. Given that the most decisive factor in the reproduction of everyday life in many Third World urban settings is the shrinkage of the state under conditions of structural adjustment, 'the broader trend is toward the decline of clientism and, conversely, the growing autonomy of urban low-income groups.'[50] As states lose their patronage capacity to channel social surpluses to supporters, social movements can cast off the worst influences of corporatism and corruption associated with urban civil society under populist regimes. As this becomes a more generalised political process, the urban poor consequently transcend spontaneous and unsustainable reactions to economic crisis such as the classic IMF riot.

But for this to be the case, it would seem, the form of urban organisation, the style of mobilisation, and the durability of the democratic process within the movement must all be carefully considered. We recognise that some Marxist theorists and socialist organisers express discomfort with either a celebratory class analysis of social movements (in the spirit of Petras and Morley) or advocacy of new relations of production and reproduction (along the lines of Frank and Fuentes) at the scale of the urban 'community.' Hirsch, for instance, has questioned the scope of urban movements' 'individual concrete demands and goals. These must remain limited no matter what, and they are repeatedly called into question by the socio-economic restructuring processes.'[51] And in a seminal Marxist study of urban politics, Cockburn argued that '"Community" belongs to capital' because 'Community action points not to deficiencies in the mode of production but in the products' and because of its 'populist formulation, open to all classes, groups and interests.'[52] Marx's own rejection of utopianism serves as an important precursor to such debates.

The left critiques we take seriously – but as a challenge to always expand the socio-economic demands (based on their feasibility) and to avoid potentially conservatising populism, not as a rationale to ditch the project of building working-class civil society. In South Africa, the tendency to exclude from any socialist project those social movements based in the sphere of extended reproduction (ie, not political parties drawing their cadres from struggles at the point of production) was briefly flirted with during the early 1980s within several trade unions (through 'workerist' syndicalism, as it was known). But it has very little purchase today, and residual calls for a distinct Workers' Party by even the powerful National Union of Metalworkers at a 1993 congress failed to resonate within the left as a whole, which instead cohered behind (working-class) civil society as watchdog on the new government.

In addition to the traditional Marxist critiques of utopianism, which require social movement strategists to continually reevaluate the conditions around which they struggle, it strikes us that there are other impediments to the maturation of urban social movements as forces for socialist transformation. Consider the trajectory of an urban movement which has its deepest origins in the form of community cooperation and networking via mutual aid systems (especially among women). As local grievances become the basis for political mobilisation, the group solidifies as a community-based organisation (with or more often without technical NGO involvement, though often taking up unfortunate patriarchal structures and styles). Along the way, it may consciously or subconsciously experiment with decommodified, destratified (and environmentally- and gender-sensitive) forms of people-centred development to meet basic needs. It experiences repeated conflicts with state bureaucrats over resources and local-level capitalists over investment decisions. And eventually it evolves as an important social force in contesting national economic policy, even linking up to discuss common strategies and tactics with similar forces in other societies.

Impediments along the way are increasingly to be found embedded within the neoliberal ideology of civil society, particularly the premise that the citizenry must not make demands for state services as entitlements. In South Africa and across the world, therefore, it is now crucial to recognize the ideological lacunae and diversions represented within the many new development organisations that have emerged in response to the broader failure of capitalist modernisation and of the state. In dozens of wretched Third World cities (including now Los Angeles) where organisation and democratic traditions of struggle are simply lacking, matters quickly degenerate into desperate IMF riots. In many other situations, the opposite – petty-bourgeois professionalisation – has taken hold. Given the class groundings, the often patriarchal form and the occasionally imperialist sponsorship of some Third World (and many First World) organisations engaged in development work, it should not be surprising that upon closer examination their progressive rhetoric is merely rhetoric and their practices quite consistent with neoliberalism. Drawing out their relationships to establishment actors (foundations, aid agencies, development banks, consultants and lawyers, construction and civil engineering capital, etc.) becomes more and more important at levels of both micro-implementation and macro-policy advocacy.

The dangerous ideology of 'neoliberal populism,' as Vivian puts it, assumes 'that if diverse interest groups and social structures are able to compete within a strong and open social "market," efficient – and by implication equitable – social institutions will result.'[53] Across the world, thus, pliant NGOs are now considered to be an integral component of the modernisation process by virtue of their efficiency and flexibility, corresponding with the desire of the international agencies to shrink Third World states as part of the overall effort to lower the social wage.[54] Even indigenous NGOs and some CBOs have been drawn into the process, which highlights long-standing distinctions between technicist, apolitical development interventions and the people-centred strategies (and militant tactics) of either small-scale CBOs or mass-based social movements of the oppressed.

This dichotomy is amplified and complicated when we move to development advocacy at the international scale. On the one hand, some Northern – and a few notable Southern – NGOs are now serving enthusiastically as transmission belts for neoliberalism.[55] But, on the other, efforts are underway among diverse progressive forces to link up and amplify existing grassroots social movement challenges to GATT and the World Bank. In the latter struggle, an important obstacle has emerged in the form of surprisingly durable reformist (as opposed to non-reformist) reformism within the radical petty-bourgeois intelligentsia. This class (to which we also belong) has more than its share of dilettantes, is sometimes politically capricious, and often wavers at key conjunctures which can be crucial for progress towards a broader internationalism. One significant result is that for reasons relating largely to its own 'insider' technocratic positionality, many intellectual and strategic campaigners within these international movements argue for reform, not defunding, of the World Bank. In contrast, increasing numbers of other organisations are coming to the conclusion that a vigorous and potentially decisive campaign to shut down the Bank – for example, through divestment (of Bank securities purchased by government, pension and university funds) in the North and popular boycotts in the South – is eminently feasible.[56]

It remains to be seen whether in coming months and years, the '50 Years Is Enough' network comprising Northern groups and dozens of excellent grassroots social movements which have fought and sometimes won struggles against the Bank – from Costa Rica, Haiti, India, Mexico, Nepal, Nicaragua, Papua New Guinea, and the Philippines, to name a few sites of intense recent activism – can come up with a consensus and cohere as an international movement. If this does occur – if, in other words, those local and national social movements with a more explicitly anti-capitalist development ideology do begin thinking globally and acting globally – it will be, in part, because of opportunities such as the *Socialist Register* consistently provides to discuss and debate the roles and responsibilities of movements and of socialist political parties.

It will also be because of strong organisational commitments and efforts. From the South African experience, we believe that social movements are capable of being tightly networked, and that their immediate territorial base can be expanded regionally, nationally or even internationally. As this happens, movements cement their common norms, practices and collective strategies and tactics, in order to advance both local agendas and larger political campaigns. This experience is still ahead, of course, but not too far off if the World Bank remains such an inviting target. (In this, the international anti-apartheid movement provides inspiration, but also important lessons about the dangers of demobilisation.)

We may ultimately agree with Navarro and so many other traditional Marxists that 'The mass struggle carried out in its many different forms needs to be carried out in the area of representative politics as well as by instruments such as political parties which need to present and articulate the demands made by these movements.'[57] Indeed, in *Socialism for a Sceptical Age* Ralph Miliband conceptualised 'dual power' not only in the proto-revolutionary terms with which we are familiar from South Africa, but also as 'a partnership between socialist government on the one hand and a variety of grassroots agencies on the other.'[58] (Such is the conception currently being theorised by the South African Communist Party.)

But until the terrain is better prepared for representative politics to emerge at the world scale,[59] or until wider cracks open in the present hegemony that neoliberal institutions maintain over nation-states, it is our sense that broad-based social movement activism grounded in struggles against both capitalist production and reproduction is where the most portentous political challenges to the international system lie. It is hence our personal hope and expectation that comrades around the world will gain most inspiration from the South African struggle, and will most effectively contribute to its deepening over the coming difficult period, by recognising the parallels through which urban (and so many other) social movements have contested uneven capitalist development.

If we can make progress in the intellectual sphere in this respect, it will be because the movements themselves begin to demand the global analysis which helps draw out the similar conditions and processes, and assess which strategies and tactics work. It will also be because the movements of working-class civil society we have come to know and respect continue to ward off any tendencies to sink into neoliberal conceptions of civil society by accepting TINA, and instead move towards THEMBA!: international forms of organisation that ardently resist capitalist development.

ACKNOWLEDGEMENTS

The authors warmly thank Leo Panitch, John Saul and Colin Leys for editing suggestions, and our institutional hosts during 1995 (Johns Hopkins University School of Public Health and Pratt Institute) for providing the space to consolidate our thoughts.

NOTES

1 Ruben Zamora, 'Toward a Strategy of Resistance,' *NACLA Report on the Americas*, v.29, #1 (July-August 1995), p.8.
2 Boris Kagarlitsky, *The Mirage of Modernization* (New York, Monthly Review, 1995).
3 For more background on South Africa during the early 1990s from Marxist perspectives see Alex Callinicos, *Between Apartheid and Capitalism* (London, Bookmarks, 1992); Neville Alexander, *Sowing the Wind* (Cape Town, Buchu, 1993); John Saul, *Resistance an Recolonization in Southern Africa* (Lawrenceville, NJ, Africa World Press, 1993); Martin Murray, *The Revolution Deferred: The Painful Birth of Post-Apartheid South Africa* (London, Verso, 1994); and Mzwanele Mayekiso, *Township Politics: Civic Struggles for a New South Africa* (New York, Monthly Review, 1996).
4 See, e.g., Mayekiso, *Township Politics*, Chapters 13–15; and South African National Civic Organisation Commission on Development Finance, *Making People-Driven Development Work* (Johannesburg, 1994).
5 For Marxist perspectives on mid-1980s possibilities, see Martin Murray, *Time of Agony, Time of Destiny* (London, Verso, 1987) and Alex Callinicos, *Between Reform and Revolution* (London, Bookmarks, 1988).
6 *The Star*, 15 September, 1992.
7 For a breathless but revealing account see Alister Sparks, *Tomorrow is Another Country* (New York, Hill and Wang, 1995).
8 See, e.g., Phillip Dexter, 'The RDP,' *South African Labour Bulletin*, v.19, #4 (September 1995), and two articles – John Pape, 'South Africa's Year One,' and Dan Connell, 'What's Left of the South African Left?' – in *Against the Current* #58 (September/October 1995).
9 Anton Harber, 'The World's Longest Honeymoon,' *Mail and Guardian* (April 21–27,

1995).

10 John S. Saul, 'Globalism, Socialism and Democracy in the South African Transition,' in Ralph Miliband and Leo Panitch (Eds), *Socialist Register 1994* (London, Merlin Press, 1994).

11 This was most notable (and resented) in the KwaZulu-Natal province, but nationally the ANC leadership also decided to reduce its electoral margin from above two-thirds of the April 1994 vote to less than 63%, thus requiring parliamentary alliances with firmly neoliberal parties for any constitutional changes. The well-publicised ballot-trading five days after the voting ended (two days before results were announced) was accepted as necessary by a wide range of elites; as Mandela himself put it, he was 'relieved' his party did not secure the two-thirds majority because of growing fears by whites and potential foreign investors that the ANC would 'write our own final constitution.' In the wake of extensive fraud, millions of lost ballots and extraordinary incompetence (and sabotage) by government officials administering the elections, the final tally (ANC, 63 percent; NP 20; Inkatha 11; others 6) was ratified by the discredited head of the electoral commission, Judge Johann Kriegler: 'We have never been asked to certify that the result is accurate. We have been asked to certify that the particular political process is substantially free and fair... You can't work in a brothel and remain chaste.' (News reports, early May, 1994.) Such was the birth of South Africa's version of low-intensity democracy.

12 Indeed Slovo's policy appeared, one business journalist conceded (in a typically arrogant rebuttal to the new minister), 'remarkably like the discredited site and service schemes advocated during the apartheid era... But housing is a key ministry. It is arguably the one which will determine how the populace judges the government's performance. It requires at the helm a political heavy-weight [i.e., not Mthembi-Nkondo] who has the support and ability to carry a controversial housing [i.e. toilets-in-the-veld] policy through to fruition.' (Robyn Chalmers, 'Housing Policy Founders in Mist of Uncertainty,' *Business Day*, 21 July, 1995, p.6.)

13 Patrick Bond, 'Undermining the RDP,' *Southern Africa Report* v.10, #5 (July 1995), pp.23–29.

14 From the same speech, in much the same spirit: 'Everything must be done to encourage a significant upward movement in the rate of investment to increase the productive capacity of the economy, to modernise and restructure the economy, to create jobs and to increase our international competitiveness. With regard to these economic issues, I would also like to emphasise our continuing commitment to fiscal discipline, including the reduction of the budget deficit, the reduction of the share of the national income that accrues to government and the reorientation of government expenditure away from recurrent disbursements towards investment.' (Address of President Nelson Mandela on the Occasion of the Opening of the Second Session of the Democratic Parliament, Cape Town, February 17, 1995.)

15 'Operation Masakhane,' for instance, was the new government's attempt to reverse widespread rent boycotts in the black townships, and was endorsed by SANCO as part of its strategy for hastening improved social services and winning more democratic forms of transitional municipal government. After a momentary upsurge in payments – in some townships to levels of 80 percent of bills paid in early 1995 – the repayment rates quickly dropped back to pre-1994 levels of below 20 percent. No visible changes warranted payment, many believed; the economic recovery had not reached the townships; nor had chaotic transitional local governments found a means of billing more than about half of township customers. Moreover, the ministry responsible for the RDP had reneged on earlier pledges to finance SANCO organisational capacity-building to support Masakhane.

16 There was, naturally, the occasional step backwards along the way, particularly as businesses persuaded some SANCO leaders to support ill-considered joint ventures in township marketing, and as bourgeois funders (such as the German Social Democratic

Party's Friedrich Ebert Stiftung) overlaid their own neoliberal bias upon SANCO's policy agenda. Nevertheless, cases of corruption by civic cadres were generally punished, and in spite of the US Agency for International Development's effusive support for civics – especially the national headquarters – a powerful critique of that agency emerged in SANCO's major pre-election policy report, *Making People-Driven Development Work*. A recounting of challenges facing the contemporary civic movement can be found in Mayekiso, *Township Politics*, Chapters 14 and 15.

17 Andre Gunder Frank and Marta Fuentes, 'Civil Democracy: Social Movements in Recent World History,' in Samir Amin, Giovanni Arrighi, Frank and Immanuel Wallerstein, *Transforming the Revolution: Social Movements and the World-System* (New York, Monthly Review, 1990), p.161.

18 Richard Sklar, 'Development Democracy,' in *Comparative Studies in Society and History*, v.29, #4 (1987), p.708.

19 David Moore, 'The Crisis in Development Discourse and the Concepts of Sustainability, Equity and Participation: A Way Out of the Impasse?,' in Moore and Gerald Schmitz (Eds), *Debating Development Discourses: Institutional and Popular Perspectives* (London, Macmillan, 1995), p.1.

20 To illustrate the dilemma with a concrete example, the housing cooperative has been alternately a solid element of socialist practice or the preferred vehicle of neoliberal state managers for privatising public housing stock (and through which to encourage banks to provide group loans with lower administrative costs), whether in the United States, as pioneered by the 1989–92 Bush Administration housing secretary, Jack Kemp, or in more than 80 other countries where USAID and its consultants have promoted the concept.

21 Ronaldo Munck, 'Political Programmes and Development: The Transformative Potential of Social Democracy,' in Franz Schuurman (Ed), *Beyond the Impasse* (London, Zed Press, 1993), p.120.

22 In particular, some of the more materially-grounded discourse critiques – such as James Ferguson, *The Anti-Politics Machine: Development, Depoliticization and Bureaucratic Power in Lesotho* (Cambridge, Cambridge University Press, 1990) and much of Arturo Escobar's *Encountering Development: The Making and Unmaking of the Third World* (Princeton, Princeton University Press, 1995) – are welcome, indeed vital additions to the critique of neoliberalism. On the one hand, development theory has been infused with new discourses from psychoanalysis, feminism and the analysis of subjectivity and action. On the other, as David Booth acknowledges, this has 'tended to lead in practice to the abandonment of the terrain of "political economy"' ('Development Research: From Impasse to a New Agenda,' in Schuurman, *Beyond the Impasse*, p.60). Instead, Escobar and his allies – such as Vandana Shiva, Ashish Nandy, Shiv Visvanathan, Gustavo Esteva, and the journals *David y Goliath* and *Neueva Sociedad* – stress common *anti-modern* themes in exploring social movements which resist development, in part because their 'processes of identity construction were more flexible, modest, and mobile [than those of previous political strategies], relying on tactical articulations arising out of the conditions and practices of daily life. To this extent, these struggles were fundamentally cultural.' As for alternatives, 'Out of hybrid or minority cultural situations might emerge other ways of building economies, of dealing with basic needs, of coming together into social groups' (Escobar, *Encountering Development*, pp.216,225); the operative word is 'might.'

23 Karl Marx, *Capital*, Volume III, various publishers, Chapter 27.

24 Based largely on dependency perspectives, social movements and progressive intellectuals have made sporadic attempts to devise broader strategies for people-centred development, especially in Africa, where the intellectual influence of dependency theory lives on in the *African Alternative Framework to Structural Adjustment Programmes for Socio-Economic Recovery and Transformation*, the *African Charter for Popular Participation in Development and Transformation*, and *The Kampala Document: Towards a Conference on Security, Stability, Development and Cooperation in Africa*.

25 See, e.g., David Harvey, *The Limits to Capital* (Chicago, University of Chicago Press, 1982) and Neil Smith, *Uneven Development* (Oxford, Basil Blackwell, 1990).
26 Michael Berry, 'Industrialisation, De-industrialisation and Uneven Development: The Case of the Pacific Rim,' in Michael Gottdiener and N. Komninos (Eds), *Capitalist Development and Crisis Theory: Accumulation, Regulation and Spatial Restructuring* (London, Macmillan, 1989); Walden Bello and Felicia Rosenfeld, *Dragons in Distress* (San Francisco, Food First, 1991); Martin Hart-Landsberg, *The Rush to Development* (New York, Monthly Review, 1993).
27 John Cavanagh and Robin Broad, 'No More NICs,' in Gerald Epstein, Juliet Schor and Jessica Nembhard (Eds), *Creating the World Economy* (Philadelphia, Temple University Press, 1993).
28 Samir Amin, *Delinking* (London, Zed, 1985).
29 There is evidence from the late 1960s of the generalised overaccumulation – the advance of the forces of production (reflected in a rising organic composition of capital) beyond the capacity of the system to consume; specifically, gluts of raw materials, consumer goods, capital goods, financial capital, even excess labour – that would plague the world economy for subsequent decades. The overaccumulation crisis has not yet been resolved, but rather temporarily but recurrently displaced through time and across space. See Simon Clarke, *Keynesianism, Monetarism and the Crisis of the State* (Aldershot, Edward Elgar, 1988), pp. 279–360; and David Harvey, *The Condition of Post-Modernity* (Oxford, Basil Blackwell, 1989), pp. 180–197.
30 Giovanni Arrighi, Terence Hopkins and Immanuel Wallerstein, *Anti-Systemic Movements* (London, Verso, 1989), p.74.
31 The authors of recent popular books on capitalist globalisation – Richard Korten, *When Corporations Rule the World* (West Hartford, Kumarian, 1995); Richard Barnet and John Cavanagh, *Global Dreams* (New York, Simon and Schuster, 1994); Bennett Harrison, *Lean and Mean: The Changing Landscape of Corporate Power in the Age of Flexibility* (New York, Basic Books, 1994); Jeremy Brecher and Tim Costello, *Global Village or Global Pillage: Economic Reconstruction from the Bottom Up* (Boston, South End Press, 1994) – offer exemplary critiques. But they avoid explicit theoretical groundings and tend to let idiosyncratic or partial reforms (never revolution, nor even systematic social movement strategies) overwhelm their 'what is to be done' chapters. Likewise the intellectual popularity of 'regulation theory,' with its inordinate focus on the norms, practices and institutions associated with particular stages and spaces in global capitalist history – to the neglect of more durable processes of capital accumulation – has not led to any particularly impressive social strategies of resistance or revolution; indeed in South Africa it has served as the left intelligentsia's main theoretical basis for thus-far fruitless class compromise.
32 Dick Bryan, *The Chase Across the Globe: International Accumulation and the Contradictions for Nation States* (Boulder, Westview Press, 1995), p.32.
33 Respectively, (latest-edition) examples of CST, articulations, Poulantzian, racial capitalism, and regulation theories include South African Communist Party, *The Path to Power* (London, SACP, 1989); Harold Wolpe (Ed), *Articulations of Modes of Production* (London, Routledge, 1980); Rob Davies, Dan O'Meara and Sipho Dlamini, *The Struggle for South Africa* (London, Zed Press, 1986); John Saul and Stephen Gelb, *The Crisis in South Africa* (New York, Monthly Review, 1986); Stephen Gelb (Ed), *South Africa's Economic Crisis* (Cape Town, David Philip and London, Zed, 1991).
34 Here we refer to an extraordinary social phenomenon, based on what seemed to be ceaseless individual meanderings – all, we stress, by white males in their 40s and 50s – from mid-1980s grassroots to early 1990s 'class roots' politics: the lead Marxist critic of the Anglo American Corporation turned to advertising his consulting services (as a trade union insider) to Anglo and other firms; the two leading Marxist critics of the Urban Foundation (Anglo American's social policy think-tank) became two of its key strategists

(within a few months of viciously denigrating that neoliberal, neo-apartheid institute); numerous academic Marxists did top-secret consulting work for the Urban Foundation on land invasions (contemporary and historical) at precisely the time the UF's land speculation strategy was most threatened by the invasion tactic; the two leading Marxist critics of orthodox pension fund management became important exponents and practitioners of orthodox financial packaging through the big institutional investment firms; the lead Marxist critic of export-led growth strategy debuted in the *Financial Mail* by endorsing Taiwan as a model for post-apartheid SA; the most influential Marxist economist within the trade unions turned from advocating social democracy in the pages of the SACP's *African Communist* to free trade, fiscal discipline and high interest rates within the Finance Ministry; and last and certainly least, South Africa's lead Marxist peasant scholar, who was jailed for his SACP ties during the 1960s and later (as dean of the Sussex Institute for Development Studies during the 1970s) supervised the doctoral theses of leading South African neo- Poulantzians, eventually became the strategist of 'homegrown' African structural adjustment at the World Bank (and presently serves as the Bank's London representative).

35 A review of the critiques is included in Patrick Bond, 'Urban Social Movements, the Housing Question and Development Discourse in South Africa,' in Moore and Schmitz, *Debating Development Discourses.*

36 Again, we defer to others for parallel Marxist theoretical innovations applicable to rural, workplace, environment, peace, gender, household, cultural and other movements and sites of struggle. Unfortunately, the literature on social movements in advanced capitalist as well as Third World settings is generally hostile to Marxist theoretical traditions, often because most studies are excessively oriented to practical, organisational, historical and conjunctural concerns, or, drawing on classical political theory, focus on state-civil society relations: see, e.g., Carl Boggs, *Social Movements and Political Power: Emerging Forms of Radicalism in the West* (Philadelphia, Temple University Press, 1986); Alberto Melucci, *Nomads of the Present: Social Movements and Individual Needs in Contemporary Society* (Philadelphia, Temple University Press, 1989); Sidney Tarrow, *Power in Movement: Social Movements, Collective Action and Politics* (Cambridge, Cambridge University Press, 1994). Empirical evidence of urban social movements is also covered by a wide range of literature, some of which draws on theories of urban class conflict and accumulation but much of which does not. Contemporary works on urban movements include Manuel Castells, *The City and the Grassroots: A Cross-Cultural Theory of Urban Social Movements* (Berkeley, University of Caliifornia Press, 1983) and Franz Schuurman and Tom van Naerssen (Eds), *Urban Social Movements in the Third World* (London, Routledge, 1989).

37 L. Pye, *Aspects of Political Development* (Boston, Little, Brown, 1965), p.8.

38 Shlomo Angel, 'The Future Lies in a Global System of Competitive Cities,' *Countdown to Instanbul*, #1 (February 1995), p.4.

39 World Bank, *Urban Policy and Economic Development: An Agenda for the 1990s* (Washington, DC, World Bank, 1991). For a practical critique of this approach, see Gareth Jones and Peter Ward, 'The World Bank's "New" Urban Management Programme: Paradigm Shift or Policy Continuity?,' *Habitat International*, v.18, #3, 1994.

40 To reiterate the thrust of those policies, a Bank report specifies that 'the overall model chosen to integrate the economy into the international markets. . . should aim at avoiding the appropriation of rents by suppliers of nontradables and workers. That is, they should maintain the real wage low, so that excess profits accrue to capital. . . In carrying out all these activities, a close alliance between Government and private agents must be developed.' (Manuel Hinds, *Outwards vs. Inwards Development Strategy: Implications for the Financial Sector* [Washington, DC, World Bank, 1990], pp.15–17.)

41 Urban Institute, *Urban Economies and National Development*, Report prepared for the US Agency for International Development, Washington, DC, 1990.

42 Franz Schuurman, 'Urban Social Movements: Between Regressive Utopia and Socialist Panacea,' in Schuurman and van Naerssen, *Urban Social Movements in the Third World.*
43 James Petras and Morris Morley, *US Hegemony Under Siege: Class, Politics and Development in Latin America* (London, Verso, 1990), p.53.
44 Petras and Morley, *US Hegemony Under Siege*, p.54.
45 No doubt, a number of other features – for example, within the reproduction process the evolving situation of women, of the young and aged, and the exploitation of the local environment – remain for more rigorous eco-feminist socialist theorizing (James O'Connor's journal *Capitalism, Nature, Socialism* being a key site).
46 Reported in Franz Schuurman, 'Modernity, Post-Modernity and the New Social Movements,' in Schuurman, *Beyond the Impasse*, pp.200- 201. See also, in Spanish, E. Tironi, 'Pobladores e Integracion Social,' *Proposiciones* #14, 1987.
47 For more balanced treatments of black youth see Jeremy Seekings, *Heroes or Villains?* (Johannesburg, Ravan Press, 1993).
48 Charles Carter, 'Comrades and Community: Politics and the Construction of Hegemony in Alexandra Township, South Africa, 1984- 1987,' DPhil thesis, University of Oxford, Oxford, 1991. See Mayekiso, *Township Politics*, for context.
49 Karl Marx, *The Civil War in France*, various publishers.
50 John Walton and David Seddon, *Free Markets and Food Riots* (Oxford, Basil Blackwell, 1995), p.336.
51 Joachim Hirsch, 'The Apparatus of the State, the Reproduction of Capital and Urban Conflicts,' in Michael Dear and Alan Scott (Eds), *Urbanization and Urban Planning in Capitalist Society* (London, Methuen, 1981), p.606.
52 Cynthia Cockburn, *The Local State* (London, Pluto, 1977), pp.158, 161.
53 Jessica Vivian, 'Non-Governmental Organizations, Institutional Reform, and Rural Development: Findings from Zimbabwe,' Unpublished PhD Dissertation, Cornell University Planning Department (Ithaca, NY, 1993), p.29.
54 By the early 1990s, two out of five World Bank projects involved NGOs (including well over half in Africa), and in projects involving population, nutrition, primary health care and small enterprise, the ratio rose to more than four out of five. During the 1970s and 1980s, more than six per cent of Bank operations included some NGO participation, but Paul Nelson found that NGOs were 'primarily implementors of project components designed by World Bank and government officials.' Moreover, especially since an upsurge in such participation began in 1988, NGOs have often been used to 'deliver compensatory services to soften the effects of an adjustment plan'; in some cases the NGOs were not even pre-existing but were 'custom-built for projects' and hence could 'neither sustain themselves nor represent poor people's interests effectively.' (See Paul J. Nelson, *The World Bank and Non- Governmental Organizations: The Limits of Apolitical Development* [London, Macmillan, 1995].)
55 See David Sogge (Ed), *Just Trying to Help: Compassion and Calculation in Private Foreign Aid* (London, Pluto, 1996).
56 See Korten, *When Corporations Control the World*, for a justification of defunding the Bank; see also the popular education and campaigning materials from the San Francisco NGO Global Exchange (e-mail globalexch@igc.apc.org).
57 Vicente Navarro, 'The Nature of Democracy in the Core Capitalist Countries: Meanings and Implications for Class Struggle,' *The Insurgent Sociologist*, v.10, #1 (1980), p.12.
58 Cited in Hilary Wainwright, 'Once More Moving On: Social Movements, Political Representation and the Future of the Radical Left,' in Leo Panitch (Ed), *Socialist Register 1995* (London, Merlin Press, 1995), p.83.
59 Until, perhaps, the conditions for a 'World Party' can be seriously debated. See Warren W. Wagar, *A Short History of the Future* (Chicago, University of Chicago Press, 1992).

# THE USE AND ABUSE OF JAPAN AS A PROGRESSIVE MODEL

Paul Burkett and Martin Hart-Landsberg

## I. Introduction

The repression, economic strangulation, and cooptation of revolutionary movements and post-revolutionary regimes throughout the world has produced a new 'end-of-history' craze which makes the 1950s 'end-of-ideology' fad seem pale by comparison. Yet, more than two decades of socio-economic crises and restructuring, of pressures on workers and their communities to adjust their work and living conditions and aspirations to capital's rising bottom line, have only served to widen the disjuncture between capitalism's competitive priorities and the crying need for a more socially and ecologically sustainable economic system. As we move into the 21st century, it therefore becomes clear that beneath the manufactured picture of 'capitalism triumphant' exhibited by the mainstream media is a system that can only legitimize itself by denying that there is any alternative. The 'end of history' is thus the ideology of a decadent system whose legitimation is self-referential, its power structure and socio-economic organization justified in terms of its own internal criteria (competitiveness and profitability) rather than by its ability to empower and satisfy the needs of human beings.

Given the rightward movement of establishment politics and discourse alongside public and private sector attacks on working-class conditions, there has been an understandable tendency for progressives to engage in a strategic retreat and regrouping. Hoping to win a wider hearing for their policy initiatives or even for reasoned defence of previously institutionalized reforms in the areas of business regulation, welfare, education, health care and civil rights, many are now trying to craft new modes of argumentation and political platforms which will be viable in today's more conservative mainstream terms. One outcome of this process is the increasingly popular argument that progressive public policies are the most appropriate vehicle for promoting a healthy economy, even when using capitalist criteria such as investment growth, output per worker hour, and the international competitiveness of domestic production to define good health. Thus, proposals for reduced work time, increased worker input into management decisions, regulation of financial speculation, popular control over financial markets and institutions, and democratized corporate governance structures are being defended not so much on grounds that these measures could – by mobilizing different working-class groups and providing a framework for articulation and reconciliation of their needs and priorities – help trigger some important first steps beyond capitalism. Rather, such policy initiatives are defended largely on grounds that they can improve conditions for workers because they make the economy more efficient and competitive in capitalist terms.[1]

In this essay we deal with one important, perhaps even dominant tendency within this 'progressive competitiveness' movement, namely the framing of policy proposals in terms of the superior competitiveness of certain national capitalisms in whole or in part. We focus on a particular case of national-capitalist 'success' which has become a common reference point for many progressive policy platforms in the U.S.: that of Japan.[2] Our concern with Japan stems partly from its influential status as an 'economic superpower' and as one of the main 'competitors of the U.S.' Another source of concern is the extreme discordance between the true exploitative, socially-irrational and imperialist character of Japanese capitalism, on the one hand, and the relatively sanguine characterizations of some or all elements of the 'Japanese model' often encountered in U.S. left and liberal writings, on the other. Perhaps our most important reason for examining the use of Japan as a model, however, is that the recent plethora of non-holistic, undialectical, and a-historical references to the Japanese experience in left-liberal writings reveals quite a bit about the analytical and political dangers of using capitalist criteria as a positive reference point for the formulation and articulation of progressive priorities. More specifically, it reveals that those who advocate using Japanese capitalist practices and institutions as guides to progressive change offer a distorted, strategically disastrous perspective on capitalism's exploitative underpinnings and historical tendency towards maturation and stagnation, and thus of the objective and subjective conditions shaping working-class politics.

To create a framework for analyzing recent positive left-liberal references to Japan, the next section describes the main elements of an emerging left-liberal consensus on Japan. Sections III and IV criticize this consensus from methodological and political angles, respectively. The essay concludes with a final section that briefly describes our own alternative political vision and strategy.

## II. Japanese Capitalism as a Progressive Reference Point

Three basic claims often appear in progressive evaluations of Japanese capitalism; indeed, these claims appear to define an emergent left-liberal consensus on Japan as an historically progressive reference point. This consensus sees Japanese capitalism as superior to U.S. capitalism because of its greater rate and more efficient allocation of productive investment, more cooperative and efficient approach to labour-management relations, and more humane and efficient approach to structuring international economic relations. In what follows we highlight the arguments underlying each of these claims.

### *The Japanese Investment Regime*

Both socialists and liberals have argued that Japan's superior economic performance can, in large part, be explained by the country's rapid rate of industrial capital accumulation, which is itself the result of both a traditionally high rate of household savings and the efficient channeling of these savings into private- and public-sector investments in capital goods, new technologies, and supporting infrastructure. The U.S., by contrast, is said to have a lower household savings rate and, more importantly, channel a larger share of its savings toward unproductive activities which erode – or at least fail to enhance – industrial competitiveness: financial speculation, leveraged buy-outs and other merger activity, bloated corporate managerial and marketing bureaucracies, and military-related activities.

Clinton and Gore (1992: 6, 143), for example, in line with the writings of their liberal advisor Robert Reich, note how in the 1980s 'our competitors' economies grew three or four times faster than ours – because their leaders decided to invest in their people and Washington did not.' They suggest that a crucial reason why Japan 'threaten[ed] to surpass America in manufacturing by 1996' was that the Japanese 'were investing more than twelve times what we spend on roads, bridges, sewers, and the information networks and technologies of the future'.

Walden Bello makes the same point when he uses 'the Japanese model of state-led capitalism' as a positive reference point for his left-populist analysis of conservative 'Reaganite' economic policies:

> In 1989 Japan invested 23.2 per cent of its GNP in plant and capital equipment and R&D, while the U.S. invested 11.7 per cent. In non-defense R&D spending, U.S. expenditures as a percentage of GNP in the 1980s came to 1.8 per cent, while the figures for West Germany and Japan were 2.6 per cent and 2.8 per cent respectively. It is hardly cause for surprise then that the U.S., which pioneered the development of most high technologies, has lost the lead to Japan in memory chips, semiconductor manufacturing equipment, robotics, numerically controlled machine tools, optoelectronics, and other strategic areas. (1994: 73, 99)

In addition to praising the Japanese state's industrially oriented credit-allocation policies,[3] progressives also point to the relative patience of investment fund suppliers and the shared long-term profit orientation of non-financial firms and their financiers as another important reason for the Japanese investment regime's competitive efficiency. For example, when recently interviewed by the popular U.S. left magazine *Dollars and Sense*, the renowned liberal Japan-scholar Ronald Dore suggested that Japanese 'joint venture partners, distributors, banks, and insurance companies' engaging in 'cross-shareholding . . . see stock ownership as a long term mutual commitment' (McDermott and Tilly, 1994: 20). This is in sharp contrast to the behaviour of the U.S. financial system where systemic short-termism and speculative pressures rule the roost to the detriment of long-term investments, corporate commitments to productive 'stake-holders' including workers and their communities, and long-term industrial competitiveness (Stanfield, 1994; Goldstein, 1995).

*The Japanese Work Model*

The left-liberal consensus also credits Japan's more cooperative and efficient approach to labour-management relations for making a significant contribution to the country's superior competitiveness. The rapid labour-productivity growth in, and overall cost-effectiveness of, Japanese production are ascribed to the less bureaucratic and more worker-participatory structure of production in leading sectors and firms – with worker participation enhanced by a greater security of employment, especially for 'core workers'. Just as for the Japanese investment regime, an important underpinning of this second claim is the belief that exogenous Japanese cultural factors, by rewarding values such as patience and cooperation, help to reinforce economic relationships which depend upon shared responsibility and mutual long-term commitments.[4]

Admiration for the Japanese work model was clearly evident in Clinton-Gore campaign proposals for 'a partnership between business and labour and education and government, committed to compete and win in the global economy' – including measures for 'reorganizing the workplace [to] encourage greater cooperation between labour and management" (Clinton and Gore, 1992: 126, 69). Appeals to learn from the Japanese labour experience are often made by liberal writers. Dore, for example, views "the Japanese system [as] a cohesive, decent society, with relatively limited inequality.' He suggests that in Japan 'the intensification of work' has been bound up with 'greater initiative, greater respect for workers, and a greater sense of achievement' (McDermott and Tilly, 1994: 38). Similarly, worker participation advocates Levine and D'Andrea Tyson include Japan (alongside Sweden) as one of the countries where businesses have, in order to 'increase productivity . . . increased worker participation – giving workers a substantive say in the production process, including training new employees, dealing directly with suppliers, setting the work pace, and keeping the firm's financial records' (1989: 20).

The use of Japanese work relations as a positive reference point has also become common on the left, especially in connection with 'progressive competitiveness' strategies. In an early post-election evaluation of Clintonomics, David Gordon emphasized the fast growth of labour productivity in Japan compared to the U.S., explaining this in terms not only of the greater rate and more efficient allocation of private and public investment in Japan, but also of Japan's more enlightened labour-management practices as manifested in an apparently lower ratio of administrative and managerial employees to total civilian employment. Gordon suggests that '[t]he President wants to prepare us for the twenty-first century, but U.S. labor-management practices reek of the nineteenth' and that 'U.S. corporations are losing ground to . . . Japanese competitors in part because they continue to rely on the stick, not the carrot, in the workplace' (1993a: 344). In order to 'build a 21st-century production system' – one based on 'visionary corporations which [have] improved their competitiveness by involving their workers' – the U.S. should follow the example of Japanese firms which 'are more likely to stimulate their workers with the carrot, seeking cooperation rather than conquest' (1993b: 21–2).

Bello (1994: 100–2) offers similarly high praise for the Japanese work model:

> The much-vaunted Japanese teamwork, the initiative of workers in the production process, the constant efforts collectively to upgrade and diversify the work team's skills – all this stems from a system of production where much of the conflict between labor and management has been reduced or softened . . . [M]ost Japanese 'core workers' – the dynamo of the firm – are far less alienated from management than American workers are. Moreover, management knows that non-alienated workers are the key to competitiveness . . Whereas automation has been used to enhance worker skills in Japan, it has been utilized by American managers to deskill and reduce their workforces.

*The Japanese Globalization Model*

The third basic left-liberal claim regarding the cooperative and efficient nature of Japanese capitalism is that it provides a more progressive and humane basis for the globalization of economic relations than does the coercive, inefficient, and imperialist nature of U.S. capitalism. This extension of the Japanese model's global-historical progressivity to the external investment and production activities of Japanese capital is also based on the notion that military power is increasingly being eclipsed by economic power in determining the political-economic position of nations within an increasingly interdependent global system. The more general assertion then, is that since Japanese capitalism is more internationally competitive and less military-oriented than U.S. capitalism, the only feasible (competitive) programme for achieving a more progressive and humane U.S. economy is one that can join working-class aspirations and political actions to a neo-mercantilist economic strategy modelled along the lines of Japanese capital's more cooperative, efficient *and increasingly globalized* corporate operations.

This position is clearly enunciated in Tabb's (1992: 81) critical analysis of the 'vampire capitalism' practised by 'the U.S. ruling class' during the Reagan-Bush years, i.e., the 'strategy of growth through redistribution – a redistribution from everyone in the world to the U.S. ruling class – based not on the productive capacities of the United States, but on its coercive talents, its military muscle, and its political and ideological domination.' Tabb includes Japan among the 'nations' which 'offer modes of capitalist development that are more efficient, and even kinder and gentler, than our increasingly social-Darwinist version' (1992: 83).

Tabb suggests that 'the United States should emulate Japan . . . in a more productive use of imperial power,' and that the left should orient its strategies toward such a more 'progressive variation of capitalism,' i.e. a 'Reichian approach to competitiveness, based on improving domestic factors of production, [which] could become the conventional wisdom of a revitalized liberal progressivism in the United States and reunite elements of the old liberal social-change constituencies'. In this 'realist' vision, the left would build 'a strong coalition of trade unions, women's groups, environmentalists, and minority groups, all pressing their demands as part of a coherent national development strategy . . . stressing policies that strengthen the competitive position of the geographical United States and the well-being of its residents.' In short, the best option for the left is to go for a 'social-democratic agenda' of 'a humanized capitalism brought about by reforms that increase productivity and dispense its benefits more broadly' while drawing economic sustenance and dynamism from state industrial and mercantilist policies modelled on the 'German and Japanese imperial states [which] put their bureaucrats to work, not in Pentagon or Langley-type occupations, but in drumming up export business and restructuring industries through intelligencing the latest technologies and marketing information' (1992: 86, 90–3, 85).

Although we have drawn upon the works of various left and liberal writers to highlight the central tenets of what we believe is an emerging left-liberal consensus on Japan, we do not mean to equate the politics of the former with those of the latter or to argue that this consensus represents the viewpoint of a consolidated political movement with a common political vision. The left writers we have quoted have all made clear in their political writings and work – in sharp contrast to the quoted liberal writers – their rejection of capitalism and their commitment to the creation of a new social order. What concerns us, however, and what we mean when we speak of a left-liberal consensus on Japan, is that many leading scholars, both left and liberal, are increasingly turning to, as well as sharing, a common perspective on the Japanese experience, even while seeking to advance very different political agendas. Not surprisingly, but unfortunately, this shared understanding of the Japanese experience has helped to establish Japan as a positive political reference point for many in the progressive community. We say unfortunately because, as we argue next, the left-liberal consensus is seriously flawed and, as a result, politically destructive for building an effective left politics in the U.S.

## III. A Methodological Critique of the Left-Liberal Consensus

To put it simply, the left-liberal consensus is flawed because of its a-historical and non-holistic 'smorgasbord' approach to the study of the Japanese experience. This consensus is underpinned, first, by a simple association of the historical progressivity of socio-economic relations and institutions with their contribution to global competitiveness. Certain elements of the heretofore highly competitive Japanese political economy are then torn out of their historical and structural context and used as positive reference points for a progressive industrial policy. Aspects of the Japanese model which are particularly difficult to define as progressive – the long and physically and mentally debilitating work and commuting times, and the extremely high housing costs for Japanese workers compared to U.S. and West European workers, for example – either go unmentioned or are treated as unrelated to Japanese competitiveness. In this manner the purportedly more progressive elements of the Japanese model are deemed transplantable to a reconstructed left-liberal socio-economic project in the U.S. This is also how the contradictions of capitalist globalization and competitiveness are bypassed, thereby allowing progressives to define the imperative of global competitiveness as natural and inevitable, and to define progressive as the most efficient and humane form of global competitiveness. We concretize this methodological critique of the left-liberal consensus by examining, in turn, each of its three basic claims.

### *The Japanese Investment Regime*

Progressive competitiveness advocates applaud Japan's high rate and strategically efficient allocation of productive investment and, by extension, the high household savings rate which helps to support it. Logically, then, the U.S. left should include in its 'progressive competitiveness' platform institutional measures modelled along the lines of those most responsible for producing the high rate of Japanese household savings. However, an examination of the sources of this household behaviour in terms of the particular material and class circumstances of the Japanese economy raises serious questions about the desirability of such a step.

Such an examination shows, for example, that the high savings rate is related to the extremely high housing costs (and generally high costs of consumption goods caused by import barriers, an inefficiently organized retail sector, and domestic production oriented toward capital goods and exports) faced by Japanese workers. It is also a response to the country's relatively small welfare state which requires workers to store up funds to cover possible lay-offs and real wage cuts (especially non-core workers, women workers in particular) as well as self-finance their own retirement (Steven, 1988). In short, it appears that the 'traditionally' high savings rates of Japanese households are bound up with a system whereby the material reproduction of the working-class is thoroughly subordinate to, indeed organized to enhance, the goal of maximum capital accumulation in forms determined by capital (including the imperatives of capitalist competitiveness) rather than by workers themselves. This leads to the healthy suspicion that the inclusion of those particular institutional modalities which underpin Japanese household savings behaviour in a 'progressive' platform must involve either a simple identification of 'progressive' with capitalist accumulation and competitiveness, or, instead, a belief that the determinants of the high Japanese household savings rate are separate (or separable) from the most alienating and oppressive aspects of Japanese capitalism—a belief which is hard to sustain.

The left-liberal consensus also considers Japanese capitalism more progressive than U.S. capitalism insofar as Japanese capital is or has been relatively patient and planned, and relatively less speculative and anarchic than U.S. capital. Here, the assumption is that Japanese capital's greater patience and more 'efficient' planning has little to with the fact that both the goals and the process of accumulation and industrial policy formulation (including the planning operations of government agencies like the Ministry of International Trade and Industry) are undemocratically determined. It assumes, in other words, that even if the basic priorities to be served by accumulation and the planning process were democratically determined, capital would (or *could*, presumably given the right constellation of political forces) be just as patient. By contrast, it seems more likely to us that the relative patience of Japanese capital was based firmly on the relative weakness of the Japanese working-class, i.e., on the strictly subordinate status of workers' priorities in the Japanese political economy. Indeed, Steven (1990: pp.12–3) suggests that the nationalist-industrialist form and ideology of the post-World War II Japanese state were based on Japanese capital's complete domination of the Japanese working class, which allowed the state to focus on external competitiveness and the management of inter-imperialist rivalry more so than in any other developed capitalist country.[5]

Crippled by its a-historicism and lack of holism the left-liberal consensus has, in fact, misunderstood Japan's basic post World War II industrialization dynamic. In contrast to progressive claims that the Japanese investment regime enabled the country to enjoy a relatively smooth, well-balanced, and non-contradictory process of economic growth, Japanese accumulation has in reality been driven by an unstable and class-conflictual process of 'scrap and build' (Steven, 1990). For example, Japan's early post-war growth was largely the result of the successful production of light manufactures for export to Asia by highly exploited Japanese female workers. Success, however, eventually forced up wages, costing light manufactures their competitive edge. Japanese capitalists, with the help of the state, therefore began their first 'scrap-and-build' cycle. Starting in the late 1950s, light manufacturing industries were gradually run down and transferred to Asia while new more profitable heavy and chemical industries were built. This industrial transformation was supported by a corporate-led offensive designed to keep labour costs as low as possible and by the flexibility of labour power initially employed in the light manufacturing sector, e.g., the crowding of female workers out of the industrial labour force and into Japan's ultra-backward service sector (Ogawa and Clark, 1995: 294–5).

This basic cycle was repeated again after 1973, when the rising price of oil and other basic commodities undermined the profitability of Japan's raw material dependent basic materials industries. These 'problem' industries were gradually run down and shifted to Asia. Machine industries, in particular transport and electrical, were selected to become the country's new growth centre and a new offensive was launched against the working class (including the expansion of temporary labour and subcontracting systems) to ensure their competitive success. The rapid growth in production and export of products such as automobiles, colour televisions, stereos, and cameras, especially to the U.S., did power a new round of rapid growth. This export drive, however, eventually led the U.S to successfully demand, in the mid-1980s, that the Japanese sharply revalue their currency. The resulting 'high Yen crisis,' by threatening the competitive position of many of Japan's machine industries, forced Japanese firms into yet another scrap and build cycle. This time, Japan scrapped and relocated large parts of its consumer goods branch to both the U.S. and Asia (creating an expanded international division of labour), concentrated on modernizing its capital and luxury goods producing machine industries, and as always during a period of transition, repressed labour. Significantly, however, Japan was unable to establish a new growth centre. With profit margins still low, Japanese firms appear, in the 1990s, to have begun a new cycle based on a further shift of production activity to Asia and the re-export back to Japan of both consumer goods and components. Clearly, the increasing lack of attractive domestic industrial investment opportunities is leading to the hollowing out of the Japanese economy – revealing the scrap-and-build strategy to have been only a temporary and socially costly palliative for capitalism's maturity dilemma.

Unable to understand the logic of Japan's industrial development, it is not surprising that progressive competitiveness advocates are unable to appreciate the significance of recent Japanese financial developments. The left-liberal consensus tends, for example, to view the 1980s growth of Japan's speculative 'bubble economy,' and concomitant pressures toward liberalization of the financial system leading to financial instability, as basically exogenous to the more progressive aspects of the Japanese investment regime rather than as an outcome of the economy's maturation and accompanying overproduction of surplus value relative to productive and privately profitable investment opportunities (Pollin, 1993; Goldstein, 1995). This interpretation ignores the possibility that

> . . . a selective credit policy . . . designed to stimulate priority sectors . . . represents an approach that, on the basis of its own maturity, will give rise to pressures for liberalization as the masses of capital increasingly begin to demand access to all possible forms of production and financial enhancement (Macedo Cintra, 1994: 45).

Indeed, as Tsuru (1993: 162–9, 188ff) indicates, by the late-1970s the internal funds of Japanese manufacturing corporations exceeded their domestic investments, and this growing surplus of funds fuelled not only expanding foreign investment but also increases in (domestic and foreign) real estate holdings by 'non-financial' corporations. The fact that exploding real estate prices underpinned rising stock prices of many corporations (and *vice versa*) certainly gives new meaning to the purported 'insulation' of these firms from outside speculative pressures. Indeed, insofar as the banks' relative shift from corporate loans to corporate share purchases resulted from, and contributed to, this phenomenon, we may say that the associated 'mutual commitment' of corporate fund suppliers and users was basically a function of capitalist maturity and the attendant shift toward finance-led accumulation – i.e., hardly separable from the 'bubble economy' (Tsuru, 1993: 189). The fact that the current Japanese financial mess appears increasingly similar to the 1980s U.S. situation, with the Japanese authorities openly using the U.S. savings & loan bail-out and financial-regulatory reforms as a model for their own clean-up operations, makes one wonder how historically progressive Japanese financial relations actually were and are apart from the quite normal war-aftermath boom and maturation phase of accumulation after World War II (Sweezy, 1980).[6]

When liberal scholars do recognize the problem of capitalist maturity, they usually fail to reconcile it with the purported progressivity of the Japanese model. Dore, for example, has the following to say about the Japanese economy:

> I'm not sure what potential there is for utilizing their current manufacturing capacity for the domestic market. There's a problem of transition comparable to the conversion problem faced by U.S. defense industries . . . I doubt if Japan can escape for much longer the consequences of the forces of technological change and imports from other countries that are reducing employment opportunities for people of low learning ability (McDermott and Tilly, 1994: 21).

One is left wondering how he can find the Japanese model so desirable if it expended its labour and other productive resources (including the region's ecology) to build an industrial structure which outlived its economic usefulness within a generation or so – an industrial structure which turned out to be just as irrational as that churned out by the Cold War military-industrial complex in the U.S.! Moreover, if Japan's earlier high-investment, scrap-and-build strategy is no longer viable, it becomes problematic to simply assume that market forms of investment finance – however 'patient' and 'mutually committed' they may be – are the best instruments for a left financial policy. The choice of financial-institutional modes (e.g., government budgets versus self-financing of worker- and community-controlled production units versus market forms of credit allocation) must therefore be considered afresh, must become contingent on the values and goals to be served by production.

By not questioning the historical progressivity of capitalist accumulation and competitiveness the left-liberal consensus surrenders to mature capitalism's alienated ideology and Japan's new imperative to move toward a more moderately paced, financially-driven, and 'high consumption' pattern of real economic growth—*to become in effect more like the U.S.* (Williams, 1994a). Insofar as this outcome is avoided, it will not be because of any historical progressivity built into capitalist competitiveness. Rather, it will only be because Japanese workers, reclaiming their past history of anti-capitalist and anti-imperialist struggles, are able to once again challenge capitalist priorities in the realms of production, exchange and distribution in and through an expanding struggle to replace capitalist relations with new, more collective-democratic forms of material reproduction.

*The Japanese Work Model*

Even for those who work in Japan's core corporations, the Japanese work model appears considerably less progressive, and more efficient only as a framework for exploitation, once it is treated as an organic system. 'Lifetime employment' is based on early retirement at or below 55 years of age, after which core workers are normally farmed out to smaller- and medium-sized enterprises at much lower wages. Accelerated seniority wage scales, retirement bonuses, and other corporate welfare features are used (in conjunction with an underdeveloped welfare state) to raise workers' 'cost of job loss' and force them to accept long work-hours and high labor intensities that would be socially unacceptable to U.S. workers. Meanwhile female workers are predominantly marginalized from core production jobs (not to speak of managerial positions), and relegated to superexploitation in smaller manufacturing and service enterprises – with this class process being legitimized by Japan's patriarchal 'family' ideology (Steven, 1988; Dassbach, 1993; Nakamura, 1993; Watanabe, 1993, Hideo, *et al.*, 1994; and Parker, 1994).

It must be emphasized that the dependence of corporate accumulation on the super-exploitation of workers in subcontracting firms (and of temporary workers in core enterprises) is not an incidental or conjunctural aspect of the Japanese model. Progressive competitiveness interpretations applaud the apparent insulation of Japanese corporations from short-term financial pressures while ignoring their use of subcontractors as a buffer for cyclical *and* financial pressures (Yamamura, 1967: 160–6; Halliday, 1975: 226; Tsuru, 1993: 109). Currently, pressures by the big corporations on their subcontractors have reached an historic extreme, producing widespread bankruptcies among small- and medium-sized enterprises despite government loans financed by the postal savings of the working class.[7] These pressures are a prime source of Japan's growing unemployment crisis – a crisis not fully appreciated until it is realized that Japanese unemployment rates are at comparable (or perhaps higher) levels than found in the U.S. if common standards of measurement are used (Steven, 1990: 49–50; Elder and Sorrentino, 1993; Chriszt, 1993; Sapsford, 1995a; *Economist*, 1995).

The whole scrap-and-build strategy of industrial accumulation employed by Japanese capital (in response to the maturation of the Japanese economy and the rising wages of its workers) was predicated upon, and in turn reinforced, the subjection of Japanese workers to levels of insecurity and competitive pressures unparalleled in the rest of the developed capitalist world (Steven, 1990: 8–14, 66–89). This strategy required not only secularly high rates of exploitation underpinned by long and intensive workdays, but also a high degree of inter-sectoral transferability and conjunctural (downward) flexibility of real labour costs during crisis-and-capital-restructuring periods. What Jon Halliday wrote two decades ago in this connection remains true today: 'there is no evidence that Japanese business has had difficulty dealing with recessions or other questions (such as accelerating capital accumulation) through manipulations of the labor force' (1975: 227).

Needless to say, the oft-heard culturalist and technocratic explanations of Japan's competitiveness bypass the patriarchal *and* class-exploitative fabric, functions, and historical roots of the familial ideology underpinning the systemic division of and capitalist hegemony over the Japanese working class – an ideology whose roots stretch back to Japan's super-exploitative brand of feudalism and elite adaptations of feudal ideology to the emerging capitalist framework during and after the Meiji period. These explanations also ignore the fact that the relatively 'productivist' appearance of post-World War II Japanese capitalism is a class-exploitative transmutation of the massive workers' production-control movement immediately after World War II, a transmutation that was underwritten by the authoritarian repression of Japanese workers by U.S. occupation forces in alliance with the same ruling class that had helped design Japan's pre-war imperialism (Moore, 1983, 1988).[8]

Although many of those who share the left-liberal consensus view of the Japanese work model are not unaware of its obviously less progressive aspects, their associated qualifications tend to be a-historical and unsystematic. For example, Dore, while noting that 'lifetime employment' applies only to the minority of core workers, and that the on-the-job experience of core workers is 'much more fun for the managers than for the workers', does not bother to mention how Japanese core capitals' efforts 'to get the workers sharing in a common sense of endeavor' may be underpinned by the threat of being relegated to even more exploitative and insecure labour-market segments, based on the gender- and education-based factionalization of the Japanese working-class (McDermott and Tilly, 1994: 38; Steven, 1988). Similarly, Juliet Schor recognizes that 'excessive hours are a serious problem in Japan,' but then goes on to suggest that:

> [w]hat we should learn from the Japanese, and from our own history as well, is not the need to reduce wages, or raise hours, but the importance of productivity. In the international market, what matters in the long run is not how many hours a person works, but how productively he or she works them . . . And efficient production itself will yield rising wages, as the cases of Japan and Korea reveal. Instead of pushing their employees' standard of living even farther down the international hierarchy, American management should be figuring out how to make the hours they buy more productive (1993: 153).

Her analysis not only ignores the intrinsic connections between long work hours, high labour intensity and the overall structure of Japanese capital-labour relations (including the relations of core workers' exploitation to the super-exploitation of temporary labourers and workers in subcontracting firms – relations bound up with the extreme gender-segmentation of the Japanese working class, an aspect which Schor is normally quite sensitive to), but also presumes that both Japanese and U.S. capitalists do not know what it takes to compete and be profitable.

The flawed perspective underlying progressive competitiveness interpretations of the Japanese work model is perhaps best illustrated by their failure to recognize that one cannot determine the true character of either 'cooperation' or 'participation' without knowing the goals and extent of worker control over the conditions, process, and results of production. The fact is that neither 'cooperation' nor 'participation' necessarily connotes 'progressive' (let alone 'liberating' or 'emancipatory'). Attacks on the cooperative and participatory aspects of Japanese institutions by publications such as the *Wall Street Journal* may raise an instinctive reaction to defend these aspects, but this is ultimately a dead-end reaction. True emancipatory visions must have a prominent place for individuality and variety.[9] We should not play into the Right's hands by supporting non-liberating – indeed exploitative and patriarchal – forms of cooperation and participation, especially at a time when capitalism's end-of-history ideology trumpets the lie that all cooperation and participation (at least all not firmly harnessed to, or confined within the limits of, the market and private profitability) leads straight to the Gulag. Moreover, the assertion that Japanese labour relations are more progressive than US labour relations implies that US workers are unprogressive insofar as they reject Japanese management methods – even though this rejection may be based not only on the unacceptable length and intensity of worktimes associated with these methods, but also on the fact that US workers understandably don't wish to 'participate' in a process in which they have no control over goals, conditions, or results.

*The Japanese Globalization Model*

The left-liberal consensus suggests that, given the recent trends toward globalization of capitalist production and finance under the rubric of transnational corporations and banks, one can do no better than fight for a progressive *and* competitive version of capitalist globalization. And, since the more cooperative and efficient Japanese capitalism has demonstrated the ability to support highly competitive domestic export industries as well as the outward expansion of Japanese corporations and banks, this progressive globalization project should be informed by the productivist features of Japanese capital's domestic and global operations. Underlying this position is the assumption that capitalist globalization is the inevitable wave of the future and – by logical extension – that popular struggles against capitalist globalization are utopian and even unprogressive insofar as they interfere with the further development of productive forces. Class struggle – in the sense of a struggle for a movement beyond capitalism toward socialism – can therefore begin only *after* the process of capitalist globalization is in some sense 'completed'. By contrast, we reject both the argument that Japan offers a model of a 'better imperialism' with positive lessons for U.S. progressives and the assumption that capitalist globalization represents an historically progressive form of development which cannot and should not be resisted.

Many liberal and even socialist oriented writers have tended to uncritically accept Japan's post-World War II scrap-and-build strategy, and evolving corresponding pattern of external trade, finance, and production activities, as historically progressive. The one-sided nature of this view is well illustrated by its treatment of Japan's recent stepped-up regional foreign direct investment activity. The overall impression often given is that by drawing regional-peripheral countries more-and-more tightly into its own network of finance, technology and trade, Japan is helping to develop the forces of production in those countries, thereby playing a uniquely progressive role in the global economy. Apart from whether Japanese expansionism is really progressive for those countries receiving its investment – an issue we consider below – the question remains as to how socially rational this process is from the standpoint of Japanese workers, a question that is commonly avoided by downplaying the distinction between Japanese capital and the Japanese people. Based on this implicit assumption of identity of interests, progressives have often been content to conclude that this new wave of expansionism strengthens the Japanese economy in some generic non-class sense. We challenge both the assumption and the conclusion.

There is no doubt that from the viewpoint of Japanese capital, it has been rational to relocate industries when domestic labour costs are higher than in the periphery, or when the domestic environmental movement reduces the feasibility of imposing environmental costs on the domestic population (Halliday and McCormack, 1973; Nester, 1990; Steven, 1990; Ofreneo, 1993). It has also been 'rational' for Japanese capitalists to satisfy their tremendous (and still increasing) appetite for raw material (including food) products by extracting such materials from neighbouring and other peripheral countries, and to respond to rising energy costs by promoting nuclear power development (Steven, 1990; Tsuru, 1993; Yoko, *et al.*, 1993; Ofreneo, 1993). But viewing what is rational for Japanese capital as progressive or rational in terms of the historical advancement of human needs satisfaction is quite a different matter. To equate them requires assuming that options like environmentally friendly conversion of domestic production (instead of relocation), reductions in the raw material intensity of domestic production and consumption, and reductions in worktime with movements of workers from industrial and unproductive-service activities into social service areas, would not be preferable, from a working class point of view, to current Japanese business practices. It may be thought that such alternatives must involve an overly-nationalist or autarkic stance, thereby undermining third world efforts to develop their productive forces. This need not be the case, however, since an alternative strategy could have different, perhaps superior, forms of economic linkage with the current periphery. Is the export of dirty, capital intensive industries, or of low-wage subcontracting production, from centre to periphery the most progressive form of interaction which is conceivable for the future? We do not believe an affirmative answer to this question can or should be assumed (Brecher and Costello, 1994).

More generally, the competitive pressures of capitalist globalization (Japanese-style or otherwise) themselves reduce the scope for reforms which the left-liberal consensus argues are necessary to make capitalism more humane and progressive (Foster, 1989; Panitch, 1994). In fact, these pressures are intensified insofar as developed national-capitalist models are successfully competitive. As Hymer (1979) presciently argued, success in global competition, occurring in and through the globalization of corporate operations, has tended to increase, not reduce, competitive pressures on workers in the 'home countries' of successfully competing enterprises. Hence even if a humane and progressive form of capitalist competitiveness were possible in the initial phases of such globalization (and we don't think it is), the conditions for its continuation would naturally be eroded by its own competitive success.

Japan itself offers an example of this process, as even core workers are now under increasing pressure to lower their real wages and accept ever longer and more intensive worktimes in order to protect a 'lifetime employment' which is itself increasingly insecure.[10] As the Labor Research Association (1994: 7) observes, Japanese

> real wages have been dropping, falling 1.6% from July 1992 to July 1993. The reason Japanese firms give for not raising wages will sound familiar: A recent Japanese Federation of Employers Association report said a wage hike 'would invite a loss of international competitive force and deindustrialization'.

Growing numbers of Japanese workers are literally working themselves to death for stagnating or falling real wages at the same time that the country faces a growing crisis of female and youth unemployment and underemployment (Sapsford, 1995a). Moreover, the increasingly crass, corporate-consumerist character of Japanese social life is 'progressively' destroying much of what was most valued in the country's cultural heritage while the 'greening' of the archipelago with new networks of highways, golf courses, and other speculative real-estate developments is doing the same to the country's environmental heritage (McCormack, 1990, 1991; Greenfield, 1992; Tsuru, 1993; Williams, 1994a).

Unfortunately, Japanese globalization also promises a bleak future for working people in the periphery because of what may be termed the hyper-super-exploitation of their human and natural resources for the sake of Japanese corporate profitability. Japanese transnational manufacturing, mining, forestry, fishing, and agricultural operations are known world-wide for the absolute ruthlessness and slash-and-burn methods with which they exploit local workers and the natural habitat (Steven, 1990; Howard, 1993; Yoko, *et al.*, 1993).[11] Nor is such behaviour anything new: it represents an historical continuity between the pre-1945 'Greater East Asia Co-Prosperity Sphere' strategy and the post-War recovery of Japanese imperialism under the rubric of the General Trading Companies and their associated financial-industrial conglomerate *keiretsu* (formerly *Zaibatsu*).[12]

This pattern of development only promises to maintain the growth of productive accumulation in any particular peripheral country or zone as long as the producers' work and living conditions do not rise above 'competitive' levels – defined in terms of the minimum level available to Japanese corporations in their entire global operating arena. It should also be noted that much of Japanese capital's recent foreign investment activity has been concentrated in financial and commercial real estate activities (including construction of hotels, golf courses, and the like in connection with the development of vacation spots for higher-income Japanese professionals and managers; the sex industry is also a major 'beneficiary' of this activity) (McCormack, 1991; Tsuru, 1993: 201–204). In this way, peripheral countries (and many workers even in other core countries like Australia – where Japanese capital is very prominent) wind up serving the luxury recreational-consumption needs of the Japanese elite before addressing the more basic needs of their own domestic majority.

The historical legitimation of Japanese capitalism would certainly be enhanced if the sacrifices of Japanese workers under the scrap-and-build (now deindustrialization) strategy were part of the development of an historically progressive regional or even global system of production pointing toward an integrated process of global development of productive capacities and human needs satisfaction. Unfortunately, there is no evidence that this is the actual tendency of Japanese imperialism. The international operations of Japanese capital, like all forms of capitalist globalization, are oriented toward maximum profit regardless of the human, social, and environmental effects; to put it differently, these effects are viewed as costs that must be managed or externalized onto society, rather than avoided or internalized into the goals of production itself.

It is also necessary to briefly comment on the argument that Japanese capitalism has gained a progressive-competitive edge over the U.S. because it is less dependent on military power. We believe that the recovery of Japanese imperialism in the post-World War II era occurred symbiotically with the evolution of U.S. imperialism, as the U.S., in order to redistribute the costs of its own hegemonic activities, encouraged and supported Japanese efforts to reconstitute its sphere of influence in East Asia. This symbiotic development occurred interactively with, but was by no means reducible to, the post-World War II boom of the Japanese economy generated by U.S. military spending associated with the Korean and Vietnam Wars (Halliday and McCormack, 1973; Sweezy, 1980; Tsuru, 1993). One could even say that Japan enjoyed many of the benefits, but none of the drawbacks, of the powerful U.S. military-industrial complex and global-imperialist network. This history challenges the misguided notion (or wishful thinking along the lines of the pre-World War I Kautsky) that military power has been eclipsed by some kind of militarily-unconnected economic power.[13]

In terms of this last point, it is important to recall that Japanese capitalism, including the basic elements of the post-World War II Japanese model, was formed in the thoroughly imperialist environment of the late-19th century and the inter-war years. This environment greatly accentuated the military *and* economic expansionist tendencies that were already built into the fabric of Japanese capitalism's fundamental class relations (Halliday, 1975). Japan was never fully demilitarized after World War II, and it now possesses a modern military machine based on the second largest military budget in the world. This machine is top-heavy with officers and actual and potential weapons-production capacity; it would thus be easy for Japan to rapidly expand its military in terms of numbers of fully-equipped personnel.[14] It appears, moreover, that the Japanese military is currently being prepared for active international use: Japan has already participated in the UN's 1992 Kampuchean peacekeeping operation in direct violation of Japanese constitutional law; even the traditionally pacifist Japanese Socialist Party has 'abandoned [its] longstanding claim that Japan's military forces are unconstitutional . . . [and] pledged to uphold the U.S.-Japan military alliance, which the party once violently opposed' (Itoh, 1994: 49; Associated Press, 1994). In short, claims by leftists and liberals regarding the progressivity of Japanese capitalism vis-à-vis military power are another figment of their near total lapse of both structural perspective and historical memory.

Finally, before offering our political critique of the left-liberal consensus, it is useful to note the close parallels between our methodological critique and Rosa Luxemburg's critique of Bernstein's more original form of revisionism. Luxemburg notes, for example, how Bernstein takes certain (positive or negative) aspects of capitalism out of their class-exploitative, hence contradictory, structural context:

> Bernstein's theory does not seize these manifestations of contemporary economic life as they appear in their organic relationship with the whole of capitalist development, with the complete economic mechanism of capitalism. His theory pulls these details out of their living economic context. It treats them as the *disjecta membra* (separate parts) of a lifeless machine. (Luxemburg, 1970: 61)

As a result, says Luxemburg, Bernstein's revisionism has a close affinity with the viewpoint of 'the isolated capitalist [who] sees each organic part of the whole of our economy as an independent entity . . . as they act upon him, the single capitalist'. For, insofar as revisionism limits its analysis to an uncritical acceptance of 'the economic facts . . . just as they appear when refracted by the laws of competition,' then 'revisionism is nothing else than a theoretic generalization made from the angle of the isolated capitalist'. Luxemburg then argues that such an a-historical, non-holistic perspective necessarily 'ends in utopia' because it is incapable of seeing how 'the contradictions of capitalism mature'; indeed, like the isolated capitalist, revisionism 'wants to lessen, to attenuate, the capitalist contradictions' (1970: 60–3).[15]

The similarity between Luxemburg's classical critique of revisionism and our critique of the left-liberal consensus on Japan becomes even clearer when we consider the political implications of the latter. As we shall see, because this consensus is based on an understanding of capitalism that also 'pulls . . . details out of their living context,' views the economy 'from the angle of the isolated capitalist,' and 'is guided by the . . . possibility of the attenuation of the contradictions of capitalism,' it must also, like Bernstein's revisionism, 'end in utopia'.

## IV. The Political Bankruptcy of the Left-Liberal Consensus

In our opinion, the attempt to build a progressive political-economic project on the basis of non-holistic and a-historical interpretations of the key underpinnings of Japanese competitiveness is not only methodologically flawed, it is also politically dangerous. The left-liberal consensus not only creates a picture of a capitalism that is capable of being reformed into a humanized and socially progressive system, it poses progressive capitalist competitiveness as the only alternative for the foreseeable future. In fact, this consensus views progressive reforms as not only possible within the capitalist framework but as actually leading to superior performance in capitalist terms of profitability and competitiveness. The logical implication of this perspective is that if capitalists and the capitalist state think and behave rationally, they can be counted on to see and act upon the wisdom of such progressive reforms.

The left-liberal consensus thus undermines any motivation for popular participation in grassroots political activity in favour of an approach to politics which emphasizes the dispensation of technocratic advice at an elite level in and through think tanks, lobbying and participating in mainstream media and politics. In short, the presumption of a natural affinity between capitalist competitiveness and progressive reforms tends naturally to limit the role of any grassroots movement to periodic visits to the ballot box or monetary contributions to progressive organizations and their media. Meanwhile, the fact that the entire political terrain is moving rightward under the intensifying competitiveness pressures of capitalist globalization is nowhere addressed (much less directly confronted and fought). In this way, the left-liberal consensus bypasses the realization that what is needed for truly progressive change, and even for a more effective defence of past popular gains, is not 'a progressive competitive state' but rather a 'transformation of the state' into 'a state whose functions are not tied to guaranteeing the economic *res publica* for capitalism' (Panitch, 1994: 87).[16]

Progressives who accept capital's globalization and competitiveness imperatives as their starting point hope, of course, that social arrangements (*e.g.*, the 'social structure of accumulation') can be constructed which will protect and benefit working people *while* boosting competitiveness. Indeed they go so far as to argue that these two goals are complementary rather than intrinsically contradictory as Marxists would have it. But unfortunately, by its uncritical acceptance of capitalism's basic structure, the left-liberal consensus fails to come to grips with capitalism's basic shortcomings, especially in its mature and globalized stage. Apparently overlooked, for example, is the fact that Sweden and Germany were once the primary models for 'progressive competitiveness' visions of a humane and efficient capitalism, that is, until the pressures and contradictions of capitalist globalization encouraged their respective ruling classes to reshape their domestic political economies along lines more similar to that of the U.S.[17] As a result, left-liberal perspectives and strategies are on a greased incline leading from European Social Democracy to Japanese capitalism.[18] With Japan's growing economic difficulties in the 1990s, the next stop is unclear.

It should be obvious that the inherent tendency of progressive competitiveness thinking to produce political demobilization will only intensify as its 'model' countries (Sweden, Germany, and Japan) continue to experience systemic economic problems, especially if workers and other popular sectors in these countries respond by criticizing and moving to transform the main features of their respective political economies. If such movements do develop, the progressive movement here (insofar as it has been influenced by the left-liberal consensus) will be placed in a difficult position, unable to explain or even acknowledge them, because to do so would undercut its own arguments that these countries have systems (or at least some crucial systemic features) that are workable and superior. Just as obviously, this quandary makes international solidarity difficult if not impossible to build. How can we join with Japanese workers to challenge capitalism, for example, when the main features of Japanese capitalism are held out as progressive and desirable? This tendency toward frittering away conjunctural (crisis-based) potentials for enhanced solidarity and revolutionary change on a global scale is, perhaps, the most tragic characteristic of both left and liberal variants of progressive competitiveness thinking.

While the left-liberal consensus puts hypothetical progressive interests or strategies – derived from a capitulatory interpretation of recent capitalist history – ahead of the actual movement of the working class, we believe that to obtain politically useful insights into capitalism's dynamics one must engage with workers' movements as much as study the human, social and ecological preconditions of capitalist competitiveness.[19] This is especially the case in our current era when capitalism's tendency to erode its own conditions of existence seems to be increasingly overriding its previous materially progressive character on a global scale. As the global crisis of capitalist human-material reproduction intensifies, it thus becomes more important for people struggling against this crisis to revive their historical consciousness, their historical memories of, and objective unity and solidarity with, past popular struggles in their own and other countries. By focusing on a false, a-historical affinity between progressive reforms and capitalist competitiveness, the left-liberal consensus stands objectively opposed to this crucial historical-ideological moment of popular organization, vision, and struggle.

To be clear, our objection to the left-liberal consensus is not that it is interested in policy but that its formulation of progressive analyses and policy proposals is divorced from any attempt to mobilize people in a way that, while helping to defend their immediate material interests, simultaneously generates an alternative vision of society. The result of progressive competitiveness thinking is, in fact, a mirage of a capitalism that can be technically restructured in such a way that its problems can be solved without a revolutionary push beyond capitalism. This is a mirage because it is concocted by deriving both the problems of U.S. capitalism and their solutions from other, 'better' capitalisms in a-historical and non-holistic fashion.

## V. Conclusions: Towards a Left Vision and Strategy

In contrast to the left-liberal consensus, it is our position that we *should* fight capitalist globalization because it is exploitative as well as socially, culturally, politically, and ecologically irrational and oppressive – in short, because it is does not offer an historical path toward human progress (or even survival) in cooperation with nature. We also believe that we *can* fight capitalist globalization precisely because it is an historically limited and contradictory, hence not an inevitable, process.[20] In other words, rejection of progressive competitiveness thinking need not entail any sectarian 'ultra-leftism,' i.e., a belief that there is nothing that can be done except wait for the collapse of capitalism.[21]

While capitalism, for historical reasons, works differently in different countries, it is crucial, in our opinion, that left intellectual work recognize and make clear the underlying isomorphism of these different capitalisms. This isomorphism stems precisely from the fact that since all are capitalist, all are class-exploitative and all have an in-built historical tendency toward maturity and decay in terms of their progressivity as modes of human needs satisfaction. Such work should also investigate and articulate how it is *capital's* logic (not workers') that is creating regional and global processes that do not allow for the building of the kind of societies we want, how it is *capital's* global motion that is narrowing the space for national reform efforts, and finally, how this narrowing of capitalist-reformist space reveals the inadequacies of supposedly 'progressive' capitalist models as vehicles for a worker-led movement toward a better society.

A left analysis of capitalism need not and should not objectively align itself *against* grassroots movements that challenge capital's competitiveness line; such an anti-popular alignment (as is logically implied by the left-liberal consensus) presumes that it is capital's priorities, rather than the individual and collective use-value oriented struggles of workers and other popular groupings, that are historically progressive. Once one critically investigates this presumption, it becomes clear that true progressivity, in the current era of humanly and socially immiserizing capitalist globalization, lies in support for *anti*-competitiveness struggles and in our ability to transform such struggles into a better world *via* the envisionment, development and implementation of non-capitalistic, cooperative and democratic, socio-economic arrangements.[22] In short, progressive competitiveness

> reasoning is inverted in the sense that it places the needs of capital first, and thus only serves to reinforce an unnecessary disjuncture between the subjective experience and practice of workers and the presumably objective needs of capital. The real cunning of history in our time lies in the fact that the straightforward struggle of labor against capital at every point along the line constitutes the only way to secure the objective economic environment in which people live and work, simply because it means placing limitations on the hegemony of private property itself. (Foster, 1989: 296)

Thus, in order to serve popular struggles for a better world in truly progressive fashion, we must ensure that capitalism's priorities do not determine our own priorities and strategy. This means that our values (in particular those involving our conceptions of individuality and collectivity, solidarity and competition, security and meritocracy, peace and justice, etc.) must be consciously articulated *before* worrying about the best instruments to employ toward their historical fulfillment. This effort to clarify our values and world-vision must be informed by, indeed firmly rooted in, the historical development and struggles of working people in the past and present. And, once clarified, they should serve as both inspiration and guidepost for the development of our political strategy and policy proposals. This value base is absolutely essential, for without a clear sense of vision, there will always be a tendency for capitalist values to fill the resulting vacuum – and such a value displacement will quite often create a strong tendency for 'the immediately possible' to displace, or to be redefined as, 'the historically progressive'. In short, the primary value dimension is crucial if we are to avoid all kinds of self-constrictive, self-fulfilling, and ultimately regressive prophecies concerning what is possible, especially in an environment in which capital is becoming less-and-less accommodative to anything other than its own profit-driven priorities.

Our conception of a primary value dimension can be contrasted with the left-liberal consensus which basically assumes that a progressive movement's values can be plucked out of their 'progressive capitalist' contexts (*e.g.*, the values of 'cooperation' and 'participation' taken from the idealized Japanese work model abstracted from its patriarchal class-exploitative context). It then treats these values as *universal* values in the sense that they are said to complement – indeed to provide the most advanced forms for fulfilling – the competitive dictates of an increasingly globalized or universal capitalism. This universalization-by-abstraction of values renders the value basis of the left-liberal consensus completely a-historical – highly appropriate given the previously discussed failure of this consensus to come to grips with the historical development and contradictions of Japanese capitalism and of capitalist globalization in terms of their class-exploitative content.

Focusing on the importance of the primary value dimension allows us to see that the political shortcomings and quandaries associated with the left-liberal consensus are not completely original. Indeed, there is a striking parallel between recent searches for progressive inspiration in the relative competitiveness of external capitalisms, and the longtime search by U.S. socialists (especially self-proclaimed left vanguardists) for inspiration from external varieties of 'socialism'. For, in the latter search too, U.S. leftists' conceptions of historical (in this case 'socialist') progress tended toward idealizations of certain components of other systems abstracted from their historically developed class contexts – and this greatly affected the values and visions of the future promulgated by the left. Taking an essentially exploitative and authoritarian country like the U.S.S.R. as a model 'socialist' country, for example, led to the identification of socialism with a system where the state, not the direct producers, maintained ownership and control over the conditions and results of production. Such an identification cannot help but vitiate one's conception of socialism and socialist values and discredit them *vis-à-vis* progressive working class traditions in the U.S..[23]

Just as for the left-liberal consensus, then, the earlier harnessing of left analysis and policy to external (and idealized) 'socialist' models implicitly presumed that left values and visions could be plucked from their external historical and class-exploitative contexts. Given the contradictions in Soviet society, left visions were gradually reduced to bringing mystical capitalist ideals ('efficiency,' 'harmony,' etc.) closer to reality in impeccably technocratic fashion (e.g., through 'planning' – just as advocates of progressive competitiveness now call for a more enlightened 'industrial policy' to bring the U.S. closer to the idealized Japanese capitalist model). Need it be added that this search for ideals in external 'socialisms' led many leftists down their own greased incline – from the U.S.S.R., to China, and in some cases even to Albania – in step with ongoing revelations concerning the horrific work and living conditions and political and cultural repression experienced by workers in these countries?

The unfortunate results of both sides of the above-described parallel reinforce our argument for a more historical, holistic, and value-based mode of analysis. We believe that, given the still central role of U.S.-based capital in reproducing and extending the power of an increasingly exploitative, oppressive and irrational global-capitalist system, the U.S. left should be a *leader*, not a follower, in the global struggle to defend peoples' conditions against capitalist attacks and to move forward to a more sane, post-capitalist system of global human-material reproduction. To be sure, this leadership should be informed by the lessons of capitalism's development, and of popular struggles, in other countries. But these lessons should be conceived in terms of their implications for a workers' movement which, while developing in solidarity and coordination with popular struggles in other countries, builds and expands upon our own history of development and struggle (which of course includes the history and struggles of indigenous peoples [Churchill, 1993]). Our view is that given 'triumphant' capitalism's crisis of human-material reproduction, we need to begin the construction of an alternative global system in the here and now, and that left analyses should directly serve this all-important task rather than trying to concoct humanized versions of *Business Week*-style corporatist capitalism.

## NOTES

1. For the productivity and competitiveness argument for reduced work time, see Schor (1993, Chapter 6). Levine and Tyson (1989) present the case for workers' control to improve US competitiveness. Several chapters in Dymski, *et al.* (1993) offer proposals for regulating financial speculation and increasing popular control over non-financial corporations and financial institutions (including the Federal Reserve)—proposals defended largely in terms of their ability to enhance the US economy's investment, productivity and competitiveness. These are only representative examples.

2. We concentrate on the U.S. variant of progressive competitiveness thinking with respect to Japan because that is the case we are most familiar with. We will let leftists in other countries decide for themselves the extent to which our outline and critique of this kind of thinking applies to their own circumstances. Nonetheless, we would hope that the present essay contributes to further cross-national discussion of, and struggle against, progressive competitiveness arguments.
3. Marxist economist Robert Pollin (1993: 341–2), for example, refers to 'Japan's success with a credit allocation-centered planning system' as 'the outstanding example of how an economy can use credit allocation techniques to promote financial stability and long-term growth.'
4. Progressive-feminist economist Nancy Folbre puts forward the claim 'that the Japanese are successfully competitive in world markets primarily because they are so cooperative at home' (1994: 27). J. R. Stanfield (1994: 11), working from a left-institutionalist perspective, argues the same point even more strongly: 'Japan . . . must be interpreted in light of the population's nationalist commitment and respect for hierarchical authority. Beyond one's firm, there is one's *keiretsu*, beyond one's *keiretsu*, there is one's country. Such rank ordered commitments are less evident in an individualistic economic setting . . . *solidaristic sentiment plays a more pervasive role in Japanese economic relationships and calculations than in the American instance*' (emphases in original).
5. In fact, to the extent that the greater patience of Japanese core-capital, based on the relative 'insulation' of Japanese corporations from short-term financial pressures, was and is gained at the expense of increased insecurity and immiseration for workers especially in the smaller subcontracting enterprises, it largely represents an 'efficient' *transfer* of financial pressures downward in the corporate (and class) hierarchy rather than a reduction *per sé* of these pressures. We take up this issue below in the context of our discussion of the Japanese work model.
6. Indeed, by October 1995, in the wake of the Daiwa Bank scandal and other related problems, US authorities indicated that they were standing by to help troubled Japanese banks (Gonzalez, 1995). Japanese banks are paying a premium between 0.30 and 0.41 percent in global interbank markets at this writing, after having received new, lower credit-ratings from Moody's in August (Sapsford, 1995b; Steiner, 1995). The role of the real estate bubble in the crisis is emphasized in Williams and Sapsford (1995), Jenkins (1995), Sapsford (1995d) and Pacelle (1995). For the similarity between Japanese and earlier US clean-up operations, and the connection of Japanese regulatory reforms with Japan's surprisingly weak and understaffed bank inspection system, see Williams and Steiner (1995), Sapsford (1995c,e,f) and Williams (1995c).
7. It must be reiterated that the super-exploitation of (predominantly female) workers in small- and medium-sized workplaces has been a primary source of capital for the commanding heights of Japanese capitalism ever since its initial phase of development in the Meiji period. This historical continuity – indicating that such super-exploitation may well be intrinsic to the Japanese accumulation regime – is completely passed over amidst the recent praise from liberals and leftists for the progressively competitive labour-management techniques of core Japanese corporations.
8. In this sense, progressive supporters of the Japanese work model objectively, albeit unconsciously, align themselves with the bourgeois distorters of the immediate post-World War upheavals – including the outright vulgar-apologetic ones like Reubens (1946) and Taira (1988) who take pleasure in downplaying the role of repression and capitalist economic sabotage in order to assert that workers' production control was and is simply a utopian project.
9. Harvey (1993: 44–5) makes this same point from an ecological perspective when he argues that '[s]ocialism is not necessarily about the construction of homogeneity. The exploration of our species potential can presumably also be about the creative search for and exploration of diversity and heterogeneity . . . much more in tune with resolving

questions of alienation and opening up diverse possibilities for self-realization . . . as fundamentally part of some socialist future'.

10. For details on the intensifying crisis in the Japanese world of work – a crisis accentuated by recent recessionary tendencies – see Dassbach (1993), Watanabe (1993), Schregle (1993), Shimada (1993), Moody (1994), Williams (1994), Hideo, *et al.* (1994) and Itoh (1994).
11. Japanese capital's environmental destruction of peripheral Asian countries – a destruction 'progressively' attained without contributing to the achievement of a sustainable pattern of industrial and agricultural development – has unfortunately reached an advanced stage. See, for example, Ofreneo's (1993) detailed discussion of the Philippine case.
12. Hence, to characterize the latest form of this 'co-prosperity sphere' as historically progressive is to align oneself, objectively speaking, with apologists for pre-World War II Japanese imperialism such as Kimura (1993, 1995), who argues that the Japanese colonization of Korea actually improved the material living standards of the Korean working population. See Hamilton (1986) and Hart-Landsberg (1993) for more balanced views of the human impact of this colonial development experience.
13. Nester's (1990) analysis of the recovery of Japan's economic hegemony in East Asia is well worth reading as a compendium of potential quandaries of imperialism without military domination.
14. Japan's military machine contains not only up-to-date conventional weaponry but also high nuclear capabilities: even if Japan does not already have nuclear weapons it has the capability of producing them within a short period of time given its large number of relevant scientific and engineering personnel and weapons-grade plutonium generating capacity (Itsunori, 1994; Leventhal, 1994; Nadler, 1994).
15. In short, the revisionist 'procedure is not guided by a consideration of the development of capitalism, by the prospect of the aggravation of its contradictions. It is guided by the attenuation of these contradictions' (Luxemburg, 1970: 60).
16. The exact institutional forms of such a radically progressive transformation of the state must, of course, be qualitatively a function of the goals, values and visions of the movement doing the transforming (see Section V on this point).
17. See Cohen (1994) for a Marxist analysis of the developing crisis of the Swedish model and of the cosmetic and incoherent explanations for this crisis advanced by the model's progressive supporters. The post-World War II West German class compromise – once touted as perhaps the most 'progressively competitive' – is now being subjected to a frontal assault by German capital (and transnational capital generally) engaging in investment strike, capital flight and an intensive propaganda campaign against the constraints imposed on its ability to freely exploit German workers and dominate German socio-material reproduction (Steinmetz, 1995; Gumbel, 1995; Shlaes, 1995a,b; Bartlett, 1995; Marshall, 1995a,b,c).
18. This shifting focus itself manifests the fact that, with the collapse of Soviet style socialism and the crisis of Western European social democracy, many progressives have lost any vision or sense of alternatives to capitalism. See Anderson (1986) and Meiksins Wood (1986) for some acute observations on the socio-economic and political underpinnings of this historical-intellectual development.
19. Indeed, the movement of the working class (its exploitation and alienation, and its human-social reactions against these dehumanizing tendencies) is in our view an integral part of capitalist dynamics including the eventual socialist transformation of this system. This viewpoint need not, and should not, entail an uncritical stance *vis-à-vis* popular movements and organizations; nor does it entail any over-romanticization of the working class. One cannot serve one's class – much less oneself – effectively by means of self-delusion and fantasy. See Hart-Landsberg (1994) for an example of the kind of sympathetic but critical analysis of developing popular movements we have in mind.
20. The 'progressive competitiveness' perspective includes an evident tension over global-

ization. One view sees globalization as an inevitable trend which cannot be significantly altered by national state policies (thereby implicitly assuming that nation states are helpless hostages to a capitalist globalization whose emergence is given apart from state policies). The other view sees national state policies as a crucial determinant of global capitalist competitiveness (which obviously presumes – more accurately as Panitch (1994) and others have pointed out – that national state policies are crucial to the process of capital globalization itself). The fact that capitalist globalization appears less inevitable in the second view is never systematically addressed by progressive competitiveness advocates.

21. The basic text for this conception of revolutionary reform is Luxemburg (1970). See Reynolds (1993) for a useful analytical retrospective on Luxemburg's approach to revolutionary politics. Our perspective on reform and revolution also draws upon the work of Sweezy and Magdoff (1982), Foster (1990), Mandel (1992: Chapters 3 and 5) and Magdoff (1995). As Mandel (1992: 128) indicates, '[i]n order to avoid the twin pitfalls of opportunism and sectarianism, it is necessary to assimilate the historical lessons of concrete class struggles, and to enrich them through critical examination of current experiences.'
22. For alternative perspectives on this task see Hymer (1979), Radice (1989), Brecher and Costello (1994) and Hart-Landsberg (1994).
23. Insofar as advocates of progressive competitiveness policies address their arguments to neoclassical economists and policymakers rather than directly to workers, this kind of alienation *vis-à-vis* working-class traditions may seem less applicable to the left-liberal consensus. Unfortunately, however, as was documented in Section II, the technocratic bent of progressive competitiveness arguments does not preclude them from being prominent in the popular progressive and (to a lesser degree) mainstream media. Indeed, the danger of popular political demobilization would not be nearly as great if this were not the case.

## REFERENCES

Anderson, Perry. 1986. 'Social Democracy Today,' *Against the Current*, Vol.1, No.6, November-December, pp.21–8.

Associated Press. 1994. 'Japanese Socialist Party Abandons Pacifist Policies,' *Tribune-Star*, Terre Haute, September 4.

Bartlett, Bruce. 1995. 'Steffi's Not the Only German with Tax Woes,' *Wall Street Journal*, October 31, p.A22.

Bello, Walden (with Shea Cunningham and Bill Rau). 1994. *Dark Victory: The United States, Structural Adjustment, and Global Poverty*. London: Pluto Press.

Brecher, Jeremy and Tim Costello. 1994. *Global Village or Global Pillage: Economic Reconstruction from the Bottom Up*. Boston: South End Press.

Chriszt, Michael J. 1993. 'Are International Comparisons of Inflation and Employment Valid?' *Economic Review*, Federal Reserve Bank of Dallas, Vol.78, No.6, November-December, pp.23–36.

Churchill, Ward. 1993. *Struggle for the Land*. Monroe, ME: Common Courage Press.

Clinton, Bill and Al Gore. 1992. *Putting People First: How We Can All Change America*. New York: Times Books.

Cohen, Peter. 1994. 'Sweden: The Model That Never Was,' *Monthly Review*, Vol.46, No.3, July-August, pp.41–59.

Dassbach, Carl H.A. 1993. 'The Japanese World of Work and North American Factories,' *Critical Sociology*, Vol.20, No.1, pp.3–30.

Dymski, Gary A., Gerald Epstein and Robert Pollin. 1993. *Transforming the U.S. Financial System*. Armonk, NY: M.E. Sharpe.

*Economist*. 1995. 'Japan: One in Ten?' July 1, pp.26–7.

Elder, Sam and Constance Sorrentino. 1993. 'Japan's Low Unemployment: An Update and Revision,' *Monthly Labor Review*, Vol.116, No.10, pp.56–63.

Folbre, Nancy. 1994. 'Capitalists All,' *In These Times*, Vol.18, No.19, August 8, 1994, pp.26–7.

Foster, John Bellamy. 1989. 'The Age of Restructuring,' In, *Instability and Change in the World Economy*, Arthur MacEwan and William K. Tabb, eds., New York: Monthly Review Press, pp.281–97.

____. 1990. 'Liberal Practicality and the US Left,' In, *Socialist Register 1990: The Retreat of the Intellectuals*, Ralph Miliband and Leo Panitch, eds., London: Merlin, pp.265–89.

Goldstein, Don. 1995. 'Financial Structure and Corporate Behavior in Japan and the U.S.: Insulation vs. Integration With Speculative Pressures,' Paper Presented at the Meetings of the Union for Radical Political Economics, Washington, DC, January 6–8, 1995.

Gonzalez, Michael. 1995. 'Prices of Stocks and Bonds Sink in the U.S.,' *Wall Street Journal*, October 24, p.C1.

Gordon, David M. 1993a. 'Clintonomics: The Upsides and the Downsides,' *The Nation*, Vol.256, No.10, March 15, pp.325, 329, 344.

____. 1993b. 'Generating Affluence: Productivity Gains Require Worker Support,' *Dollars and Sense*, November/December, pp.20–2.

Greenfeld, Karl Taro. 1992. 'Children of the Bubble,' *The Nation*, Vol.255, No.22, December 28, pp.807–12.

Gumbel, Peter. 1995. 'Kohl Criticizes Germans for Losing Their Work Ethic,' *Wall Street Journal*, October 17, p.A14.

Halliday, Jon. 1975. *A Political History of Japanese Capitalism*. New York: Pantheon Books.

____ and Gavan McCormack. 1973. *Japanese Imperialism Today: 'Co-Prosperity in Greater East Asia.'* Harmondsworth, Middlesex, England: Penguin Books.

Hamilton, Clive. 1986. *Capitalist Industrialization in Korea*. Boulder, CO: Westview Press.

Harvey, David. 1993. 'The Nature of Environment: The Dialectics of Social and Environmental Change.' In, *Socialist Register 1993: Real Problems, False Solutions*, Ralph Miliband and Leo Panitch, eds., London: Merlin, pp.1–51.

Hart-Landsberg, Martin. 1993. *The Rush to Development: Economic Change and Political Struggle in South Korea*. New York: Monthly Review Press.

____. 1994. 'Post-NAFTA Politics: Learning from Asia,' *Monthly Review*, Vol.46, No.2, June, pp.12–21.

Hideo, Totsuka, *et al.* 1994. 'Myths of the Managed Society,' *AMPO*, Vol.25, No.1, pp.10–39.

Howard, Michael C. 1993. 'Introduction,' In, *Asia's Environmental Crisis*, Michael C. Howard, ed., Boulder, CO: Westview Press, pp.1–35.

Hymer, Stephen. 1979. 'The Multinational Corporation and the International Division of Labor,' In, *The Multinational Corporation: A Radical Approach*, New York: Cambridge University Press, pp.140–64.

Itoh, Makoto. 1994. 'Is the Japanese Economy in Crisis?' *Review of International Political Economy*, Vol.1, No.1, Spring, pp.29–51.

Itsunori, Ikeda. 1994. 'Giving the SDF New Fangs,' *AMPO*, Vol.25, No.2, pp.7–9.

Jenkins, Holman W., Jr. 1995. 'Japan's Quiet Bank Bailout,' *Wall Street Journal*, October 17, p.A19.

Kimura, Mitsuhiko. 1993. 'Standard of Living in Colonial Korea: Did the Masses Become Worse Off or Better Off Under Japanese Rule?' *Journal of Economic History*, Vol.53, No.3, September, pp.629–652.

____. 1995. 'The Economics of Japanese Imperialism in Korea, 1910–1939,' *Economic History Review*, Vol.48, No.3, August, pp.555–74.

Labor Research Association. 1994. 'Japanese Workers Feel the Squeeze,' *Economic Notes*, Vol.62, No.3, March, p.7.

Leventhal, Paul L. 1994. 'The New Nuclear Threat,' *Wall Street Journal*, June 8.

Levine, David I. and Laura D'Andrea Tyson. 1989. 'No Voice for Workers: U.S. Economy

Penalizes Worker Participation,' *Dollars and Sense*, December 1989, pp.20–2.
Luxemburg, Rosa. 1970. 'Reform or Revolution,' In, *Rosa Luxemburg Speaks*, Mary-Alice Walters, ed., New York: Pathfinder Press, pp.33–90.
Macedo Cintra, Marcos Antonio. 1994. 'Financial Repression and the Latin American Finance Pattern,' *CEPAL Review*, No.53, August, pp.31–47.
Magdoff, Harry. 1995. 'A Note on "Market Socialism",' *Monthly Review*, Vol.47, No.1, May, pp.12–18.
Mandel, Ernest. 1992. *Power and Money: A Marxist Theory of Bureaucracy*. London: Verso.
Marshall, Matt. 1995a. 'German Chemical Giants Wary of Future: High Costs at Home Mean Shift to U.S. and Asia May Be Key to Survival,' *Wall Street Journal*, November 10, p.A12.
____. 1995b. 'Kohl's Failure to Cut Spending is Faulted,' *Wall Street Journal*, December 7, p.A6.
____. 1995c. 'Outlook Dims for Germany's Economy With GDP Unchanged, Jobless Rate Up,' *Wall Street Journal*, December 8, p.A8.
McCormack, Gavan. 1990. 'Capitalism Triumphant? The Evidence from 'Number One' (Japan),' *Monthly Review*, Vol.42, No.1, May, pp.1–13.
____. 1991. 'The Price of Affluence: The Political Economy of Japanese Leisure,' *New Left Review*, No.188, July/August, pp.121–34.
McDermott, John and Chris Tilly. 1994. 'Japan in Recession: A Conversation with Ronald Dore,' *Dollars and Sense*, March/April, pp.20–1, 37–8.
Meiksins Wood, Ellen. 1986. *The Retreat from Class: A New 'True' Socialism*. London: Verso.
Moody, Kim. 1994. 'Toyota's Leanness Hits the Limit,' *Labor Notes*, No.184, July, pp.16, 10.
Moore, Joe. 1983. *Japanese Workers and the Struggle for Power, 1945–1947*. Madison: University of Wisconsin Press.
____. 1988. 'Production Control: Workers' Control in Early Postwar Japan,' In, *The Other Japan: Postwar Realities*, E. Patricia Tsurumi, ed., Armonk, NY: M.E. Sharpe, pp.14–35.
Nadler, Eric. 1994. 'North Korea's Nuclear Neighbors,' *The Nation*, Vol.259, No.1, July 4, pp.17–9.
Nakamura, Masao. 1993. 'Japanese Industrial Relations in an International Business Environment,' *North American Journal of Economics & Finance*, Vol.4, No.2, Fall, pp.225–51.
Nester, William R. 1990. *Japan's Growing Predominance Over East Asia and the World Economy*. New York: St. Martin's Press.
Ofreneo, Rene F. 1993. 'Japan and the Environmental Degradation of the Phillipines,' In, *Asia's Environmental Crisis*, Michael C. Howard, ed., Boulder, CO: Westview Press, pp.201–19.
Ogawa, Naohiro and Robert L. Clark. 1995. 'Earnings Patterns of Japanese Women: 1976–1988,' *Economic Development and Cultural Change*, Vol.43, No.2, January, pp.293–313.
Pacelle, Mitchell. 1995. 'Japan's Banks Sell More Real Estate in U.S. at Big Losses,' *Wall Street Journal*, December 5, p.A5.
Panitch, Leo. 1994. 'Globalization and the State,' In, *Socialist Register 1994: Between Globalism and Nationalism*, Ralph Miliband and Leo Panitch, eds., London: Merlin Press, pp.60–93.
Parker, Mike. 1994. 'Trouble in Paradise: Election of Dissident Reveals Discontent at Model 'Team Concept' Plant,' *Labor Notes*, No.184, July, p.2.
Pollin, Robert. 1993. 'Public Credit Allocation through the Federal Reserve,' In, *Transforming the U.S. Financial System*, Gary A. Dymski, Gerald Epstein, and Robert Pollin, eds., Armonk, NY: M.E. Sharpe, pp.321–54.
Radice, Hugo. 1989. 'British Capitalism in a Changing Global Economy,' In, *Instability and Change in the World Economy*, Arthur MacEwan and William K. Tabb, eds., New York: Monthly Review Press, pp.64–81.

Reubens, Beatrice G. 1946. '"Production Control" in Japan,' *Far Eastern Survey*, Vol.15, No.22, November 6, pp.344–7.

Reynolds, David B. 1993. 'Rediscovering Marxism's Heritage: Rosa Luxemburg and the Revolutionary Party,' *Nature, Society, and Thought*, Vol.6, No.3, pp.267–98.

Sapsford, Jathon. 1995a. 'Yen's Climb Causes Jobless Rate to Rise to 3.2% in Japan,' *Wall Street Journal*, May 31, p.B9.

____. 1995b. 'Japanese Banks Get New, Lower Ratings,' *Wall Street Journal*, August 22, pp.A2, A6.

____. 1995c. 'Japan to Propose New Bank Safeguards,' *Wall Street Journal*, September 25, p.A10.

____. 1995d. 'Japan Posts Rise in Bank Loans Unlikely to Be Repaid; Facts May Be Even Worse,' *Wall Street Journal*, November 15, p.A16.

____. 1995e. 'Tokai Bank to Aid in Japanese Rescue of Credit Union,' *Wall Street Journal*, December 8, p.A8.

____. 1995f. 'Japan Approves Unpopular Bailout Plan,' *Wall Street Journal*, December 20, p.A10.

Schor, Juliet B. 1993. *The Overworked American: The Unexpected Decline of Leisure*. New York: Basic Books.

Schregle, Johannes. 1993. 'Dismissal Protection in Japan,' *International Labor Review*, Vol.132, No.4, pp.507–20.

Shimada, Haruo. 1993. 'Recession and Change in Labor Practices in Japan,' *International Labor Review*, Vol.132, No.2, pp.159–60.

Shlaes, Amity. 1995a. 'Does German Business Need Germany?' *Wall Street Journal*, October 24, p.A23.

____. 1995b. 'A Germany That Kills Science,' *Wall Street Journal*, November 7, p.A22.

Stanfield, J.R. 1994. 'Learning from Japan About the Nurturance Gap in America,' *Review of Social Economy*, Vol.52, No.1, Spring, pp.2–19.

Steiner, Robert. 1995. 'Daiwa Scandal, Loan Woes Boost Rate Japanese Banks Pay to Borrow Money,' *Wall Street Journal*, October 25, p.A17.

Steinmetz, Greg. 1995. 'German Firms Sour on System that Keeps Peace with Workers,' *Wall Street Journal*, October 17, pp.A1, A14.

Steven, Rob. 1988. 'The Japanese Working Class,' In, *The Other Japan: Postwar Realities*, E. Patricia Tsurumi, ed., Armonk, NY: M.E. Sharpe, pp.91–111.

____. 1990. *Japan's New Imperialism*. Armonk, NY: M.E. Sharpe.

Sweezy, Paul M. 1980. 'Japan in Perspective,' *Monthly Review*, Vol.31, No.9, February, pp.1–14.

____ and Harry Magdoff. 1982. 'The Responsibility of the Left,' *Monthly Review*, Vol.34, No.7, December, pp.1–9.

Tabb, William K. 1992. 'Vampire Capitalism,' *Socialist Review*, Vol.22, No.1, January-March, pp.81–93.

Taira, Koji. 1988. 'Economic Development, Labor Markets, and Industrial Relations in Japan, 1905–1955,' In, *The Cambridge History of Japan*, Vol.6, Peter Duus, ed., New York: Cambridge University Press, pp.606–53.

Tsuru, Shigeto. 1993. *Japan's Capitalism*. New York: Cambridge University Press.

Watanabe, Ben. 1993. 'Promise of "Lifetime Employment" is Disappearing in Japan,' *Labor Notes*, No.170, May, pp.1, 13.

Williams, Michael. 1994a. 'Japan's Shoppers Bring a New Era to Economy,' *Wall Street Journal*, June 20, p.A1.

____. 1994b. 'Japan's Labor System Survives Recession,' *Wall Street Journal*, November 8.

____. 1995c. 'Japan Will Improve Supervision of Branch Banks, Add Inspectors,' *Wall Street Journal*, November 13, p.A11.

____ and Jathon Sapsford. 1995. 'Japan's Slow Response to Bank Crisis Shows Its Big, Basic Problems,' *Wall Street Journal*, June 14, pp.A1, A8.

____ and Robert Steiner. 1995. 'Japan Finally Begins Its Huge Bank Bailout, Seizing Two Lenders,' *Wall Street Journal*, August 31, pp.A1, A5.

Yamamura, Kozo. 1967. *Economic Policy in Postwar Japan: Growth Versus Economic Democracy*. Berkeley: University of California Press.

Yoko, Kitazawa, *et al.* 1993. 'Black Paper on the Economic Superpower,' *AMPO*, Vol.24, No.4, pp.14–38.

# A KINDER ROAD TO HELL? LABOR AND THE POLITICS OF PROGRESSIVE COMPETITIVENESS IN AUSTRALIA

John Wiseman

> When this government introduced a market economy, when it opened us up to the world and implemented programs of micro economic reform, every step we took towards a more competitive Australia was a step towards a fairer Australia.
>
> *Australian Prime Minister Paul Keating, 1992.*[1]

> Australians and Australian companies need to come to terms with the fact that traditional Australian egalitarianism and views of fairness are not what is needed today . . . because the race to prosper in a more competitive world [is] endless.
>
> *Virginia O'Farrell, director of an Australian firm of 'remuneration consultants', defending the payment of million dollar salaries to business executives.*[2]

> [The international credit rating agencies] would think social justice is a horse running at Saratoga.
>
> *Former Victorian Labor Premier, John Cain.*[3]

After twelve years and five election victories the Australian Labor Party (ALP) is one of the few social democratic parties to have been in government continuously throughout the 1980s and the first half of the 1990s. For this reason the record of the ALP – and of the Australian labour movement – has been of increasing interest to labour movement activists and political parties in many parts of the world where electoral success has been more elusive.[4]

The ALP's impressive electoral record has provided the basis for extensive trade union access to government decision-making forums and social policy outcomes which have provided some targeted protection to low income and disadvantaged groups during a period in which the Australian economy and labour market have been dramatically restructured. The long period of Labor government in Australia has also provided some breathing space and room to move for those sections of the labour movement and other social movements who continue to challenge the inevitability and irreversibility of globalisation. However the dominant force driving the Australian Labor government has been the restructuring and deregulation of the Australian economy so as to increase competitiveness in global markets. In the end this strategy of 'progressive competitiveness' is likely to lead to the same mix of social polarisation and loss of political and economic sovereignty which has been the result of more openly right wing, neo liberal responses to globalisation.[5]

The Australian experience of progressive competitiveness provides a disturbing picture of the dilemmas facing social democratic parties and trade unions in a period of globalising power, fragmenting values and shifting loyalties. In such times it has become both harder and more urgent to open up debate about alternative policies and strategies at local, national and international levels which can begin to challenge the logic of 'competitiveness at all costs' on the ever expanding global racetrack.

Globalisation, the great political buzz word of the 1990s, has become a much used – and much abused – way of explaining the transformation of institutions and relationships at local, national and international levels in the concluding years of the twentieth century. Too often the language of globalisation has been used simplistically to suggest that global corporate power has become an overwhelming juggernaut extinguishing all geographical and historical differences, leading inevitably to the creation of a completely global economy and policy and an effective end to the sovereignty of nation states and the identity of local cultures.

An alternative view is that globalisation implies a more complex and dialectical process of 'action at a distance', varying in its nature and effects in different locales and subject to ongoing contestation from some sections of the state as well as from non government organisations and social movements.[6] From this perspective globalisation encompasses the increasing interdependence of national ecologies, economies and societies; the expansion of international trade, investment, production and financial flows; the growing significance of regional trading blocs and international economic agreements; more influential roles for international financial institutions and transnational corporations; greater mobility of capital (particularly finance capital) and the spreading of individualised and commodified economic, social and cultural relations into ever more spheres of human activity.[7] These trends have significant consequences in relation to capital formation and productive investment, the distribution of wealth, work and income and the integrity and sovereignty of national democratic decision-making processes.

First, even fervent supporters of financial deregulation have discovered that the volatility of globalized money markets creates a climate of escalating economic and political instability which can undermine the creation of sustainable long term investment strategies.[8] Economies such as that of Australia, with a small capital base and a high level of dependence on commodity exports, are particularly vulnerable.

Second, the fierce pressure to attract footloose capital, expand exports and compete on more open world markets generates a process variously described as 'downwards harmonisation', a 'race to the bottom', 'competitive austerity' or 'the low road to restructuring' in which there is constant downwards pressure on wages, working conditions, social programmes and environmental protection.[9] This means that, while the gap between richer and poorer nations deepens there is also a process of polarisation within industrialised nations between a privileged minority with access to well rewarded jobs and a growing majority of citizens excluded to the economic and social margins.[10] This polarisation has a significant gender dimension. While some women have benefited from the opening up of paid work opportunities, many others have been forced into the bottom end of the labour market at the same time as declining expenditure on health and community services increases demands on women to carry out unpaid caring and domestic work.[11] Rising inequalities within and between nations have also forced many people to move from rural to urban regions and across national borders in an attempt to flee poverty and unemployment.[12]

Third, the relative autonomy and sovereignty of national and sub national decision making forums in both state and civil society is undermined by the mobility of capital and the power of international financial institutions, credit rating agencies, transnational corporations and largely unaccountable global institutions such as the IMF and the World Bank.[13] The internationalisation of corporate power, the flexible localization of production networks and the concentration of producer services in particular urban centres have also led to pressures which, when combined with tensions over cultural and linguistic identities, tend to fragment national states and societies into competing and, at times conflicting interests.

For the champions of global capitalism national boundaries and destinies are barriers to be overcome. Enhancing the bargaining power of the corporation and undermining the legal and political regulatory power of national state institutions become the primary goals, with the construction of regional treaties and agreements protecting the rights of property and capital as key tools in this process. No doubt this is what Walter Writson, the former Chair of Citicorp Bank, was referring to when he enthused that '200,000 monitors in trading rooms all over the world now conduct a kind of global plebiscite on the monetary and fiscal policies of the governments issuing currency . . . There is no way for a nation to opt out'.[14]

Such naked defences of the interests of transnational capital are harder to legitimate at the national level where an acceptance of the inevitability of globalisation is more likely to be combined with strategies designed to maximise the competitiveness of national and regional economies. This commonly involves cost cutting policies such as labour shedding, wage reductions and deregulated labour markets as well as the promotion of productivity through technological innovation and improvements in infrastructure, training, production processes, marketing and distribution.

Much of the trade union movement in industrialised economies has accepted the inevitability of the competitiveness agenda but has attempted to protect union members through productivity trade offs designed to minimise job losses and protect working and living conditions. Similarly, as Albo and Panitch have argued, some social democratic parties have explored alternatives 'to austerity competitiveness' through strategies of 'progressive competitiveness' which aim to limit the social dislocation and polarisation of economic restructuring by redistributing some of the fruits of export-led growth so as to compensate those who have suffered most.[15]

Progressive competitiveness is an apt description of the overall political strategy pursued for over a decade by the Australian Labor Party and there has been a clear aim of targeting resources to group most disadvantaged by economic restructuring.[16] However the 'core business' of the government has increasingly been defined in terms of competitiveness, global integration and export growth. Fundamental problems in relation to production, distribution and regulation have deepened over this period and the stage has been set for a more extreme and openly right wing agenda of 'austerity competitiveness' to be pursued by a future Liberal/National Party government.

### *From a farm and a quarry to the global racetrack*

At the time of the ALP's victory at the 1983 election, the Australian economy remained a highly protected 'farm and quarry', heavily reliant on agricultural and mining exports, with a small uncompetitive manufacturing sector focussed mainly on the domestic market.[17] The Australian welfare state remained a fragile and residual creation based on assumptions of full employment and high wage levels defended by centralised wage fixing.

The uniquely Australian 'labourist' combination of legally arbitrated wages and residual welfare provisions began to emerge in the early twentieth century in the context of a neo-colonial economy still heavily dependent on agriculture and mining and increasingly reliant on protectionism to defend manufacturing industries and employment. Fifty years later the construction of the expanded post-war Australian welfare state by the Curtin and Chifley Labor governments occurred in the context of high levels of economic and employment growth resulting from demand built up during the war, the expansion of Fordist mass production and consumption and the initial success of Keynesian demand management policies. For the twenty years following World War II it was possible to achieve relatively high standards of living for households with access to the income of employed, unionised, male workers. However these arrangements provided substantially less support to those citizens, predominantly women, who were excluded from the workforce. Despite the struggles and achievements of the Australian women's movement the gendered division of labour and the assumption that women would normally be dependent on the male breadwinner also remained deeply entrenched.[18]

The central features of this economic and social policy framework were not fundamentally altered by the Whitlam Labor Government's ambitious but short lived efforts between 1972 and 1975 to expand the Australian welfare state and regain control of mineral and energy resources. Despite a limited shift in the direction of neo-liberal economic policies the 1975 to 1983 Liberal/National Party government remained committed to protectionism and a resource based economy until it was overwhelmed by the severe recession of the early 1980s. However the story of the 1980s and 1990s in Australia is the story of the shattering of the economic and social assumptions on which the Australian settlement between labour and capital had been constructed, and of the attempt by the ALP to manage the transition to a 'modern', post Fordist and globalised economy. Probert effectively captures the dilemmas which this has created for the ALP, noting that

> the impact of the rise of post Fordism on institutional politics is most apparent in the rise of New Right politics which appears to take on the cause of restructuring most transparently. However it can be argued that it is traditional social democracy which has suffered the greater crisis. This is particularly true of the Australian Labor Party which has been trying to manage the transition to a new, globally restructured economic order, and to ensure a share of the new global functions for Australia while at the same time trying to maintain the loyalty of its traditional working class supporters, whose livelihoods are being devastated by the very same policies.[19]

The immediate aim of the Hawke Labor government, elected in 1983, was to deal with the impact of the recession and to generate economic and employment growth through fiscal expansion while holding down inflation. This latter objective was to be achieved through the establishment of the Accord agreement between the government and the trade union movement which guaranteed that wages would not rise faster than prices in return for the government's commitment to employment generation and improvements in health and other social programmes. Trade union access to key governmental decision-making forums and processes was also a central part of the bargain and led to the establishment of a wide range of tripartite economic and industry consultative forums involving government, union and business representatives.[20]

The initial neo Keynesian optimism was soon overtaken by international pressures. In December 1983 Treasurer Keating overcame spirited opposition within the parliamentary Labor party to achieve support for the view that the rising speculative activities and power of international financial institutions meant that it was no longer possible to maintain a managed Australian exchange rate. For Keating and his supporters within both Treasury and the business community this reform also had the positive effect of ensuring Australia's rapid integration into the harsh realities of global competitiveness. The 1983 decision to float the Australian dollar and abolish exchange rate controls was the first step down the path of financial deregulation completed over the next two years by the removal of interest rate ceilings and the entry of foreign banks. As the editor of the *Australian*, Paul Kelly argued

> the float transformed the economics and politics of Australia. It harnessed the Australian economy to the international marketplace – its rigours, excesses and ruthlessness . . . The move to financial deregulation was the decisive break made by the Hawke-Keating government with Labor dogma and Australian practice . . . It was based on the belief that deregulation would mean a more efficient financial sector and that market forces, not official intervention could better direct capital to achieve a more efficient economy.[21]

By 1986 in a climate of economic recovery the financially deregulated Australian economy faced the problems of rapid currency depreciation and a balance of payments crisis arising from the triple pressures of worsening terms of trade, rising imports and the cost of servicing foreign debt (which was largely the result of private sector borrowing). There was serious talk of IMF intervention and ongoing critical comments from credit rating agencies such as Moody's about the over reliance on commodity exports and 'economic and structural weaknesses [which] could cloud the nation's flexibility for servicing long term external debts'.[22]

In May 1986 Treasurer Keating provided the famous warning that Australia would become 'a banana republic' unless economic restructuring was accelerated to ensure the competitiveness of Australian exports. From that point on the policy agenda of the Hawke and Keating Labor Governments was driven by the view that the central task was to transform Australia from 'a farm and a quarry' into a competitive producer and exporter of high value added manufactured products and services. Looking back from the perspective of 1990 Keating summarised the dominant themes of government policy in the following way. 'The question at issue is whether we build on our approach of the last seven and a half years – of deregulation, of removing the meddling hands of bureaucracy from the operation of markets, of forcing our businesses and our workers to confront the realities of world markets and international opportunities – or to retreat to the failed policies of the past'.[23] Competitiveness was to become both the diagnosis and the cure for all kinds of economic and social ills, with the choice of remedies underpinned by the increasingly pervasive dominance of 'economic rationalist', neo liberal economic policies.

The deregulation of financial markets, exchange rates and financial institutions in the expectation that this would encourage productive investment was only the first step onto the global racetrack. The second step involved the deregulation of trade through tariff cuts and lobbying in support of free trade on both a bilateral and multilateral basis. The emphasis on energetic and high profile trade diplomacy was based on the belief that Australia's multipolar trade profile meant that its interests would best be served by the encouragement of multilateral free trade agreements. To this end Australia was an influential leader of the Cairns Group of commodity exporting nations lobbying for the freeing up of multilateral agricultural trade in the Uruguay round of the GATT negotiations. The possibility of seeking membership of the North American trading bloc was considered and rejected in the mid 1980s but greater effort began to be focussed on the Asia Pacific region through the development of the Asia Pacific Economic Conference (APEC) in the early 1990s.

The third significant element in the competitiveness agenda was an extensive programme of micro economic reform designed to improve the productivity and competitiveness of Australia's export industries. Reductions in tariff protection were associated with a number of sectoral strategies for restructuring key industry sectors including, in particular, the automotive, steel, textiles, clothing and footwear industries. Despite bitter battles within the ALP the privatisation and commercialisation of public sector activities such as banking, transport and telecommunications was vigorously pursued as was a contested but continuing process of tax cuts, public sector expenditure cuts and reductions in grants to the States.

The close connection between the ALP and the Australian Council of Trade Unions (ACTU) meant that the government could not pursue full labour market deregulation as quickly or completely as the business community would have liked. Nonetheless the Accord processes provided a framework for a fundamental shift away from arbitration and the award system towards far more decentralised enterprise bargaining arrangements.[24] As balance of payments problems worsened during the mid 1980s new Accord agreements were negotiated which traded off reductions in real wages against tax cuts and improvements in superannuation. By the late 1980s and early 1990s the Accord negotiations had also become a mechanism for winding back working conditions (often referred to as 'restrictive work practices'), boosting productivity and moving rapidly down the path towards enterprise level bargaining.

Finally there was a renewed emphasis on training and skills development through the 'Active Society' principle of encouraging (and at times threatening) the unemployed into an expanded range of labour market programmes. This policy direction was first articulated by the Social Security Review in 1987 and given further impetus through the White Paper on Full Employment in 1994.[25] These training measures were associated with social security reforms designed to provide higher levels of income support to people on the lowest incomes by targeting payments more closely through tighter means testing and eligibility requirements.

The central aim of the entire competitiveness strategy was to provide a supportive climate within which private sector investment would surge into productive export industries. Unfortunately much of the surge was into an orgy of unproductive (and in some cases criminal) financial speculation, company takeovers and other 'get rich quick' schemes. Such speculative investment actually made the balance of payments problems worse as large sums of money were borrowed abroad, leading to a sharp rise in private sector foreign debt. Throughout the latter part of the 1980s the terms of trade continued to worsen, imports continued to rise and inflation was again becoming a problem. The choice of high interest rates to slow economic growth accelerated and deepened the recession of the early 1990s.

The government argued that this recession was part of the price Australians had to pay for restructuring the Australian economy but of course some people paid a higher price than others. Official rates of unemployment rose to over 11 per cent in 1993, the highest levels since the Depression. Nearly one million Australians were unable to find a job and many others were forced into low waged and insecure casual employment. Facing a public outcry about unemployment and a sharply deteriorating electoral situation the government began to shift ground. The 1992 *One Nation* economic policy statement signalled a rediscovery of the social costs of unemployment and some expansion of public expenditure in infrastructure development, education and training and community services.[26] Wrapping himself in the nationalist symbolism of Republicanism Prime Minister Keating managed to stir up sufficient fear about the divisive impact of the Liberal/National Party's radical New Right *Fightback* platform and its central component of a goods and services (consumption) tax to win the 1993 election.

After the election the government continued to focus on unemployment and commissioned a major inquiry into employment options for Australia leading to the publication of a White Paper on Unemployment in May 1994.[27] Yet the heart of this White Paper remained business as usual with the primary answer to unemployment defined in terms of export growth driven by free trade, deregulated financial markets, reduced business costs, privatisation, enterprise bargaining and training to improve the 'job readiness' of the unemployed. Trade and industry policies continued to be based on the view that 'Australian and international experience make it clear that protectionism, resistance to structural change and avoidance of competition are inimical to growth . . . An open economy leaves no room for subsidies that prop up uncompetitive firms, nor for detailed prescriptions for industry where government directs the flow of resources'.[28] As far as the White Paper was concerned the path to the future was simple. 'When Australia opted for an open economy, the nation committed itself to succeed in an endless race to become, and remain, globally competitive'.[29]

The last twelve years can be interpreted as a strategic triumph for the Labor Party and the labour movement in Australia. During this time the ALP has won five elections in a row and Prime Minister Keating speaks in glowing terms of the creation of 2 million jobs, the introduction of comprehensive superannuation coverage and improvements in the social wage such as Medicare, increased child care places and higher, more targeted benefits for low income earners.[30] Over the same period the ACTU has had unprecedented access to government forums and, while alarmed by falling membership figures, boasts of the victories of 'strategic unionism' defined as larger and more efficient union structures able to intervene in a proactive way in both public and private sector decision making.[31]

Labour's supporters have argued that, given there is no alternative to the goal of competitiveness, it is essential that economic restructuring be managed by a Labor government which can minimise social polarisation and dislocation.[32] For the most optimistic Labor supporters the goal was understood to be the creation of a kind of southern Sweden, combining high value added manufacturing exports with relatively humane social policies.[33] In addition Labor ministers and ACTU officials have been quick to respond to criticism of rising inequality and unemployment by arguing not only that there were no alternatives but that 'it could have been worse'. Constant reference is made to the horrors of Thatcher's England or the truly bizarre right wing social and economic experiments being carried out in New Zealand. Closer to home there are the dismal examples of Victoria, South Australia, Western Australia and Tasmania where Liberal governments have embarked on an extraordinary programme of Thatcherist slash and burn privatisation and anti union legislation.

No doubt it could have been worse and it would be foolish to dismiss the real significance of social wage programmes such as Medicare or the residual sources of protection against the full force of labour market deregulation. However an alternative interpretation is that the most lasting legacies of Labor's period in government will be a deregulated and globalised economy fully engaged in a race to the bottom with the low wage, low tax economies of South East Asia.[34] While the ALP has been clever at winning elections the price of competitiveness has been heightened inequality and a radical programme of deregulation and privatisation, which prepares the ground for more savage forms of economic restructuring when a more openly right wing Liberal/National Party government is elected. This prospect appears increasingly likely given recent by-election and opinion poll results indicating that the sharpest decline in electoral support has been among Labor's traditional male, blue collar, working class constituency and that the ALP is perceived as a hollow political machine, intolerant of criticism and with a declining base of support outside the core groupings of the organised work place.[35] While globalisation with a human face is preferable to more brutal forms of restructuring the core problem facing social democratic parties and labour movements remains. The struggle for victory at all costs on the global race track is fundamentally incompatible with the goals of sustainable production, fair distribution, co-operative citizenship and democratic sovereignty.

### *The problem of sustainable production*

The Labor years in Australia have clearly demonstrated the problems facing small resource dependent economies during the transition to globally integrated and post Fordist economic relations. As Marceau correctly points out, Australia faces the special problem of being 'caught at the apex of an uncomfortable and internally contradictory triangle: socially, politically, organisationally and proprietorially the country looks across to the Eastern Pacific and Europe while in terms of trading partners it must look north. A weak, and increasingly powerless, state combines with a "foreign" industrial base in a recipe which has been tried nowhere else'.[36] Labor's strategic mix of financial deregulation, free trade, micro economic reform, low taxes and a social contract with the unions to hold down wages has had only limited success even on its own terms. While the record in relation to economic growth, export growth, employment and inflation is reasonable in comparison with other OECD countries, the underlying structural problems have worsened.[37]

In relation to capital formation, domestic savings remain low while foreign investment and ownership rise sharply. The cost of servicing foreign debt has been a key factor in the ongoing deterioration of Australia's balance of payments position which has also been undermined by poor commodity prices and strong demand for manufactured imports. The government continues to claim that substantial reductions in tariff protection were essential to encourage international competitiveness and that foreign investment will finally form the basis for the expansion of Australian high value-added export industries. But there is little evidence that foreign investors are particularly interested in the long term development of Australian export industries other than mining. Much of the foreign investment has been directed into speculative activities and assets such as tourist resorts, hotels and office blocks. As Melbourne *Age* economics editor Tim Colebatch notes, 'little investment has gone into the main export earning areas. In the decade to 1993, the real net capital stock per head grew by 24 per cent in mining, fell by 24 per cent in farming, and was virtually flat in manufacturing. The re-equipping of industry was a myth'.[38] And while it is true that manufacturing exports have risen sharply, manufactured imports have risen even faster leading to a worsening of the manufacturing trade deficit.[39]

At the same time the ecological limits to growth are becoming clearer with mounting evidence of the finite nature of Australia's natural resources and the threatening implications of environmental warning signals such as global warming and ozone depletion.[40] Bitter conflicts over the logging of native forests, uranium mining and mineral exploitation on Aboriginal land continue to divide environmentalists, trade unionists and corporate interests. The family farm has become an endangered species in many areas due to the combined impact of falling commodity prices, high interest rates, soil degradation, salinity and the pollution of water supplies by toxic algae.

*The problem of distribution*

The debate about who has won and lost in Australia over the last decade has been hotly contested. The government and its supporters argue that low income and disadvantaged groups have benefited substantially from income security reforms, employment growth and the expansion of the social wage. Labor's critics on the other hand argue that, after ten years of economic restructuring poverty, inequality and unemployment remain deeply entrenched, there has been a significant shift from wages to profits and the labour market has been radically transformed with much of the employment growth limited to low paid, part time and casualised jobs.[41] The government itself boasts frequently of its success in reducing taxes and public sector expenditure claiming this as a victory for efficient management and tighter targeting of income security payments. Cuts in areas such as health and education have often been particularly severe at State and local government levels as difficult decisions are passed down the line by the Commonwealth government in the form of reduced grants and revenue sharing arrangements. In the end even the government's own Economic Planning and Advisory Council freely admits that, while 'Australia does not yet have unmanageable levels of the homeless and beggars on the streets ... even a cursory reading [of the available evidence] suggests that measured income inequality, especially that for market-based earnings had been increasing, or at best has been relatively static'.[42]

Despite the government's relatively strong record in promoting employment growth the fact remains that official unemployment rates will remain at over 5 (and probably closer to 10 per cent).[43] All 'sensible' economists – and the government – of course agree that this has now become the new 'natural rate of unemployment'. At the same time the casualisation of the Australian workforce continues at a dramatic pace with much of the employment growth in the part time and casual spheres. A distributional strategy based on a combination of mass unemployment, mass casualisation and mass training is indeed a disturbing prospect and casts a dark shadow over hopes that social democratic politics can deliver a new and progressive version of full employment if the union movement is prepared to broker the sharing out of increased productivity and reduced wages among workers.[44]

But perhaps the most disturbing development of all is the extent to which Labor has created a climate in which egalitarian and co-operative values have been swept away by the advocates of economic rationalism and the free market. The rhetoric of social justice and citizenship has been a poor defence against the avalanche of claims from business leaders and right wing think tanks that an open competitive economy makes cutting taxes and public sector expenditure an inevitable necessity. To take only two of many possible examples Ivan Deveson, former head of Nissan Australia and the Channel 7 media group makes it clear that 'there is no doubt that we cannot afford the "social net" that we have – that the size of the net must be linked to the economy – that to some degree our commitment to an efficient economy has been weakened by some excessive dependency on social support'.[45] Economist Fred Argy who was the initial architect of the Hawke government's financial deregulation strategy now draws the conclusion that 'we are losing control over our social priorities. Capital markets simply don't like high levels of government spending on health and social programs'.[46] This leads to a broader question. Who then is making the decisions – who is governing a deregulated Australian economy and society? And how can national and local democracies survive in an age of global financial markets which have become utterly contemptuous of national borders and local populations?

### *The problem of regulation and democracy*

In 1985 the international credit rating agencies and financial markets reacted savagely and the value of the Australian dollar plummeted following the suggestion that the Hawke Labor government might oppose the testing of MX missiles by the United States in Australian offshore waters. In 1993 the Labor government in Victoria was hurled from office in a climate of mounting media hysteria about the latest downgrade in credit ratings from Moodys and Standard and Poors. In 1995 Ford Australia publicly warned that it would cease its Australian operations (at a cost of 7000 jobs) unless there were substantial reductions in the costs of labour and government services. In 1993 Victoria Liberal Premier, Jeff Kennett sacked all elected local governments and replaced them with appointed commissioners. In 1995 he announced, after a show of hands by several hundred business men and women at a power breakfast, that business would be more efficient and competitive without having to deal with an elected Council for the central Melbourne area. So there would be no elections.[47]

The combined impact of low domestic savings, rising levels of private foreign debt and financial deregulations have dramatically increased the influence of international capital markets, financial institutions and credit rating agencies. In this climate it has become almost impossible to talk about higher levels of public sector expenditure or progressive taxation without being howled down by commentators shouting that, not only would this make Australian business uncompetitive but, in a deregulated financial system the international financial markets and credit rating agencies would never permit such policies to be implemented. This has led to a disturbing trend towards political self censorship with even the most progressive of Labor politicians and trade unionists simply refusing to talk about alternatives to current economic policy settings because, it is argued, there is no point in talking about things which simply cannot happen.

The full implications of financial deregulation in Australia are best articulated by H.C. Coombs who oversaw the introduction of Keynesian economic policies in post-war Australia and went on to be the founding head of the Reserve Bank and a key economic adviser to eight Australian Prime Ministers:

> The deregulation of the Australian financial system was, in my opinion, a tragedy and I think the outcome was highly predictable from the time of the decision and it was disastrous. We had a crop of bank failures, a repudiation of the rights of depositors, company crashes, millionaires all around the place but the system was not working in a stable fashion. We were progressively losing ownership of our own assets and losing ownership of the major enterprises and institutions in our society.[48]

The ALP under Paul Keating's leadership has been very effective at playing the nationalist card, proposing that Australia should break its last ceremonial ties with the British monarchy by becoming a Republic. There has also been much talk of creating 'one nation' and supporting 'the promotion of individual and collective cultural rights and expressions on the one hand and, on the other, the promotion of common national interests and values'.[49] This attempt to find an appropriate balance between principles of inclusiveness and difference may help to lessen the explosive potential for racist forms of social fragmentation which can easily be triggered by the dangerous combination of rapid economic restructuring and diverse ethnic and racial populations. However broader claims that Labor has at least defended Australian cultural sovereignty have a hollow ring given the extent to which foreign ownership of all forms of media has been actively encouraged with the control of print and electronic media effectively concentrated into the hands of the Australian Kerry Packer, the

Canadian Conrad Black and Australian/American/global citizen Rupert Murdoch.[50] Certainly the comprehensive deregulation of the Australian economy threatens to make a complete mockery of democratic decision making and sovereignty in relation to all significant aspects of economic and social policy. As the Victorian example indicates even the very idea of democratic elections has been challenged by the champions of competitive efficiency.

### *After social justice? The problem of political ideas*

In claiming victory at the 1993 election, Paul Keating referred to it as a victory for 'the true believers', presumably referring to Labor's traditional working class constituency whose ways of life are increasingly under threat due to the very changes in labour market regulation which the Labor government has supported so strongly. Unfortunately it is unclear what the believers are supposed to believe in beyond a vague commitment to 'the poor', 'the workers' – and 'social justice'.[51]

Since its formation one hundred years ago the language of 'social justice' has often served as the Labor Party's unifying vision and philosophy, at least for those sections of the party and the labour movement who wished to avoid being tainted with the image of more radical, 'socialist' projects. But of course social justice can mean many things. In 1909 one of the founding organisers of the ALP, W.G. Spence argued that Labor's social justice mission was the antithesis of rapacious capitalism:

> Labor has an ideal. It realises there never can be social justice under a capitalistic system of production, distribution and exchange. It aims at a gradual but nevertheless complete and permanent change. Capitalism, commercialism, competition, and its concomitant, wage slavery, must go.[52]

Forty years later in the heady days of post-war reconstruction Labor Prime Minister Ben Chifley articulated a vision of social justice, security and compassion as Labor's 'light on the hill':

> It is the duty and responsibility of the community and particularly those more fortunately placed, to see that our less fortunate fellow citizens are protected from those shafts of fate which leave them helpless and without hope. That is the objective for which we are striving. It is the beacon, the light on the hill to which our eyes are always turned and to which our efforts are always directed.[53]

In his 1992 Chifley Memorial Lecture Paul Keating continued to insist that 'Labor still stands for the values that Ben Chifley stood for – the primacy of social justice, social cohesion, equal opportunity – the fair go'.[54] It is certainly true that, throughout the 1980s, Labor governments at both Commonwealth and State levels struggled to articulate a renewed sense of direction through the creation of elaborate 'Social Justice Strategies'.[55] However, stripped of their rhetorical flourishes about social justice as 'access, equity, participation and rights' the major contribution of these Strategies was to provide a justification for the more effective targeting of reduced resources to groups identified as 'disadvantaged', with disadvantage largely defined in terms of exclusion from the mainstream labour market.[56] This was quite consistent with the wider strategy of progressive competitiveness or 'restraint with equity' as Prime Minister Hawke referred to it. Social justice defined as restraint with equity was unlikely to rekindle the 'light on the hill' or inspire a deeply uninspired electorate.

In the context of soaring unemployment Labor's 1993 election victory came as a startling surprise to most observers. But anecdotal and opinion poll evidence suggests that the dominant Australian social mood is one of cynicism and 'sullenness' combined with fears about the effect of rapid change in a fragmented world in which there are few sources of certainty, faith or inspiration.[57] As a wide range of commentators have noted this deepening sense of risk, anxiety and a collapse of trust in religious and political institutions is a pervasive feature of post industrial, post Fordist societies and has given rise to a variety of responses by political parties desperately attempting to recapture supporters and a sense of direction.[58]

In Australia one response has been to look backwards to the so called 'lucky country' of the 1950s, calling up the ghosts of Labor's traditional heroes and 'true believers.[59] However the supposedly more secure and prosperous world of the 1950s cannot be reclaimed in the fragmenting societies and globalising economies of the 21st century, even if it was thought desirable to return to the often rigid and oppressive relations of gender, sexuality, race and ethnicity which were also a feature of those times.

A second, more dominant response has been the technocratic language and politics of economic rationalism, public choice theory, privatisation, deregulation and managerialism. Some of these ideas are simply a reworking of neo classical economic ideas about the merits of laissez faire capitalism. But as Pusey has suggested they also involve a fundamental distrust of discourses based on morality and ethics.[60] The underlying assumption is that there can no longer be any commonly agreed on social norms or values – there are only the desires of each individual to maximise their sensory pleasure and material gain. The solution is to turn to the market as the arbiter of individual choices and to neo classical economic 'science' to ensure the market is protected. The market has finally become God.

A third possibility is to accept, and perhaps revel in the collapse of universal truths and values. After all it was Paul Keating's speech writer Don Watson who has suggested that Australians should begin to imagine a 'post modern republic' – a nation which is 'aleatory [dependent on chance], impressionistic, figurative, bebop'.[61] Some strands of post modern theory have provided a timely antidote to the arrogance of ideological certainty as well as highlighting the significance of the politics of difference. However the implications of much post modernist discourse can also be profoundly nihilistic leading down a path of moral relativism quite consistent with the reduction of all social relationships to the narrowly contractual and commercial relations of the market place.

In this arid climate one starting point is to continue to fiercely oppose the atomistic individualism of competitive 'market citizenship' and to defend and reclaim the significance of interdependence and co-operation.[62] This implies a reaffirmation of the fundamentally social nature of human life and of the ecological interdependence between all forms of life and the natural environment. It also means that debates about the nature of economic growth and the distribution of paid and unpaid work will be crucial in the process of re-imagining political ideals and programmes. From these beginnings we can then continue the struggle to identify the most desirable balances between autonomy and solidarity, co-operation and identity, rights and responsibilities – and to open up new understandings about the need to respect differences of gender, sexuality, race and ethnicity. As Rustin notes:

> it is possible to defend the value of social differentiation without abandoning universalistic and egalitarian claims as a foundation for a beneficial diversity of values and lifestyles . . . The central issue is to see that ways of life of . . . complexity and richness depend not just on individuals but on the various kinds of community which make human accomplishment, even the everyday accomplishments of parenthood, craftsmanship, or good citizenship, possible.[63]

## *After Labor? The problem of political strategy*

Many external observers have been intrigued by the seemingly remarkable electoral success of Labor in Australia. Charismatic leadership, tactical skill, good timing and a fair amount of luck are all part of the explanation. But the major reason for Labor's election victories has been the capacity of the party to continually reinvent itself in response to the progressively more difficult problems of modernising the Australian economy while maintaining cross class alliances between working class and middle class voters.[64]

The opposition Liberal party responded to its 1983 election defeat by purging itself of moderate influences and attempting to carve out a radical new right political position. However for much of the past decade the Liberal party and its allies, the rurally based National party, have struggled to present a credible programme which could reconcile extreme economic liberalism, moral conservatism and a backward looking attachment to England and the monarchy. By contrast Labor has been able to effectively portray itself as the wave of the future, turning from the monarchy to

Republicanism, expanding cultural and trade connections with Asia and promising targeted protection for the victims of deregulation and restructuring. This strategy has also provided an effective basis for maintaining the support of some sections of manufacturing capital who have shared a common interest in gaining access to Asian markets and in a managed process of privatisation and deregulation.[65]

At the same time Labor's balancing act has also included an attempt to portray itself as a champion of ecological sustainability in order to build alliances with the environment movement and increase its appeal to ecologically concerned middle class voters. However, these alliances have continually fractured under the pressure to expand natural resource exports, demonstrating again and again the difficulty of reconciling social democratic and ecological politics if it is not possible to keep increasing the size of the economic pie.

The challenges facing Australian trade unions and the ALP reflect similar concerns among all social democratic parties and labour movements. Perhaps, as many social movement activists claim, the project of social democracy is, like the vision of social justice, a worked out seam, and it is social movements, Green Parties and radical independents who are now the most significant agents of social reform. In Australia, the ecologically focussed Australian Democrats and, more recently, the Greens have held the balance of power in the Senate for all of Labor's time in government. Alongside an emerging cast of social movement based independents they have also provided part of the infrastructure for exploring new forms of extra-parliamentary political action.

If the central goal of modern social democracy is understood to be little more than the humane management of economic restructuring and global integration it is hardly surprising that many people have turned to other sources of political inspiration. Yet it is important to remember that the social democratic heritage has always contained both technocratic and emancipatory potentials. One danger of simplistically embracing the social movement 'solution' is that the significance of class as a category of both analysis and action will be completely lost. Thus Segal, while rejecting the often gender-blind, technocratic and authoritarian practices of both social democracy and Leninism asks:

> should we not also pause a moment to recognize the weaknesses of the new social movements themselves? Without access to the resources of strengthened social democratic reformist structures, as decentralised and accountable as possible, and without strong trade unions, the social movements (particularly as conceived by the theorists of difference) can offer little more than the enjoyment of an endless game of self-exploration played out on the great board of Identity.[66]

The choice between social democratic, labour movement and social movement politics is a false choice. Of course, social democratic parties will never challenge the dominant logic of the market and economic growth by themselves. It has always been silly to believe that – in Australia or anywhere else. Parliamentary parties linked to labour movements can only be expected to hold their nerve and pursue alternative economic agendas to those of globalised capital if they are constantly challenged, pushed and inspired by non parliamentary labour and social movements. The task therefore is to defend and build on the solidaristic traditions of the labour movement while exploring the space for more creative, reciprocal and differentiated social relations and political processes emerging from social movements concerned with questions of gender, sexuality, race, ethnicity and ecology.

It is possible that, over time, a formal alliance between progressive labour movement and environmental political movements might develop in Australia along the lines of the Alliance in New Zealand.[67] But the Australian historical context of a particularly tight connection between the labour movement and the Labor Party make grand coalitions an ambitious goal. Shifting networks of labour, social movement and community organisations coming together to work on particular issues of common concern are likely to be more feasible and fruitful arrangements in the immediate future. Whatever form these alliances or networks take they will have to come to terms with the politics of globalisation and the changing nature of national boundaries and the nation state.

*Alternatives to the global racetrack? The problem of national politics in borderless nations*

Unfortunately it is far easier to point to the limitations of Australian Labor's 'globalisation with a human face' than it is to articulate alternative local, national and international strategies which can seriously challenge the logic of 'competitiveness at all costs' and are consistent with the principles of ecological sustainability, social cooperation and democratic sovereignty.

The first and most important step is to believe that there are, in fact, alternatives. Globalisation does not mean we are heading for a monolithic world government run by the UN or anyone else. That way lie the dangerous paranoias of the US militias and the fundamentalist right. Nor are we facing the complete collapse of national borders and the slide into a global Bosnia of tribalism and chaos predicted by a variety of post modern charlatans and end of the world doom sayers.[68] Other prophets of globalisation argue that the massive expansion of global communication technologies allowing the virtually instantaneous transfer of vast financial flows rules out the possibility of even discussing the reregulation of financial markets. This in turn provides a formidable and demobilising weapon for those who argue, like Margaret Thatcher, that There Is No Alternative to the wildest extremes of free market capitalism. However, as Bienefeld argues, financial deregulation is a result of political choice rather than technology:

> In the final analysis, financial regulation depends on the political will to enforce adequate sanctions, so that, given the risk of discovery, the majority of people will observe the law. The fact that such laws can always be technically evaded (by some, for a time) is not an argument against them or their enforcement, any more than the existence of unsolved murders constitutes an argument against the homicide laws ... In fact, the biggest obstacle to the enforcement of financial regulations today, is not the computer or the fax machine, but the poisonous individualism of the eighties which has undermined people's willingness to observe the law by corroding the ethical and ideological foundations on which law enforcement, taxation and the ability to justify social investment ultimately rest.[69]

The task of developing creative alternatives to the destructive power of global economic restructuring has global, local and national dimensions. Globalist strategies have tended to focus on the creation of alternative political, financial and legal global institutions which can form a democratic counterweight to the power of transnational capital.[70] If corporate power has shifted to the global arena then global trade unions, environmental agencies, community organisations and governmental institutions are seen, by some, as the remedy. Such organisations could, it is argued, provide the base for the creation of international corporate codes of conduct, controls over financial transactions and the construction of new forms of international governance including the possibility of international corporate taxes such as the Tobin tax proposal.[71] Internationally based government and non-governmental organisations can also provide the basis for attempts to enshrine trade union and human rights principles in international trade agreements and create multilateral and bilateral social charters specifying minimum standards of living and standards of social service provision. The establishment of agreements about human rights and appropriate social, economic and environmental benchmarks in the Asia Pacific region certainly need to be firmly placed on the agenda in the context of the negotiations around APEC and the expansion of Asia Pacific trading relations. However, the limited effectiveness of social charter and trade union rights agreements in both the NAFTA and EC experience suggests that it would be unwise to place too much faith in internationalist strategies on their own.

At the other end of the scale are the supporters of 'globalisation from below', commonly involving the fostering of local economic networks and local community relationships as significant arenas within in which identity and difference can be protected, solidarity and mutuality nurtured and ecological values sustained.[72] Many proponents of localism have also noted the potential for making global links between local groups and developing the 'Lilliputian tactic' of tying down the corporate 'giants' of global corporate power with thousands of interconnected local grassroots movements and struggles. Part of the aim here is to counter the divide and rule, 'beggar thy neighbour' tactics of the race to the bottom agenda by creating the conditions for an 'upward' rather than 'downward' harmonisation in which workers and citizens with lower wages and working conditions are lifted upwards rather than driving down the living standards of workers in more prosperous economies. As a number of authors and activists have noted the expansion of global trade and communications creates possibilities as well as threats and the careful broadening of international and regional alliances between local trade unions, community organisations and social movements is an important and complex challenge.[73] In relation to this goal many activists within the Australian labour movement – and indeed other social movements – have begun to recognise the importance of creating networks and alliances within the Asia-Pacific region.[74] Recognising the importance of such networks is a good start. But establishing the understanding and trust to overcome deep cultural differences will require a marked increase in the resources and time devoted to this task.

As the rhetoric of 'think global: act local' becomes pervasive it is tempting to accept that the room to move at the nation state level has effectively disappeared. But while the very idea of national political identity may have been opened to question by the internationalisation of capital it has become more important than ever to reconsider the relationship between social movements, labour movements and nation states. As Mahon correctly points out 'the world has more depth than a global network of economic power extending from the centre(s) to the periphery. To problematise the coherence and durability of national societies and states, however, does call for new ways of thinking about the way that social space is organised and reorganised over time . . . the nation state is not dead but strategic horizons have to be expanded to render visible other layers of action'.[75]

Without being naive about the room to move available to national governments it will be a serious error to vacate the arena of the nation state and national parliamentary politics. That way lies the hollowed out 'street warfare' politics of Los Angeles and New York with no effective focus for contesting the control of transnational or national capital over decisions in particular societies and locales. One of the most important lessons from the last fifteen years in Australia is that, if we lose democratic control over the key decision-making forums and processes of the national and regional state, then we lose a great deal indeed for all real decision making power in relation to capital formation, production and distribution will have been effectively corporatised. The debate about the relative autonomy of the nation state is far from over but the challenge is to imagine and create new democratic institutions and regulatory processes in an age where trust is scarce, the sense of risk is widespread and the consequences of actions are often far removed from those involved in making the decisions.

More broadly the experience of Labor in government in Australia suggests that progressive competitiveness may be a kinder strategy in the short term. It may also create some room to move for the exploration of new political formations and alliances. But it will remain only a kinder road to hell if there continues to be an unquestioning acceptance of the inevitability and irreversibility of a globalised and deregulated economy. The alternative path is far from clear but an important starting point must continue to be a recognition that the goals of endless economic growth and competitiveness at all costs are finally not compatible with the goals of ecological sustainability, co-operative citizenship and democratic sovereignty.

## NOTES

1. P. Keating, Speech to Australian Council of Social Service Annual Congress, Canberra, October 1992, unp.
2. V. Farrell, cited in *The Sunday Age* March 26 1995.
3. J. Cain, in *The Age* April 11 1993.
4. As early as 1986 Panitch noted, sceptically, that the Australian Labor Party had joined the Swedish and Austrian social democratic parties as a 'new vogue' example of an electorally successful mix of incomes policies and corporatist economic strategies. See L. Panitch, *Working Class Politics in Crisis. Essays on Labour and the State*, Verso, London, 1986, p. 35. As Pilger has also documented the British Labour Party has been particularly enthusiastic in looking to the ALP as a model. See J. Pilger, 'The lessons of Australia's hard Labour' in *New Statesmen and Society*, June 10, 1994. There have also been an ongoing range of critical debates about Labor's record in Australia. See for example P. Beilharz, 'The Australian Left: Beyond Labourism' in R. Miliband, J. Saville, M. Liebman, and L. Panitch, (eds.) *Socialist Register 1985–86*, Merlin Press, London; G. Duncan, 'The Australian road to socialism' in *New Socialist*, December 1989/January 1990; R. Kuhn, 'The Limits of Social Democratic Economic Policy in Australia' in *Capital and Class* 51, Autumn 1993. I am grateful to Andrew Scott and Greg Albo for drawing my attention to a number of these references.
5. The nature of progressive competitiveness is discussed in more detail below and draws on the work of L. Panitch, 'Globalisation and the State' and G. Albo, 'Competitive Austerity and the Impasse of Capitalist Employment Policy', both in R. Miliband and L. Panitch (eds.) *Between Globalism and Nationalism: Socialist Register 1994*, Merlin Press, London, 1994.
6. A. Giddens, *Beyond Left and Right: The Future of Radical Politics*, Polity, Cambridge, 1994.
7. This understanding of the scope of globalisation draws on a range of sources including D. Harvey, *The Condition of Post Modernity*, Basil Blackwell, Oxford, 1989; A. Glynn, and B. Sutcliffe, 'Global but leaderless? The new capitalist order' in R. Miliband and L. Panitch, *Socialist Register 1992*, Merlin Press, London 1992, pp. 76–95; P. Hirst and G. Thompson, 'The problem of "globalization": international economic relations, national economic management and the formation of trading blocs', *Economy and Society*, Vol. 21, No. 4, November, 1992, pp. 357–396; D. Drache & M. Gertler (eds.), *The New Era*

*of Global Competition: State Policy and Market Power*, McGill-Queens University Press, Montreal, 1991; J. Brecher, J. Childs and J. Cutler (eds.), *Global Visions: beyond the New World Order*, Black Rose Books, Montreal 1993; M. Featherstone (ed.), *Global Culture: Nationalism, Globalization and Modernity* (A Theory, Culture and Society Special Issue), London: Sage, 1990.

8. Thus we see the World Bank noting that deregulated financial markets 'tend towards instability and fraud' and the IMF warning that deregulation may 'result in destabilizing and inefficient capital speculation' both cited in M. Bienefeld 1994. 'Capitalism and the nation state in the dog days of the twentieth century', in R. Miliband and L. Panitch (ed.), *Between Globalism and Nationalism*, Merlin Press, London, 1994, p. 109.
9. See S. Sweeney, 'What is the "New Labor Internationalism"? Comments on Upward Harmonization, Social Charters and Globalization from Below', paper presented to the Sixteenth Annual North American Labor History Conference on International and Comparative Labor History, October 27–29 1994, Wayne State University Detroit; J. Brecher, J. Childs and J. Cutler, *op. cit.*; W. Sengenberger, 'The role of labour market regulation in industrial restructuring', in G. Standing and V. Tokman (eds.), *Towards Social Adjustment: Labour Market Issues in Structural Adjustment*, ILO, Geneva, 1991, pp. 235–250.
10. See United Nations Research Institute for Social Development, *States of Disarray: The social effects of globalization*, UNRISD, London, 1995.
11. See G. Standing, 'Global Feminization Through Flexible Labour', *World Development*, Vol. 17, No. 7: 1077–1095 and A. Yeatman, 'Women's Citizenship Claims, Labour Market Policy and Globalisation', *Australian Journal of Political Science*, Vol. 27, 1992, pp. 449–461.
12. S. Sassen, *The Mobility of Labor and Capital: A study in International Investment and Labor Flow*, Cambridge: Cambridge University Press, 1990.
13. T. Sinclair, 'Passing judgement: credit rating processes as regulatory mechanisms of governance in the emerging world order', *Review of International Political Economy*, 1:1 Spring 1994, pp. 133–158.
14. Cited in J. Brecher, 'After NAFTA: Global Village or Global Pillage?', *The Nation*, December 6, 1993, p. 686.
15. See Panitch, 'Globalisation', *op. cit.* pp. 81–86; Albo, 'Competitive Austerity', *op. cit.* pp. 147–8, 156–7, 162–3. G. van Liemt, 'Economic Globalisation: Labour Options and Business Strategies in High Labour Cost Countries', *International Labour Review*, Vol. 131, No. 4–5, 1992, 453–470.
16. For an overview of the mainstream Australian debate about responses to globalisation see Economic Planning and Advisory Committee, *Globalisation: Issues for Australia*, AGPS, Canberra, 1995 and B. Lepani, G. Freed, P. Murphy and A. McGillivray, *Australia in the Global Economy*, AGPS, Canberra, 1995.
17. See F. Castles, *Australian Public Policy and Economic Vulnerability*, Allen and Unwin, Sydney, 1988; P. Beilharz, M. Considine and R. Watts, *Arguing About the Welfare State*, Allen and Unwin, Sydney, 1992; P. Boreham, S. Clegg, J. Emmison, G. Marks and J. Western, 'Semi peripheries or particular pathways: The Case of Australia, New Zealand and Canada as class formations', *International Sociology*, Vol. 4, No. 1, 1989, pp. 67–90; J. Ravenhill, 1994, 'Australia and global economy'. In S. Bell & B. Head (eds.), *State, Economy and Public Policy in Australia*, Oxford University Press, Melbourne, 1994.
18. See L. Bryson, *Welfare and the State: Who Benefits?*, Macmillan, London, 1992.
19. B. Probert, 'Restructuring and globalisation: what do they mean?' in *Arena Magazine*, April–May 1992, p. 21.
20. See P. Ewer, I. Hampson, C. Lloyd, J. Rainford, S. Rix and M. Smith, *Politics and the Accord*, Pluto Press, Sydney, 1991.
21. P. Kelly, *The End of Certainty*, Allen and Unwin, Sydney, 1992, p. 76.
22. Cited in P. Kelly, *op. cit.*, p. 222.

23. Keating cited in P. Ewer, et al., *op. cit.*, p. 63.
24. A useful summary of the Accord agreements up to 1992 can be found in F. Stilwell, 'Wages policy and the Accord' in G. Mahony (ed.), *The Australian economy under Labor*, Allen and Unwin, Sydney, 1993. See also P. Ewer, et al., op. cit. and R. Kuhn, op. cit.
25. B. Cass, *Income Support for the Unemployed in Australia: Towards A More Active Society*, Social Security Review Issues Paper No. 4, AGPS, Canberra, 1988 and Commonwealth of Australia, Working *Nation: Policies and Programs*, AGPS, Canberra, 1994.
26. Commonwealth of Australia, *One Nation*, AGPS, Canberra, 1992.
27. Commonwealth of Australia, *Working Nation: Policies and Programs*, AGPS, Canberra, 1994.
28. Ibid. p. 57.
29. Ibid. p. 52.
30. See, for example, Keating's opening address to the 1995 Australian National Social Policy Conference in Sydney, extensively reported in *The Age*, July 8 1995.
31. Union membership had fallen to 35 per cent of the workforce by 1995. See Evatt Foundation, *Unions 2000: A Blueprint for Trade Union Activism*, Evatt Foundation, Sydney, 1995.
32. See, for example, M. Costa and M. Duffy, *Labor Prospects and the Nineties*, Federation Press, Sydney, 1991.
33. This point of view was particularly strong during the 1980s with its high point being the joint labour movement and government delegation sent to the Nordic countries in 1987 to bring back lessons applicable to Australia. See ACTU and Trade Development Council, *Australia Reconstructed: A Report by the Mission Members to the ACTU and the TDC*, AGPS, Canberra, 1987.
34. As Frankel has noted one of the key contradictions which has emerged during Labor's period in government has been the idea that there could be a transition to the 'productivist culture' associated with Sweden and other Northern European countries at the same time as a comprehensive programme of financial deregulation and free trade was being implemented. See B. Frankel, *From Prophets the Deserts Come*, Arena Press, Melbourne, 1992.
35. See K. Walsh, 'Blood, sweat and jeers' in *The Bulletin*, October 10, 1995 for a summary of recent research on falling working class electoral support for the ALP.
36. J. Marceau, 'Will the Souffle Rise? Australian Business Recipes in the New World Economic Order', *Prometheus*, Vol, 10, No. 2, December, 1992, p. 189.
37. For a more extensive discussion see S. Bell, S. and B. Head (eds.), *State, Economy and Public Policy in Australia*, Oxford University Press, Melbourne, 1994.
38. T. Colebatch, 'How did the economy get into this much trouble?' in *The Age*, February 2, 1995.
39. See K. Davidson, 'First we define the real problem, then apply proper cure' in *The Age*, February 8 1995.
40. See P. Christoff, 'Environmental Politics' in J. Brett, J. Gillespie and M. Goot, *Developments in Australian Politics*, Macmillan, Melbourne, 1994.
41. For the positive interpretation see, for example, P. Travers and S. Richardson, *Living decently: material well-being in Australia*, Oxford University Press, South Melbourne, 1993 and A. Harding, 'Equity, Redistribution and the Tax Transfer System Since the Early 1980s' in M. Hogan and K. Dempsey (eds.), *Equity and Citizenship Under Keating*, Sydney University, Sydney, 1995. More critical perspectives can be found in P. Saunders, *Welfare and Inequality: National and International Perspectives on the Australian Welfare State*, Cambridge University Press, Melbourne, 1994; L. Bryson, 'The welfare state and economic adjustment', in S. Bell and B. Head (eds.) 1994, *State, Economy and Public Policy in Australia*, Melbourne: Oxford University Press, 1994; J.

O'Connor, 'Citizenship, class, gender and labour market participation in Canada and Australia', in S. Shaver (ed.), *Gender, Citizenship and the Labour Market: The Australian and Canadian Welfare States*, Sydney: University of New South Wales, Social Policy Research Centre Reports and Proceedings No. 109, 1993.

42. EPAC, *Income Distribution in Australia: Recent Trends and Research*, Economic Planning Advisory Council Commission Paper No. 7, AGPS, Canberra, 1995, pp. 80 and 69.
43. The target in *Working Nation* was 5 per cent but few credible commentators accept this figure. See, for example J. Langmore, and J. Quiggan, *Work for All: Full Employment in the Nineties*, Melbourne University Press, Melbourne, 1994.
44. See A. Glynn, 'Tackling unemployment' in *New Left Review*, 211, 1995, pp. 33–55.
45. I. Deveson, 'The Challenge of Change for Australians', in *Business Council Bulletin*, May 1993, p. 29.
46. F. Argy, cited in R. Smith, 'Caught in the current', *Time Australia* May 15 1995, p. 22.
47. After widespread public outrage Kennett finally agreed to allow the elections to proceed but still argued that he could see no threat to democracy from the proposal to cancel elections!
48. H. C. Coombs, in D. Hill, 'Nuggets of History' in *The Age Good Weekend* supplement, August 16, 1995, p. 40.
49. P. Keating cited in K. Middleton, 'Keating's good citizen' in *The Age*, April 27, 1995.
50. See B. Frankel, op. cit., *From Prophets the Deserts Come*, Arena Press, Melbourne, 1992.
51. For an extensive discussion of the connections between the historical traditions and current forms of Labor – and labour movement discourse in Australia, see P. Beilharz, *Transforming Labor: Labour Tradition and the Labor Decade in Australia*, Cambridge, Melbourne, 1994. See also S.MacIntyre, 1985, *Winners and Losers*, Allen & Unwin, Sydney.
52. W. G. Spence, *Australia's Awakening*, Sydney, 1909, p. 227.
53. B. Chifley (from the 1949 election policy speech), cited by E. G. Whitlam, *The Road to Reform – Labor in Government*, 1975 Chifley Memorial Lecture, Melbourne University ALP Club, 1975, p. 6.
54. P. Keating, cited in *The Age*, September 14, 1992.
55. See J. Wiseman, 'The Development and Outcomes of the Victorian Social Justice Strategy', in B. Costar and M. Considine, *Trials in Power: Cain, Kirner and Victoria 1982–1992*, MUP, Melbourne, 1992.
56. See P. Beilharz, 'Social Justice and Social Democracy' in *Australia and New Zealand Journal of Sociology*, Vol. 25, No. 1, May 1989.
57. See, for example, H. McKay, *Reinventing Australia*, Angus and Robertson, Pymble, NSW, 1993.
58. See, for example, D. Harvey, 1989, op. cit. and U. Beck, *Risk Society: Towards a New Modernity*, Sage, London, 1992.
59. See P. Beilharz, 1994, op. cit.
60. M. Pusey, *Economic Rationalism in Canberra*, Cambridge University Press, Cambridge, 1991.
61. D. Watson, 1993, cited in M. Hirst, 'No more "po mo" propaganda' in *The Australian Higher Education Supplement*, July 26, 1995.
62. See N. Fraser, *Unruly Practices. Power, Discourse and Gender in Contemporary Social Theory*, Polity Press, Cambridge, 1989 and Giddens, 1994, op. cit.
63. M. Rustin, 1991, 'Life beyond liberalism' in P. Osbourne (ed.), *Socialism and the Limits of Liberalism*, Verso, London, 1991: 171 and 176.
64. See P. Beilharz, 1994, op. cit.
65. By late 1995 it had become clear that this picture was changing with all fractions of capital becoming increasingly impatient about the pace of movement towards full labour market deregulation.

66. L. Segal, 'Socialism, Feminism and the Future' in R. Blackburn (ed.), *After the Fall: The failure of Communism and the Future of Socialism*, Verso, London, 1991, p. 285.
67. For a more extensive discussion of these possibilities see R. Leach (ed.), *The Alliance Alternative in Australia: Beyond Labor and Liberal*, Catalyst Press, Annandale, NSW, 1995.
68. See, for example, S. Huntington, 'The Clash of Civilizations' in *Foreign Affairs*, Summer 1993.
69. M. Bienefeld, 'Capitalism and the nation state in the dog days of the twentieth century,' in R. Miliband and L. Panitch (eds.), *Between Globalism and Nationalism*, London: Merlin Press, 1994, p. 102.
70. See, for example, UNRISD, op. cit.
71. See M. Walker, 1993, 'Global Taxation Paying for Peace,' *World Policy Journal*, Vol. X, No. 2, Summer, pp. 7–12.
72. See, for example, J. Brecher, et al., op. cit., P. Ekins, *A New World Order: Grassroots Movements for Social Change*, London: Routledge, 1992, M. Nozick, *No Place Like Home: Building Sustainable Communities*, Canadian Council on Social Development, Ottawa, 1992 and A. Liepitz, *Towards a new economic order: postfordism, ecology and democracy*, Polity Press, Oxford: Polity Press, 1989 and N. Costello, J. Michie and S. Milne, 1989, *Beyond the Casino Economy*, London: Verso.
73. See, for example, P.Marcuse, 'Globalisations forgotten dimension' in *Polis*, No. 3, July 1995, pp. 42–50.
74. See Evatt Foundation, op. cit.
75. R. Mahon, 'The "New" Canadian Political Economy Revisited: Production, Space, Identity' in J. Jenson, R. Mahon and M. Bienefeld, *Production, Space, Identity: Political Economy Faces the 21st Century*, Canadian Scholars' Press, Toronto, 1993, pp. 13–14.

I would like to thank Greg Albo, Mitchell Bernard, Boris Frankel, John Murphy, Leo Panitch, Belinda Probert and Andrew Scott for their comments and constructive criticism on earlier drafts of this article.

# IN DEFENCE OF CAPITAL CONTROLS

James Crotty and Gerald Epstein

## I. Introduction[1]

The story of the rise and fall of the Golden Age of modern capitalism is an oft told tale. But for all its familiarity, it is easy to forget that the Golden Age was, among other things, an era of effective national economic regulation. It was the age of the 'social contract'[2] or capital-labour 'accord' (however loaded in capital's favour these arrangements might have been) under which the Keynesian state, with the acquiescence of capital, was to pursue full employment and build a stronger social safety network. Golden Age central banks fixed exchange rates and determined interest rates with only sporadic interference from a relatively small class of financial speculators. Such state regulation was made possible by the emaciated condition of the domestic rentier class, capital controls on international financial flows, and the as yet quite limited size and power of multinational corporations (MNCs).

The limited extent of globalization was hardly the only important determinant of the Golden Age, nor even its most important condition of existence. But the acceleration of the process of globalization of finance and capital investment and the increase in the openness of trade that took place as the Golden Age evolved does seem to have been an essential element in the dynamics of its demise. The continuation of the globalization process over the past two decades has created tenacious impediments to the restoration of a regime of sustained full employment and real wage growth.

In this essay we will argue that a set of policies to gain more control over the international flow of money and, perhaps, goods is an essential component of any serious package of progressive structural reforms designed to achieve sustained full employment and greater equality of income and wealth. In making this argument we are in a minority, but we are not alone. Indeed, in recent years there has been renewed support for capital controls, even among policy makers and mainstream economists.

Several factors help explain this growing interest. First, speculative attacks against the EMS in 1992 drove Great Britain and Italy out of the exchange rate mechanism, generated enormous macroeconomic problems for Sweden, Spain and other countries, and forced a widening of the bands for countries that remained. A number of respected mainstream economists have wondered whether capital controls may be necessary to bring about the transition to European Monetary Union. (See, for example, Eichengreen, Tobin and Wyplosz, 1995 and the references there.) Second, the recent Mexican disaster frightened even committed neoliberals. In this sensitive environment, the International Monetary Fund, in a move that made headlines and generated a critical editorial in the *Wall Street Journal*, cautiously argued for the occasional desirability of controls on inward capital flows to developing economies (IMF, 1995).[3] Finally, the continuation of devastatingly high unemployment in Europe and wage stagnation and increased inequality in the US has led to renewed interest in capital controls among progressives as a way of allowing countries to use macroeconomic policy to promote full employment. The surprise best selling book by *The Guardian*'s Will Hutton, *The State We're In*, calls for capital controls as a way of promoting full employment. Other respected progressive academics who have recently supported controls as part of a restructuring programme include Juliet Schor, Fred Block, and Andrew Glyn.[4]

However, even proponents of controls remain ambivalent about their feasibility. Is it possible to control capital when billions of dollars can move across cyberspace in a nanosecond? Can the international cooperation that may be required to control capital ever really occur? And, maybe globalization and the constraints that it imposes aren't all that important? For example, Andrew Glyn (1995), one of the economists on the left who has written most often and most perceptively and supportively on the economics of capital controls recently seemed to shift gears, arguing that the primary impediment to full employment at present lies in the fact that labour has failed to support a binding incomes policy that commits working people to non-inflationary wage and benefit demands at full employment. He believes that the costs, tensions and pressures of sustained full employment, magnified as they are in the current environment, should be 'explicitly counted and willingly shouldered by the mass of wage and salary earners' (Glyn, 1995, p.55). The problems of globalization complicate the issue to be sure, according to Glyn, but constraints on international mobility are not an essential element in its solution.

We share Glyn's belief in the need to constitute a new set of domestic political arrangements that will commit labour, capital and the state to egalitarian full-employment policies. The problem is this: *in the absence of the enactment, or at least the credible threat of enactment, of capital controls and trade restraints, what leverage can labour and the citizenry possibly use to force capitalists to even bargain seriously over these issues, never mind to persuade them to agree to any new political understanding other than one that delivers the total and complete surrender of all progressive social and economic values?* There are a depressingly large number of costly adjustments that the working class would have to 'willingly shoulder' in such a new domestic deal as Glyn now advocates. The US, for example, suffers not just from excessive average unemployment, but from urban decay, public infrastructural disinvestment, a health care system that is not viable in the longer run, an emaciated social safety network, a growing underclass of low-paid, under employed workers, and so forth. Is the working class to voluntarily agree to pay all the costs involved in solving these problems? Under existing political conditions, it is certainly clear that the economic elites will refuse to do so. And are engorged rentier incomes to be guaranteed in this new deal along with adequate corporate profits? The point is that *world elites have no incentive at present to jettison their current economic and political agendas*. Capital controls or their threat are the means to create such an incentive.

Discussions among economists about the pros and cons of capital controls usually take place in a fairly narrow context. Would this or that control help country X maintain a moderately lower interest rate or a somewhat lower rate of unemployment? Given the problems of evasion, or the propensity of controls to induce or worsen corruption, or the inefficiencies assumed to follow any interference with market incentives, the case for controls is normally rejected more or less out of hand. We want to consider capital controls in a much broader context. We are concerned with the current and future implications for the quality of life of the majority of the world's people of the continued development and perfection of the neoliberal global economic regime. Sustained high unemployment is now taken for granted across Europe and in most of the world. Inequality is on the rise everywhere. The US, though celebrated for its less-than-very-high unemployment rate, is suffering from secularly falling real wages, rising poverty rates, massive urban decay, and rising racial tensions. Its social safety net, miserly by developed country standards, is being torn to shreds by an arrogant and ignorant Congress whose only accountability is to wealth and power. Of course, these problems cannot be contained within the economic sphere. Deep fissures in the social fabric are appearing everywhere, and the body politic is not immune to the poisons this regime is spreading around the world. Racial hatred, immigrant bashing, and neofascism have made their reappearance on the global political scene.

In this context, the key question is not whether this control or that is on balance cost effective. Rather, we need to consider whether or not capital controls can help alter the current configuration of class economic and political *power* in order to facilitate the creation of new political commitments in support of full employment macropolicy, public investment, credit allocation and income redistribution. There are three ways in which capital controls can be helpful in this regard. First, such controls directly restrict the ability of rentiers and MNCs to threaten labour and the political majority by running away. Freedom to 'run' is one of the main sources of capitalist political power in the current neoliberal regime. Second, controls can facilitate the attainment of full employment, at least in the short to intermediate run, thereby strengthening labour's bargaining power. Third, the imposition of moderate controls and the *threat* to implement comprehensive controls (on trade and the movement of real and money capital) and more powerful state economic intervention in general may be the only way to get capital to consider supporting more progressive institutional arrangements because negotiations toward a political 'new deal' will be the only way they can protect themselves against the possible emergence of an overtly anti-rentier or even anti-capitalist regime or, alternatively, the development of political and social chaos.

Fortunately, the political feasibility of capital controls may be greater than is commonly believed. The current system of capital mobility, however profitable in the short run, is not operating in the long run interests of many of those capitalists engaged in producing goods and services. It is primarily the global rentier class that consistently benefits from the current system of capital mobility.[5] While it is true that the rentier class has gained tremendously in size as well as economic and political power in the post-war period, their assets still constitute a small fraction of total capitalist wealth. Hence, the constitution of a coalition of interests between labour and fractions of industrial and commercial capital against the parasitic interests of rentiers might be attainable under the right conditions.

As for economic feasibility, the case is even stronger. Economists do not doubt that capital can be controlled. The only issue is at what cost. Neoliberal economists assume that the current economic system is operating virtually without flaws; thus any costs associated with interference in the system are automatically considered to be too high a price to pay. We agree that the costs of imposing controls must be compared with the costs of not imposing them. However, contrary to the dominant view, it seems clear to us that the costs of maintaining the current neoliberal regime are absolutely astronomical. Any reasonable estimate of the efficiency costs to the nation of a system of capital controls must pale in comparison with the costs of doing nothing. As we shall see in Part IV of this essay, a broad range of controls are possible; capital flight can be frustrated not only by international cooperation among states, but also by the appropriate sequencing of and the vigorous enforcement of various controls by individual governments.

## II. From the Golden Age to the Resurgence of the Global Rentier Class

We offer here a brief and selective chronology of events leading to the birth and death of capitalism's Golden Age in the 1950s and 1960s[6] and then discuss the construction of the global neoliberal regime in order to draw attention to five key points. First, the systems of capital controls and credit allocation put in place after the war helped make the Golden Age possible. Second, the unravelling of these controls contributed substantially to the Golden Age's subsequent demise. Third, the alliance between industrial and financial capital that emerged in this period, as well as increased competition among nations for shares of the enlarging international financial market, were central to the dynamics of its demise. Fourth, the current neoliberal regime was created by global economic elites to facilitate their victory in a one-sided class war waged against working people around the world. Fifth, this regime has given capital such power over labour and society that no attempt to create a new progressive domestic policy coalition is likely to succeed unless accompanied by a direct assault on the foundations of that regime through capital and perhaps trade controls.

By the beginning of the 20th century, a globalized economy had become a reality. London, New York and Parisian bankers could move money to the far corners of the globe in no time at all, financing trade, public works, and speculation of vast proportions (Zevin, 1992). The free movement of money – anywhere, anytime – was the keystone of a liberal society and the basis for the accumulation of massive wealth by rentiers like Morgan, Rothschild, and Aldrich. Then came the calamities which destroyed the liberal order: the two World Wars and the Great Depression (Hobsbawm, 1994). If the Great Depression and War brought about an enormous reshuffling of national fortunes, it also dramatically reshuffled the pecking order of ideologies and classes. The sacred economic ideas of the day – the gold standard, independent central banks, and free international capital mobility – had all come to be seen as purveyors of calamity rather than pillars of stability. John Maynard Keynes was only the best known of many economists who discredited the idea that free international capital mobility and unregulated private finance were the *sine qua non* of economic progress (Crotty, 1983). Indeed, in many parts of the capitalist world, no group bore more blame for the economic crisis than the rentier class and its allies, the central bankers. Among the early casualties of the depression was the independent power of many central banks, including the Federal Reserve and the Bank of England, both of which were brought under the direct control of their governments in the 1930s (Epstein and Schor, 1995).

The planning undertaken by governments to more effectively wage the Second World War hastened the maturation of a political process already in motion: the institution of financial controls and economic planning in much of the advanced capitalist world. When Harry Dexter White for the US and John Maynard Keynes for England met to begin negotiations to construct the post-war economic order, there were two things on which they agreed. Controls over international capital movements would be necessary to achieve economic prosperity in the post war world; and such controls would be most effective if countries developed comprehensive national regulation of all foreign exchange transactions and cooperated with each other in enforcement of these regulations.[7] They wrote provisions which protected countries' rights to institute comprehensive controls into early drafts of the Bretton Woods Agreement; these provisions survived more or less intact. Keynes proposed voluntary international cooperation in his drafts, while White argued that such cooperation should be mandatory. In his 1942 draft, for example, White proposed that governments be required 'a) not to accept or permit deposits or investments from any member country except with permission of the government of that country, and b) to make available to the governments of any member country at its request all property in form of deposits, investments, securities of the nationals of that member country' (quoted in Helleiner, 1994 p. 38).

The early proposals of Keynes and White met with fierce opposition from New York bankers. Mandatory controls would interfere with the profitable business of accepting flight capital, as the New York bankers had done in the 1930s. And bankers opposed capital controls because they knew they would be used to support significant government intervention in post-war domestic economies. They eventually succeeded in removing the mandatory aspects of international controls enforcement. The 1943 version of White's draft stated that countries had to cooperate in enforcing controls 'only if the IMF had recommended it' (Helleiner, p. 47). In addition, countries were no longer required to repatriate flight capital at the request of the originating government, only to provide information about it. There was virtually nothing concerning nations' obligations to help each other enforce controls included in the 1944 Joint Statement. In the end, though, the Bretton Woods Agreement did reject the sanctity of unregulated private capital flows and the liberal, open, financial order with which it is associated.

It should be noted that one reason the New York bankers were not even more effective in striking controls from the Bretton Woods agreements was that industrial capitalists in the US and elsewhere rejected free capital mobility. In particular, those industrialists – largely from capital-intensive and high tech sectors – who had provided Roosevelt with crucial business support in the 1930s strongly supported effective capital controls (Ferguson, 1984). In other important countries (such as Japan, Germany, France and Italy) both financial and industrial interests agreed on the need for controls.

Indeed, at the start of the post-war period virtually all the countries in the world, with the important exception of the US, had extensive capital controls on outflows, inflows or both. For many countries such controls were seen as necessary to protect modest foreign exchange reserves in the face of strong import demand and tempting financial investment opportunities in the US But for others, controls facilitated the creation and allocation of credit and the regulation of trade that were important parts of government directed national development plans. Countries, such as Germany, for whom controls seemed an unfortunate necessity rather than an essential element of economic planning, began to remove their controls early in the post-war period. But virtually all such countries eventually reinstated controls in some form (Goodman and Pauly, 1993). The German Government 'while opposed to capital controls in principle, also resorted to them in practice' (Henning, 1994, p. 314). A coalition of bankers and industrialists committed to an export-led development strategy saw capital controls as essential for the maintenance of a stabilized and undervalued Mark. The German government therefore reimposed controls on inflows again from 1960 to 1969, in 1971 and as recently as in the early 1980s.

Japan, on the other hand, was more ideologically committed to the use of controls as part of its industrial development strategy. Its Foreign Exchange and Trade Control Law of 1949 brought 'formal prohibitions on capital transactions and restrictive licensing for financial institutions engaged in international business. There were also informal controls, such as administrative guidance of the foreign exchange positions of Japanese banks' (Henning, 1994, p. 314; Mathieson and Rojas-Suarez, p. 9). Capital and exchange controls allowed Japan to keep the cost of credit low, to channel credit to desired uses, and to stabilize the Yen at an undervalued level to promote exports. These policies were, as in Germany, the reflection of a coalition of interests between industry and finance. In France as well, a strong alliance between the state, finance and industry supported controls as part of an overall industrialization strategy. The French had used controls since 1915; in 1966 their post-war system of controls was significantly strengthened when a new law gave the government the right to control all foreign exchange transactions between France and the rest of the world, oversee the liquidation of foreign funds in France and French funds abroad, and prescribe conditions for the repatriation of all income earned abroad. Among the developing countries, South Korea used highly restrictive capital controls most effectively

(Nembhard, 1996). Controls on both outflows and inflows were a necessary adjunct to the industrial and credit allocation policies which made South Korea one of the first developing country 'economic miracles' in the post-war period (Amsden, 1989). Of course, controls were misused in some countries. But the point is that they played an essential role in creating virtually all of the great post-war secular booms.

In sum, the creation and reproduction of the Golden Age was facilitated by several key conditions. First, the rentier class was weak. Some economies were flush with liquidity after the war years, real interest rates were modest, and capital accumulation was primarily financed by the flood of internal funds created by growth and a consistently high rate of profit. This was an age in which the interests and needs of real capital accumulation dominated those of financial capital. Second, capital controls helped keep finance primarily national while domestic financial regulations and credit controls channelled funds to priority domestic uses. Both aspects were important: domestic rentiers had little power over the accumulation process and capital controls prevented them from augmenting their power by threatening to 'run away' if interest rates and inflation rates did not suit them. Largely because of controls, the overall flow of private cross border finance was quite low in the 1950s and early 1960s. Rentiers thus had yet to gain veto power over macropolicy. Third, though the dislocations and uneven destruction wrought by the war meant that trade had to be of some significance, it was less important than it was to later become, while direct investment across borders was inconsequential. Firms thus were forced to rely primarily on strong rates of growth of domestic aggregate demand for their own expansion and profit. Industrialists as a group were unable to resolve their cost problems by national policies of high unemployment without destroying the main markets for their own goods. And with political commitments made by capital to labour during the war to cement their allegiance to the war effort still in effect, conditions were ripe for the creation and maintenance of the political and economic arrangements that led to full employment and rising social wages across Europe and, to a somewhat lesser extent, in the US.

Unfortunately, the history of the postwar financial order is one that culminates in the ultimate triumph of rentiers and MNCs and the restoration of an open global financial and economic system. A major contributing factor to this victory was that as important segments of business became more international in orientation they joined the bankers in their support of a more financially open global economy. Thus united, they became too politically powerful for most governments to successfully oppose.

In our view, the contradictions and strains that brought the Golden Age to its demise in the late 1960s and early 1970s were primarily domestic.

The economic and political power of the working classes in the advanced countries was invigorated by sustained full employment and a rising social wage. This period saw an eruption of strikes, militant demands for better wages and working conditions, and a push by labour for more democratic control of the labour process. These challenges to capital created the cost side of the squeeze on the profit rate characteristic of this period. At the same time, industrial capital was trying to undercut labour's power by shifting production to nonunion sites either at home or abroad; foreign investment and its threat became increasingly important weapons in this conflict. Meanwhile, citizens around the developed world demanded a more generous social wage, creating strains on the public purse. (See Bowles, Gordon, and Weisskopf, 1990.)

Of course this is also the initial period of the resurgence of the global rentier class. The modern global rentier class evolved through an increase in the size and power of rentier interests in many advanced capitalist countries combined with increased openness of world financial markets. As it became larger, the rentier class began to form coalitions with segments of industrial and commercial capital, in some cases as the result of the creation of huge financial/industrial conglomerates, a veritable merging of rentier and industrial interests under one corporate roof.

The clearest early signpost of this new unity occurred in the 1960s in the context of the implementation of a capital controls programme in the US and the associated rise of the Eurodollar market. When the US government set up its voluntary capital controls programme in the 1960s, it tolerated and even promoted the Eurodollar market in London in order to prevent the subversion of the programme by large US banks and multinational corporations. The Eurodollar market allowed both big banks and multinational industry to gain access to deposits and loans abroad without immediately hurting the US balance of payments. The push by British Banks and the British Government to restore London as a world financial centre, with a deregulated international financial market unhindered by capital controls, finally let the globalization genie out of the bottle.

The US had become decidedly hostile to international capital controls by the early 1970s. When the declining US trade position precipitated a run on the dollar and threatened the collapse of the Bretton Woods system, European and Japanese governments proposed extensive cooperative capital controls to help maintain the fixed exchange rate mechanism. The US government vetoed their proposal (Helleiner, 1994). Without the support of the US, the attempt to maintain international regulation of the emerging global rentier class was doomed to failure. By the middle 1980s virtually all advanced countries were in the process of loosening or even eliminating controls. Their general demise was the result of a combination of internal and external political pressures, the precise mix of which varied from country to country. Much of the external pressure emanated from the US. As noted, the US had encouraged the development of the Eurocurrency markets in London in the 1960s. Euromarkets then became the site of the freest international capital market since the 1920s; this created pressure on other countries to dismantle their own capital controls so that their financial institutions could more successfully compete in the emerging global marketplace. In the 1970s, the US succeeded in changing the language of the IMF bylaws, for the first time giving the IMF the power to force countries to reduce or even eliminate capital controls. Finally, in the late 1970s and 1980s, the U.S. directly pressured a number of countries, Japan among others, to open their capital markets. Germany played a similar role within the EMS. Nevertheless, in most cases the primary cause of the demise of capital controls was probably domestic. Domestic industry and finance, having become more globalized and more outward oriented, eventually became more unified in their opposition to controls. They had also lost much of their commitment to the social contracts that originally made capital controls attractive to them. The accumulation of these international and domestic pressures to remove controls eventually overcame the resistance offered by various OECD governments.

Symptoms of the death of the Golden Age were easy to spot. Real wage growth slowed everywhere; in the US it vanished. Average industrial and commercial profit rates declined markedly. But the rentier class continued to expand in size as well as in its propensity to cross borders. The central events in this process of expansion revolved around the creation of an ocean of petrodollars recycled by the exploding Eurodollar market to the Third World. Petrodollar recycling represented a new evolution for global rentiers since loans to developing country had previously been modest in amount, and came primarily from governments and international lending agencies, not private financial institutions. The second OPEC price increase in 1978–79 accelerated this process. Inflation spiked again. Exchange rate instability skyrocketed. The Europeans tried to delink from the US dollar and form their own exchange rate system in an attempt to insulate themselves from this chaos. Capital controls in much of Europe were temporarily reintroduced.

In political terms, the 1970s can perhaps be best understood as a time of distributional struggle among and between classes over who would bear the costs of slower growth, rising rent extraction by oil producers, and increased economic instability and insecurity. The decade saw no clear cut winner. The rentier classes in particular fared poorly. Inflation adjusted equity prices dropped rapidly over the decade; indeed share prices divided by money wages fell dramatically all across the OECD. Meanwhile, inflation at times rose above nominal interest rates in the late 1970s, giving rentiers negative real rates of return. By 1980 the economic elites in the developed world were seething with anger at their failure to win this distributional struggle. If the 1970s was their decade of discontent, the 1980s was to be their decade of revenge.

A run on the US dollar in 1979 kicked off the decisive phase of capital's war against labour and the social contract. US Federal Reserve Chairman Volcker proceeded to implement his attack on inflation and the US working class, precipitating the Third World debt crisis. Super-tight US monetary policy, along with like-minded policies implemented elsewhere in the OECD, raised world real interest rates, helping create a global recession. The global recession created an environment that permitted European elites, who were not in a political position to simply tear up the social contract, to violate it with some impunity. European unemployment rates, which had increased from about 3% to about 6% between 1973 and 1980, levitated to above 10% by the mid-eighties, never to return to their 1970s, let alone their 1960s, levels.

Thus, by the early 1980s all the pieces needed to implement the new political agenda of the more unified elites were in place. Rentiers wanted the devolution of all regulatory controls on the movement of money – within the country and across borders. They wanted inflation smashed quickly. Finally, they wanted low taxes on rentier income and on the rich. The agenda of industrial capital was generally consistent with rentier interests; only questions of the depth and length of the desired recession separated them. To raise profits and create greater managerial autonomy, they wanted to complete the job started in the 1970s and break the economic and political power of labour. They sought lower real wages and more freedom to organize work and workers as they saw fit; the weakening or even destruction of unions and the reduction of the social safety net were necessary conditions for achieving this result. They also wanted to loosen the government regulatory apparatus and cut business taxes even further. In the decade or so to follow, US rentiers and industrialists got almost all of what they wanted; their European counterparts had to settle for less.

The 1980s also saw the accelerated expansion of a deregulated financial sector swollen by high real interest rates, rapidly rising debt to income ratios in the business, household and government sectors, and speculatively driven financial asset prices. Since there had been no increase in world saving, the sustained secular rise in indebtedness, along with the rentier-dictated anti-inflation mania of central banks, kept constant upward pressure on real interest rates. The relation of the financial sector to the nonfinancial sector thus had changed dramatically from the hey-day of the Golden Age. The financial sector now absorbed a vastly increased share of the income flows generated in the real sector which it used primarily to fund its own self-expansion. Finance had become a parasite on and impediment to real sector growth.

Of course, governments everywhere became increasingly dependent on the rentier class. The post-1973 slowdown in economic growth reduced the rate of increase of tax revenues and raised demands for higher spending. Serious budget deficits first arose after 1973; they increased (relative to GDP) in the 1980s. Cuts in taxes on business and the rich further weakened the fiscal position of the state. Finally, the record high real interest rates of the period raised the cost of servicing the ever rising stock of government debt. Throughout the developed and the developing worlds, governments became burdened with their heaviest debts since WW II. With rentiers now inclined to boycott bonds issued by governments that tolerate inflation or run deficits that are considered irresponsibly large, raising their interest payments and punishing their exchange rates, fiscal as well as monetary policy had fallen under rentier dominance.[8]

The political-economic strategies implemented by capital in the 1980s were astonishingly successful in settling the distributional struggle in capital's favor in the US and in much of the Third World, and reasonably successful in the rest of the OECD. Looking at the US, we can say that the elites have substantially destroyed the old social contract. Meanwhile, the economies of the Second and Third Worlds have become increasingly open to First World exploitation. Indeed, with the acceleration of globalization, with the increasing allegiance to neoliberal policies and ideology, with further privatization, and with legally binding treaties such as GATT and NAFTA, the very concept of nationalist economic policies is beginning to seem hopelessly naive.

The central point that needs recognition is how integral the process of globalization has been to the unfolding of this story. The proximate cause of the end of the Golden Age was the collapse of US international financial hegemony and of global financial stability brought on by a run on the US dollar in the early 1970s. And the proximate cause of the onset of global monetarist terror in the 1980s was the run on the dollar in 1979 that brought Volcker to power. The policies adopted in the 1980s then produced the speculative booms and financial fragility that further enlarged and empowered the rentier class. Indeed, the general environment of uncertainty that followed the Golden Age was fuelled by waves of global hot money flooding into and then out of different countries, dramatically raising exchange rate instability. This ocean of hot money has grown ever wider and deeper as financial sectors inflate, technological and organizational innovation accelerates, and, most importantly, the ability and the desire of governments to control these flows erodes. Unless and until we restore some reasonable degree of societal control over the 'freedom' to move goods, jobs and, especially, money across borders at will, attempts to implement full employment macropolicies or to write domestic new deals will be doomed to failure.

## III. Capital Controls as Prerequisites For Progressive Macropolicy

The crucial question in this context is whether capital controls (and perhaps also trade management) are necessary conditions for the implementation of full employment and egalitarian economic policies. There are actually two important sub-questions involved here. First, do unregulated investment, trade, and financial capital flows make the implementation of a long term or sustained policy of full employment difficult if not impossible? Second, do they significantly weaken labour's ability to force capital to agree to a new, progressive, egalitarian domestic economic regime? We believe that the answer to both questions is yes, and that, therefore, capital controls are an essential precondition for the reconstruction of a regime of sustained full employment and reduced inequality. Obviously, some countries face less binding external constraints on the implementation of progressive domestic economic policies than do others. But, in our opinion, capital controls would enhance the ability of a progressive political alliance in *any* country to successfully pursue sustained full employment and a more progressive income distribution.

How do trade openness and unregulated real and financial capital flows impede the ability of government to pursue high wage, high employment, egalitarian policies? To answer this question it is first necessary to ask how extensive capital mobility really is. On the one hand, the quantity of two-way short-term flows (so called gross mobility), has increased dramatically, and is now at astronomical levels. These are the movements of capital that most observers have in mind when discussing the 'hyper-mobility' of capital. On the other, the net transfer of long term capital from one country to another is still at a lower level relative to the size of economies than it was at the turn of the century. But things are changing. With the rise of neoliberal ideology, the increased power of the global rentier class and the strengthening of international protections for foreign investment embodied in NAFTA, agreements of the EU, and other international legal arrangements promoted by the IMF, World Bank and other institutions, the pace of long-term and net capital flows is dramatically accelerating. If the current pace continues, the level of international capital mobility even on a long-term and net basis is certain to eventually increase substantially over the early 20th century peaks. In sum, short term international mobility is already extensive; and if current trends continue, long-term mobility will continue its dramatic rise as well. (See Epstein, 1995 and Epstein and Gintis, 1992 and the references cited there). In this context, let us consider the following issues.

*Direct Investment*
Changes in technology and the prying open of Second and Third world economies to unrestricted foreign investment have made it easier for multinationals to invest anywhere and to produce an increasing variety of goods and services using a broader spectrum of relatively low cost foreign labour skills. While still modest relative to domestic investment in the advanced countries, foreign direct investment is not insignificant and is growing fast. Foreign investment can have two deleterious effects on the domestic economy: it can substitute for, and thus reduce, domestic investment; and it can affect the relative bargaining power of labour and capital in the negotiations that determine wages and working conditions, primarily in those industries experiencing capital outflow, but in related industries as well.

There are arguments on both sides of the question as to whether foreign investment by domestic corporations is a complement to or substitute for domestic investment by these same companies. But taking into account the increasingly wide range of labour skills available to advanced country MNCs abroad at a fraction of the cost of domestic workers, as well as the frequent absence of unions, environmental restrictions, health and safety regulations, taxes, and so forth in less developed countries, it seems reasonable to conclude that foreign investment in the advanced countries is on balance a substitute for domestic investment (Burke, 1996; Feldstein, 1994).[9]

Under virtually anyone's theory of wage determination, the loss of capital and technology in the domestic economy caused by foreign direct investment should lower productivity and therefore the real wage, at least in the short run. The magnitude of this effect should not be large, however, because the proportion of the potential domestic capital stock that has run away is not large. But if one accepts, as we do, the more realistic view that the division of the national product among the factors of production is mediated by a complex set of institutions and practices that determine the relative power of the contending parties, it is not at all clear that the effect on wages of runaway capital is minor. How many companies have to run away, leaving behind unemployed and underemployed workers and depressed communities and regions, in order to lend credibility to the threat by other companies to do the same? In an environment of substantial secular unemployment such as we have lived through in the past 15 years, even partial credibility can frighten workers into making major concessions. Until we find a reliable way to measure the growth of such threat-credibility, we will have no way of knowing for certain what we believe to be the case: that foreign direct investment has had a major effect on wage behaviour in the advanced countries in recent years.

*Trade and Financial Capital Flows*

Consider the situation confronting a nation that wants to implement a macropolicy designed to achieve sustained full employment. Assume this nation is completely open to trade and to real and financial cross border investment flows, and that trade is a significant component of GDP. The trade-related impediments to a full employment macro policy in such an open, trade-dependent nation are many and complex. Here we simply list four. First, increased income growth will induce a rise in imports that will lessen the impact of a given degree of policy stimulus on GDP (or will lower the policy 'multiplier'). Second, the rising trade deficit will, other things equal, precipitate a fall in the nation's exchange rate that, in current speculative currency markets, could be of substantial magnitude. Third, the fall in the exchange rate will cause a deterioration in the real terms of trade – the quantity of imports earned by a given volume of exports. If traded goods and services are a large percentage of GDP, this could lead to a large reduction in real wages and in the national income. Fourth, this surge in imports itself will cause competitive downward pressure on domestic real wages. As we shall see, these trade-related problems will interact with financial capital flows to sabotage the full employment policies that spawned them.

Those who do not believe that globalization is a major cause of the deterioration in economic performance over the past twenty years often point out that while dependence on trade did increase substantially since the 1960s, its rise has not been all that dramatic, and that while direct investment did increase by dramatic proportions, it remains small in absolute terms. However, no one can deny that financial capital flows have increased dramatically and have reached unprecedented relative and absolute levels. The daily turnover in the foreign exchange market, which was about $15 billion in 1973 and about $60 billion in 1983 is now approximately $1.3 trillion, an amount perhaps sixty times the volume needed to finance trade, one that dwarfs the less than one trillion dollars available to the governments of the advanced countries for exchange rate stabilization purposes.[10]

What impediments to our hypothetical full employment macropolicy might today's global rentier class cause? The primary problems are that the fall in the exchange rate caused by the higher trade deficit and lower interest rate associated with this policy will be *larger*, will take place *sooner*, and will be *more uncertain* or unpredictable in size. The term 'rational expectations' is an oxymoron in the world in which we live. We can 'predict' the future only through guesses, hunches, rules of thumb, and social conventions. And perhaps no important world market is more subject to the speculative instability and fundamental uncertainty endemic in the real world than the current global money market. Any significant movement of an exchange rate in either direction can start a stampede into or out of any currency in this market; herd behaviour is the norm (Crotty, 1994). Thus, as our new full employment policy – with its reliance on low interest rates and its promise of higher inflation and larger trade deficits – begins to be implemented, global rentiers will jump ship, touching off an exchange rate decline which could turn into a free fall. Knowing that they don't know how fast or how deep the drop will be, even investors who are not hostile to the longer term objectives of the host government may quite sensibly decide to play it safe by shifting their funds elsewhere, perhaps with the intention of returning when the exchange rate pressure has subsided.

These problems are greatest, of course, for small, trade-dependent developing countries. But even large countries will suffer when rentiers decide to run away from their currencies. The central bank may be forced to defend the exchange rate through high interest rates, striking a blow to domestic investment. Financial instability may rise as higher interest rates undermine the stability of banks dependent on short term deposits to fund their investment in long term loans and in bonds purchased earlier when rates were low. Higher interest rates may transform a difficult fiscal deficit into a fiscal nightmare: the government will pay much higher rates to finance its deficits and turn over its debt. Heavily indebted industrial and commercial corporations are subject to the same kinds of financial shock; greater financial fragility in this case means less capital investment. In short, substantial capital flight can generate tight constraints on policy. Unfortunately, vast inflows of capital can eventually prove to be almost as damaging. The crisis in Mexico in 1994–1995 is a case in point (Grabel, 1995; Danby, 1995; IMF 1995).

The main point is that the problems caused by the decline of the exchange rate are magnified and quickened. In essence, the problems which the new expansionary policy might have generated only slowly and in concert with its benefits, are now magnified and appear *before the benefits have a chance to even be experienced*. It is easy to see why the objectives of the new policy might be impossible to attain under these conditions. It is easy to see how public support for the policy could easily evaporate in this environment. It is also easy to see, given the logic of this scenario, why even well meaning governments – an endangered species – would shy away from anything resembling a policy of sustained full employment. With central banks universally opposed to such policies and rentiers ready to severely punish any government which tries one, it is easy to understand why the majority of the world's population has had to suffer the consequence of secularly high unemployment for the past two decades.

The virtual elimination of full employment macropolicies is not the only serious problem caused by financial aspects of globalization. The existence of this ocean of hot money, subject as it is to fads and fashions, has helped create enormous actual as well as potential instability in exchange rates. This rise in exchange rate uncertainty potentially affects the decisions of all economic agents influenced by international prices and quantities; a group that grows apace with globalization. That is to say, the evolution of the global rentier class has substantially increased the deleterious impact of uncertainty on economic performance. Nowhere is this more important than in reducing the pace and changing the composition of capital investment spending. The current era is thus one in which productive accumulation is being strangled by financial capital – through debt burdens, high interest rates, fickle short-term finance, heightened uncertainty, and restraints on expansionary macropolicy. Freedom to cross borders at will has substantially enhanced the ability of the rentier class to enrich itself while impoverishing society.

## IV. What is to be Done?

We have no doubt that existing impediments to the implementation of effective capital controls are many and are powerful. The main general problem is this: the most efficient potential solutions to our current economic problems are global in character, but there are no obvious democratic political mechanisms at hand through which to design and implement global institutional change of the kind we need. Such mechanisms as we do have are national or regional in character.

To see the potential superiority of global solutions, suppose that *all* governments decided to cooperatively pursue full employment through larger budget deficits and lower interest rates. Under such global cooperation no country need confront serious problems from rising trade deficits, or capital flight, or currency devaluation. Thus, the need for capital or trade controls would be substantially diminished. If this need did arise, cooperative agreements to enforce capital controls would make them much more efficient and harder to evade. Keynes was surely on the right track when he based Britain's 1940s proposals for a new international order on the concept of an international central bank empowered to expand the world's credit supply to accommodate and sustain global economic expansion. The bank was to assist countries that develop balance of payments problems through faster than average growth, and penalize surplus countries, forcing them to grow faster.

Clearly then, the most effective method for creating global full employment is cooperative macropolicy expansion, cooperative capital controls, an international central bank in the Keynes mode, and an international Social Charter enumerating and enforcing minimum wages and working conditions, minimum social and economic rights, and appropriate environmental standards. Unfortunately, current prospects for attaining such comprehensive global agreements are dim. Governments everywhere are beholden to national and global economic elites who are either quite content with the status quo or who want to push the neoliberal agenda even further. Cross border labour and citizen alliances are developing, but they have not evolved to the point where they could have a serious impact on global economic policy. 'The focus on nation states derives primarily from a pragmatism born of a total inability to conceive, let alone construct, a meaningful political process at the global level' (Bienefeld, 1994, 122).

Thus, the best political prospects for major change exist at the national or regional levels, but here is where the economic impediments to the implementation of effective controls are greatest. Comprehensive controls in a single nation, if they remain in place for a long period of time, become increasingly difficult and costly to administer and, under the intentionally leaky enforcement procedures that normally prevail, increasingly easy for the economic elite to evade.[11] The smaller (and more politically isolated) the country and the tighter its integration in and dependence on world markets, the harder the problem becomes. It is especially hard for a small, globally dependent country to unilaterally implement powerful comprehensive capital controls designed to thwart all the forces that will rebel against permanent, egalitarian full employment policies.

This is not to say that it cannot be done. If the government's economic plan is comprehensive and coherent and consistently implemented and if the controls enforcement mechanisms are powerful and vigorously, even ruthlessly, enforced, then the successful use of long term controls by smaller countries is possible – as South Korea and Taiwan, among others, have demonstrated. Nevertheless, the political units best able to unilaterally adopt a programme of capital controls in pursuit of expansionary egalitarian policies and the eventual achievement of a new social contract are relatively large countries (especially those, such as the US and Japan, that are not excessively dependent on trade), and appropriate regional alliances, such as the EU.

Let us assume that, with the possible exceptions discussed below, it is most reasonable to consider the possibility of controls for the case of large nations or appropriate alliances. What set of capital and\or trade and\or direct investment controls would best facilitate the achievement of a new progressive full employment programme? The first thing to realize is that the answer to this question is contingent on all those things that influence the relative power and the political perceptions of the main economic classes; freedom of capital to cross borders is just one determinant of capitalist class power. *Any* combination of domestic economic policies and cross border controls that can bring industrial and rentier capital to political negotiations willing to accept a progressive social contract, or that can help unite labour and segments of industrial capital against rentier intransigence is satisfactory. In the best of circumstances moderate controls might suffice. Under more common, less propitious circumstances, it might take relatively strong capital controls accompanied by a believable threat that the refusal of capital to cooperate in bargaining will result in the rigorous control of trade, investment and financial flows and a generally more interventionist state.

*There is no single policy with respect to controls that is optimal in all countries under all circumstances.* Nevertheless, we present below a sample list of feasible national or regional capital controls to emphasize that, under the right conditions, including controls in any strategy designed to produce sustained full employment is a pragmatic political act. The claim that strong controls are not technically feasible or economically sustainable is, we will show, simply inconsistent with the facts. We cannot over-emphasize the point that the primary impediments to the successful use of capital controls are *political*, not technical. It is not support for capital controls, but the contrary belief that progressive economic restructuring can be achieved without at least the threat of such controls that is utopian.

## V. Capital Controls and International Cooperation

### *What Not to Do*

The first task facing those who want to rein in the domestic political power of MNCs and global rentiers is to stop any further liberalization of the rules governing international capital mobility. At regional as well as global levels, moves are afoot to further reduce the ability of nations to control international capital mobility. This is especially true with regard to foreign direct investment. For example, the United States is proposing an extension of the North American Free Trade Agreement to Chile and other countries in the Caribbean and Latin America. This so-called 'Free Trade' agreement is primarily an agreement to reduce the ability of communities to regulate, restrict or control foreign companies which invest there. This will only serve to diminish national policy autonomy. For its part, while the EU continues negotiations for its enlargement, the rules governing the outflow of direct foreign investment to lower wage areas must be carefully monitored and shaped so as not to further enhance capital's bargaining position.

At the global level, negotiations are continuing for an agreement on the international protection of foreign investment within the framework of the World Trade Organization. These protections, if ratified, would dramatically reduce the ability of national democratic forces to establish restrictions on foreign investment. These attempts must be resisted. Finally, we should continue to oppose conditionality requirements imposed by the IMF and World Bank which trade access to credit in return for limitations on the ability of nations to restrict capital mobility. But we should not stop here: a good offence is the best defence.

*Stand-by Controls on Capital Flight*

Instead of using international institutions to promote capital mobility, they should be used to limit destructive capital flight. A system of international stand-by controls on capital flight could be negotiated that required countries to return capital that crossed borders in violation of any nation's laws (Block, 1993, p. 170–171). Such stand-by controls would be especially helpful to the enforcement efforts of smaller, poorer countries. While small countries can and do implement capital controls, the costs of unilateral enforcement can be high, especially if the country is very dependent on imports, exports or foreign investment. There is ample precedent for such agreements. As discussed earlier, Keynes and White saw such international cooperation as a key to any sensible international financial regime, and they tried to write such cooperation into the Bretton Woods Agreements.

International cooperation in monitoring and controlling the movement of funds is already occurring, and the tightening of such controls seems virtually inevitable. Already, law enforcement officials from around the world are desperately seeking better mechanisms to restrict the laundering of drug money. For example, Switzerland has reduced its bank secrecy laws as applied to drug-related and other illicit financial movements partly as a result of pressure from the US. Efforts to reduce tax evasion by multinational corporations is another pressure point; many governments have an interest in seeking international cooperation to better identify and control the international movement of corporate funds. What is needed, then, is an extension of these ongoing efforts at international cooperation on the restriction of financial flows to include mandatory cooperation in support of national capital controls – as originally proposed by Harry Dexter White.

*An Internationally Coordinated Transactions Tax*

Another globally coordinated measure which has received wide discussion among academics and some international organizations is the so-called Tobin Tax, named after Nobel Laureate economist James Tobin (Tobin, 1978, 1994). The Tobin Tax is a small percentage tax on all foreign exchange transactions. It is designed to discourage excessive short term speculation without discouraging longer-term, presumably more efficient flows of capital and uses of foreign exchange.

The tax would work like this. Say the rate of tax is 0.5 percent on all foreign exchange transactions, both when buying and when selling foreign exchange. An investor who buys $1 million in foreign exchange, invests it in a foreign bank for 1 month, and then sells it again (and does this every month), will pay (.005) X 12 X 2 X $1 million or a total of $120,000 in tax (or a tax rate of 12% per year). If she buys and holds only for one day, and she does this every day, she will pay tax at the rate of 365% per year. Only a very large expected profit on speculative dealings could justify such foreign exchange churning. On the other hand, if she buys and holds a 1 year bond, she will pay a tax of 1% or $10,000 on a million dollar investment.

Tobin points out that such a tax would have to be levied globally or at least in all major financial sectors. Otherwise, foreign exchange transactions would simply move to an untaxed locale. Implementing such a coordinated international tax would be relatively easy. Any of the international financial institutions, such as the IMF, BIS, or WTO could implement and enforce the tax with the help of local authorities. The international coordination of financial regulation is widening and deepening in any case. Moreover, there are relatively few technical obstacles to such a tax, since the same computer technology that facilitates capital flows could be used to monitor and tax them.

However, there are serious limitations to the Tobin Tax as a mechanism for dealing with the disruptions created by contemporary international capital mobility. A small tax would not discourage massive speculation based on the expectation of a one shot, immanent, large devaluation, as in the recent British or Mexican cases. Indeed, mainstream advocates of the tax see this as an advantage: they do not want to discourage speculation against what they see as unsustainable or ill-advised policies.

Implementing an internationally coordinated Tobin Tax would be a major step forward and we strongly endorse it. But it would not be sufficient to qualitatively alter the domestic political class balance of power. While such a tax might allow for a temporarily lower interest rate in one country undertaking an expansionary policy, it would not protect countries implementing longer term policies which dramatically differ from the international lowest common denominator. Deeper and broader controls would likely be necessary to bring about the results we require. And these deeper controls are, in the present environment, likely to be implemented only at the national or regional levels.

## VI. Capital Controls at the National or Regional Levels

*Controls on Direct Foreign Investment*

Consider first controls on foreign direct investment. There is a wide range of experience with constraints on the activities of MNCs. With respect to inflows, many countries have restricted the purchase of domestic companies by foreigners anywhere in the economy (South Korea) or in certain sectors (oil, Mexico). Other countries have allowed only the purchase of minority shares in companies, or in companies of particular sectors (the media, U.S.). With respect to outflows, countries have placed general restrictions on foreign direct investment (South Korea), or have controlled particular investments, (for example, the sale of sensitive high technology production processes to potential enemies). The general considerations outlined above apply here: the point is to get sufficient control over capital to create a qualitative change in the domestic political balance of class power.

*Restrictions on Bank Lending to Non-Residents*

A widely discussed measure which would discourage shorter-term flows is based on the recognition that speculators must first obtain a currency before they can sell it. Nonresident speculators often borrow domestic currency from financial institutions for future resale. To reduce the incentive for such speculation, countries or regions could place a tax on lending to non-residents, or a requirement that a portion of all such loans be put into a non-interest bearing account (Eichengreen, Tobin and Wyplosz, 1995). In the case of a deposit requirement, the size of the requirement could be proportional to the size of the loan. Because speculators receive no interest on these deposits, they function as a tax. The higher the interest rate, the higher the interest foregone, and thus the higher the tax rate. Hence, the higher the interest rate differential between home and abroad (and therefore the greater the incentive for speculation), the higher the rate of the tax.

These controls could eventually become quite leaky. Residents may begin to borrow from domestic banks in order to lend the money to non-residents, thereby circumventing controls. Advocates of such controls, therefore, see these policies as being effective only in the short term. For longer term controls on capital, stronger medicine is clearly required.

*Using the Tax System to Reduce Capital Mobility*

Perhaps the easiest and most efficient way to reduce destructive capital mobility is to use a well developed, politically accepted institution which all advanced industrial countries rely on: the tax system. The great advantage of reliance on the tax system where feasible is that it involves no new bureaucracy and, at least in the advanced countries, is reasonably cost effective.

Consider first the imposition of a 'Keynes' tax – a tax on the sale of any financial asset held for less than a target length of time, say one or two years. (See Baker, Pollin and Schaberg, 1995)[12] The Keynes tax is a natural complement to the Tobin tax because before large sums of 'hot' money can flee the country, they must first be harvested through the sale of assets or by borrowing. Taxing the sale of the asset and taxing the foreign exchange transaction should have the same qualitative effect on the profitability of flight. And a Keynes tax can be applied unilaterally. Of course, since it penalizes domestic financial market 'churning,' a Keynes tax would also have a salutary effect on the stability of domestic financial markets. Similar results could be obtained through changes in the provisions of the capital gains tax: penalty rates (relative to ordinary income) applied to the sale of assets held for less than the target period could be very effective.

The tax system can also be used directly as a type of capital control by treating differentially income generated from foreign and domestic financial investment. For example, until this year the tax treatment of gains and losses on the foreign and domestic securities held by the very powerful Japanese insurance industry were set so as to severely limit the incentive to invest abroad. These tax laws were quite effective in achieving their desired results. Institutions such as pension funds and insurance companies hold large and rapidly rising shares of advanced country domestic financial wealth, and they are trading securities across national borders at an increasing rate. By taxing the gains from cross border investments at a penalty rate and by discriminating against the deductibility of cross border losses, governments could substantially reduce the propensity of money to move into and out of the country.

Another way to see the point that the tax systems can be used to control capital mobility is to note that in some cases tax systems already promote capital outflows. In the United States, for example, tax rules that govern multinational corporations' transactions (such as transfer pricing, deferral of tax payments and deductibility of taxes paid in foreign jurisdictions) have had the effect of promoting outward foreign direct investment. These rules could be changed to discourage such outflows.

Focusing on the tax system makes it clear that enforcing international capital controls need be no harder (and no easier) than imposing taxes. Taxes, like capital controls, are, to some degree, evaded. It costs money and takes effort to collect taxes as it does to control capital mobility. But where there is a will to collect taxes, they are collected; it would simply take a change in the tax law to extend this mechanism to reducing international capital mobility.

*Dual Exchange Rates*

Dual (or multiple) exchange rates can substitute for or reinforce the tax proposals discussed earlier. (See Dornbusch, 1989 and Glyn, 1995.) A major problem with capital flight, as noted above, is that it can significantly lower the exchange rate, greatly increase the cost of imports, and thereby substantially lower the standard of living. The destructive effects of capital flight could be reduced if their impact on the cost of imports could be attenuated or eliminated.

That is what dual exchange rates attempt to do. Separate exchange rates are established for trade and capital transactions. The government stabilizes the rate used for trade, but allows the rate used for capital transactions to float. In this system, even if capital flight greatly depreciated the value of the exchange rate, businesses would be able to obtain foreign exchange from the government at the old rate in order to import products. Hence, the attempt by speculators to sell domestic currency need not increase the cost of imports. Such dual exchange rates have been widely used, particularly in developing countries. In 1975, three industrial countries used dual exchange rates, and 22 developing countries did so. By 1990, only one industrial country (South Africa) used them, but the number of developing countries using them increased to 34 (Mathieson and Rojas-Suarez, 1993, p. 5). Andrew Glyn (1994) has recently proposed using them in Great Britain.

A difficulty with dual rates is that people try to evade them by buying the cheaper currency from the government, then using it to purchase financial assets abroad. Hence, a strong enforcement mechanism may be required to reduce the likelihood that the country will run out of foreign exchange because of illegal capital flight. Eventually the government may find that it needs to implement quantitative controls.

*Quantitative Restrictions*

The most commonly used capital controls are quantitative in nature. There have been a dazzling array of controls used by different countries at different times. In 1975, 17 industrial countries and 85 developing countries had some types of quantitative restrictions on payments for capital transactions on the books. By 1990, 11 industrial countries and 109 developing countries had them.[13] Of course, having them on the books and strongly enforcing them may be two different things. In the 1992 ERM crisis, for example, Ireland and Portugal implemented strong capital controls simply by enforcing and strengthening controls that were already law. To give the reader an idea of current practice, we list some examples of controls that have been used recently (IMF, 1995, ch. 5).

In Ireland in 1992: (1) all credits to nonresident Irish pound-denominated accounts in excess of 250,000 pounds had to be reported to the Central Bank unless the credit was trade-related; (2) residents were not allowed to make financial loans in Irish pounds for periods of less than one year to nonresidents without the permission of the Central Bank; (3) foreign currency accounts were available to residents but with restrictions: for example, deposits made with funds converted from Irish pounds had to be held for at least three months; (4) forward foreign exchange transactions in Irish pounds for speculative purposes were prohibited – minimum maturity requirements of 21 days were imposed; and (5) as the crisis developed, the law was strengthened so that all currency swaps required central bank approval (IMF, 1995, p. 104). In Portugal during the same crisis, all short term local currency lending to non-residents was prohibited.

More comprehensive quantitative controls have also been used. These could be held out as a threat to bring capital to the bargaining table if milder controls don't suffice. For example, in Argentina, in April 1982, (as in many countries in the early post-war years) all sales of foreign exchange were prohibited except for imports and for principal repayments and interest payments on foreign loans. In Mexico in the summer of 1982, all foreign exchange transactions were made subject to control, with the Banco de Mexico (and its designated agents) being the only authorized foreign exchange supplier. A 5,000 peso limit was imposed on imports and exports of domestic currency and limits were placed on the amount of foreign currency that could be taken out of Mexico by each person. Insurance of payments and other transactions in pesos abroad by Mexican credit institutions was prohibited. Profit and royalty remittances associated with foreign direct investment in Mexico were limited to 15 percent of equity subject to foreign exchange availability (IMF, 1995, p. 106). And the list goes on.

As these examples suggest, there is a whole panoply of quantitative controls which can and have been used. These range from controlling a select set of transactions to controlling all uses of foreign exchange, including trade. There is no shortage of examples and experiences to either adopt or to use as a threat.

## VII. Conclusion

Two questions immediately come to mind when assessing the case for capital controls. First, even if they worked would they be a good thing? Second, will they work, for how long and at what cost?

Even if one dismisses the notion that unfettered free market capitalism delivers the goods, one may still raise objections to capital controls. First, won't they reduce the flows of capital to poorer countries that badly need them (Block, 1993)? The best answer is that private capital markets are currently doing a poor job of transferring useful capital to most poor countries. In fact, the net flow of capital to poorer countries is much smaller than is commonly realized. There are substantial two-way flows, but little net transfer of funds; and much of what does flow is short term and unstable (Block, 1993; Epstein, 1995; Epstein and Gintis, 1992). The citizens of Mexico as a whole did not benefit from the huge flow of mutual fund money that went their way (Danby, 1994; Grabel, 1995). What is needed is a much better public mechanism for capital transfers to poorer countries, not more unstable two way flows.

Second, won't controls drive financial business away from a country's financial centre and cost income, revenue and jobs? This threat is often highly exaggerated. Andrew Glyn argues that the City of London's dealings in sterling (as opposed to other business), actually brings in very little revenue to the UK. He notes that 'The City's contribution to the balance of payments is indeed invisible in more ways than one' (Glyn 1994, p. 196). But even if this financial business is lost, that may not be such a bad thing. Many financial sector jobs in the US and other financial centres are not by most accounts socially productive.[14] These clerks and MBA's could be much better used elsewhere in the economy. Indeed, that is one point in favour of capital controls: they can facilitate policies that will achieve a more socially rational use of physical and human resources.

There is evidence based on statistical analysis and case studies that suggests that capital controls can be effective, at least in the short to medium term. Marston (1995) shows that capital controls on outflows were effective in keeping domestic interest rates in Britain, France, and Germany below international levels in the 1960s and 1970s, before they were dismantled. Grilli and Milesi-Ferretti (1995), in a study of 61 developed and developing economies, find that countries with exchange and capital controls tend to have lower inflation adjusted interest rates than those that don't. Epstein and Schor (1992) report econometric work indicating that in the 1970s and early 1980s countries with capital controls tended to have lower unemployment rates. Manuel Pastor (1987) and James Boyce and Lyuba Zarsky (1989) both report econometric studies which suggest that capital controls reduced capital flight in the 1980s in a number of developing countries. Most of these studies refer to controls on outward flows. The International Monetary Fund report (IMF, 1995) on the experience of many countries with inward capital controls during the last five years or so found that such controls have been effective in stabilizing exchange rates and interest rates.

The strongest and most convincing evidence that relatively strict capital controls are not only technically feasible, but can be used successfully as a crucial component of a national interventionist strategy to achieve long term growth and stability has already been presented. The so-called 'economic miracles' of late 20th century capitalism – including Japan, South Korea, Germany and Sweden – all used capital controls in conjunction with a whole set of interventionist policies to achieve decades-long prosperity. These cases provide compelling evidence that controls, when implemented properly and embedded in a coherent national economic plan, can work brilliantly. Of course, progressive economists have no desire to simply replicate the Japanese and South Korean development experiences. The design and implementation of an effective long term interventionist growth plan requires a prior political 'contract' or agreement that forces all major class strata to accept the roles and responsibilities given to them in the plan. In both Japan and South Korea, this political commitment was imposed by force on the weaker classes by the stronger. Japan smashed labour's political power in the late 1940s (with the help of US occupation forces) while Korea 'still enforces tough anti-strike laws that go back to the years of military rule' (Tsuru 1993; Wall Street Journal, Oct. 20, 1995, p. A9A). We hope to see the enactment and\or threat of controls used to help democratically create the political preconditions required for the constitution of an effective and progressive economic programme. Unless and until working people can substantially reduce the economic and political power of rentiers and globally oriented industrialists, no such progressive economic programme will be possible. Capital controls can help solve this *political* problem. Whatever their other flaws, the experience of the 'economic miracle' countries demonstrates conclusively that there are no economic or technical impediments to the successful use of controls.

But haven't things changed? Aren't Japan, Korea and the other 'success stories' dismantling their controls? To some extent, they are. But, as we have stressed, the primary reasons are *political, not economic or technical.* An extremely interesting study by Daniele Checchi (1992) suggests one reason why even countries that have used controls effectively are retreating from them to some degree. In a careful econometric analysis he found that in two out of three countries he studied (that is, in Great Britain and Japan, but not in Australia) more intensive use of capital controls was associated with a higher labour share of income. Hence, capital controls, possibly by contributing to lower unemployment and more rapid economic growth, may have enhanced labour's power vis-a-vis industrial capital and rentiers.

The evidence reviewed here supports our thesis that capital controls are technically feasible, and that even comprehensive controls can be maintained for long periods of time with very positive effects on economic performance. Thus, as we see it, it is a mistake for the debate about controls on the left to continue to focus on their technical feasibility. That is not really in dispute even on the right: as *The Economist* put it recently, those 'who demand that the trend of global integration be halted and reversed, are frightening precisely because, *given the will, governments could do it*' (Oct. 7, 1995, p.16, emphasis added). Indeed, as we noted at the beginning of this essay, it is not at all clear that even if progressives fail to support capital controls they will stay off the political agenda. It is virtually inevitable that another financial earthquake such as global rentiers recently experienced in Mexico will erupt in the future, perhaps next time in the more dangerous form of a financial meltdown in a major country. One of these events is likely to trigger a demand for the reinstitution of controls by rentiers and industrialists. The left had best come to grips with the question of controls before they are unilaterally imposed on us by our political enemies.

It is often argued that the implementation of capital controls by a progressive government is self-defeating because capital will flee the country as soon as the policy is given serious political attention, before the controls can be implemented. There is some validity to this argument, but it applies as well to *any* serious policy proposal (such as low interest rates, higher taxes on the rich or tighter financial market regulation) perceived to be against the interests of rentiers. Should we abandon support of all progressive policies out of fear of such retribution? In any case, several considerations suggest that the problem may be manageable. If capital controls are part of a sensible, believable overall plan to raise the rate of economic growth and reduce economic uncertainty over the longer run, some holders of longer term real and financial assets might not see flight as their most profitable option. More important, the *sequence* in which various controls are introduced can affect the degree of severity of the problem. Suppose relatively moderate Keynes and Tobin taxes are introduced first. If more powerful controls are contemplated thereafter, they can be preceded by a substantial rise in the magnitude of these taxes. In the same vein, taxes on some transactions involved in the flight of capital can be applied retroactively, again limiting the gain from flight. And it is possible to enact *standby controls* in conditions where there is no immediate plan for their implementation. At some future time when more comprehensive controls are considered, the standby controls can be used without prior notice to prevent anticipatory capital flight. That is, under proper sequencing, the cost of flight can be raised just as the incentive to flee goes up.

In sum, these problems are indeed serious, but not in principle insurmountable. What remains most relevant is the potential contribution of capital controls to the economic success of a progressive full employment policy regime and their ability to change the political power of the contending classes.

Politically, the real question is whether it is likely to be possible for a democratically constituted majority coalition to wrest effective control over government economic policy in all its dimensions from rentiers and industrialists in the absence of controls or, at bare minimum, the credible threat of their implementation. That is, can the veto power over economic policy currently held by an increasingly powerful, arrogant and pitiless capitalist class be broken by working people without the use of controls? Is Andrew Glyn correct that the most effective way to solve the severe problems of the current conjuncture is for the working class to unilaterally agree to pay any and all costs that arrogant capital might demand for its permission to move the economy closer to full employment?

Our answers to these questions are clear. We believe it will not be possible to restore the political and economic position of working people to anything resembling their Golden Age status (never mind improving on it) unless we can successfully challenge the domestic political power of capital. Since one of the crucial pillars of capitalist power is the unrestricted freedom of rentiers and MNCs to roam the world in search of economic profit and political dominance, constraints on this freedom in the form of capital and trade controls are a necessary precondition for the creation of a more favourable class power balance. Without a substantial structural rise in the power of labour relative to capital, the hoped for constitution of a 'new deal' committing capital, labour and the state to the pursuit of sustained full employment, greater economic equality and a more adequate social welfare system may turn out to be nothing more than a dream. And if that turns out to be the case, if the neoliberal regime continues to deepen and strengthen, the cost to humanity may prove to be incalculable.

NOTES

1. We are grateful to Leo Panitch and Ilene Grabel for helpful comments on an earlier draft.
2. The term 'social contract' is used in this essay in a metaphorical rather than a literal sense. It refers to the multiplicity of laws, formal agreements, and informal arrangements, conventions and practices through which capital, labour and the state, or various segments thereof, coordinated their actions in pursuit of agreed-upon economic objectives. When in the course of this essay we argue in favour of the use of controls over international economic flows as a means to force capital to 'negotiate' a progressive new 'social contract' or a 'New Deal' with labour and the citizenry, we do not mean to limit our political vision to some grand national convocation of labour, capital and the state. A new 'social contract,' should one eventuate, is more likely to evolve from a wide range of economic and political agreements negotiated at various private and public sites.
3. However, the report maintained the IMF's strong opposition to controls on outflows.
4. See also the excellent collection of articles in Michie and Smith (1995), especially the chapters by Akyuz, Cornford and Kelly.
5. By global rentier class we mean national rentiers with an interest in the free flow of capital across borders. While such rentiers do not, strictly speaking, constitute a class, they do have important economic and political interests in common. Moreover, these common interests are institutionally represented by the World Bank, the IMF, and most of the central banks of the world.
6. For other discussions of the rise and fall of the Golden Age and the Bretton Woods System, see Block, 1977 and Marglin and Schor, 1990.
7. The discussion here draws very heavily on Henning (1994), Goodman and Pauly (1993), and especially Helleiner (1994).
8. A growing proportion of this increasing pool of public debt is held by nonresident rentiers. And government bonds held by foreigners have a much higher rate of turnover than bonds held domestically. Thus, 'the opinions of international bondholders have become increasingly important in countries with big public-sector debts. In recent years

bond markets have passed votes of no confidence [in the fiscal policy of] several heavily indebted governments, including those of Canada, Italy and Sweden.' Moreover, 'when the global capital market dislikes an economic policy it moves fast' (*The Economist*, Oct.7, 1995).

9. A recent *Wall Street Journal* article on the transfer of technology and high skilled jobs from the US to China by the Boeing Corporation noted that the cost to Boeing of equivalent labour in China and the US was $120 and $3,530 per month respectively (Oct. 10, 1995, p.1).
10. *The Economist*, Oct. 7, 1995. Glyn (1995, p. 48) reports that daily turnover is 'four times the total gross central bank intervention during the 1992 ERM crisis ($270 billion).'
11. Since small country governments are often tightly controlled by economic elites, it is not surprising that they normally permit themselves modes of evasion of their own capital controls. Controls are not in principle unenforceable. Consider for example the case of South Korea, where 'violations of prohibitions on overseas capital transfers were punishable by a minimum sentence of ten years in prison and a maximum sentence of death' (Grabel, 1995, 28–9). Since the Korean government was serious about enforcement, its controls were quite effective for decades.
12. As Baker, Pollin and Schaberg note in their Table 1, numerous industrialized countries have financial transactions taxes, including the U.S., which has a .0004% tax on stock sales. As discussed above, since domestic currency can also be borrowed and then sold abroad, deposit requirements or taxes on borrowing may also be required to get maximum effectiveness from the Keynes tax. But since a large portion of the run away funds will come from the sale of domestic financial assets, the Keynes tax should be reasonably effective even on its own.
13. The total number of countries included in the sample increased from 128 in 1975 to 153 in 1990 (Mathieson and Rojas-Suarez, p. 5, Table 1).
14. See Crotty and Goldstein, 1993, on the allocational inefficiency of US financial markets. Robert Fitch (1994) has vividly described how reliance on global and domestic banking, real estate and insurance has helped bring the city of New York to its knees.

## REFERENCES


Amsden, Alice, 1989. *Asia's Next Giant.* Oxford: Oxford University Press.

Baker, Dean, Robert Pollin, and Marc Schaberg, 1995. 'The Case for a Securities Transaction Tax: Taxing the Big Casino', Washington, DC: Economic Policy Institute, mimeo.

Banuri, Tariq and Juliet B. Schor, 1992. *Financial Openness and National Autonomy*. Oxford: Oxford University Press.

Bienefeld, Manfred, 1994. 'Capitalism and the Nation State in the Dog Days of the Twentieth Century', *The Socialist Register*, pp. 94–129.

Block, Fred L. 1977. *The Origins of International Economic Disorder*. Berkeley: University of California Press.

Block, Fred, 1993, 'Remaking Our Economy; New Strategies for Structural Reform', *Dissent Magazine*, Spring, pp. 166–171.

Bowles, Samuel, David Gordon and Thomas Weisskopf, 1990. *After the Wasteland.* Armonk, New York: M.E. Sharpe.

Boyce, James, and Lyuba Zarsky. 1988. 'Capital Flight from the Philippines, 1962–1986,' *The Journal of Philippine Development*, Vol. 15, No. 2 (1988), pp. 191–222.

Burke, James, 1996. 'The Effects of Foreign Direct Investment on Investment, Employment and Wages In the United States', mimeo. University of Massachusetts, Amherst.

Checchi, Daniele. 1992. 'Capital Controls and Distribution of Income: Empirical Evidence for Great Britain, Japan and Australia', *Weltwirtschaftliches Archiv*, 128, pp. 558–587.

Crotty, James, 1983. 'On Keynes and Capital Flight', *Journal of Economic Literature* Vol 21, pp. 59–65.

Crotty, James, 1993. 'The Rise and Fall of the Keynesian Revolution in the Age of the Global Marketplace', in Gerald Epstein, Julie Graham and Jessica Nembhard, eds. for the Center for Popular Economics, *Creating a New World Economy; forces of change and plans for Action.* Philadelphia: Temple University Press.

Crotty, James and Don Goldstein, 1993. 'Do U.S. Financial Markets Allocate Credit Efficiently?', in Dymski, Epstein and Pollin eds, *Transforming the US Financial System.* Armonk, New York: M.E. Sharpe, pp. 253–286.

Crotty, James, 1994. 'Are Keynesian Uncertainty and Macrotheory Compatible? Conventional Decision Making, Institutional Structures, and Conditional Stability in Keynesian Macromodels', in Robert Pollin and Gary Dymski, eds., *New Perspectives in Monetary Macroeconomics,* Ann Arbor: University of Michigan Press, pp. 105–42.

Danby, Colin, 1995. 'Constructing a Crisis: Mexican Financial Liberalization, 1989–1994', paper presented to the Eastern Economic Association, March, 1995.

Dornbusch, R. 1989. *Exchange Rates and Inflation.* Cambridge, Ma.: MIT Press.

Dymski, Gary, Gerald Epstein and Robert Pollin, eds. 1993. *Transforming the U.S. Financial System.* Armonk, NY: M.E. Sharpe.

Eichengreen, Barry, James Tobin and Charles Wyplosz, 1995. 'Two Cases for Sand in the Wheels of International Finance', *Economic Journal,* 105, January, pp. 162–172.

Epstein, Gerald A. and Juliet B. Schor, 'The Structural Determinants and Economic Effects of Capital Controls in the OECD', in Banuri and Schor, pp. 136–162.

Epstein, Gerald A., 'The Federal Reserve-Treasury Accord and the Construction of the Post-War Monetary Regime', *Social Concept,* forthcoming.

Epstein, Gerald A. and Herbert Gintis, 1992. 'International Capital Markets and the Limits of National Economic Policy', in Tariq Banuri and Juliet Schor, 1992, pp. 167–1987.

Epstein, Gerald A. 1995. 'International Financial Integration and Full Employment Monetary Policy', *Review of Political Economy,* Vol. No. 2, pp. 164–185.

Feldstein, Martin, 1994. 'Foreign Direct Investment and National Investment', NBER Paper.

Ferguson, Thomas, 1984. 'From Normalcy to New Deal: Industrial Structure, Party Competition, and American Public Policy in the Great Depression', *Industrial Organization,* Vol. 38, pp.41–94.

Fitch, Robert, 1994. 'Explaining New York City's Aberrant Economy', *New Left Review,* 207, pp. 17–48.

Glyn, Andrew, 1994. 'Market dual: jobs vs. currency', *New Economy.*

Glyn, Andrew, 1995. 'Social Democracy and Full Employment', *New Left Review,* 211, pp. 33–55.

Goodman, John B. and Louis Pauly, 1993. 'The Obsolescence of Capital Controls? Economic Management in an Age of Global Markets', *World Politics,* Vol. 46, Oct., pp. 50–82.

Grabel, Ilene, 1995. 'Marketing the Third World: The Contradictions of Portfolio Investment in the Global Economy', mimeo, Graduate School of International Studies, University of Denver.

Grilli, Vittorio and Gian Maria Milesi-Ferretti, 1996. 'Economic Effects and Structural Determinants of Capital Controls', IMF Staff Papers, forthcoming.

Helleiner, Eric, 1994. *States and the Reemergence of Global Finance.* Ithaca: Cornell University Press.

Henning, C. Randall, 1994. *Currencies and Politics in the United States, Germany and Japan.* Washington: Institute for International Economics.

Hobsbawm, Eric, 1994. *The Age of Extremes.* New York: Pantheon.

Hutton, Will, 1995. *The State We're In.* London: Jonathan Cape.

International Monetary Fund, 1995. *International Capital Markets; Developments, Prospects, and Policy Issues.* Washington: IMF.

Marglin, Stephen A and Juliet B. Schor, eds., 1990, *The Golden Age of Capitalism,* Oxford: Clarendon Press.

Marston, Richard C. 1995. *International Financial Integration; A study of interest differen-*

*tials between the major industrial countries*. Cambridge: Cambridge University Press.
Mathieson, Donald J. and Liliana Rojas-Suarez, 1993. *Liberalization of the Capital Account; Experience and Issues.* International Monetary Fund Occasional Paper 103. Washington, D.C.: International Monetary Fund, March.
Michie, Jonathan and John Grieve Smith, eds., 1995. *Managing the Global Economy*, Oxford: Oxford University Press.
Nembhard, Jessica Gordon, 1996. *Capital Control, Financial Regulation and Industrial Policy in South Korea and Brazil.* Westport, Ct: Praeger Publishers.
Pastor, Manuel, Jr. 1990. 'Capital Flight from Latin America'. *World Development*, Vol. 18, No. 1, pp. 1–12.
Schor, Juliet B., 1994. 'A Sustainable Economy for the 21st Century', New Party Papers, New York: New Party.
Tobin, James, 1978. 'A Proposal for International Monetary Reform', *Eastern Economic Journal*, 4, pp. 153–159.
Tobin, James, 1994. 'A Tax on International Currency Transactions', in United Nations, *Human Development Report*, p. 70.
Tsuru, Shigeto, 1993. *Japan's Capitalism: Creative Defeat and Beyond.* Cambridge: Cambridge University Press.
Zevin, Robert, 1992. 'Are World Financial Markets More Open? If so, why and with what effects?' in Banuri and Schor, pp. 43–84.

# THE CHALLENGE FOR TRADE UNIONISM: SECTORAL CHANGE, POOR WORK AND ORGANISING THE UNORGANISED

Anna Pollert

The subject of union survival in a climate of high unemployment, casualisation, and low labour movement morale is a child of the 1980s and 1990s. The decline of manufacturing, the former mainstay of trade unionism, has brought into sharp relief the urgency of securing collective organisation in the service economy – in maintaining it where it is established and extending it to the rapidly growing numbers of the unorganised. The case of Britain from 1979 to 1995 presents a stark scenario in which neo-liberal policy has encouraged multinational capital flight and de-industrialisation; the rise of a low-wage/low-skill service economy; the erosion of the state sector and introduction of market values and competition into public service; the further deregulation of an already unregulated labour market; and the disempowerment of trade unionism by a persistent stream of new legal restrictions.[1]

Within the overall context of high unemployment, government hostility towards trade unions, a string of new legal curbs on union activity, the dismantling of the state service sector and messianic zeal for labour market and wage deregulation, British unions face a formidable challenge. The most important of these is arguably trade union decline through the decimation of the organised (and mainly male) manufacturing base of the economy and expansion of the service sector based on women's low-paid, 'non-standard' jobs – a trend common throughout Europe (Bakker 1988, and more generally Jenson et al 1988)[2]. The proportion of part-timers among employees in Britain had grown to 28.2 per cent by 1993 (1993 Labour Force Survey) and the significance of women in this employment segment is illustrated by the fact that around 90 per cent of part-timers are women, while 44.3 per cent of British women employees work part time. The consequences of de-industrialisation and tertiarisation cannot be divorced from the wider problems of employers' exclusionary strategies towards trade unions. With regard to the object of this paper, the service sector, we therefore have to look both at the problems of maintaining union organisation where it already exists and is under increasing attack; and recruiting and organising the unorganised in the growth sectors of the economy.

Attention focuses first on the British experience of restructuring in the public service sector, especially the challenge to collective organisation posed by the new management strategies of employee participation, total quality and the like, which have proliferated across all economic sectors. In addition, however, the public sector is experiencing a specific attack on its traditionally centralised national system of industrial relations through employment restructuring implemented with the introduction of market disciplines and values. Fragmentation in the public sector is not, however, only a question of decentralised bargaining arrangements. It also adds to the growing numbers of exposed, isolated and casualised workers – a trend affecting the entire economy. Analysis therefore turns to some British examples of trade union attempts to organise the unorganised. In all these cases, a common theme is the need to reconsider the 'traditional' model of trade unionism as collective bargaining for full-time, male employees, and find ways of redrawing it as a recruiting and organising agent to mobilise other workers and their communities. A key thread in this discussion is gender and feminisation of the unions, and it must be stated at the outset that limits of space and time unfortunately eclipse other dimensions which should be incorporated into the analysis, such as race, ethnicity and age.

## PUBLIC SECTOR RESTRUCTURING AND THE CHALLENGE FOR TRADE UNIONISM

For workers in the public sector, privatisation and increasing emphasis on work and employment flexibility, blur the distinctions between public and private sectors, and between services and manufacturing. Across the economy, managements have attempted to marginalise trade union organisation by fragmenting it, creeping de-recognition of managerial strata, marginalisation of collective channels of consultation and negotiation, increasing use of personal contracts and performance appraisal, and by the use of various versions of engaging employee commitment to business goals such as employee share ownership, team working and total quality management. Free-market rhetoric has fetishised the customer: customer-supplier relations pervade the 'total quality' jargon of both the assembly line and service provision, while 'customer-care' is supposed to replace an older 'service ethic'. Both at the ideological level and in the increased pressures of budgetary measurements of work, there has been a convergence between the manufacturing and service sectors. This also opens a new area of shared experience for trade unionism.

The lived experience of trade unionism is that of cost-cutting, employment insecurity, labour intensification and increased corporate financial controls. The language of quality improvement, commitment, participation and devolution of responsibility has not, in general, 'won hearts and minds' because unequal power relations and conflicts of interest continue to confirm an us and them relationship in the workplace (Kelly and Kelly 1991, Guest and Dewe 1991). In manufacturing, there is also evidence for the resilience of shop floor control (Heaton and Linn 1989). But while 'new' systems, such as team working may not have succeeded in total union exclusion in some sectors and production systems, such as routine assembly, since trade unions have been able to exploit the shallowness of labels and the tensions and inefficiencies of such fads, workplace representatives nevertheless walk a constant tight-rope between maintaining control over new initiatives by negotiating within them, and propping up the system – thereby assisting their own demise (Pollert 1995). In the privatised public utilities, unions have also been able to subvert new management techniques: the language of total quality has highlighted deteriorating services, and the unions have been able to 'play with the resource implications of the quality message in their negotiations with the company' (Ferner and Colling 1991:401). Similarly, in retail, the shop workers' Union of Shop, Distributive and Allied Workers (USDAW), produced a policy statement, 'Retailing in the 1990s', arguing how 'customer care' programmes have implications for staffing levels, work loads and training, which employers must meet if they want quality service for customers (Heery 1993, IRS 1995).

The attempts by employers to neutralise, marginalise and exclude trade unions continues both openly and insidiously, and the danger remains of union incorporation and weakening in playing the partnership game. Debate continues among practitioners and academics as to whether union survival is best achieved by such social partnership with management, or by independence and opposition. Kelly (1995) makes a convincing case for the benefits of union militancy versus moderation (defined by five criteria of goals, membership resources, institutional resources, methods and ideology): partnership, he argues, is a chimeral aim in the face of overwhelming evidence of employers' hostility to unions per se. Gains from moderation in the 1980s were meagre, whether measured by membership increases or union influence and its extreme form eroded the willingness and capacity of members to challenge employers demands. Militant trade unionism which recognises the antagonism of the capitalist employment relationship and defends workers' interests builds on the only reliable foundation, namely its membership and their willingness to act (ibid.: 102) and has demonstrated membership increases in the 1980s, with the left-wing Fire Brigades Union showing Britain's second largest growth of 73 per cent between 1979 and 1992, the banking union, BIFU – an organisation which had become increasingly militant in the 1980s – coming next with a 17 per cent growth in this period (Kelly 1995: 92).

As part of the wider attack on trade unionism in the 1980s, there have been distinctive strategies directed at the formerly strong, nationally organised trade unionism of the public sector, which resulted from government policies specifically targeted at state employment. Since 1979, there has been a sustained government drive to privatise and introduce market mechanisms into the public sector. The strategy has been aimed at destroying national systems of tripartite consultation and regulation and fragmenting and weakening collective bargaining. How far, and in what ways, this has affected collective bargaining and trade unionism more widely, has been the subject of considerable debate in Britain. Looking across the spectrum from those industries actually privatised, to services still in state hands but increasingly operating under competitive imperatives, there is evidence that growing exposure to 'market discipline' is strengthening managerial prerogative and undermining a former consensus-forming pattern of public sector industrial relations. In the following, the main parameters of change in the British public sector since 1979 are outlined, and the signs of both union survival and weakening are discussed.

### *Privatisation of Public Services: Continuity or Radical Change in Industrial Relations?*

Privatisation has been a major plank of Conservative Party policy since it came to power in 1979. All the major state industries have been sold off: British Telecom (BT) in 1984, British Gas in 1986, British Airways in 1987, British Steel in 1988, the water industry in 1989, electricity distribution in 1991; and British Shipbuilders and the National Bus company were broken up and sold off piecemeal (Ferner and Colling 1991). The TUC survey of practices in privatised companies revealed major cut-backs in employment, deteriorating pay and conditions and worsening of industrial relations, including the break-up of national bargaining machinery in the water industry, removal of bargaining recognition from managerial staff in BT and major flexibility initiatives in gas and telecommunications. Whether these changes were due to privatisation, and how far similar practices were being enacted in the public sector is a moot point. But it is arguable that pressures to reduce staff numbers increased after privatisation to send the right kind of signals to financial opinion formers in the City (ibid.) At the same time, it appears that there are sectoral differences in managers' interpretations of these pressures, their response to competition, and their strategies towards industrial relations. Ferner and Colling (1991) identified differences between BT and British Gas, with the first more confrontational than the second, but both demonstrating a trend towards a duality in industrial relations, maintaining stability and continuity in their 'core' business, while using their new subsidiary activities as possible test-beds for non-union management. Strategies for union survival in the 'core', according to this analysis, must eventually face the challenge of organising the 'periphery' of the non-union, or poorly organised 'peripheral' businesses. The privatised water utilities present a different challenge for trade unions: here, the national industry was broken up into 10 water plcs and 25 water-only companies, which compete with each other on costs. In response to this pressure, managements decided to abolish national bargaining giving scope to the development of a variety of industrial relations and restructuring strategies – some committed to working with unions, others hostile, and some making a radical turn to subcontracting, and others maintaining in-house employment (O'Connell-Davidson 1993, Ogden 1994). This clearly fragments trade unionism, making it difficult to develop a concerted response to change.

### *Fragmentation and Marketisation of Public Services: Union Survival, Renewal or Death?*

In the (remaining) public services of local government, health and education, the introduction of market relations has brought a catalogue of changes. Public service restructuring took place in two phases: from 1979 to 1987, management reform included appointing managers with private sector experience, greater use of budgetary control and the introduction of performance related pay. After 1987, the more radical programme of developing a service market took place, with competing providers, cost cutting and 'value for money' budgeting with state provision depending on market outcomes (Bach and Winchester 1994:266). In 1991, an internal market was developed in the National Health Service, with 'purchasers' (district health authorities and doctors) separated from 'providers' (hospitals), which opted out of district health authority control as independent and competing National Health Service (NHS) Trusts, with flexibility to determine employment conditions, bargaining and consultation arrangements. Similarly, in education, local authority and teacher control has been eroded: the 1988 Education Reform Act devolved financial responsibility and staff management to school governing bodies, while schools now competed, with funding linked more directly to pupil numbers. Schools could opt out entirely from local authority control by seeking Grant Maintained Status and being funded directly by the state.

A first assault on public sector industrial relations was the abolition in 1981 of the concept of 'fair comparison' between occupational groups as one criterion of wage determination. Instead, in health, a nurses' pay review body was set up, while in education the tripartite teachers' Burnham Committee – originally established in 1960 – was abolished in 1987, after widespread industrial action in 1985–6, and replaced by unilateral powers by the Secretary of State to impose terms and conditions, modified only by some consultation (ibid.: 270). Yet marketisation of public services has caused its own organisational and managerial difficulties which may undermine government plans to weaken public sector consultation. Bach and Winchester (1994:271) point to the resilience of national pay determination, with objections to fragmentation not only from unions, but also from managers unable to cope with its disorganising impact, and from members of the very institutions set up to replace traditional consultative arrangements, such as the nurses pay review body, who themselves helped to set up new 'quasi-bargaining' forums. However, pessimists stress the degree to which fragmentation has occurred, especially to NHS Trusts as units of employment (Beadle 1995). Despite differences regarding the effectiveness of state policy to decentralise pay bargaining, most observers agree that, at the level of the workplace, staff reductions and the intensification of labour are key responses to public sector pay limits. The implications of such restructuring on the labour movement are ambiguous. In some cases, there has been a radicalisation of rank-and-file trade unionism. For example, in the summer of 1995, the normally conservative Royal College of Nurses voted for the first time to reverse its ban on industrial action, while teachers considered action against increasing class sizes. On the other hand service unions are always very wary of alienating public opinion, a fear which is readily exploited by the government and the media.

While most debate as to the continuities or disruption of national pay bargaining implies that fragmentation undermines trade union power, others have a more optimistic reading of events and suggest that, paradoxically, decentralisation of industrial relations to the workplace offers workers the chance to strengthen and democratise grass-roots organisation (Fairbrother 1995). Widening the area of analysis from pay negotiations to responses to work restructuring, the thesis is that while public sector trade unionism was formerly remote, centralised, bureaucratic and non-participatory (Fosh 1993) decentralisation is moving the centre of gravity from national leaders and consensus-building committees, to workplace representatives and local, more democratic forms of bargaining and trade unionism. Yet, while examples of possibly emerging union renewal are drawn from civil service and social services union branches, it is arguable that such optimism is based on specific sectors and occupations. A more sombre reading of public service fragmentation points to the dangers of parochial enterprise unionism emerging and division between stronger and weaker bargaining groups – particularly full-time male workers and women working part-time and on contracts – in a fragmented structure (Colling 1995, Colling and Ferner 1995). While Fairbrother provides the example of greater visibility of women's needs under new workplace-based bargaining in the civil service, with women's requests for an extension of part-time work with pay parity being satisfied, in other areas, such as cleaning and catering in the health and education sectors, there are many more examples of women service workers becoming more vulnerable than before, particularly as a result of the increasing trend to subcontract services.

The contracting out of services has increased in both manufacturing and services throughout the 1980s. But in the public sector, the introduction of Compulsory Competitive Tendering (CCT) in the 1988 Local Government Act was explicitly drawn up both to introduce market discipline and to minimise union presence and influence in the public sector (Colling 1995). The aim is both to cheapen labour, by making 'value for money' – usually translated into cost – the criterion in the tendering process, and increasing managerial prerogative, by severing the former links of union-management joint consultation over service provision into separate 'clients' and 'contractors', with the client 'service manager' dictating the quality and conditions of service. The impact of CCT on service provision has been to intensify labour and reduce employment, with membership loss for the unions. Although in the majority of cases, council workforces have been successful in retaining contracts for themselves (69 per cent of contracts went to 'in-house' direct service organisations, or DSOs in 1994), they have been under pressure to cut costs to beat outside competition, although they have not cut jobs as drastically as outside contractors (for example, LRD 1994a showed that on average, contractors cut 31 per cent of jobs in refuse collection, while DSOs cut 23 per cent).

The unions response to public sector workplace fragmentation has been slow and most resources and initiatives have remained at a centralised, national level (Colling and Ferner 1995). This has led to concentration on legal issues, such as the UK's version of the European Union's Acquired Rights Directive – the Transfer of Undertakings (Protection of Employment) Regulations (TUPE). Under union pressure, this was revised in 1993 to come into line with the European Court of Justice, so that employers had to protect terms and conditions upon take-over, including trade union recognition. While this has assisted workers, it is only of short-lived use for workers transferred to new employers, and of no help to those employed by DSOs. Nor is it a substitute for strategies towards workplace restructuring, which has been left to workplace trade unionism. Research on local responses to CCT (Colling 1995) in the early 1990s is less sanguine about the potential of decentralisation for union renewal than Fairbrother, revealing a patchwork of service managers' styles ranging from conciliatory to confrontational, while union response varied from a 'strained' form of participation, to one of opposition. It appears that CCT has provoked only defensive strategies, with no signs of proactive tactics. Moreover, the contracting process has clearly been divisive on gender lines: stronger, more centralised occupational groups, such as male full-time employees in refuse collection or ground maintenance, where levels of unionisation were already high, successfully defended their pay and conditions, while fragmented, part-time employees in cleaning and catering which were poorly unionised, and nearly all female, lost out, and suffered worsening conditions, shorter hours and less take-home pay. A 1993 study found increased casualisation and pressures undermining equal opportunities, since DSO managers 'felt that they could not afford to implement equality initiatives (LRD 1994a), while another (EOC 1995) revealed that women's overall employment fell by 22 per cent, while men's fell by the smaller 12 per cent since 1989 and in building cleaning, it fell by as much as 31 per cent (LRD 1995a). Women's earnings were reduced by 25 per cent as a result of cuts in hours, and some even suffered basic pay rate cuts where local bargaining was implemented (LRD 1995a).

While there are sound arguments for transforming the remote, bureaucratic nature of centralised bargaining, the potential for union renewal through more democratic, less centralised trade unionism needs to be highly sensitive to the gendered segregation of service work and the problems of fragmentation and weak bargaining strength.

## POOR WORK AND ORGANISING THE UNORGANISED

Both the political and managerial premium placed on a 'flexible workforce' during the 1980s have made visible the previously invisible but vast contribution of casualised, feminised 'poor work' to capital accumulation – from early industrialisation, to the nineteenth century, and now globally (Berg 1985, Rowbotham 1994, Mitter 1994). There has also been an increase in low-paid and non-standard employment everywhere, and in Britain, women part-time workers accounted for half of the low-paid[3] in 1991 (Rubery 1995: 547). The tertiarisation of the economy together with the rise of non-standard employment have impressed on many trade unions the urgency of organising the unorganised. Legal action to improve employment protection and confront low pay, including use of equal value legislation to increase womens pay, is an important element of union strategy to help the unorganised. However, it is not a substitute for collective organisation. Unfortunately, there is ample evidence of the poor inroads of trade unionism into 'non-standard' and fragmented employment, which is partly a result of deliberate government attempts to isolate the unionised sector (ibid.: 543). The evidence for part-time workers' unionisation in Britain is not encouraging. A survey of part-time workers' representation in trade unions in 1993 found it was lower than their representation in the labour force and did not reflect their increasing numbers (LRD 1993): they accounted for only 16 per cent of the combined membership of the 20 largest TUC unions, compared with 28 per cent of the workforce. Moreover this showed a relative decline compared with a similar survey in 1989, which had found they comprised 17 per cent of TUC membership compared with 25 per in employment. This deterioration was also reflected at the aggregate level of union density as a percentage of employees, which showed that, while part-time workers' density had held steadier than full-time workers', it showed a decline after 1992 (Table 1).

*Table 1.* Union density (%) by full/part time working 1989–94.

| | *No. of workers covered (1994)* | *Density* | | | | | |
|---|---|---|---|---|---|---|---|
| | | *89* | *90* | *91* | *92* | *93* | *94* |
| Full-time | 16.1m | 43 | 42 | 42 | 40 | 39 | 36 |
| Part-time | 5.4m | 22 | 21 | 22 | 22 | 21 | 20 |

*(Source: 1994 Labour Force Survey; in LRD 1995b).*

There has been a similar slight decline in all women employees union density, which, having remained steady at 32 per cent through the 1990s, dipped in 1994 to 30 per cent (Table 2).

*Table 2.* Union density (%) by sex 1989–94.

| | *No. of workers covered (1994)* | *Density* | | | | | |
|---|---|---|---|---|---|---|---|
| | | *89* | *90* | *91* | *92* | *93* | *94* |
| All | 21.5m | 39 | 38 | 37 | 35 | 35 | 33 |
| Men | 11.2m | 44 | 43 | 42 | 39 | 38 | 36 |
| Women | 10.3m | 33 | 32 | 32 | 32 | 31 | 30 |

*(Source: 1994 Labour Force Survey; in LRD 1995b).*

Although less steep than the decline for men – from 39 to 36 per cent – it was particularly worrying as women's percentage of all employees continued to creep up to 49.2 per cent by 1993 (LRD 1994a:9; figures based on 1993 Labour Force Survey).

The low unionisation of part-time workers and women is echoed in the small firm sector, and, indeed, there is likely to be considerable overlap between 'non-standard', women's and fragmented work. In 1993–94, union density in the small firm was 12 per cent in those employing less than eleven employees, and 26 per cent in those with 11 to 50 employees (1994 Labour Force Survey, LRD 1995b). Yet the potential for unionisation may be considerable; as indicated earlier, some 43.3 per cent of service employees worked in firms employing fewer than 20 employees, where, according to a recent survey (Abbott 1993) not all employers reported hostility to union recognition. Admittedly, most (39.9 per cent) would resist their employees setting up a union, but a significant 30.9 per cent said they would accept requests for union recognition – although stated intention should be treated with caution. Yet of considerable concern was the finding of employees' resistance to unionisation: across all occupations covered in the survey, from advertising and marketing, to computer services, secretarial training, and the restaurant, public house and wine bar sector, over half employees interviewed reported they would not join a trade union, suggesting that they either felt they could manage without one, or that trade unions as they perceived them, could not help them.

The above study obviously covered a wide range of employees, from skilled professionals to routine service workers; but it does underline the need for unions to find ways of connecting with small employment units. Narrowing the problem to the low-paid end of the spectrum, the challenge facing unions in recruiting and organising involves overcoming two main obstacles to change: one is the image of trade unionism as white, male and directed at full-time, permanent workers. The other is the practical difficulty of reaching workers, recruiting them, organising them, gaining union recognition and retaining them. Obviously, the two go hand in hand; for unless the culture of trade unionism alters to appeal to the unorganised, there will be little success in winning support.

### *The male union image and feminising the unions*

Women's under-representation in the top decision making bodies of trade unions is one barrier to altering the climate of trade unions. In Britain, although 12 of the 56 seats on the TUC General Council are reserved for women, only some unions have reserved seats on their national executives, and in only three unions is women's representation on the national executive close to their proportion of membership (the General, Municipal and Boiler Makers Union, the GMB; the Manufacturing, Science and Finance union, MSF; and the shopworkers' union, USDAW; LRD 1994c). Women's worst representation is among full-time officials (FTOs): in

1993, only four out of 68 TUC union general secretaries were women, and in none of the top 10 unions did the proportion of women FTOs – either nationally or regionally – reflect the numbers in membership. Thus, in UNISON, now Britain's largest union with 1,400,000 members since the merger of three major public sector unions in 1993, only 20 per cent of senior national officials are women compared with 68 per cent of the membership (LRD 1994c). The situation improves, but is not much better, as one goes down the FTO hierarchy to the branch or workplace. There have been attempts to offset this deficit with the creation of national women's and equality officers in 7 of the 10 top unions, while some, such as UNISON, have set targets for women to comprise 30–40 per cent of senior FTOs by the end of the century.

Clearly, one cannot simply assume that the presence of women at senior and FTO levels in unions will automatically mean that women's issues will be raised, or that the culture and image of unions will change. Research has demonstrated the difficulties, senior women union officers faced, especially when trying to raise womens issues, in the meetings behind closed doors where policy decisions were really shaped – even though many unions were now presenting a far more women-friendly face publicly (Dorgan and Grieco, 1993). Pressure to conform to the conventional male image was expressed as gaining respect, while local women FTOs saw their senior sisters gradually incorporated into a men's trade union world where it was hard to pursue a women's agenda: thus, although Women's National Officers could legitimately pursue womens and equal opportunity interests, General Secretaries were regarded as having a responsibility to 'all members' – a 'unisex' model with male gendered undertones - even though female union recruitment is arguably the major priority for union survival.

Greater numbers of women at senior, paid-officer levels would arguably shift the balance in their favour and there is evidence of an upsurge in female recruitment to FTO level during the 1980s. A study of women FTOs (Heery and Kelly 1988) found that 59 per cent had been recruited to these posts during the 1980s, suggesting some positive steps were being taken to redress their under-representation. However, the initiative appeared to be women's rather than the unions', with only one fifth of the FTO sample reporting that their unions had policies to encourage more women bargainers, while only one sixth said their union was actively looking for a women to do their job when they were appointed. Union recruitment practices therefore display limited commitment to positive action to reverse existing imbalances. Moreover, most women officials tended to work in certain types of unions – mainly in those with large numbers and percentages of women members – and even in many of these, the percentage of women FTOs fell far below the membership percentage.

If a small number of women at very senior union levels become isolated and overpowered, a key question is whether more women FTOs throughout the union organisation have different agendas from the majority of male colleagues who, as some have argued, pursue strategies which maintain male privileges over women (Cockburn 1985). Heery and Kelly's research established first that the majority of the women FTOs studied felt the fight for women's equality was central to the labour movement, 88 per cent saying they took a special interest in women's issues such as equal pay, parental leave, sexual harassment, women's health, problems of part-time workers and low pay, regardless of whether they served a predominantly female membership or not, and most felt their priorities differed from men's. This was borne out by more detailed comparisons between what men and women FTOs regarded as 'women's issues in collective bargaining' – women having a much broader conception, including the integration of paid and domestic labour (Heery and Kelly 1988: 495). Further, only 13.3 per cent of male FTOs saw these as a major priority; if however, bargaining issues could be presented in a gender blind way, such as 'help for the low paid', over 60 per cent of male FTOs saw this as a priority. In sum, the evidence suggests that the priorities of FTOs are gender related, and that union feminisation would alter both the image and the practice of unions.

In terms of women FTOs effectiveness, it is significant that just 76 per cent said their jobs allowed them to pursue women's interests, suggesting that the rest could not, echoing again the pressures to 'conform' of more senior women officers. Nevertheless, the field study observing women FTOs through collective bargaining processes did identify success in pursuing issues such as equal pay, where male colleagues were less enthusiastic – although the authors caution that they also observed male FTOs pressing for 'women's issues' – arguably because of the growing influence of feminist ideas in the labour movement (Heery and Kelly 1988: 498). Despite this, it appeared that there was a difference in the work routines of women and men, with more women (almost half) prioritising organising and recruitment rather than routine office work and conducting negotiations, than men (less than a third). More women FTOs also guided lay representatives and attended branch meetings. While the above could simply reflect that women FTOs tended to work in unions where recruitment had to be a priority because membership organisation was weak – and therefore that they were following union policy, rather than a woman's agenda – it is difficult to separate the two. As Heery and Kelly (1988) conclude, since the recruitment of women to unions is a priority for union renewal, the role of women in promoting women's causes in collective bargaining, as well as their emphasis on organising, underlines the importance of feminising the unions, since the gender of officers does seem to make a difference to their priorities.

The above discussion, while highlighting the connections between the gendering of trade unions and their culture and orientation, should not be over-stretched as a simplistic equation with feminisation of the unions and a new womens agenda and culture. Clearly, there are divisions among women FTOs and lay members on numerous criteria, including those based on whether they are newly active or with previous experience, and on various union allegiances and priorities. There may also be divisions among union activists between old and young, not to mention links based on ethnicity, nationality and so forth, which transcend sexual division. This said, the power and influence of women in unions is arguably one vital strand towards making trade unions more inclusive, less sectionally divisive, and as concerned with recruitment and organisation as with collective bargaining.

Several case studies of different unions' attempts to address the needs of 'non-standard' workers and recruit the unorganised reiterate the need to establish a recruitment culture at the grass roots. They chart the problems encountered both in the external environment, such as high labour turnover of 'non-standard' workers, and employers' recognition refusals, as well as internal barriers to change – not least the reluctance of both FTOs and lay union workers to activate an organising trade unionism.

## UNION RECRUITMENT DRIVES: CASE STUDIES

### *1. The Union of Shop, Distributive and Allied Workers (USDAW) Recruitment Drive in the late 1980s*

USDAW's recent attempt to recruit shop workers demonstrates the many difficulties confronting a union attempting to organised a fluctuating, largely part-time and fragmented labour force; the potential opportunities provided by concentration in retailing; and the barriers to unionisation where access to the workplace is denied by employers. Union organisation among Britains 3.2 million retail and wholesale workers was only 11.7 per cent in 1990 – a decline from 13.46 per cent in 1982 (Upchurch and Donnelly 1993:61).[4] Between 1980 and 1990 USDAW lost 20 per cent of its members; partly during the recessionary slump of the early 1980s, when both sector employment and recruitment dropped, but also because membership declined faster than the drop in employment from 1988–1990. The sector has major problems for union organisation: half the 2.1 million retail workers are in family or single-employer shops; a high proportion of workers are part-time (25 per cent of union members are part-time); and turnover is extremely high, so that the union must annually recruit one third of its membership merely to stand still.

Although traditionally regarded as a moderate union, following a national leadership change in 1986, USDAW adopted a more campaigning style, with a prioritisation of recruitment activity for FTOs, and several issue campaigns, such as a campaign against Sunday trading, and a Part-Time Workers' Charter. However, research on the effectiveness of the campaigns revealed a contrast between successful recruitment in already unionised workplaces, and failure to penetrate non-union areas. Thus, where there were concrete examples of effective workers defence on local issues in already unionised workplaces, such as countering attempts to force up working hours in two London West-End stores, union recruitment as a result was successful (Upchurch and Donnelly 1992). Similarly, a number of successful equal-value pay claims in unionised retail supermarket chains between women checkout staff and male warehouse staff brought advances to the union in unionised workplaces including invitations to join job-evaluation panels, provision of check-off facilities, as well as encouraging recruitment campaigns elsewhere (ibid.: 67). However, hopes that the creation of large supermarkets would necessarily assist union organisation were disappointed: in some cases, unionisation in such workplaces was successful – but this was arguably due to the transfer of already unionised workers to these premises. In new shopping-malls, where stores were unwilling to offer recruitment facilities, the presence of security officers obstructed access to union workers.

On the other hand, despite the difficulties of generating a 'recruitment culture' in unions generally, it appears that USDAW's focus on this activity bore some fruit: one fifth of new members in 1991 were a result of organisers' direct efforts. The importance of locally relevant issues for recruitment was also revealed: while USDAW attempted to target key groups such as women and young workers with particular campaigns, it appears the mobilisation has only been successful where a local campaigning issue arose, such as the outbreak of Legionnaires' Disease in a number of London's West End shops in 1989, when membership in smaller shops rose by 20 per cent. Considering the major obstacles to collective organisation of temporary and part-time work, and a young workforce unfamiliar with trade unionism, USDAW has been quite successful in simply stopping a landslide of union membership.

### *2. The Transport and General Workers' Union (TGWU) Link Up Campaign*

The Link Up campaign, like the TUC's 'Union Yes' campaign, was largely inspired by the US example of increasing emphasis on targeted recruitment campaigns, following the critical decline in membership in the early 1980s. Its declared aim was to reach the unorganised in the frontiers of trade unionism – part time, contract and temporary workers, particularly since

TGWU membership had declined by 34 per cent between 1979 and the start of the campaign in 1987. Whether the Link Up campaign succeeded either in the short term, in increasing TGWU membership, or in the longer term, in altering the union's culture and mobilising its full-time officers and lay members behind the recruitment campaign are the two issues to examine (Snape 1994).

The first stages of the campaign were aimed at convincing those inside the union of the need to prioritise recruitment and involved the establishment of a National Co-ordinating Committee, Regional Organisers reporting local progress, a Link Up 'Organiser's Pack' for lay activists which included a TGWU Charter for Temporary and Part Time Workers, and a model collective agreement. It aimed to address community and welfare issues and the union organised a conference to discuss them in 1987. To counteract the male, white, middle aged image of the union, Regional Women's Advisory Committees, as well as Regional Race Advisory Committees were set up, and a National Women's Secretary and an Equalities National Officer were appointed to promote equal opportunities. A national youth conference and national officer responsible for youth affairs were established, and in 1991, advisory youth forums were set up at regional and national levels. Agriculture, construction, commercial and road transport and public services were the major targets in the first phase of Link Up in 1988, with a schedule of quarterly trade group meetings on recruitment campaigns. Phase Two of the campaign, started in 1989, aimed both to consolidate existing membership and continue to recruit part-time and temporary workers, with the emphasis on health and safety, training and equal opportunities. Again, national and local events were organised on equal opportunities, child care and Health and Safety, and card inspection and membership audits were conducted for branches and workplaces to involve branch secretaries and shop stewards in a bid for 100 per cent membership. In 1990 the union announced a further two year programme, including a national 'Recruit-a-Mate' campaign. Regions selected their own targets, combining a mixture of extending membership where there was already union recognition and entering virgin territory.

However, evaluation of the campaign by the union in the early 1990s endorsed Kelly and Heery's (1994) findings on the low priority given to recruitment by FTOs and revealed problems in developing a 'recruitment culture' among officers. Among lay union activists the experience was mixed, with some reporting small 'core' teams as effective recruiters, while others displayed a pattern of disillusion after meeting with indifferent responses to their efforts. Although there were some successes, such as the recruitment of contract cleaners in the North West area, Link Up's declared aim in terms of membership growth was disappointing in terms of failing to halt annual membership decline, with the outflow of members greater than the inflow, although this improved in the late 1980s. Many officers interviewed by Snape saw the problem of union decline more in terms of membership loss through high turnover, than recruitment failure: 'peripheral' workers could be recruited but could not be retained since isolation and small numbers prevented the consolidation of collectivism. Thus, as Link Up continued in 1990, retention became more of an issue than recruitment. This was addressed at a number of levels, including reduced membership dues for the unemployed and offering financial and legal advice services. However, it appears that Link Up failed in a widespread winning of recognition deals.

A number of factors inhibited the success of this campaign; external factors – the rate of unemployment, problems of reaching small, isolated workplaces and employees on diverse, fragmented shifts and a hostile political economic climate – all figure. At the same time, as another study argued (Hudson 1989), factors internal to the union must be addressed: these included not only financial and time constraints on full-time and lay officers, but hindrances to the long term aims of the campaign in changing the culture of the TGWU from its traditional manufacturing, male, full-time worker model to one responsive to the contemporary employment. Hudson's research suggested that, although the campaign organised events, set up institutions and committees targeted at specific groups such as women and youth, and produced publicity material, there seemed insufficient provision for local organisers to creatively respond to local issues. Standardised 'packages' and big events did not necessarily connect with issues on the ground which could have mobilised and empowered people. Shortage of resources may have been a major obstacle, but it appears that an over-centralised, standardised strategy here replicates the problems discussed regarding the slow response of public sector unions to fragmentation in the public service sector.

### *3. Organising the Unorganised: Race and Poor Work*

A third case study charts the experience of the TGWU in a specific local recruitment campaign of ethnic minority women cleaners at London's Heathrow Airport in 1990 (Wrench and Virdee 1995). The problems already raised in relation to unions becoming more women-friendly in terms of developing a recruitment and organising culture and responding to womens specific needs are overlaid in the case of minority women with the critical need for involvement in locally based communities.

The processes of migration have made ethnic minority women one of the largest groups of vulnerable workers across the world. Trade union responses to ethnic minorities in Britain have been through several phases since the post-Second World War entry of commonwealth immigrants, from racism, to a policy of equal treatment at a time when both sex-blind and race-blind approaches to trade unionism prevailed, to the beginnings in the late 1970 and early 1980s, of more pro-active policies to combat racial discrimination and address ethnic minority needs, whether of language, rights of dress or other issues (Wrench and Virdee 1995). Recently, despite the fact that the first generation of Asian and West Indian workers had an above average propensity to join unions, unions have begun to pay greater attention to the recruitment of minority workers, partly because second generation workers no longer display any particular predilection towards unionisation (possibly because of negative experiences), but also because of the swelling numbers of under-unionised ethnic minority/migrant workers in the unregulated sweat shop and service sector.

The recruitment drive by the TGWU of mainly female South Asian cleaners at Heathrow can hardly be called a success story: in two years, union membership rose from six to fifty – just five per cent of the total of 1000 workers. Beside the hostile political environment and demobilising trade union legislation which inhibited better organised workers at Heathrow from taking solidarity action to defend the more vulnerable, external difficulties included the employers' refusal to grant union recognition and the union's inability to organise at the workplace, which forced recruitment tactics into a time consuming door-to-door effort. The cleaners' shift work, long hours and often second jobs to supplement their low pay, made them more intractable during home visits. However, Wrench and Virdee (1995) also point to avoidable organisational errors, such as the failure to hold a single branch meeting of the fifty new recruits, the replacement of the special officer for the cleaners by another who had to share his time between the cleaners and another group, and the unwillingness of the local branch to take special measures for Asian workers: the local branch office was all-white, and there had been no co-operation with the local Asian community.

Following a review of the campaign, it appears that some lessons had been learned and the local TGWU began working with the Indian Workers' Association. However, Wrench and Virdee also highlight some of the potential difficulties encountered where co-operation between a trade union and a community organisation is attempted. The example is drawn from a strike for union recognition at a metal-finishing sweat-shop subcontractor to the motor industry, Burstall, in the West-Midlands in 1992 – 1993, led by the General, Municipal and Boiler Workers' Union (the GMB). After sustained picketing for two years, the fight was lost, largely because workers in other firms failed to boycott Burstall's products, both through apathy and intimidation by laws against secondary action preventing the boycotting of goods, while a mass picket of the firm itself was rejected by the union on the grounds that it would have exposed it to major fines – (British picketing laws have made mass pickets illegal). In the context of the paralysing effect of anti-union legislation under the Conservative Government, this strike highlighted the tactical and organisational problems of operating within the law, or outside it. The ensuing bitter attack by local Asian support groups, including the Indian Workers' Association, on the GMB for 'betraying' the workers by confining its action to remain within the law, demonstrated the divisive impact of such legislation on co-operation. The union, on the other hand, pointed out it had paid strike pay, managed to get entitlement to social security benefits for the strikers and done all it could. Breaking the law would have threatened the union with sequestration of its funds rather than the support groups'. The community group, on the other hand, argued that unless workers began to challenge such laws, they would remain disempowered. In general, while both of these cases point to the importance of community support for union recruitment and recognition drives, they also depressingly illustrate how the increase in 'poor work' creates major obstacles for organisation in a hostile union legal framework which encourages selfish insularity among better organised groups and intimidates solidaristic behaviour, and poses a genuine threats to union finances. It also points to the need to develop the political means to challenge the state.

## CONCLUSIONS

The discussion of both the public and the private service sectors has returned to the consistent theme of decentralisation and fragmentation of employment and bargaining units and the rise of 'non-standard' and poor work. The evidence on the British union response suggests that attempts are being made to confront this situation, not necessarily for the moral reasons of greater sensitisation to the needs of the unorganised who, while increasing in numbers, have always been there, but for very basic reasons of union survival. In some unions there have been attempts to move the agenda away from the male, full-time, manufacturing model – but successes in organisation and recruitment have been equalled and probably outnumbered by failures.

As the last two cases illustrate, the strategies needed to organise casualised work transcend sectoral boundaries. Whatever their inadequacies, the recognised and established organisations of the labour movement are essential for the organisation of the unorganised. As Mitter (1994: 32) found, successful alternative strategies of organisation, such as the Self-Employed Women's Association in India, or co-operatives, have been in areas where the trade union movement is strong, which points to the need to strengthen existing labour movement institutions, as well as seeking new forms of organising. She also points out that the most self-critical and imaginative union developments have been in Canada, both in terms of affirmative action to increase the numbers of women in leading union posts, in integrating more women and family-friendly issues, such as equal pay and opportunities and child care, into mainstream union concerns, and in working with communities. Briskin (1994) outlines in more detail Canadian unions' strategies such as the Canadian Auto Workers' store-front workers' centre to attract non-union workers and possibilities of establishing union centres which are based in communities as well as workplaces, to respond to the reality that many people's employment fluctuates between workplaces, as it does between employment and unemployment.

In the context of such a 'leading-edge' free market state as Britain, debate continues as to whether trade unionism has weathered the storm, or is undergoing terminal decline. Whether one takes sides with the pessimists, or the optimists, several questions of union strategy have emerged. One is the issue of union centralisation and decentralisation. This has arisen in the context of public sector trade unionism, which, unlike the decentralised pattern increasingly typical of British manufacturing – and the norm in North America – has been centralised on national bargaining lines. The evidence regarding its fragmentation, as a result of privatisation and marketisation, is uneven, with some pointing to the resilience of national pay bargaining, and others, the increase in single-employer bargaining and fragmented industrial relations. Within this framework of unevenness, there has been debate as to whether fragmentation augurs union 'renewal or rigor mortis' (Colling 1995): some have pointed to the potential of workplace democracy and participation posed by management decentralisation as a welcome challenge to a former over-centralised, bureaucratic and distant form of national industrial relations system. Others stress the exposure of vulnerable groups to casualisation in a divisive development in which there may be winners – the well organised – but only at the expense of the losers. It seems that there is something to be learned from both these positions, and to equate centralisation with non-participatory trade unionism may be misleading: certainly, there is evidence that a turn to workplace bargaining in the service sector may degenerate into parochial enterprise-unionism, leaving part-time, subcontract and isolated workers – especially women and ethnic minorities – out in the cold (Colling and Ferner 1995). This suggests that the unions' policy of defending a broad-based, national bargaining system against the attempts to fragment it are in labour's interests. At the same time, this is not to condone over-centralised, bureaucratic trade unionism. New forms of democratic participation are not an optional extra if the values of collectivism are to survive the challenges of a managerial agenda of participation in the form of business values and individualism.

It is here that the analysis of maintaining union organisation in the unionised sector meshes with the wider concerns of redefining trade unions in order to make them relevant for 'non-standard' employees in 'poor work'. The question of feminising the unions, both in response to the feminisation of the labour force, and as a force to alter the organisational culture and priorities of trade unions has been a significant theme of this paper. Unless trade unions alter their image of white, male, middle aged manufacturing workers, they will have little appeal to women, people of colour, the young, part-time, temporary workers and other workers. But the problem is not just one of image: unions need to defend their existing members, but also change from a negotiating culture, to one of recruitment and organisation. As we saw, this is proving a very long-term task; pressure from women, minorities and others will have to be sustained to effect change. But as well as attitudinal and organisational problems, under-resourcing remains a constant barrier to change. In these circumstances, devising simple, imaginative means of organisation will undoubtedly need to draw on local resourcefulness, which, in turn, would lead to a more inclusive democratic model of trade unionism, in which workers and their communities had real input into the agenda.

## NOTES

1. Dickens (1988) analyses the ways in which most non-standard workers fall through the safety net of Britain's limited employment protection. For a discussion of British employment and industrial relations legislation in the context of Western Europe, see Hyman 1994. For details of British legislation since 1979, see Dickens and Hall 1995.
2. Trade union decline has been the main trend in Europe from the end of the 1970s and accelerating during the 1980s, particularly in the private sector. (Sweden, Finland and Norway avoided it by an expansion of the public sector, and Denmark, by the unions' involvement in unemployment insurance administration: Visser 1994: 82). Germany, Austria and Switzerland remained stable, but Britain, France, Ireland, the Netherlands, Spain and Portugal experienced severe decline. By 1994, Britain's aggregate union density had fallen to 33 per cent. Disaggregation by gender reveals the major drop in male union density in the total: while this was 66.9 per cent in 1979, it fell by 30.9 per cent to 36 per cent in 1994. Women's union density in 1979 was only 40.4 per cent, but fell by only 10.4 per cent to 30 per cent in 1994 (Employment Gazette 103, no. 5, May 1995). This underlines the importance of major secroral restructuring and the loss of former male manufacturing union strong-holds.

   The picture for the service sector is worrying given the decline of public sector employment from 27 to 22 per cent of the labour force between 1971 and 1991 (Thompson and Beaumont 1978 and Economic Trends 1991). While high membership density in the public sector continues, with, for instance, 75 per cent of energy and water workers, 86 per cent of posts and telecommunications, and 70 per cent of local government employees unionised in 1990, in private services, with the exception of the well organised banking, finance and insurance sector (53 per cent employees unionised), it is extremely low. In 1990, there was 3 per cent union density in hotels, catering and repairs, 11 per cent in business services and 25 per cent in retail distribution (Main indicators of union presence by industry, 1990, Table 3A, in Millward et al 1992). Furthermore, this data covered only workplaces employing 25 or more workers; the low figures for many parts of the service sector are likely to overestimate union density, since many employees in the service sector (43.3 per cent in 1987) work in firms with fewer than 20 employees (Abbott 1993).

3. Low pay defined by £3 per hour, or the legal minimum wage as defined by wages councils in 1991, or 60 per cent of median earnings.
4. Source USDAW Annual Reports, which gives only USDAW membership and is therefore lower than 25 per cent density for retail in 1990 in Millward et al 1992, which includes other unions.
5. Kelly and Heery (1994) found that FTOs (with the sample dominated by men) considered that negotiating better pay and conditions for existing members was more important than recruiting new members: 55 per cent ranked higher basic pay as their priority, compared with 21 per cent citing recruitment and 11 per equal opportunities. In other words, they were more responsive to members as 'economic insiders' pressing for better pay and conditions, than to top union policies, which emphasised recruitment, or to 'economic outsiders on the periphery of the labour market'.

## REFERENCES


Abbott, B. 1993 'Small firms and trade unions in services in the 1990s' *Industrial Relations Journal*, Vol. 24, No. 4, Dec., 308 – 317.

Ackers, P., Smith, C. and Smith, P (eds.) 1996 *The New Workplace and Trade Unionism*, London: Routledge.

Bach, S. and Winchester, D, 1994 'Opting Out of Pay Devolution? The Prospects for Local Pay Bargaining in UK Public Services' *British Journal of Industrial Relations*, Vol. 32., No. 2, 263 – 282.

Bakker, I. 1988 'Women's Employment in Comparative Perspective' in J. Jenson et al (eds.).

Berg, M. 1985 *The Age of Manufacturers 1700–1820*, London: Fontana.

Beadle, R. 1995 'Opting out of Pay Devolution? The prospects of local pay bargaining in UK Public Services: A Comment' *British Journal of Industrial Relations*, Vol. 33, No. 1, 137 – 142.

Briskin, L. 1994 'Equity and Economic Restructuring in the Canadian Labour Movement', *Economic and Industrial Democracy*, Vol. 15, No. 1, 89 – 112.

Cockburn, C. 1985 *Machinery of Dominance*, London: Pluto Press.

Colling, T. 1995 'Renewal or rigor mortis? Union responses to contracting in local government', *Industrial Relations Journal*, Vol. 26, No. 2, 134 – 145.

Colling,T. and Ferner, A. 1995 'Privatization and Marketization' in P. Edwards (ed.).

Dickens, L. 1988 'Falling through the net: employment change and worker protection', *Industrial Relations Journal*, vol. 19, Summer, 139–153.

Dickens, L. and Hall, M. 1995 'The State: Labour Law and Industrial Relations' in P. Edwards 1995 (ed.).

Dorgan, T. and Grieco, M 1993 'Battling Against the Odds: the emergence of senior women trade unionists', *Industrial Relations Journal*, Vol. 24, No. 2, June, 151 – 164.

Economic Trends, 1991, No. 458, December, p.98, London: HMSO..

Edwards, P. (ed.) 1995 *Industrial Relations: Theory and Practice in Britain*, Oxford: Blackwell.

EOC 1995 *The gender impact of CCT in local government*, Escott, K. and Whitfield, D., Centre for Public Services, Manchester: Equal Opportunities Commission.

Fairbrother, P. 1995 'Workplace trade unionism in the state sector' in P. Ackers, C. Smith and P. Smith (eds.).

Ferner, A. and Colling, T. 1991 'Privatisation, Regulation and Industrial Relations', *British Journal of Industrial Relations*, 29:3, 390 – 409.

Fosh, P. 1993 'Membership Participation in Workplace Unionism: the Possibilities of Union

Renewal', *British Journal of Industrial Relations*, Vol. 31, No. 4, 577 – 592.

Guest, D. E. and Dewe, P. 1991 'Company or Trade Union: Which Wins Workers' Allegiance? A Study of Commitment in the UK Electronics Industry' *British Journal of Industrial Relations*, Vol. 29, No. 1 75 – 96.

Heaton, N. and Linn, I. 1989 *Fighting Back: A report on the shop stewards response to new management techniques in TGWU Region 10*, Barnsley: TGWU Region 10 and Northern College.

Heery, E. and Kelly, J. 1988 'Do Female Representatives Make a Difference? Women Full-Time Officials and Trade Union Work', *Work, Employment and Society*, Vol. 2, No. 4, 487– 505.

Heery, E. 1993 'Industrial relations and the customer', *Industrial Relations Journal*, Vol. 24, No. 4, 284 – 295.

Hudson, M. 1989 'An analysis of the short-term and long-term recruitment aims of the TGWU Link Up Campaign', MA Dissertation, University of Warwick.

Hyman, R. and Ferner, A. 1994 (eds.) *New Frontiers in European Industrial Relations*, Oxford: Blackwell.

Hyman, R. 1994 'Industrial Relations in Western Europe: An Era of Ambiguity?' *Industrial Relations*, Vol. 33, No. 1, January, 1–23.

IRS 1995 '"The customer is boss"': matching employee performance to customer service needs', *IRS Employment Trends* 585, June 1995, London: Industrial Relations Services.

Jenson, J., Hagen, E. and Reddy, C. (eds.) 1988 *Feminisation of the Labour Force: Paradoxes and Promises*, Cambridge: Polity.

Kelly, J. and Kelly, C. 1991 'Them and Us: Social Psychology and the New Industrial Relations' *British Journal of Industrial Relations*, Vol. 29, No. 1, 25 – 48.

Kelly, J. and Heery, E. 1994 *Working for the union – British trade union officers*, Cambridge: Cambridge University Press.

Kelly, J. 1995 'Union Militancy and Social Partnership' in P. Ackers, C. Smith and P. Smith (eds.).

LRD 1993 'Unions failing on part timers', *Labour Research*, September 1993, Vol. 82, No. 9, London: Labour Research Department.

LRD 1994a 'Local Services – A Contract Killing', *Labour Research*, May 1994, Vol. 83, No. 5, London: Labour Research Department.

LRD 1994b 'Do part timers have equal rights?', *Labour Research*, July 1994, Vol. 83, No. 7, London: Labour Research Department.

LRD 1994c 'Still a long road to equality', *Labour Research*,March 1994, Vol. 83, No. 3, London: Labour Research Department.

LRD 1995a 'Compulsory competitive sex bias', *Labour Research*, June 1995, Vol. 84, No. 6, London: Labour Research Department.

LRD 1995b 'Work changes take toll on unions', *Labour Research* May 1995, Vol. 84, No. 5, London: Labour Research Department.

Millward, N., Stevens, M., Smart, D. and Hawes, W.R. 1992 *Workplace Industrial Relations in Transition*, Aldershot: Gower.

Mitter, S. 1994 'On organising women in casualised work: a global overview' in S. Rowbotham and S. Mitter (eds.).

O'Connell-Davidson 1993 *Privatization and Employment Relations, the case of the water industry*, London: Mansell.

Ogden, S. 'The Reconstruction of Industrial Relations in the Privatized Water Industry', *British Journal of Industrial Relations*, Vol. 32, No. 1, 67 – 84.

Pollert, A. 1995 'Team work' on the assembly line: contradictions and the dynamics of union resilience' in P. Ackers, C. Smith and P. Smith (eds.).

Rowbotham, R. 1994 'Strategies against sweated work in Britain, 1820 – 1920' in S. Rowbotham and S. Mitter (eds.).

Rowbotham, S. and Mitter, S. (eds.) 1994 *Dignity and Daily Bread: New forms of economic*

*organising among poor women in the Third World and the First*, London: Routledge.
Rubery, J. 1995 'The Low-paid and the Unorganised' in P. Edwards (ed.).
Snape, E. 1994 'Reversing the decline? the TGWU's Link Up campaign' *Industrial Relations Journal*, Vol. 25, No. 3, 222 – 233.
Thompson, A. W. J. and Beaumont, P. B. 1978 *Public Sector Bargaining*, Farnborough, Hants.: Saxon House.
Upchurch, M. and Donnelly, E. 1992 'Membership Patterns in USDAW 1980 – 1990: survival or success?', *Industrial Relations Journal*, Vol. 23, No. 1, June, 60 – 68.
Visser, J. 1994 'European Trade Unions: the Transition Years' in R. Hyman and A. Ferner (eds.).
Wrench, J. and Virdee, S. 1995 'Organising the Unorganised: 'Race', Poor Work and Trade Unions' in P. Ackers, C. Smith and P. Smith (eds.).

The original version of this paper was first presented to the Conference co-ordinated by the Centre for Research on Work and Society, York University, Canada: *Service Sector Revolutions: Innovations in Work Restructuring and Worker Representation in the Canadian Service Economy*, November 2–5 1995, Canadian Autoworkers Conference Centre, Port Elgin, Canada.

# THE TOWER OF INFOBABEL: CYBERSPACE AS ALTERNATIVE UNIVERSE

Reg Whitaker

Fin-de-siècle capitalist culture is awash with prophecies of revolution. We are told that we are in the process of a transformation so profound that we can barely discern its implications. But this time the spectre is not that of revolution from below, but from *outside*, through the miraculous agency of that *deus ex machina*, technology. The Agricultural Revolution and the Industrial Revolution are now to be surpassed by the Information Revolution. The computer is transforming economy, society, culture, human beings themselves.

To the prophets, the digital futurologists of capitalism, this is not revolution as spectre at all, rather it is a beacon pointing the way forward. The future will be entirely different from the present, yet *plus ça change, plus c'est la même chose:* capitalism will be the engine of this transformation because it is capitalism that taps the wellsprings of technological change, capitalism that knows how to put technology to practical use and capitalism that can market the new technologies. Some capitalists will be thrown off by the great wheel of *laissez innover*, but those who learn to ride it will be rewarded with positions on the commanding heights of the new world.

Against this siren chorus of conservative revolutionaries there stands a smaller, less electronically articulate and less media-literate but equally enthusiastic, group of leftish prophets who see the seeds of social revolution in the new technologies. Democracy will spring not from the barrel of a gun but from the personal computer and modem. States and corporations will lose control over the flow of information. The People will rule the Internet.

Both camps are united at least on the principle that it is technology that is the autonomous engine of history. It is as if some cosmic dice are cast, and we await nervously, excitedly, to see if our number comes up. There is a third camp, not politically identifiable under traditional labels, that also shares this understanding of how the universe unfolds and our place at the table as spectators. But these are pessimists who think the results will be bad, destroying jobs, displacing values, degrading society and stunting our culture.

Finally there is a fourth camp, also politically uncategorizable, that rejects the technological determinism of the others, derides the prevalent infohype, and argues that we can turn back the great wheel or at least stop it in its tracks, if we recognize the flimsiness and pretence of the prophecies. The Information Revolution is in their eyes no more than an incremental change in the way we do things, far from a qualitative leap into the unknown.

Given the extreme trendiness of so much discussion of this question, its breathless up-to-the-minute quality, it is something of a shock to discover that the most haunting image of the Information Age was penned some forty years ago by an Argentinian writer innocent of any interest whatever in the technology of the present or the future. This is Jorge Luis Borges' remarkable vision of the 'Library of Babel'[1]:

> *The universe (which others call the Library) is composed of an indefinite and perhaps infinite number of hexagonal galleries. . . . From any of the hexagons one can see, interminably, the upper and lower floors. The distribution of the galleries is invariable. Twenty shelves, five long shelves per side, cover all the sides except two; their height, which is the distance from floor to ceiling, scarcely exceeds that of a normal bookcase. One of the free sides leads to a narrow hallway which opens into another gallery, identical to the first and to all the rest. . . . Also through here passes a spiral stairway, which sinks abysmally and soars upward to remote distances. In the hallway there is a mirror which faithfully duplicates all appearances. . . . The Library is a sphere whose exact centre is any one of its hexagons and whose circumference is inaccessible.*

Given the frenetic and feverish manner in which the information revolution is being hyped, it is worth pausing to ask just what is actually involved in this revolution. The initial answer is deceptively simple. Essentially there are two closely linked technological departure points: the computer and instantaneous communication systems. Both technologies have been developing in an exponential, explosive trajectory, but it is in the *fusion* of computing and communications (*networks*), that the truly revolutionary potential lies. Just as the capacity of the human mind to store, sort, retrieve and manipulate vast amounts of information is being enormously enhanced by means of ever-smaller, ever-faster and ever-more powerful microprocessors, the reach of individuals is being immeasurably extended through fibre optic cable and satellite communication to form 'real-time' networking of all computers.

This technological fusion has literally created a new world, a new space – *cyberspace*. Cyberspace exists nowhere and everywhere[2], it is a *tabula rasa* in the sense that it is constantly being constructed and reconstructed, written and rewritten, by the simultaneous interaction of all those networking in the medium. With Virtual Reality – which eventually will shed its present clumsy apparatus of goggles and gloves for something more akin to StarTrek's Holodeck, an all-encompassing artificial interactive environment – cyberspace will actually become a lived space, with its own landscape and geography, into which people will 'move' and inside which they will 'act' (and be 'acted upon'). The discovery of such a new world, and more, a world that is apparently plastic, that can be moulded (closer to our heart's desire, unlike the intractable and often perverse real world?), is bound to bring out the Faustian in those who first glimpse its expansive, seemingly limitless, contours. They stand with wild surmise upon a peak in Darien.

With Faust, let us give the devil his due. The possibilities are endless, intoxicating. Space – old-fashioned physical space, distance – already shrunk by technologies like the telephone, is finally dissolved in cyberspace. People communicate with one another without regard to physical location: communities (systems of communication?) can transcend not only locality but the artificial constructs of the nation and political boundaries. New languages are born out of the new forms of communication, and with them, humanity reshapes its own consciousness.[3]

Already, not in some speculative future, but in the here and now, cyberspace is giving birth to new, 'artificial' life forms. In computer labs, programs have been designed to replicate particular environments (say, an 'ocean') and into these environments a 'species' (for instance, 'fish') has been introduced that is programmed to adapt to changing conditions. Generations pass and adaptations are made quite independent of the original program. The fish swim about, eat, reproduce and die in cyberspace. They are not 'real', they have no physical materiality, yet they behave just like 'real' fish, they interact with their environment, and they make something of themselves in the process.[4] In the most recent Star Trek spinoff series, Voyager, there is a brilliant creation, the Emergency Medical Hologram, a computer program containing the most advanced medical knowledge projected holographically as a 'doctor' who must serve as the starship's chief medical officer in the absence of a human doctor. This hologram behaves remarkably like a human being when interacting with 'real' humans; he is self-conscious, he experiences anxiety, irritation, affection.[5] And why not? How does 'real life' differ from its 'artificial' replication in cyberspace, presuming only that the program is complex enough?

*Of course, the Library is not really the 'Universe', its architecture is not the architecture of matter. It is an analogical 'universe'. Its shelves store information in the form of texts which contain 'data' that mirror or reproduce the material universe. Borges advances two axioms about the nature of the Library that he considers indisputable. The first is that it exists* ab aeterno. *The architecture of information is too complex and elegant to have been the product of man, the 'imperfect librarian'. Call it*

*God or Nature as you please, but remember that information is about something, it is not that thing itself. But this is easily obscured when the focus shifts to what is in the Library. Borges' second axiom is that 'The orthographical symbols are twenty-five in number' (the letters of the alphabet plus the period, comma and space). This has allowed the formulation of a General Theory of the library. All books are made up of the same elements, but in the 'vast Library there are no two identical books'. From these premises it may be deduced that the* 'Library is total and that its shelves register all the possible combinations of the twenty-odd orthographical symbols *(a number which, though extremely vast, is not infinite.)*[6] *In other words, 'all that it is given to express, in all languages. Everything: the minutely detailed history of the future. . . .'*

> *When it was proclaimed that the Library contained all books, the first impression was one of extravagant happiness. All men felt themselves to be the masters of an intact and secret treasure. There was no personal or world problem whose elegant solution did not exist in some hexagon. The universe was justified, the universe suddenly usurped the unlimited dimension of hope.'*

Thus our own era of infohype, the unlimited promise of the great Internet (the embodiment of Borges' Library condensed into millions of individual computer screens as [W]indows into cyberspace, a 'sphere whose exact centre is any one of its hexagons and whose circumference is inaccessible'). These are no small matters. The devil's promises are enthralling, enchanting, alluring. No wonder so many have been drawn by the siren's song. But wait . . . cyberspace is not another universe into which we can escape via a magic doorway. Dream worlds exist in the minds of dreamers, who live in *this* world, breath air, eat food when hungry and drink water when thirsty - or not, depending upon their material circumstances. Cyberspace is a dreamed world, but the dreamers dream it through the mediation of computer hardware, fibre optic cable, complex telecommunications networks, and specific social and economic systems that support and deliver these technologies. Cybernauts are *wired*, in more ways than one. There is, or at least there should be, a *political economy* of cyberspace. Yes, even in the free-floating delirium of this new world, the old dismal science, like gravity, drags the cybernauts back toward earth.

Some uncomfortable but unavoidable facts: most of the people of the present real world not only lack computers but even lack access to telephones. To most of the world, the Information Revolution is not even a rumour. The IBM television ads that portray "solutions for a small planet" with cute clips of people in traditional and exotic settings discussing (with subtitles) various arcana relating to the latest IBM technologies perhaps tell us more about the imperial delusions of corporate power, or about the penetration by new products of Third World elites, than about any reality of 'solutions' for a 'small' planet. The Information Highway may be opening out like a vast autobahn across North America and Europe and the hyper-developed parts of Asia, but when it reaches into Africa and Latin America and the less developed parts of Asia, it reaches as narrow fingers into privileged islands; for much of the Third World, it simply stops short altogether.[7] Nor is there any rational reason to think that the information revolution offers a magical solution to the endemic problems of poverty and underdevelopment. It is rather the latest name given to the enduring and ever deepening domination of the many poor by the wealthy few. Access to the Internet is as much use to a Bangladeshi peasant as hitching a ride on the Challenger space shuttle; but it is very useful to the multinational corporations that rule the global economic system that maintains Bangladesh as a ghetto of misery.

There are similar arguments against facile idealism applicable within Western societies. A reasonably up-to-date computer clone, pirated software, modem and monthly connect charge may not represent a huge investment. Yet it excludes a great many, as does the specific context of computer culture. The result is that the Information Highway has a decidedly middle-class look. Users tend as well to be disproportionately male, white, and the other familiar categories of privilege. Of course, over time these things may change. But just as with the case for Third World development, there are overheated notions afloat in political and bureaucratic circles (viz., the frenetic mind of Newt Gingrich) that a computer in every kitchen will somehow solve the problem of unemployment and regional economic decline. It is, of course, out of the question that right-wing neo-liberal politicians (who tend to be the ones that babble most about the transformative power of the computer) can devise and execute and pay for a vast public works scheme for actually putting the hardware and software required into the hands of the poor and the unemployed. Unfortunately, social democrats have been equally complicit, if less utopian, in talking up the computer as empowerment. Even the limited schemes undertaken by some social democratic governments to 'retrain' (a mantra of contemporary capitalist crisis) redundant fishermen with no fish stocks, coal miners with closed pits, or workers with skills tied to vanishing heavy industries, via the route of imparting 'computer skills' quickly disclose their derisory limitations. At best, these retrained workers hunching over their consoles have instantaneous access to the intelligence that no jobs are available. At least lining up outside the unemployment office provided some minimal human contact with others of like predicament, even if the end result is the same.

The attraction of neo-liberal politicians to infobabble has little to do with any notions of redistribution of wealth and power. The computer as 'empowerment' is a wonderfully ambiguous piece of rhetoric. This 'empowerment' offers a convenient and trendy rationale for further slashing the public sector. Who needs armies of public sector workers to offer support services when former state clients have the opportunity to plug in directly? Who needs expensive capital investment in physical infrastructure and maintenance when services can be accessed on the Net? Right-wing politicians in North America who are tired of seeing tax dollars going to universities and colleges have started talking about the 'Virtual University', where courses are on offer to clients (formerly called students) receiving information designed by programmers (formerly called professors) and tapping in assignments and answering exam questions, without ever leaving their home computers. In the fullness of this vision, the entire support and maintenance staffs, most of the teaching staff and the administrative apparatus can be lopped off the public rolls, and the physical plant (formerly known as the campus) can be sold to the private sector for more productive and profitable use. This is a paradigm for other such schemes for a 'Virtual Public Sector' or the 'Virtual State'. Like Virtual Reality, users allow their senses to delude them into believing that they are somewhere they are not, that they are really doing things that are not happening at all. The opiate of the masses indeed.

There is an ideology among many of today's cybernauts, especially the Americans, that can best be described as frontier capitalism, or rugged individualism. The self-image is that of the lone frontiersman out there on the cutting edge of civilisation armed with his [the gendered pronoun is used advisedly] contemporary equivalent of the six-gun, the high-speed modem. It is expressed in a powerful aversion to the traditional enemy of the frontiersman, government and its attempts to regulate and domesticate his wild energies. Thus there have been ferocious reactions to the clumsy attempts of the Clinton administration to impose surveillance over the Internet, from the 'Clipper Chip' and the embargoing of exports of various encryption programmes; to the FBI's ham-handed attempt to enforce tapping of digital communication (and make the users pay for the privilege!); to censorship initiatives from various levels of government against cyberspace pornography and hate mail. These are probably reasonable responses under the circumstances, but they are also classic examples of navigating via the rear view mirror.

Neither individual free enterprise nor an aggressive interventionist state are particularly relevant to the new political economy of cyberspace. Hardware and software are produced by corporate giants like IBM and Microsoft, and the infrastructure of the Internet is currently a bone of contention between the telephone and media/cable giants. The real frontier is the commodification of information by capital. To shift metaphors, cyberspace is like the commons under attack from enclosures. The relentless emphasis in recent years on 'intellectual property' as a crucial element in international trade agreements points us clearly in the direction that the so-called information revolution is travelling. The architecture of cyberspace may well look very much like the dark vision of William Gibson in his 1984 science fiction novel *Neuromancer* that first invented the very term 'cyberspace': vast mysterious collections of data looming like mega-fortresses fiercely guarded by giant corporations – while the 'real world' wallows in urban squalor, petty criminality, violence and tawdry escapism.

Information is a resource whose relation to late twentieth century capitalism is like that of oil to the capitalism of the early twentieth century. This is not to say, as some have unwisely extrapolated, that industrial capitalism is dead. Automobiles still provide the basic means of transportation for much of the world, and oil must still be tapped to feed the voracious appetite of automobiles for fuel. Information has not displaced older resources, just as postindustrialism has not displaced industrialism. But the computer and the new communications technologies have redefined how production and distribution take place. Mass production and mass consumption have, in the process of fulfilling their promise of growth, been transmuted. Production (including services) requires fewer workers and greater 'flexibility', and mass consumption of mass-marketed goods is increasingly matched by 'niche' marketing of specifically targeted production. On both sides of the equation, information and high-speed communication of that information is a crucial resource. The shift from the primary to the information-intensive services sector that is evident throughout the rich industrial nations is another indicator of this same change. Command over information and its transmission will be the key to success in the capitalist world of tomorrow.

The notion that this crucial resource will be allowed to become a public good is idealism at its most inane.[8] Thus the cyberspace commons is enclosed as rapidly as its space expands. The advocates of 'electronic freedom' have their hearts in the right place but their heads in the sand. More apposite to the realities are the young freelance cyberpunk hackers who for their own fun and profit break into the dark corporate information towers that loom over the wired world. The first (anti)hero of the first cyberpunk novel was Gibson's Case, cyberspace cowboy who had made too many powerful enemies. Yet even these latter-day information highwaymen are themselves gobbled up by the very corporations they have successfully targeted: the electronic safe-crackers are hired on as smart high-tech security guards to keep out others (and, who knows, to crack their competitor's security as well?). Already we may be moving into a new era that leaves behind the individualistic hacking frontier: organized electronic warfare employing disciplined teams of corporate hackers setting about systematically to break into or to sabotage the data banks and operational software of economic competitors may become the order of the day.[9] Computer viruses, first transmitted by freelancers out of malice or just for the hell of it, will increasingly be utilised as weapons targeted at specific competitive information systems (the biological warfare of cyber-space, attacking the synapses of the enemy's information economy). This is a long way from the 'promise of the Internet', from the limitless vistas of information laid open to each and all who wish to browse its fields and pluck its free flowers of truth. Let us be blunt: this is a vision of Never-Never-Land, Lucy in the Sky with Diamonds.

We should consider carefully why the promise of the Internet is such a pleasing delusion. It is not because capitalists are evil persons, or because corporations are conspiring against the public interest (both propositions might be true, but still be beside the point). Information is a product. Raw, unprocessed data is not yet information – and even that requires someone to collect it in the first instance and store it in accessible form. Already there are claimants expecting compensation for their work. Processing data into a finished product useful to potential consumers is even greater value added. All this will be reflected in the final price. Only in the for-profit private sector are there the resources both to produce sophisticated information and to purchase the finished product on a commercially viable scale. Public sector information services were once fairly widely available on a free or relatively low-cost basis, but in this neo-liberal era, market principles of user-pay, cost recovery and servicing 'clients' have led to the virtual privatization of public sector information. Even those once-privileged bastions of state information secrecy, the security and intelligence agencies, are flogging their information services to the highest bidders in the private sector. Governments increasingly post free information on the Internet, but this is mainly for democratic legitimation of their cost-recovery supply to the private sector: the very fact that information is freely available is generally proof of its relatively low value as commodity.

Cyberspace will be a treasure trove of information only for those who already have treasuries to spend. For the rest of us, beneath the false promise of the Internet lies an overstuffed, cluttered, anarchically disorganized jumble of infotrash, so worthless that it has been discarded to lie along the sidewalks of the information highway for the casual use of anyone who cares to pick the odd item up. As time goes by, even this litter will be cleaned up and replaced by smaller business ventures selling baubles and beads: North American television viewers have already seen the future in the Shopping Channels.

Information is a valuable commodity, and it is power in the form of competitive advantage. But it is crucial to understand that information is power in a deeper sense. Ever since Foucault's *Surveiller et Punir: Naissance de la Prison* was published in 1975, we have been alerted to the importance of *surveillance* as a primary mechanism of social control in the modern world. With Foucault, the Panopticon – Bentham's plan for a prison designed in such a way that each prisoner was under constant hidden surveillance, or what amounts to the same, would believe that he might be watched at all times – became the quintessential metaphor for a modern technology of power. Others have elaborated Foucault's insights into a concept of the 'surveillance society'.[10] This technology of power rests on the accumulation of coded information used to administer the activities of individuals about whom it is gathered. In contrast to earlier political forms, the modern state lays less stress on overt coercion to sustain its rule. Instead it favours pervasive, and penetrative administrative power, primarily through the collection, storage and retrieval of information within an administrative context of regulated definitions of tasks, functions and roles that situate individuals and groups in relation to other individuals and groups in an administrative or organizational framework. Under a surveillance regime, people disappear into abstract, bureaucratic categories: 'client', 'customer', 'taxpayer', 'functionary', 'law enforcement officer', 'supervisor', 'shop steward', 'teacher'. The routinized exercise of surveillance *implies* coercion, but overtly involves only the marshalling of information as a means of regulating behaviour.

The lineaments of the surveillance state have been apparent for a long time, but the explosive advances in computer and communication technologies provide a powerful and ever-expanding toolbox of surveillance. From the workplace to the streets to the home, people are being subjected to ever more sophisticated, ever more specific, ever more invasive, scrutiny. Although many of these technologies were initially developed through the military-industrial complexes, force-fed by the national security states during the eras of world war and cold war, they are now very much central elements of contemporary capitalism, in two main ways. First, corporations are enhancing their surveillance capacities to increase competitiveness, both in terms of the productive process and marketing/distribution. Second, surveillance is increasingly relied upon by capital in general to reduce risks and provide a more stable environment for doing business, both domestically and globally. Indeed, the privatization of surveillance has proceeded to the extent that it is perhaps more appropriate to talk about the surveillance *society* rather than the surveillance *state*. In effect, many of the aspects traditionally associated with the state's political rule – authoritative allocation of roles and regulation of behaviour, for example – are being quietly transferred to the private sector.

To look first at surveillance for *competitiveness*: fewer workers in more automated work environments are also more closely-watched workers. 'Smart-cards' permit controlled entry to workplaces and also allow supervisors to keep electronic track of where employees are at all times. Electronically encoded identification of tools and parts not only permit better inventory control but also block employee pilfering. Increasing use of computers as an integral part of the productive process not only enhances efficiency but also provides a cumulative and precise record of the productivity of the employees operating them, as well as of the workers that the computers are tracking. None of this need be confined to individual workplaces: global corporations carry out global surveillance of operations and employees; managers are in constant electronic touch through E-Mail, teleconferencing, etc., and their performances closely monitored and evaluated.

When we turn to the marketing and distribution side, the scope of surveillance is equally impressive. Mass marketing – which still of course continues – is a very blunt instrument, a bit like the bombs dropped from air planes in World War II: a visual or radar sighting of the target area was made from thousands of feet in the air, the doors were opened, the bombs dumped, and the crew hoped for the best. Today's niche marketing is more like the military's contemporary smart weapons: the targeting is precise and the delivery is monitored and guided all the way to impact. The key to the new smart marketing is information. Consumers are identified not as mass, undifferentiated markets, but as subgroups with very specific information about purchasing patterns and purchasing power. Data banks on consumer preferences, with information gathered from myriad sources, can be cross-referenced and specific potential customers for specific products can be identified and targeted. Mass media move from broadcasting to 'narrowcasting': 500 channel television via direct broadcast satellites permits a proliferation of specialized programming with specific audiences whose particular buying preferences will be sensitively accommodated by the advertisers on those channels. Most of the data gathering goes on quite unnoticed by the targets, or is seen to be facilitating consumption. For instance, electronic checkouts at video rental shops speed up the process for customers. Few realize that information on each rental becomes part of a data profile of each customer's preferences in films.[11]

Supply and distribution have been similarly revolutionized by the new technologies. Bar codes on products can provide instant readout of sales and inventories all the way to the factory door; readjustments and resupplies can be underway within seconds of consumer decisions recorded at checkout counters.

Surveillance as *risk aversion* moves the private sector closer to the traditional concerns of the state. Credit-worthiness is a crucial entrée into the consumer society. Anyone judged a credit risk can not hold a credit card, or borrow money for a house or car, and may even be barred from renting accommodation or transportation. Once named a credit risk, on the basis of data matching from private data banks, a process which allows little recourse for the targeted person to crosscheck the validity of the sources of the negative information, an individual may find it very difficult to get off this electronic blacklist, leading to a downward spiral in personal economic circumstances. Insurance companies, basing decisions on data banks to which they have privileged, sometimes exclusive, access, can deny people access to insurance policies, or arbitrarily set rates at prohibitively high levels. In the case of automobile drivers in most jurisdictions, this may amount to effectively preventing someone from driving – and in many cases, from making a living. Even more ominous is the increasing use of screening for employment: drug testing, evidence of previous legal offences, medical problems, even lack of credit-worthiness, may be reason for denying employment or sacking an existing employee, often without appeal. Information upon which such significant decisions are made are based upon immediate access to vast data banks, many of them privately-held and controlled. Even in the case of public data banks, funded by taxpayer dollars, the subjects of the information may have little or no access to data on themselves, either because they are prohibited by law, or because only corporations with a high commercial stake can afford to pay for the added value of ordering the design of the data in forms accessible for their particular purposes. Again, in the case of public data banks, citizens often feel that these are actually helpful to them in their daily lives. For example, 'smart' health cards that encode personal medical information (blood type, allergies, medications, etc.) offer holders security that they will be properly handled in medical emergencies. Less obvious is that such cards may contain credit information about health insurance coverage that could lead to being turned away at hospital doors, or worse, medical information (a history of drug addiction, for instance, or having been tested positive for certain conditions such as HIV) that may have devastating consequences for the holder in various situations. DNA banks might seem to offer protection for peaceful citizens against criminals, but what of the (admittedly very small) chance of an innocent person's DNA sequencing matching that of an offender?

The Cold War national security state pioneered the process of security screening of broad categories of people: state employees; workers in defence and other industries of national significance; immigrants and citizenship applicants. The criteria were political: membership in the Communist party or in some other left-wing groups; association with known Communists, or past membership in alleged Communist 'front' organizations. The political prejudices of conservative politicians and police were given free reign under the purportedly impartial cover of security screening – as if this were like objective screening for a disease. It did not stop there. Homosexuality was targeted as an alleged character weakness that left persons vulnerable to blackmail and thus security risks. Rabid homophobia was never far from the surface, and has in the case of the American and British military outlasted the Cold War that provided the ostensible rationale. There were many things going on in this process, many different fish being fried. But what was in common was the growth of data banks on citizens, first in the primitive and clumsy form of card indices and paper files, and then later in electronic form, in cyberspace. This was (and *is*, it still very much exists) a *shadow world*: it exists in the thick shadows of state secrecy, and its information shadows, or parallels, the real world. Owen Lattimore, the Asian scholar who was bizarrely persecuted by the Washington witch-hunters in the 1950s as a Soviet spy, said it best in his autobiography when he referred to the dossiers compiled on him by the FBI and congressional committees as the profile of a "*man who might have existed*."[12] There was a real Lattimore and then there was the Lattimore of the files who *might have* existed. And only the latter one mattered in the eyes of the powerful.

Today, in the time of the Information Revolution, we are all, in a sense, Owen Lattimores. The private and public data banks that form the high-security skyscrapers of cyberspace contain the shadow selves of almost every citizen and consumer. These data profiles, or shadow selves, in important ways *overshadow* our real selves.[13] People who have protested bad credit ratings, for instance, have found that even simple cases of mistaken identity have been almost impossible to rectify. Just as the guardians of state security always argued that doubt must be resolved in favour of the state, never the individual, the powerful motive of risk aversion on the part of capital means that doubt is resolved in favour of the corporation. Corporations do not care if mistakes are made, or injustices perpetrated against individuals (except in the rare cases where sufficient bad publicity is generated that their public image suffers), because it does not *pay* to be attentive to such possibilities. They are in the business of avoiding risks on behalf of their shareholders; data profiles indicate risk categories and actions are taken to avoid anyone whose profile places them in the category. The result is a kind of social *triage*. Some are effectively excluded from full citizenship not in the state but in civil society.

Our cyberspace selves tend to overshadow our real selves for both good and bad reasons. Data banks mirror the real world but, necessarily, imperfectly. Just as a perfect scientific/mathematical model of the material universe – one that established a one-to-one relationship with reality – would be an absurdity, a theory as vast and complex as the actual universe, so too data profiles are always simplifications of reality. The key points are who asks the questions and sets the parameters of the data search, for what purposes. The answer of course is that those with wealth and power get to shape the questions and thus the kind of simplifications that emerge. Corporate data banks, and the public data banks to which corporations buy privileged access, are there to answer corporate questions. The simplified, perhaps simplistic, data profiles are patterned to answer corporate needs. Real world selves are inveterately messy, maddeningly complex, irritatingly inconsistent, full of contradictions – in a word, difficult. That is what it means to be human, after all, and why we so often throw up our hands in personal relationships, write poems and novels and plays to contemplate the inexplicable, toil over biographies, and vainly try as social scientists to explain individual behaviour through metatheories of the collective. But our cyberspace shadow selves are not messy, not complex, not inconsistent, not contradictory: they are simple, easy constructs that can be quickly and cheaply drawn from the database and cost-efficiently used by the customers who pay for them. These cartoons crowd out the messy reality because the world of economic transactions is structured in such a way that only certain kinds of information can be fed into it. If you don't fit the programme, you will have to be cut down to size, or stretched, or whatever it takes. It's the Mad Hatter's Tea Party; if the mouse can't be stuffed into the teapot he will just have be excluded – a *risk*.

*But this is, after all, the Library of Babel. The biblical Tower of Babel was an audacious attempt to build a direct link between earth and heaven. A jealous God cursed the architects and builders with a multiplicity of languages so that no-one could communicate with any other. The Tower fell and the languages were dispersed across the earth. So the extravagant happiness of the revolutionaries armed with the General Theory of the Library soon gives way to doubts, heresies, strife and despair as it becomes apparent that 'everything' includes nonsense, mistakes, even deceptions. One book consists of nothing but "the letters MCV, perversely repeated from the first line to the last." The era of infohype passes into the era of infobabble. 'Purifiers' are despatched through the endless halls to seek out and destroy false texts. There are struggles and librarians are murdered; others commit suicide.*

Seen in a sceptical light, cyberspace is not such an enthralling field of possibilities after all. It is a threatening terrain with dark towers of data brooding on the horizon, old-fashioned exploitations and conflicts transposed into new and disturbing forms, haunted by strange shadow distortions of our material selves that menace us in our daily lives. It is an *alienated* world where the products of our own invention and imagination come back to torment us.

This picture too is just a *possible* world, drawing on elements already present and extrapolating a plausible, if unpleasant, future. Like all possible worlds it will probably not come about exactly as pictured; it may indeed look quite different. Futurology is a treacherous endeavour, especially when premised upon the whims of that most illusive of masters/mistresses, technological innovation. But the bottom line of my argument is that any speculation that fails to take into account the thread of continuity in terms of power and wealth will be seriously off the mark. The networked computer may change us in ways that can be both foreseen and yet unforeseen. It is unlikely to effect, by itself, a fundamental transformation in the political economic structure of the very system that gave rise to it, that marketed it, and enthusiastically incorporated it into its organizational strategy for competitive success. If real change is to come about, it will have to be because people make it happen, by learning to use the new technologies against their owners, not because a technological *deus ex machina* does it for them.

What then of the left-wing cyberenthusiasts and their prophecies of cyberspace as a democratic frontier? One must immediately qualify any response by granting that in authoritarian regimes, the new communication technologies can be liberating and empowering. The capacity of any repressive regime to shut out the outside world, to hold its subjects captive in mind as well as body has been rapidly eroded. The fax machine and E-Mail have indeed become revolutionary weapons in the hands of dissidents, and satellite television, for all that it symbolizes cultural imperialism and the penetration of traditional cultures by Western capitalist values, also destabilizes brutal regimes and police states. But when we turn to the so-called 'advanced' liberal democracies, the democratizing potential seems far less substantial.

Take the fashionable chatter about 'virtual communities' in cyberspace as new nodes of social resistance. Some have even spoken of Internet affinity groups as 'electronic cafés' like the European cafés of the early twentieth century where radical and revolutionary ideas and movements were spawned. But these 'virtual communities' are entirely lacking in the social and cultural context that could give rise to actual revolutionary movements. They are literally disembodied, disconnected from the social roots of their participants, floating in cyberspace without the identities that enable and drive people to carry out actual struggles against real enemies. People who communicate with one another only in cyberspace often mediate these communications through masks, false identities that they consciously adopt as playful/deceptive shields to protect their real identities.[14] Some would have us believe that this represents a new evolving consciousness that transcends class, ethnicity, gender and national borders. It sounds more like escapist game-playing: *Nintendo players of the world unite, you have nothing to lose but your identities*! In any event, it is already a notorious fact that it is the Right, not the Left, that has made the most of the political opportunities of cyberspace, in many cases the ugliest elements of the Right, offering racism as political pornography on the Internet.

Another take on this is to argue that cyberspace eliminates from communication the hierarchical cues that infect face-to-face communication. Women need not be silenced by domineering male voices, discussion can be colour-blind, etc. It is true that studies of the impact of E-Mail communication in multinational corporations suggest a slight weakening of hierarchical order, a certain limited democratization. Unfortunately, there is a downside to this democratization. Unable to effect genteel putdowns by the body language of status and privilege, or unable to catch the cues that would signal retreat and submission, participants resort to verbal violence: the phenomenon of '*flaming*' one's opponents. The democratic frontier turns out to be a Hobbesian frontier, the verbal war of all against all. The moral lesson? The fault, dear Brutus, is not in the stars. . . . An aggressive, competitive society is not transformed when beamed into cyberspace; rather cyberspace takes on some of the colouration of that society.

Does the Information Revolution offer an *alternative*? Yes and no. It does offer an alternative capitalist future, but it is unlikely, under present circumstances, to offer an alternative *to* capitalism. On the other hand, the profound impact of this revolution cannot be ignored by those seeking real alternatives. Cyberspace is a new reality, a spectre haunting the world. As some of the old terrains of struggle shrink, cyberspace expands as a new terrain to be studied, and to be acted upon. It is emphatically *not* itself an answer to problems that we ourselves must solve, with or without the aid of technology.

*At the end – or is it the beginning (the Library is "unlimited and cyclical")- we are left with the great conundrum of the Library: by containing everything it contains nothing. Indeed, even if humanity were to extinguish itself, "the Library will endure: illuminated, solitary, infinite, perfectly motionless, useless, incorruptible, secret".*

*In the* Hitch Hiker's Guide to the Galaxy, *the ultimate computer, 'Deep Thought', after cogitating for seven and a half million years, finally delivers the answer to the 'great Question of Life, the Universe and Everything'. The answer: 'forty-two'. When complaints are raised about how disappointing this is, Deep Thought suggests that the problem is in the question. But the question is . . . everything. '"Exactly!" said Deep Thought. So once you do know what the question actually is, you'll know what the answer means.'*[15]

## NOTES

1. Jorge Luis Borges, *Labyrinths: Selected Stories and Other Writings* (New York 1964) pp. 51–58.
2. See Julian Stallabrass, 'Empowering technology: the exploration of Cyberspace', *New Left Review* 211 (May/June 1995) pp. 3–32.
3. Mark Poster, *The Mode of Information: Poststructuralism and Social Context* (Cambridge 1990).
4. Claus Emmeche, *The Garden in the Machine: the Emerging Science of Artificial Life*

*(Princeton 1994)*. The virtual fish actually do exist, in a computer at the University of Toronto: see Stephen Strauss, 'Artificial Life', *The Globe and Mail* (Toronto) Sept. 10, 1994, p. D8.

5. The doctor thus represents one further step along the road pioneered by the earlier brilliant creation of *StarTrek: the Next Generation*, Data the android, who raises the same troubling questions about the alleged uniqueness of humanity.
6. Actually Borges is mistaken: there *are* an infinite number of combinations of a limited number of characters. I am indebted to George Comninel for pointing this out to me.
7. A recent survey indicated there are about 3.4 million computers hooked up to the Internet in the United States (70% of the global total) and just over 500,000 in Western Europe. By contrast, Africa has just 27,100, Central and South America 16,000 and the Middle East 13,800. A report by a non-governmental foundation warned about a new form of poverty – "information poverty" – that threatens the developing world. "There is a danger of a new information elitism which excludes the majority of the world's population. . . .The technology could actually increase the gap between rich and poor." Mark John, 'Third world faces "information poverty"- report', Reuters (London) Oct. 11, 1995. Even this survey may have missed the degree of domination of the Internet by US users: on its heels came another survey showing that the number of Americans who use computer on-line services shot up in the first half of 1995 to 12 million. 'On-line-services', AP (New York) Oct. 15, 1995.
8. For an example of how vapid any discussion of these issues that avoids or ignores the underlying reality of capitalist ownership of information can be, see Anne Wells Branscomb, *Who Owns Information? From Privacy to Public Access* (NY 1994). After 185 pages of consideration of the question asked in her title, she concludes with breath-taking banality that "we [?] will build the kind of legal infostructure that we [?] want and need." (p. 186)
9. At a recent conference on 'Infowar' an American electronic warfare specialist told of a bizarre plan by a group of American hackers, allegedly motivated by patriotic rage at French economic espionage against the US, to mount an "electronic assault on the main nerve centres of the French economy". Although apparently technically capable of inflicting considerable damage, the plan was called off when the FBI threatened them with arrest. 'Dawn of the Infowar era', *Intelligence Newsletter* 271 (14 September 1994) p. 1.
10. Anthony Giddens, *The Nation-State and Violence* (Berkeley 1987); Christopher Dandeker, *Surveillance, Power and Modernity* (Cambridge 1990); Oscar H. Gandy, Jr., *The Panoptic Sort: a Political Economy of Personal Information* (Boulder, Colo. 1993); David Lyon, *The Electronic Eye: the Rise of Surveillance Society* (Minneapolis 1994).
11. Republican Supreme Court nominee Robert Bork learned about this to his dismay when undergoing Senate confirmation a few years ago: enemies got hold of the information that he had in the past rented pornographic films.
12. Owen Lattimore, *Ordeal by Slander* (Boston 1950) p. 28.
13. Mark Poster was one of the first to point out the existence and some of the significance of this shadow world: *The Mode of Information*, op. cit.
14. In Douglas (*Generation X*) Coupland's 1995 novel *Microserfs*, set among a group of ex-Microsoft 'techies' running their own software start-up in Silicon Valley, one character falls in love with an E-Mail correspondent in Waterloo, Ontario, whom he knows only by the address BARCODE, sex, age, etc. unspecified.
15. Douglas Adams, *The Hitch Hiker's Guide to the Galaxy* (London 1979) p. 136.

# 'SACK THE SPOOKS': DO WE NEED AN INTERNAL SECURITY APPARATUS?

PETER GILL

### *Introduction: The Security Totem*

For fifty years a central concern of the Left has been the development of 'national security *states*' defined in terms of their political domination by military and security elites and consequent repression of democratic rights.[1] More recently, however, the focus has shifted to the increase in surveillance and accompanying 'disciplinary' measures employed by both state and non-state organisations, variously described as the rise of 'surveillance'[2] or 'maximum-security'[3] *societies*.

Surveillance practices have developed over centuries within specific institutions – the prison, the factory – but it is only during the last few decades that they have extended from sites of confinement and production to those of consumption. The gathering, collating, buying and selling of personal data is directed at refining marketing and credit-evaluation techniques while the simultaneous mushrooming of CCTV schemes combine in a drive to make cities safe for consumption. Thus 'security' is a totem of the contemporary world and the numbers of those – especially in the private sector – whose livelihood depends in some way on its provision (or purported provision) grows to an extent matched in few other employment sectors.[4] For some, notably Foucault, apparatuses of security are the very heart of modern government – 'governmentality'.[5] Although modern capitalist states may be choosing to withdraw from various markets through processes of privatisation they still play a central role in unifying the dispersed patterns of domination in capitalist societies,[6] for example, as the 'strong state'[7] that enforces the parameters within which those markets operate.

However, it is important not to succumb to 'postmodern paranoia'[8] regarding the malign aspects of surveillance, whether the chosen metaphor is Orwell's *1984* or Huxley's *Brave New World*.[9] It is clear that the growth of surveillance cannot be reversed, not least because so many are convinced of its benign impact, for example, in providing safer opportunities for consumption and leisure. Rather, the case must be made for some greater 'specificity' of the knowledges sought by otherwise excessive surveillance schemes,[10] more robust regulatory and inspections systems, and, as here, appropriate organisational changes aimed at minimising the 'gaze' of those surveillance apparatuses seen as most malign to the democratic political process. This paper considers what if any political action the Left can take, particularly what any Labour government elected in the UK in 1996 or 1997 should do, particularly regarding the British Security Service (MI5).

As befits a modern totem, security is an 'expertise' that is very difficult for 'outsiders', including elected governments, to challenge: it is not just what those working in security claim to know that secures their position; it is also their 'monopoly on the lack of knowledge that counts'.[11] In the estimation of present and future 'unknowns' with respect to 'risks', 'threats' and 'vulnerabilities' their pronunciations are privileged in the 'hierarchy of credibility'[12] by their expert status. Yet, total security is unobtainable; some degree of security can be obtained by the professional assessment of 'threats' but when it comes to analysing that large area of uncertainty regarding the significance or intensity of the threats posed by political and social movements this must not be left up to 'experts'. Democratic control requires the involvement of elected 'non-experts'.

History records no example in which security experts concluded there were no threats justifying their continued employment: their methodologies and organisational interests are bound to lead to the identity of new 'threats' which may occur at some future time. Specifically, what has occurred since the collapse of the Soviet Union has been a rush by the agencies to 'colonise' fresh areas of threat and to advertise the utility of their traditional skills as counters, for example, regarding 'economic intelligence', 'economic security' and 'transnational organised crime'. The consequent rather frantic pace of organisational activity suggests not just that the agencies are trying to keep up with global political shifts but also that they would prefer to have a new security intelligence policy edifice in place – to match their new headquarters buildings on opposite banks of the Thames – should a Labour Government come to power in 12–18 months' time. There may be little in Labour's record in Opposition to alarm the agencies but enough questions are already being asked and budget cuts being made to give them some cause for concern.

It is clearly futile to expect a state to organise itself without reference to protecting its interests and foreign intelligence agencies (in the UK specifically the Secret Intelligence Service [SIS] and Government Communications Headquarters [GCHQ]) might be legitimately tasked to develop intelligence regarding those interests; but a consideration of the foreign intelligence structures so deeply embedded in the modern state system, particularly since international economic competition between states becomes even more Hobbesian,[13] is beyond the scope of this paper.

*What is the problem?*

Between 1947 and 1991 the proclaimed mission of western internal security agencies in general was the surveillance and countering of perceived Soviet agents and domestic communist parties. In fact these surveillance activities spread far and wide to cover all forms of organised dissent under the pretext of combatting 'subversion'. In Canada the Security Service developed as a special section within the Royal Canadian Mounted Police (RCMP) and only received its first executive guidelines when it asked for them in 1975; these were rapidly overtaken by the McDonald Commission inquiry into Service activities particularly in Quebec in the 1970s, resulting in legislation for the new civilian Canadian Security Intelligence Service (CSIS) in 1984.[14] In Australia the Australian Security Intelligence Service (ASIO) was set up in 1949 and a statutory mandate followed in 1956, subsequently being revised in 1979 and 1986 in the light of royal commissions. The UK Security Service was established amid the spy-scares of 1909 and by means of 'secrecy, duplicity and chicanery'[15] but only received a statutory mandate eighty years later. In both the Australian and British cases the decision to legislate reflected, to a greater or lesser extent, the fears of the relevant Service that subsequent Labour governments might impose greater restrictions, if not, in Australia, actually abolish the agency. Present internal security structures therefore reflect the fact that legislation has been passed primarily to 'legalise' already existing agencies and, in the Canadian case, to reform a structure discredited by scandal. A similar effort to provide a congressional charter for the domestic security functions of the FBI in the wake of the revelations of the corruption of the Hoover years failed in the late 1970s. Over the years the main challenges to the continued autonomy of these agencies have tended to come from bureaucratic rivals rather than democratic pressures, for example, the UK Security Service survived threats to its autonomy after both world wars.[16]

Otherwise, the autonomy of specific national agencies has been most compromised by the US intelligence hegemony. This was organised formally through intelligence-sharing treaties such as UKUSA that divided up the world into areas of SIGINT responsibility and informally through networks of information exchange. US domination of this 'intelligence community' was established by its provision of disproportionate finance that in turn enabled it to write the 'rules' for exchange and largely to set the tone for domestic political intelligence gathering.[17] For example pressure from the US and UK was able to oblige the Australian Labour Party in 1948 to reverse its integration of the remaining wartime security service into the police and establish the new, free-standing ASIO.[18] Slightly earlier the Attlee Labour Government had expressed some independence from the security apparatus by appointing a police chief constable as the new head of MI5 in 1946 but this initial scepticism did not survive the desire to share in the developing US nuclear programme as exampled by Labour's adoption of US-recommended vetting procedures.[19]

By the 1960s the succession of British security 'scandals' – Burgess, Maclean, Philby, Blunt, Vassall, Bossard and the Profumo case – indicated so far as the US was concerned that not only was the British Security Service incapable of catching 'spies' unaided but, more significantly, that it had probably itself been penetrated at a high level by the Soviet KGB. Accordingly President Johnson commissioned a study of British intelligence in 1965 as a consequence of which some in the Central Intelligence Agency (CIA) – James Angleton in particular – appear to have hoped that they would soon have their own officials working within MI5. The Security Service was able to resist this but in 1967 those officials in MI6, MI5 and the CIA who shared Angleton's views on the omnipotence of the KGB and the extent of Soviet penetration of the West initiated the series of CANZAB counter-intelligence conferences which was intended to further the US hegemony. Since Angleton's demise in 1975 US pressure may have been less overt but in a general sense its focus has shifted rather than been reduced. What has been called the 'internationalization'[20] of US law enforcement has been developing alongside anticommunism during the twentieth century but, with the decline of the latter, has become much more significant amidst the 'new world disorder'.

In Britain the official response to these scandals was primarily a series of 'damage-limitation' policies but the tight grip of secrecy retained around security intelligence structures[21] has minimised the examination of not just whether the Security Service could effectively protect security but also the allegations from former security intelligence insiders – Miranda Ingram, Jock Kane, Cathy Massiter, Peter Wright, Colin Wallace, Fred Holroyd[22] - that its operations infringed the democratic process. Hitherto the reaction from the Labour Party in general to this range of most serious allegations and revelations has been timid. In part this is explained by the success of 'Thatcherism' in appropriating popular fears and insecurities in order both to protect the security apparatus from outside scrutiny and to strengthen it as an essential context for its liberalisation of the economy. However much these fears were aggravated by 'moral panics', they always had some material base in people's experience of the consequences of capitalist restructuring.

The challenge facing Labour is to develop an alternative position which enables it both to face down the Right's rhetoric on any issue relating to security or public order and to assert democratic control over domestic security apparatuses whose autonomy has been deployed on behalf of predominantly right-wing causes. If and when Labour takes power enormous pent-up expectations of social and political improvement will descend upon it and, to the extent that some of these are likely to be disappointed, a further challenge facing Labour will be to avoid simply making use of both the traditional and newer mechanisms of repression, for example, the Criminal Justice and Public Order Act 1994.

In meeting this challenge Labour must consider, first, what threats to national security actually exist and, only then, what organisations would be most appropriate to gather information about and counter those threats.

*What is National Security?*

Hitherto the political left within capitalist democracies has not really subjected the notion of 'national security' to detailed scrutiny because it perceived, quite correctly as we see below, that it was itself viewed by state security intelligence agencies as a major 'threat' to that security. Consequently there was a tendency to regard the entire notion of 'national security' as nothing but a veil behind which state agencies and their private sector allies would seek to repress dissent. It is now well-documented that notions of 'subversion' came to mean in practice that any activity on the left, even if entirely peaceful and legitimate, would be routinely surveilled by the state and, possibly, subject to disruption.[23] This could take a variety of forms but most involved some degree of 'information control'. Records released by the Public Records Office in August 1995 have confirmed the establishment by the 1945–50 Labour government of the Information Research Department (IRD) within the Foreign Office that, until its abolition in 1977, provided the primary vehicle for anticommunist propaganda. Significantly, Labour's initial desire that the IRD adopt a 'third way' between anti-communism and pro-capitalism was rapidly eroded by the military and intelligence officials primarily running the Department.[24] The IRD was primarily aimed at foreign audiences but did make its materials available to anticommunist British trade unionists. So also did Industrial Research and Information Services (IRIS) formed in 1956 as an off-shoot of Common Cause. Providing a platform for anticommunist propaganda this was financed primarily by private companies through tax deductible charitable donations but, when it became independent of Common Cause in 1963, was tided over by the Macmillan government with £40,000 from the intelligence services budget.[25]

Such close connections between the security intelligence services and the private sector date from the immediate aftermath of the first world war and the establishment of the Economic League (by the former head of Naval Intelligence) which conducted not just anticommunist propaganda but also ran its 'blacklisting' service into the 1990s.[26] Security Service information gathering regarding trades unions was most often carried out on the basis of unionists' membership or association with the Communist Party, a pretext that legitimised surveillance on the grounds that the Party was 'subversive'. But the use to which resulting 'intelligence' might be put went far beyond 'threats to national security', for example, a Security Service transcriber was instructed to listen particularly for any reference to the Ford Unions' bottom line in their pay negotiations late in 1978 when she received the material from the permanent telephone tap on Syd Harraway, a communist convenor at Fords Dagenham.[27]

Security intelligence agencies have always taken advantage of divisions within the labour movement, but this has not prevented the agencies employing disinformation more generally against the Labour Party. For example, Colin Wallace worked as a public relations officer for the Army in Northern Ireland from 1968 until 1974, latterly concerned with a variety of disinformation campaigns directed at paramilitary groups. During 1974, however, an intensive period of political activity in Britain including the NUM strike, Heath's 'who governs Britain?' election in February and a second election in October, Wallace became concerned that the raw material he was receiving from MI5 increasingly dealt with the financial and sexual vulnerabilities of British, especially Labour, politicians.

Wallace's evidence is just part of a broader picture that looks very like a campaign by, among others, members of the Security Service to discredit the Labour Party in general and Harold Wilson in particular.[29] Official rubbishing of these allegations has never been very convincing and none of the records that the British government has so far chosen to release in any way amends the picture. If nothing else, the history of these years should be a salutary lesson to any new Labour government that if it does challenge the security intelligence apparatus then it must be prepared for the possibility of similar disinformation campaigns appearing through the media outlets historically used for the dissemination of unattributable 'information'.

Operations against the NUM culminating in the 1984–5 strike were a central feature of the Security Service's operations after 1972. Then, resources began to be switched from the traditional targeting of Soviet representatives to 'domestic subversion' in the face of the growth of political and industrial struggles. Seumas Milne has recently produced a compelling account of the campaign involving the British state and private interests, notably Robert Maxwell, not only to break the strike but also to discredit Arthur Scargill. Alerted by some GCHQ employees to the fact that the three main security intelligence agencies had combined forces in a concerted effort to 'Get Scargill', Milne recounts the extensive human and technical surveillance operation mounted by MI5, including the use of agents provocateurs, the recruitment as sources of as many as three-quarters of media labour correspondents, the placing of a high level informer into the NUM's Sheffield HQ – Roger Windsor, the Chief Executive, and the extensive interception by GCHQ of European banking transactions in order to advise the court sequestrators where the NUM had sent its money.[30]

One problem with Milne's analysis is symptomatic of the challenge facing a future Labour government. In places the evidence in support of his account is rather thin yet, despite the seriousness of the allegations, remarkably little political fuss was made by senior members of the Labour Party at the time of the book's publication. In part this no doubt reflects the Party's embarrassment at its failure to challenge the Thatcher Government's handling of the strike, but it also reflects a lamentable lack of determination actually to ascertain the extent and propriety of the Security Service's operations against the strike. An inquiry into these operations, among others, would provide an excellent agenda for the post-election Intelligence and Security Committee established by the Intelligence Services Act 1994.

Since 1989 domestic security intelligence agencies have been at pains to point to the small proportion of their resources that are now devoted to the surveillance of 'subversives',[31] and there is independent evidence that certainly this is much reduced from earlier years.[32] But the extremely broad definition of national security still pertaining in the UK is a potential pretext for widespread political surveillance: 'the safeguarding of the state and the community against threats to their survival or well-being.'[33] Outside the UK inquiries into security intelligence abuses have resulted in a number of efforts to *narrow* similarly broad national security mandates but this has been resisted in Britain. First, there has been no public inquiry; second when ministers have been invited to narrow the official definition they have declined. Douglas Hurd, for example, during the passage of the Security Service Act said that the Government did not want to exclude *anything* from the Service's mandate which might one day become a threat.[34]

It is not, in fact, impossible to define this concept in such a way that it will concentrate security intelligence resources on genuine threats and reduce the risk of interference with legitimate political activities. This issue has most recently been addressed by Laurence Lustgarten and Ian Leigh who argue that, contrary to notions of the need for some 'balance' between security and rights that predominate in the security intelligence literature,[35] political and civil rights are actually a major constituent of national security. Consequently the national security of any state that fails to protect human rights is not worth defending. Therefore governments must elaborate precisely what they see as threats, respond to them proportionately and with appropriate mechanisms of oversight. The core security task to which, they argue, governments must be confined, is to defend democratic practice from foreign manipulation along with the ability to defend the nation's independence and territory against military attack.[36]

Their analysis can be criticised for resting on a somewhat idealist view of the role of law in defining areas of core state concern, for example, judges in the UK have shown themselves perfectly able simultaneously to affirm the importance of rights *in general* while denying them in individual cases,[37] but their 'minimalist' definition of national security provides a significant critique of officialdom's preference for 'maximalism'.

### *Challenging the extension of domestic security*

Formally, domestic security intelligence threats are enumerated as espionage, 'subversion', 'terrorism' and foreign influence. More recently, 'economic well-being' has been added to this list.[38] The central issue is to distinguish the genuine element of these 'threats' from that which is contrived and facilitates generalised political intelligence gathering.

#### *From espionage to 'economic well-being'.*

Espionage, we are told, has not ended with the end of the Cold War. There are some residual areas in which the traditional concern with protecting military secrets still applies, but officials are now more likely to refer to 'illegal technology transfer' and 'proliferation'. One reason for scepticism as to the security intelligence role here is that security agency action regarding 'technology transfer' will not be unambiguously determined by any legal prohibitions. Organisational interests must be considered: if an agency's primary mandate is intelligence-gathering then it may well connive at illegal technology transfers if, as a consequence of those transfers, it is receiving useful information. Thus the very utility to the SIS and Security Service of those who became the Matrix Churchill defendants was the access they gained to Iraqi factories and officials through supplying them illegally with machinery.

But more generally, 'counter-espionage' is being supplanted by the protection of 'economic well-being'. Since all states will define protection of the basic socio-economic structure as a fundamental task of governing, and in modern times governments expect their performance to be judged by the electorate largely in terms of the economy, we should not be surprised if 'national security' is viewed increasingly through the prism of economic 'well-being' but, again, there must be a challenge. The specific concern here is not whether states should seek intelligence regarding their vulnerabilities and threats faced within the global economy, but what role is to be played by domestic security agencies?

The issue is not whether economic activities require security – clearly they do, but it is normally provided by those economic sectors themselves and the costs passed on to consumers. In the UK where neo-liberalism has been in the ascendant for the last twenty years it would be ironic if state security intelligence agencies were to enter the economic field in order to provide national firms with protection against the operations of the market system. If this were to happen these agencies would presumably find themselves opposing the agencies of precisely those countries with whom they were formerly allied during the Cold War.[39]

The UK Security Service claims its interest is in the 'leakage of selective technology'[40] and the Security Service Act only mandates the Service to counter the actions of people outside Britain[41] but the present economy provides a crucially different context from that of the Cold War. This was conceptualised, however falsely, as a two-person zero-sum game: and domestic security agencies developed their organisational policies, practices, and culture accordingly. The 'Free World' and the 'Communist bloc' competed in such a way that the 'gains' of one equalled the 'losses' of the other.

The contemporary global economy is neither two-person nor zero-sum. The longevity of capitalism is partly accounted for by the fact that it is a variable sum game, though the winnings and losses are highly unequally divided and the numbers of competing states and corporations is now such that the global economy is an n-person game. Therefore, for security intelligence agencies it follows that there will be greater difficulties in identifying 'us'. Historically, this was defined in national-state terms even as patterns of economic ownership and control became steadily transnational. Now, patterns of ownership and production are such that identifying what is a 'Canadian' 'American' or 'British' company' (in order to advise/protect it) will be difficult. For example, an American writer on this issue lamented the failure of the US Government to provide leadership by re-defining national security to include economic competition and the need to counter 'competitive espionage', yet noted also that 'much' of the economic espionage reported by US companies in a 1992 survey was conducted by other US companies![42]

Alternatively, it has been argued that defensive economic intelligence should be based more on regional rather than national concerns[43] but this barely simplifies the issue since competition within regional blocs may be as fierce as that between them. A primary reason for the development of regional trading blocs is the degree of intra-bloc trade, much of which involves companies in direct competition with each other.

Another problem with current developments is that 'us' is officially defined in corporate terms. Clearly, 'economic well-being' should not be seen as simply a synonym for 'corporate profitability': in the following quote from Robert Reich any country might be substituted for 'America':

> ...American ownership of the corporation is profoundly less relevant to America's economic future than the skills, training, and knowledge commanded by American workers – workers who are increasingly employed within America by foreign-owned corporations. So who is us? The answer is, the American work force, the American people, but not particularly the American corporation.[44]

*From 'subversion' to 'terrorism'.*

Historically, security agencies within liberal capitalist states have regarded 'subversion' as synonymous with left-wing dissent – that never was justifiable in any terms other than the self-interest of the political elites themselves and maintaining this mandate perpetuates the risk of improper state surveillance of political activity. 'Subversion' in Britain is not a criminal offence and is defined so broadly as to permit the security surveillance of political activities that are neither illegal nor violent. The recent history of the equivalent provision in Canada is instructive: when the new CSIS was established in 1984, having been separated out from the RCMP, it was to operate for the first time with a statutory definition of what constituted threats to Canadian security. This included 'subversion' though, as is also the case in the UK, the actual word was not used in the statute. After a few years the new overseers of CSIS concluded that the old discredited ways of the RCMP Security Service remained essentially intact and, after a further government inquiry, the counter-subversion branch of the Service was disbanded. Over the next few years almost all its case files were closed and destroyed or sent to the public archives. Of the cases that were re-assessed relatively few were re-allocated to either counter-intelligence or counter-terrorism branches. Subsequently a parliamentary Committee conducting a five-year review of the CSIS Act concluded that the subversion section of the mandate was essentially redundant and should be repealed. The Government, however, adopted the Hurdian position of wishing to keep the provision 'just in case'[45].

After the defeat of the NUM strike the political violence associated with Northern Ireland became the primary threat addressed by the Security Service: in its 1993 corporate brochure MI5 said that 70% of its resources were allocated to terrorism (44% 'Irish and other domestic', 26% 'International').[46] What impact the Irish ceasefire has on these figures remains to be seen but a crucial question will be: how to ensure that there is some legitimate state structure for the gathering of information as to threats of serious political violence – whether directed at political structures or particular groups within the population – while preventing 'terrorism' simply replacing 'subversion' as the pretext for the widespread surveillance of political dissidents. This tendency within security intelligence agencies has been brought about not just by the conservatism of their personnel but also by the logic of targeting and surveillance. Any individuals who are planning illegal political violence will do so covertly and thus be harder to detect. By comparison, political activists organise and propagandise openly and thus are relatively easy to surveill – thus agencies develop large banks of data on the latter but frequently struggle to identify the former.[47]

*'Foreign Influence'*

'Foreign influence' is closely related to subversion and terrorism because western elites have assumed not only that domestic political conflict can only arise as a consequence of conspiracies[48] but most probably these conspiracies will be foreign-directed.[49] Again, the left has been particularly prone to this because it has explicitly avowed the centrality of international solidarity to its struggles. This category for surveillance has been particularly pernicious because, in its most extreme form, there is no way in which an individual can 'disprove' the proposition that she is an agent of foreign influence. The only 'evidence' required for a positive threat-assessment is that someone takes public positions that are consistent with those of a foreign state. Typically, during the Cold War, therefore, arguing for British unilateral disarmament was 'evidence' simply because that was consistent with Soviet aims to achieve military superiority.

The bizarre and potentially damaging consequences of this 'logic' were illustrated most recently when *The Sunday Times* headlined 'KGB: Michael Foot was our agent' on the front page of its February 19, 1995 issue. The following story was based primarily on the recollections of Oleg Gordievsky, the former KGB officer who had worked for the British as a 'defector-in-place' between 1974 and 1985 when he finally defected and whose memoirs commenced their serialisation in the paper the following week. The substance of the story was that Foot, among others, had been targeted by the KGB as a potential 'agent of influence' in the 1960s because of his editorship of *Tribune*. Soviet officials, including KGB officers, with whom he met made small donations to the paper. *The Sunday Times* argued that its 'disclosures' were given such prominence because they showed how the Soviet Union had sought influence, that the British Left and communism had a 'shared philosophy' and because Foot had later become a party leader.[50] Neither of the first two reasons was remotely novel which leads to the conclusion that it was the opportunity to damage a former leader of the Labour Party that most appealed to editors and publishers of *The Sunday Times*, ignoring completely the fact that neither Foot personally nor *Tribune* had ever toed a Soviet line. The fact that these views will have coincided on occasions is the only 'support' for such a classic smear. When Foot sued for libel *The Sunday Times* retracted, offered 'sincere apologies' and paid Foot a six-figure sum in costs and damages.[51]

However, there remains the possibility that foreign influence may be exerted in a manner against which any state has the right to protect itself, for example, Canada's concern at the clandestine activities of foreign intelligence officers within their large ethnic communities is understandable.[52] Concomitant to this, however, is the danger that security agencies alleged 'concern' with the safety of their ethnic communities actually arises from their pursuit of inquiries on behalf of the security agencies of allied states. Should these states face major political challenges then the 'concern' may actually be to surveill foreign sympathisers with that challenge. This certainly occurred in the FBI's investigation of the Committee in Solidarity with the People of El Salvador (CISPES) during 1983–5[53] and something similar may have happened also in Canada in 1995 when CSIS 'interviewed' a number of Canadian human rights workers who had been working in Chiapas, the area of the Zapatista uprising against the Mexican government – Canada's partner in NAFTA.[54]

Therefore the issue becomes how to achieve protection without infringing on democratic liberties? At the very least, this concept must be defined more restrictively than it is at present in the UK ('the activities of agents of foreign powers') so that it is limited to covert activities. All nations use a variety of public relations techniques in order to influence each others' policies that are not appropriate concerns for security agencies, but covert funding of domestic publications or political organisations are.[56]

*From 'domestic security' to 'law enforcement'*

Although not seen historically as matters of 'national security', the final collection of threats that are currently receiving increased attention from domestic security services relate to law enforcement. This is perhaps the most crucial area for current concern. The UK Security Service Act 1989 did not include a role for MI5 regarding crime, except permitting it to pass on 'collateral' information, but the Intelligence Services Act 1994 that sets out for the first time in statute the jobs of the SIS and GCHQ specifically includes 'the prevention or detection of serious crime' as a function in addition to those regarding 'national security' and 'economic well-being'.[57] In the US a string of cases from the 1980s onwards – Noriega, BCCI and BNL – led to considerable controversy as the organisational interests of intelligence agencies in information and of law enforcers in prosecutable cases clashed loudly.[58]

In Canada, CSIS is treading very warily given the fact that it is barely over a decade since it was created by the removal of the Security Service from the RCMP – the federal police force, but the UK Security Service is far less reticent about colonising areas of law enforcement, despite its initial protestations to the contrary. In her Introduction to the corporate brochure the Director General, Stella Rimington, wrote in July 1993:

> . . . the work of the Service is strictly limited to countering activities which are assessed as threatening national security, or safeguarding the economic well-being of the United Kingdom. *There are therefore no plans for the Service* to become involved in the investigation of, for example, the misuse of illegal drugs, or organised crime.[59]

But by October 1995 the Security Service had successfully positioned themselves to take on an increasing role with respect to 'organised crime'. The speed of this shift, accelerated by the ceasefire in Northern Ireland, raised even sharper questions as to the future role for the Security Service while the main alternative – the National Criminal Intelligence Service set up in 1992 including police, customs and civilian analysts – suffered from under-resourcing and the unwillingness of chief constables to allow it to become operational. Thus Stella Rimington's public lecture to the English-Speaking Union in October 1995 offering 'the same strategic approach, the same investigative techniques' to counter the threat of organised crime as had been developed to deal 'with the more familiar threats'[60] previewed John Major's announcement to the Tory Party Conference the following week that legislation would be prepared to extend the Security Service's mandate accordingly.[61]

The ease with which a potentially underemployed Security Service has been able to occupy this turf can be explained in part by the essential similarity of security and criminal intelligence methods (discussed further below). The only real respect in which they have differed has been in targets: those of security intelligence have been explicitly political – dissidents, peace campaigners, those employing political violence – while criminal intelligence has been concentrated primarily against the provision of illegal markets – drugs, gambling, smuggling and the laundering of the proceeds of these markets. Contrary to the impression sometimes given,[62] these pre-date the end of the Cold War although the extent of some has increased with the globalisation of computerised information-exchange. While some of these phenomena are capable of causing significant (if poorly quantifiable) harms to both public and private interests and there is certainly scope for utilising intelligence in support of law enforcement, for example, countering nuclear proliferation, the wholesale application of security intelligence methodology would be highly inappropriate. But it is not only Stella Rimington for whom 'International Organized Crime' promises to fill the void left by the collapse of 'International Communism'; Roy Godson cites US counter-espionage of the 1940s and counter-terrorism of the 1970s as 'roadmaps' for a US, indeed international, strategy against organised crime,[63] ignoring the fact that 'organised crime' is an endemic part of most capitalist economies (including that of the US). Following this map will certainly ensure lifetime employment for security intelligence personnel but is as likely to contain or defeat international organised crime as it is to eliminate sin.

Meanwhile clear dangers are posed by inserting unreconstructed security intelligence agencies into the criminal justice process. The traditional 'targeting' practices of security intelligence agencies have led them inexorably towards the surveillance of dissent. 'Organised crime' is already viewed by police in essentially ethnic terms, for example, 'Italian-', 'Asian-', and, most recently, 'Russian'. Additionally the new European security architecture is dominated by official concerns with population movements and defined largely in terms of ethnicity.[64] Consequently one particularly negative aspect of this change might be yet greater generalised surveillance of ethnic minorities.

Further, there is a clear gulf between the agencies' traditional practices and the requirements for open and fair trials. Apparently, it is the trial process that will be reconstructed in order to close the gulf, for example, the use of Public Immunity Interest certificates to prevent disclosure of prosecution evidence to the defence and witnesses appearing anonymously.[65] Such practices have infamously contributed in the past to the succession of major miscarriages of justice revealed in the UK since 1989. However, are current developments – domestic security intelligence agencies supporting or supplanting the police – the only alternative?

### *Alternative Organisational Futures*

In the UK domestic security intelligence is currently the responsibility of the Security Service and police special branches (SB). The former is primarily an intelligence agency and has no police powers but it may use a variety of countering techniques short of arrest. The latter is the junior partner – in the words of its 1994 Guidelines it is 'to assist the Security Service in carrying out its statutory duty',[66] and it is to gather information with respect to those same threats as does the Security Service in addition to making 'public order assessments'. Both agencies are involved in 'security': personnel vetting is carried out in part by the Service and partly by other departments, SB advises on and provides personal protection for prominent people while the Service advises government on the security of buildings and information. Are both these agencies necessary?

The arguments for keeping the role of a domestic security intelligence agency distinct from that of a police force have been most systematically considered by the Canadian McDonald Commission (1977–81). Their detailed discussion is re-examined here because of its relevance, though, of course, it cannot be assumed that what suits Canada will necessarily be appropriate elsewhere. The Commission's Report explained first why it thought government needed counter-intelligence, -terrorism, and -subversion capabilities,[67] why it thought these functions could not be achieved by reliance on conventional policework[68] and why it thought the function should be carried out by a separate civilian security agency rather than by a special section within the RCMP.[69] Generalising from the Canadian experience, it is argued that the police's gathering of information is for more specific purposes and by more restricted means than is appropriate for a government's need for security intelligence. The specific purpose is prosecution and the means of gathering information for that purpose are governed by rules of evidence and disclosure determined by judges. Given future security uncertainties, it is argued, the state requires more general information and sources should not be restricted only to those that will be admissible in court. Therefore, the argument continues, the kinds of people traditionally recruited into police forces and trained in a culture that emphasises obtaining relatively short-term 'results' are ill-equipped for the longer-term and more analytical nature of security intelligence work.

A second argument is that denying police powers to a security intelligence agency is a check on any potential abuse of power. For example, it might be argued that an agency with police powers of arrest and charge will find it easier to coerce people into providing information. In part this argument reflects the well-placed fear of a 'political police' in which the very vagueness and permissiveness of 'political crime' laws[70] adds immeasurably to the power of an agency that may arrest and detain people for 'thoughtcrimes'.

McDonald pointed to the benefit that could accrue from having a security intelligence agency, without police powers, separate from a police agency with certain residual security functions, namely that they would check and balance each other by having to co-operate on certain operations and also potentially providing information about the other's misdeeds.[71] In 1994, addressing herself to a related question – the suggestion that the UK required a single, unified 'counter-terrorist structure', Stella Rimington argued that co-ordination and focusing of the necessary expertise would not necessarily be achieved by centralisation. Rather, she argued, the existing structure in which several government departments, the police, Customs and Excise and the Crown Prosecution Service all 'added value' without eroding their specialist skills or losing the flexibility to turn to other work, had demonstrated its effectiveness.[72]

Whether the 'successes' of these arrangements outweigh the 'failures' generated through inter-organisational struggles is not known, but the general argument that more agencies, competing and co-operating, might be preferable has been recently supported also by a radical critic of the UK security regime, Richard Norton-Taylor, pointing out that the current disputes between police and MI5 over 5 may not promote efficiency:

> Yet it may have one, unintended, benefit – rivalries will prevent the creation of an over-

arching national agency, with the threats to civil liberties that the history of the FBI has so clearly demonstrated in the US.[73]

Perhaps the FBI is not the best example to use since in the US liberties have been as much assaulted by other federal agencies such as the DEA and its predecessors and the 'Red Squads' established by many municipal police forces.[74] However, the point is taken that one of the factors strengthening political dissent has been the simple inefficiencies of the state's attempts to surveill and repress it.

What are the arguments against such a separation? Organisationally it can be argued that the number of separate agencies that should be maintained with overlapping functions should be minimised. As we have seen, a problem with maintaining a separate domestic security intelligence agency is that it has an ongoing bureaucratic interest in the discovery of fresh 'security' threats. Jurisdictional disputes ('turf wars') between agencies are an indispensable feature of bureaucracy but they can be particularly intensive within the security intelligence area because of the compartmentalisation of knowledge ('need-to-know') which aggravates the reluctance to share information and co-operate with other agencies for fear of compromising valued sources. Further, having more than one agency, possibly under different regimes of ministerial control, if any, may result in some sub-contracting of sensitive operations between agencies, specifically towards those in which control and accountability are less developed.

Given organisational jealousies it might be proposed as a general rule that enforcement agencies will prefer to act on the information provided by their own intelligence 'heads'. There is some evidence, therefore, that agencies which are 'only' intelligence agencies might seek some way of acting on their intelligence, that is developing their own 'arms', while those with executive functions will seek to develop their own means of generating intelligence.[75]

Another argument for separation is that security intelligence work requires ministerial control while policework must remain independent but ministerial control or direction of security intelligence work is a double-edged sword. While it is important to prevent security intelligence agencies from enjoying so much autonomy that they become 'independent security states',[76] they may also be mis-used for partisan purposes by the party in power.[77] Within the current UK security framework, neither the Security Service nor police are tasked by political authorities (as are SIS and GCHQ). Therefore, to shift the security intelligence function from the Security Service to the police would involve no great innovation constitutionally. In the UK the notion of ministerial control of police, however, is seen officially as anathema. But what does this doctrine of 'constabulary independence' actually mean? Its primary value is as political myth which conceals the extent of the increasing central government influence over policing as manifest in its role in budgeting, regulations and Home Office circulars regarding policy. The myth has been utilised mainly as a means of rebutting the attempts of left-wing local governments in the 1980s to have greater influence over local policing policies,[78] but its symbolic importance can also be seen in the efforts of the British government to conceal their direction of police policy with respect to the NUM strike in 1984–5.

The central core of the doctrine that should be preserved is that the prosecution of individuals should not be subject to partisan political pressures; would this be violated if security intelligence functions were to be carried out by the police? If, as is argued here, as much as possible of the security intelligence mandate should be defined in terms of the criminal law, then there is no principled objection to political control of the *investigative* priorities of the police. Historically the Attorney General has been given control over security-related *prosecutions* precisely because of their political 'sensitivity'. The rhetoric of the rule of law, however, does not permit the political direction of the criminal justice process and so, we are told, the Attorney General acts as an individual, not as a member of the government, when making decisions over prosecutions. This fiction has been exposed on a number of recent occasions in the UK as Attorneys General have acted, or have been used as, 'presentational' devices to conceal Cabinet manipulation,[79] for example, in the Westland and *Spycatcher* cases. Should the police take over the security intelligence function, however, the prospect of political manipulation of prosecutions would be no worse, or possibly a little less given the somewhat lower susceptibility of the police to partisan political pressures.

The argument here is not, in any event, for the creation of some super-agency performing all domestic security intelligence functions, but the more limited one of suggesting the removal of one agency on the grounds that its existence is neither beneficial nor necessary. Police, special branch or whatever, will still need to co-operate with other enforcement agencies such as Customs and Excise. Also, to the extent that national police intelligence units become more significant as a consequence of shifts in functions, it is important to reiterate the point that this must be conducted only within a broader context of re-structuring and democratising state structures in the UK so that any tendencies for such units to become 'firms within the firm' are minimised.

### *Conclusion: Sack the Spooks?*

It has been argued that current trends towards extending the surveillance activities of a domestic security agency such as MI5 should be resisted.

Their most extensive abuses of power have resulted from excessively vague mandates and a lack of democratic oversight. Modern states do require some means of assessing the extent of genuine threats to their security and public safety, but these should be defined in terms of the criminal law and minimalist definitions of 'national security'.

Therefore it is proposed that any new Labour government inquire into the domestic security structure with a view to abolishing the Security Service; those of its functions and personnel still being required being reallocated to the appropriate section of the police. The vehicle for such an inquiry could be the Intelligence and Security Committee already in place but the limited access to information enjoyed by that Committee would be a problem. Rather, a free-standing committee of inquiry would be a better vehicle for the necessary examination of precisely what threats to public security and safety, if any, are deemed to require special investigative powers and then the most appropriate organisation for the task.[80] The current regime of control and oversight of both security intelligence and police is inadequate; consequently a simple transfer of functions from one to the other would not be helpful. For example, it can be argued that the current accountability regime for national-level police squads such as the Metropolitan Police special branch and the National Criminal Intelligence Service is no more transparent than that for the Security Service. It is equally important that Labour applies critical scrutiny to the plans of some chief constables for a 'British FBI'. Any reconstruction of the police and security apparatus must take place within a broader context of constitutional reform: particularly the incorporation of a bill of rights and access to information that goes beyond the cosmetics of the present 'Open Government' package in the UK.

It is assumed that the state will continue to gather foreign intelligence both by HUMINT and SIGINT. Domestic intelligence, once 'threats' come to be defined entirely in terms of the criminal law, would be the investigative responsibility of the police and other law enforcement agencies, presumably with some continuing organisational specialisation between special branches (for explicitly 'political' threats) and other special squads for 'non-political' criminal threats such as fraud and drugs. Since threats do not conveniently fall into exclusive 'foreign' or 'domestic' categories there will of course need to be arrangements for liaison between the relevant law enforcement and foreign intelligence agencies. As regards covert foreign influence, for example, information as to this may be generated abroad (by a foreign intelligence agency) or domestically in which case the investigative peg would be existing laws relating to corruption.

Some have argued that applying a 'criminal standard' to security intelligence activities unduly restricts the state's ability to defend itself against undemocratic attack.[81] However, not restricting agencies in this way has historically led not to proven effectiveness against 'spies' and 'terrorists' but to the accumulation of large quantities of information about many varieties of perfectly proper political activities. Consequently limiting security intelligence surveillance to some criminal standard will actually concentrate the minds of officials on the difficult task of identifying those few who may be planning some criminal activity and/or developing information about those actions that can inform some form of countering action.

Clearly this proposal is no panacea – controlling state surveillance or 'political policing' will remain extremely difficult and contentious; Turk argued that:

> . . . the process of intelligence-gathering always tends to flow through and around legal constraints, and to be limited only by political considerations and the available technology.[82]

However, the role of law is not one-dimensional – certainly it is no guarantee of correct behaviour by the state but neither can it be dismissed as irrelevant to the calculations of state officials. If only for reasons of self-protection, they will prefer to act within legal parameters and therefore the first part of the process of controlling excessive state surveillance is to ensure that as far as possible it is confined to activities that are actually illegal, that is, excluding such categories as 'subversion'. This will be easier if state surveillance is the responsibility of law enforcement bodies rather than intelligence agencies lacking enforcement functions. Since the 'new threats' discovered by security agencies since the end of the Cold War are predominantly criminal – drugs, money laundering, etc. – this strengthens the argument that the police will be the better locus for security intelligence gathering.

As long as capitalism remains the dominant form of economic organisation, and 'economic well-being' remains of central concern to elected governments, then, other things being equal, it is inevitable that one dominant interest of state security apparatuses will continue to be those seeking to challenge the dominance of the capitalist form. Hitherto the essentially unchecked autonomy of security intelligence agencies has meant that such dissenters were the primary targets of surveillance even though their opposition took place legally and peacefully within a democratic political process. The task now is to curtail that autonomy so that only those challenges that are expressed illegally and violently come within the legitimate frame of state surveillance. It is the present contention that this is most likely to be achieved by a Labour government committed, first, to a thorough auditing of the massive democratic deficit incurred by domestic security agencies and, second, to the development of a security regime under better control and properly accountable. No Labour, or any other, government will be able to reverse the general rapid growth of security surveillance, but by asserting some control for the first time of those most secret parts of the state machinery it can demonstrate its commitment to the progressive development of a more democratic state in the UK.

## NOTES

The author gratefully acknowledges the helpful comments given on an earlier draft by Annie Demirjian, Ian Leigh, Richard Norton-Taylor, Leo Panitch, Reg Whitaker and some anonymous others.

1. For example, on the US see M. Raskin, 'Democracy versus the National Security State,' *Law and Contemporary Problems*, 40(3), 1976, pp.189–220; on the UK see T. Bunyan, *The History and Practice of the Political Police in Britain*, Quartet Books, London, 1977.
2. For example, D. Lyon, *The Electronic Eye: the rise of surveillance society*, Polity, Cambridge, 1994.
3. G.T. Marx, *Undercover: police surveillance in America*, University of California Press, Berkeley, 1988, pp.219–33.
4. L. Johnston, *The Rebirth of Private Policing*, Routledge, London, 1992, pp.71–86; also, see T. Jones & T. Newburn, *How Big is the Private Security Industry?*, Policy Studies Institute, London, 1994.
5. M. Foucault, 'Governmentality,' in G. Burchell *et al* (eds.) *The Foucault Effect: studies in governmentality*, Harvester Wheatsheaf, London, 1991, pp.102–3.
6. Bob Jessop makes the point that both Foucault and Poulantzas agree on this despite the differences in their approaches to state power: *State Theory: putting capitalist states in their place*, Polity, Cambridge, 1990, p.235.
7. A. Gamble, *The Free Economy and the Strong State: the politics of Thatcherism*, Macmillan, Basingstoke, 1988.
8. Lyon, *Electronic Eye*, pp.218–9.
9. Marx, *Undercover*, suggests that Huxley is a better guide than Orwell to current developments in modern capitalist states because of the pre-eminence of the 'velvet glove' over the 'iron fist', pp.231–2.
10. Lyon, *Electronic Eye*, p.217.
11. W. van den Daele, 'Scientific Evidence and the Regulation of Technical Risks: twenty years of demythologizing the experts,' in N. Stehr & R. Ericson (eds) *The Culture and Power of Knowledge*, de Gruyet, Berlin and New York, p.332.
12. H.S. Becker, 'Whose Side Are We On?' in Becker, *Sociological Work: Method and Substance*, Allen Lane, London, 1971, pp. 123–34.
13. R. Whitaker, 'Security and Intelligence in the Post-Cold War World,' *Socialist Register 1992*, p.113.
14. For a summary of these events see, for example, G. Weller, 'The CSIS Under Stress,' *Canadian Public Administration*, 31(2), Summer 1988, pp.279–302.
15. R. Thurlow, *The Secret State: British internal security in the twentieth century*, Blackwell, Oxford, 1994, p.43.
16. F.H. Hinsley & C.A.G. Simkins, *British Intelligence in the Second World War: security and counter-intelligence*, HMSO, London, 1990, pp.6–7, 177–8.
17. UKUSA is fully explored in J.T. Richelson & D. Ball, *The Ties That Bind*, Unwin Hyman, London, 2nd edition, 1990.
18. See, for example, D. McKnight, *Australia's Spies and their Secrets*, Allen & Unwin, St Leonards, NSW, 1994, pp.6–25.
19. For details see I. Linn, *Application Refused: employment vetting by the State*, Civil Liberties Trust, London, 1990, pp.9–10.
20. E.A. Nadelmann, *Cops Across Borders: the internationalization of US criminal law*

*enforcement*, Pennsylvania State University Press, Pennsylvania, 1993. A recent US State Department Survey found that eight American law enforcement agencies employ 1,649 people permanently assigned overseas. (*CASIS Intelligence Newsletter* #24, Fall 1995, University of New Brunswick, Frederickton, p.23).

21. The Major governments have proclaimed that they are embarking on 'Open Government' – the title of a White Paper published in 1993. This has resulted in some volunteering of historical files on certain security intelligence issues, eg, surveillance of the British Union of Fascists, but these releases remain solely at government discretion. There is no right to access nor any means, as in Australia, Canada and the US, to challenge the government before some independent tribunal. For discussion see R. Aldrich, 'The Waldegrave Initiative and Secret Service Archives: new materials and new policies,' *Intelligence and National Security*, 10(1) January 1995, pp.192–7.
22. These are summarised in P. Gill, *Policing Politics: security intelligence and the liberal democratic state*, Frank Cass, London, 1994, pp.20–27.
23. eg see Commission of Inquiry concerning certain activities of the RCMP, Second Report, Volume 1, *Freedom and Security Under the Law*, Minister of Supply and Services Canada, 1981, pp.445–511 (hereafter 'McDonald').
24. *The Guardian*, August 18, 1995, pp.3, 9.
25. D. Osler, 'Anti-red, and alive,' *New Statesman and Society*, February 10, 1995, p.18.
26. M. Hollingsworth & C. Tremayne, *The Economic League: the Silent McCarthyism*, NCCL, London, 1989, provides a good summary of the league's history and operations.
27. Interview in *MI5's Official Secrets* broadcast on Channel 4, March 8, 1985.
28. P. Foot, *Who Framed Colin Wallace?* Pan, London, 1990, pp.41–2.
29. The clearest expositions of this are: D. Leigh, *The Wilson Plot: the intelligence services and the discrediting of a prime minister 1945–76*, Heinemann, London, 1988 and S. Dorril & R. Ramsay, *Smear! Wilson and the Secret State*, Fourth Estate, London, 1991.
30. S. Milne, *The Enemy Within: MI5, Maxwell and the Scargill Affair*, Verso, London, 1994, pp.252–85.
31. The proportion of Security Service resources allocated to 'subversion' was officially said to be 5% in 1993 (*The Security Service*, HMSO, London, July 1993). Stella Rimington described this as 'only a tiny fraction of what it was ten years ago.' ('Intelligence, Security and the Law.' James Smart Lecture, London, November 3, 1994).
32. Security Intelligence Review Committee, *Annual Report for 1987–88*, Minister of Supply and Services, Ottawa, 1988, pp.13–14.
33. As given by Douglas Hurd, House of Commons Debates, March 23, 1984, col.591.
34. House of Commons Debates, January 17, 1989, cols. 213–4.
35. For example, the Report of the Canadian Senate's Special Committee on the CSIS was entitled *Delicate Balance: a security intelligence service in a democratic society*, Minister of Supply and Services, Ottawa, 1983.
36. L, Lustgarten and I. Leigh, *In From the Cold: national security and parliamentary democracy*, Clarendon Press, Oxford, 1994, pp.4–26.
37. D.J. McBarnet, *Conviction: Law, the State and the Construction of Justice*, Macmillan, London, 1983, pp.154–68.
38. For instance, Security Service Act 1989, s.1.
39. Documentation regarding French targeting of US and UK corporations during 1989–91 provides the basis for a brief chapter in J. Adams, *The New Spies: exploring the frontiers of espionage*, Hutchinson, London, 1994, pp.121–6.
40. *The Security Service*, 1993, p.16.
41. Security Service Act, s.1(3).
42. J.T. Strong, 'Tilting with Machiavelli: fighting competitive espionage in the 1990s,' *International Journal of Intelligence and Counterintelligence*, 7(2), 1994, pp.165–6.
43. S. Porteous, 'Economic Espionage: issues arising from increased government involvement with the private sector,' *Intelligence and National Security*, 9(4), 1994,

pp.743–4.
44. Quoted in R.M. Fort, *Economic Espionage: problems and prospects*, Consortium for the Study of Intelligence, 1993, p.9
45. See Gill, *Policing Politics*, pp.107–12 for further details.
46. *The Security Service*, HMSO, 1993, p.12.
47. E.g., Jean-Paul Brodeur, 'On Evaluating Threats to the National Security of Canada and to the Civil Rights of Canadians,' Paper for Security Intelligence Review Committee Seminar, October 1985, pp.7–9.
48. See S. Hall *et al*, *Policing the Crisis: Mugging, the State and Law and Order*, Macmillan, Basingstoke, 1978, pp.309–10.
49. See B. Porter, *Plots and Paranoia*, Unwin Hyman, London, 1989, *passim*; R. Thurlow, *The Secret State: British internal security in the twentieth century*, Blackwell, Oxford, 1994, p.396.
50. February 26, 1995, p.5.
51. *The Guardian*, July 7, 1995, p.1; July 8, 1995, p.3.
52. The Canadian Security Intelligence Review Committee has recently reviewed some of the activities of CSIS in this regard. SIRC, *Annual Report 1994–95*, Minister of Supply and Services, Ottawa, 1995, pp.17–19, 21–23.
53. G.M. Stern, *The FBI's Misguided Probe of CISPES*, Center for National Security Studies, Washington DC, 1988, pp.2–16.
54. *Toronto Star*, April 22, 1995, A1; April 25, 1995, A3. SIRC, *Annual Report 1994–95* refers to the Review Committee's 'serious reservations' regarding CSIS' liaison arrangements with security agencies in one Latin American and one African country, 1995, p.25. It noted also that CSIS assessments of foreign agencies paid inadequate attention to human rights abuses and corruption, pp.29–31.
55. Security Service Act, 1989, s.1(2).
56. Lustgarten & Leigh, 1994, pp.408–10.
57. Intelligence Services Act, 1994, s.1(2).
58. A joint task force established by the Justice Department and CIA eventually reported in August 1994 with 23 recommendations, short of new legislation, for ways of improving the co-operation of the intelligence and law enforcement communities. Joint Task Force on Intelligence and Law Enforcement, *Report to the Attorney General and Director of Central Intelligence*, August 1994.
59. *The Security Service*, 1993, p.5.
60. 'National Security and International Understanding', London, October 4, 1995, p.13.
61. *The Guardian*, October 14, 1995, p.7.
62. For example, Stella Rimington talked of the phenomenon of 'organised crime' as being 'comparatively new'. 'National Security and International Understanding', October 4 1995, p.13.
63. R. Godson, 'The Crisis of Governance: devising strategy to counter international organized crime,' *Terrorism and Political Violence*, 6(2) Summer 1994, pp.163–77.
64. For example, see T. Bunyan (ed), *Statewatching the New Europe: a handbook on the European state*, Statewatch, London, 1993.
65. For example see C. Foley, *Northern Ireland: human rights and the peace dividend*, NCCL, London, 1995, pp.38–40. Also interview with Michael Mansfield QC, *Red Pepper*, April 1995, pp.23–4.
66. *Guidelines on Special Branch Work in Great Britain*, Home Office, London, July 1994.
67. McDonald, 1981, pp.414–7.
68. McDonald, 1981, pp.418–21.
69. McDonald, 1981, pp.753–76.
70. A.T. Turk, *Political Criminality: the defiance and defense of authority*, Sage, Beverley Hills, 1982, p.54.
71. McDonald, 1981, p.759.

72. Rimington, November 3, 1994.
73. 'The Fearful State,' *The Guardian*, March 7, 1995.
74. F. Donner, *Protectors of Privilege: Red Squads and Police Repression in Urban America*, University of California Press, Berkeley, 1990.
75. For example, Jean-Paul Brodeur accurately predicted that one consequence of the removal of the Security Service from the Canadian RCMP, while leaving it with responsibility for certain security offences, would lead to the RCMP developing its own intelligence unit. 'Criminal Justice and National Security,' in P. Hanks & J.D. McCamus, *National Security: surveillance and accountability in a democratic society*, Les Editions Yvon Blais, Cowansville, Quebec, 1989, p.66.
76. As has been argued was the case with some FBI programmes in the 1960s: W.W. Keller, *The Liberals and J. Edgar Hoover: the rise and fall of a domestic intelligence state*, Princeton UP, Princeton, 1989.
77. Gill, *Policing Politics*, pp.217–26 for detailed discussion.
78. L. Lustgarten, *The Governance of Police*, Sweet & Maxwell, 1986 provides a thorough critique of this notion of constabulary independence.
79. Gill, *Policing Politics*, pp.221–2.
80. Gill, *Policing Politics*, ch.9 discusses in more detail the issues surrounding any such inquiry.
81. K.G. Robertson, 'The Study of Intelligence in the US' in R. Godson (ed.) *Comparing Foreign Intelligence*, National Strategy Information Center, Washington DC, 1988, p.20; A. Shulsky, *Silent Warfare*, Brassey's, McLean Va., 1991, pp.152–6.
82. Turk, 1982, p.123.

# SPORT, GENDER AND POLITICS: MOVING BEYOND THE O.J. SAGA

Varda Burstyn

## INTRODUCTION

For the last half of 1994 and the first nine months of 1995, North America was fascinated and sickened by the O.J. Simpson saga. Between January and October, coverage of the former football player accounted for more minutes of air-time on ABC, CBS and NBC prime-time news than Bosnia and the Oklahoma bombing combined; and thirteen times as much as the debate on Medicare.[1] Part gladiatorial combat, part soap opera, part show trial, part pornography, part police-and-courtroom drama – the Simpson trial generated an economy of hundreds of millions of dollars in television, publishing and novelties, and in lawyers, experts, legal and prison services. The trial alone cost taxpayers eight million dollars, and it was the very least of it. The gold rush is still on. Now that he has been acquitted, Simpson stands to make multimillions himself. 'The obvious precedent,' wrote Howard Witt of the *Chicago Tribune* in early October, 1995, was 'last month's pay-per-view Mike Tyson boxing match, which netted the convicted rapist a quick $25 million.'[2] As this article is being completed, Simpson is negotiating to do a pay-per-view television appearance for $40 million. He has also applied for trademarks on 120 commodity items, including placemats, pyjamas, aprons, and – yes – 'squeeze dolls' for little girls.

The effects of all this have been palpable, indeed inescapable. While it ran its course, the trial served as a textbook-case lightning rod for social and political disaffection. It was a massive circus that captured energy, exacerbated ugly and perverse attitudes with respect to race, sex and gender, and bred even deeper cynicism about the law, police and justice than existed before. On the one hand, the defence did not convincingly establish Simpson's innocence, so that large sectors of the (primarily white) North American public were angered by the verdict of 'not guilty' and the *National Enquirer* ran headlines such as 'O.J. targeted for death by Right wing groups'. On the other hand, the stunning revelations by the defence of racism, misogyny, corruption and tampered evidence in the Los

Angeles Police Department mortally undermined the prosecution's credibility and legitimacy as well. Following on the Rodney King beating by LAPD officers and the acquittal of the police by an all white jury, the Simpson trial further deepened convictions among African Americans that the police and justice systems are thoroughly rigged against them in the most spectacular of ways. And women of all colours wondered why, even if not guilty of murder, O.J. the batterer was being cast as a hero on his acquittal.

O.J. Simpson the black athlete and Mark Fuhrman the white cop seemed during the long months of the trial to be consummate antagonists, each stirring fierce passions of loyalty and hatred among his respective supporters. Yet notwithstanding appearances, these two men actually share a common ideology that unites them as much as the colour of their skins and their traditional political ideologies divide them. They share an ideology – a 'feeling-idea' that animates emotion and action – of coercive entitlement; and they share it as *men*. At its most blunt, it sounds like this. 'I like to hurt women when I make love to them,' Mike Tyson was quoted as saying in a recent issue of *Sports Illustrated*.[3] 'I like to hear them scream with pain . . . to see them bleed . . . it gives me pleasure.' The authors of the article in which these words appeared repeated them with some incredulity. But Tyson likes to relate to *men* this way, so why not to women? Judging by the size of the audiences Tyson is commanding now that he has been released from prison, this ideology links him not only to Simpson and Fuhrman but to millions of other men as well. This ideology is actively constructed in the ritual formations of men's culture – above all, in sport; and it is celebrated and popularized by the mass media.

That the Simpson saga was profoundly entwined with issues of gender, colour and class in the U.S. today has been acknowledged with more or less depth in the mass media. Crucially, however, the saga is also linked to the specific cultural practice of sport, and the world of men's culture which sport both exemplifies and organizes. Like Tyson the rapist, Simpson the batterer is a not just one good boy gone bad for idiosyncratic reasons; but a predictable example of the inevitable spillage of values and modes of behaviour from the stadiums and arenas of contemporary sport into 'real life'. The complicity of sport in the violent actions of such athletes (and of many other men who emulate them) is not addressed in public discourse. To the contrary, the subject is conspicuous by its absence.

Were the Simpson drama to fully highlight its own tributary structures it would properly provoke not just a general breast-beating about racism and sexism (O.J. as victim of one, Nicole as victim of the other); but also a specific and overdue interrogation of the cultural practice of sport that made O.J. a hero in the first place, and placed him like a god in the popular pantheon. For it is in teaching the culture of masculinity and masculinism,[4] with their specific values and modes of behaviour, that contemporary sport provides a school for authoritarian, punitive and vengeful ideologies for males; ideologies which then serve to animate other ideologies of inequality and associated behaviours of domination.

Despite the way that sport has largely been accepted across political lines as a benign and even positive cultural practice, in this essay I argue that in fact, as a central institution for the rehearsal and regeneration of masculinity and masculinism, sport is a central institution for the regeneration of anti-social and, by direct extension, anti-socialist, values in contemporary society.[5] Far from being the democratic and fraternal force its supporters have claimed, sport constitutes a master narrative of competition and domination – indeed a narrative of masters – through its inflection of gender, in an age when other master narratives are crumbling. As an embodied ideological practice, sport should be considered a central material and discursive institution that reproduces relations of inequality and strife. Because of the dominance of men's culture within mixed culture as a whole, and the dominance of sport within men's culture, sport's celebration of aggressive conquest has great influence and power, shaping personal and communal ideals and political reflexes.

The elaborate attention accorded to heavyweight boxing champion Michael Tyson a few years ago, and now – on a much grander scale – the media energy devoted to O.J. Simpson, are examples in grotesque but accurate caricature of the way the media exploit the charismatic celebrity of sport heroes more generally. Athletes are special because they are able to stir deeper regions of collective disturbance, desire and fear than most other men, even famous ones. With African-American athletes such as Tyson and Simpson, that ability includes the mobilization of racist beliefs about African-American males and their sexuality, a feature that carries an extra charge symbolically, economically and, in Tyson's and Simpson's cases, judicially. Had O.J. Simpson been a heart surgeon or an accountant – even an African-American one – the coverage of his trial would not have commanded nearly the degree of attention it has. Even Clarence Thomas' controversial nomination to the U.S. Supreme Court received only a fraction of the attention heaped on Simpson.

Professional athletes are our greatest culture heroes. Collective projections of ideal manhood are cathected to famous athletes in unusually intense ways – not least because the sport nexus has fiercely marketed sport figures to draw on these emotions and identifications. A good warrior, the athlete, our champion, is supposed to turn his violence outward against designated Others, against our enemies, not against us. When a famous athlete is accused of a violent crime in which he does turn against us, society is potentially confronted with a major contradiction: the dichotomy between the behaviour it approves in one arena (athletics) and the behaviour it officially disapproves in most others. By omitting a discussion of the complicity of sport and the media in the violence of athletes and men as a group, television, newspaper and magazine discourses have prevented a potential tear in the ideological fabric that might have been effected by any discussion that questioned the values and nature of our most popular and celebrated pastimes.

My aim here is to help motivate on the part of the left and progressive social movements precisely what the mainstream media discourse about O.J. Simpson has so assiduously avoided: a political examination of the role of sport in society today, within the context of still-neglected matters of gender relations, family arrangements and culture. Let me be clear from the outset about my terminology in this exposition. When I employ the term 'sport' here, I am referring to a delimited and specific field of activities within the broad field of physical culture. I am *not* referring to all physical activity (for example, the generic activities of running, jumping, throwing, swimming); nor all physical disciplines (for example, yoga, t'ai chi, dance). The distinction between active physicality and sport – though often blurred – is essential, for sport is only one way of being physically active and organizing physical activity. When I use the term sport I am speaking of physical contests, individual or team, based on the zero-sum objectives of taking territory and/or overpowering an opponent; contests that possess codified, standardized rules and measurements; and are organized into formal associations, with official records and designated champions. As well, for the purposes of this exposition, when I use the term sport I am using shorthand to refer exclusively to the *dominant sports* in the industrial world and transnationally (football, basketball, baseball, hockey, Olympic individual sports such as track and field and gymnastics, tennis, boxing and auto racing most specifically; not to more marginal or minoritarian sports like lacrosse or water ballet). There are important differences among these dominant sports – with American football and boxing weighing in clearly as the most agressive and violent, while baseball and tennis appear the most gentlemanly, and hockey and basketball somewhere in between. However, there are also important generalizations to be made about all of these sports and their promotion, and I make them here. Further narrowing the field for the purposes of this article, I discuss these dominant sports almost exclusively as they include men and exclude women. There is a great deal to be said about the active relationship between women and sport, but it cannot be said adequately in this forum.[6]

In my thirty years as a socialist activist, I have become convinced that gendered institutions, values and behaviours shape 'small p' political culture (the politics of interpersonal and social life) in ways that *directly* affect 'large p' political culture (the politics of government and the state) much more than has yet been taken into account in theories of political formation and social(ist) change. It is in this sense that developments in contemporary gender culture – organized and exemplified by the case study of sport – bear directly on the crisis of collective political agency today. While a critical attitude to sport is by no means generalized among socialists and Marxists, many of the scholars of sport within these traditions share a negative assessment of sport's broadest socio-political functions. A number of writers take pains to assert important positive by-products which sport has delivered to working class and oppressed individuals and groups (e.g., active physicality, group coordination, physical mastery, group identity and differentiation). Nevertheless, there is broad consensus among many socialist thinkers that these benefits need not be tied to sport; and that they are generally appropriated, outweighed or negated by the broad negative valences and functions of the dominant sports and their culture.

To explain why sport, however contradictory, is more reactionary than progressive, most critical socialist scholars attribute its negative qualities directly to those of the capitalist mode of production. 'Modern competitive sport is a product of industrial society, the concentrated symbolic representation of its fundamental principles; this is the reason why it fascinates the masses in all industrialized countries, and in all countries moving toward industrialization.'[7] Thus, according to this succinctly articulated view by Christian Graf von Krakow, the subordination of co-operation to domination occurs because *capitalism* is not a humane socio-economic system. The fundamental relationships sport validates are competition and ranking; the fundamental good that of high performance; the fundamental actions those of overpowering and dominating because all these are inherent in and constitutive of the capitalist system.

Without rejecting the rich acquisitions of this school of thought, however, something extremely important has been left out of its account. I am speaking here of sport's relationship to men organized as a gender-class; of the way sport is the concentrated symbolic representation of the *masculinist system* and its fundamental principles. Further, I am convinced that masculinism must be understood as the primary, constitutive core of sport and its culture. Masculinism and gender class are not 'add-on' categories to capitalism and economic class where sport is concerned. Rather, masculinism lies at the heart of what sport organizes and achieves. It is what is mobilized via the ideological reflexes sport nurtures and sustains to energize the other traditional political identifications – locality, ethnicity, nationality, and so forth – to which socialist sport scholars have paid so much attention by virtue of their more obvious relationships to economic class. Insofar as sport is our way to prepare young males to act as physical enforcers of a vigorously defended economic and gender order grounded in inequality and domination, sport is not fun and games. Instead, it should be understood as a proto-military cultural practice that serves to demarcate undemocratically the ownership of physical coercion, a territory that is still almost exclusively men's; and that spreads the values of domination within the larger social sphere.

## SPORT AND THE GENDER ORDER

Just as every known human society has an *economic* order – a system for organizing how it gets the means of subsistence from the environment – it also has a social order for daily and generational reproduction which organizes and gives cultural meaning to the biological existence of two sexes and the in-built, bodily drive for sexual pleasure. The term I will employ for this system henceforth is the *gender order*.[8] When a gender order 'constructs' its ideals of masculinity and femininity – what the boys and men, women and girls are supposed to be like, or to try to be like – it is attempting to fix overlapping predispositions and potentials, shared by children of both biological sexes, into predictable behaviours ('roles') so that the work of daily and generational reproduction can proceed in a stable fashion.[9]

Gender identity and gendered consciousness are products of the articulation of socially organized modes of economic activity and family organization with the biophysical and psychological needs, predispositions and potentials of humans. The biological givens place limits on the social possibilities – minimally, needs for food, air, water, shelter, clothing and procreation must be met. As well, however, given the psychoneurological equipment of humans, needs for identity formation and the formation of ideation must also be addressed.[10] The larger point flowing from these propositions that socialists need to integrate into the heart of their political theory and programme development is a simple one: specific arrangements for childrearing create, and are reflected in, specific patterns of adult behaviour. Matters such as the presence or absence of parents of either gender, the use of harsh punishment and general attitudes to children, the degree and kind of integration or segregation of the sexes – all these matters of childrearing, among others, will have consequences for the way adults conduct their personal and political lives.

In pre-capitalist patriarchal economies, the site of production and reproduction was the same – the family household. Fathers, uncles and older brothers were present in the lives of children, especially boys, throughout their childhood.[11] In these families, the omnipresence and omnipotence of the family father could be very oppressive. Regardless, his presence and involvement in the socialization of children, especially boys, was an important feature of traditional agrarian and artisan family arrangements. This changed with the advent of capitalism. Capitalism severed the site of daily and generational reproduction (the home) from the primary site of production (the factory, the office), and radically changed the place of the familial father in the daily childhood experience of boys. Throughout much of the nineteenth century, the father's involvement in domestic and childhood life was limited largely to matters of authority and discipline. At the end of that century, with the establishment of a new family norm for urban capitalism in the 'family-wage system', it became possible for some fathers to become more present in the lives of their sons through the pursuit of leisure and recreation activities – most notably, around sport. The 'absent father family' is the usual term applied to the gender division of labour in the family-wage system; but the 'remote father family' would probably be more correct.

The remoteness of the family father and older men had its corollary in the 'overpresence' of the mother and women in childhood life – and these twin characteristics initiated a very particular pattern of parenting and childhood response, leading in turn to particular patterns in gender identity formation. These, interacting with the needs and motifs of capitalism and historical patriarchal traditions and values, have had major consequences for the development of cultural idealizations of masculinity and for the behaviours and actions of men as a class, and men in groups.[12] The deficits in parenting arising from this arrangement, produced according to some a virtual 'crisis in masculinity'[13] in the nineteenth century; one that has parallels today, with largely negative consequences for society as a whole.

Most notably, in creating a primary identification in boys with the women who preside over their childhood – an identification which must be superseded by a secondary and often antagonistic identification with men in adolescence; and in compelling boys to construct ideals of masculinity on the basis of remote and even fictive examples,[14] this parenting arrangement ensures that large numbers of adult men will fixate on super-aggressive masculine ideals and identifications – what I have called 'hypermasculinity' – in over-compensation for the qualities associated with disowned femininity.[15] These ideals, valuing the qualities of overpowering strength and gender entitlement, have been seen as a powerful overcompensation for early feminine identifications. But they predispose those who hold them against the qualities – and the politics – of the more 'feminine' (liberal, socialist) attitudes and values.

Institutions of male-exclusive culture, with their initiation ceremonies and ongoing ritual languages, are the numinous, charismatic heart of masculinist ideology. According to psychologist John Whiting initiation ceremonies 'serve psychologically to brainwash the primary feminine identity and to establish firmly the secondary male identity' in father-absent societies . In his study of a diverse sample of sixty-four societies with male initiation ceremonies, Whiting hypothesized that 'in societies where the father is absent or plays a minor role in child rearing, the male infant perceives the mother as all-powerful, envies her role, and then adopts a feminine identification. Yet when he begins to notice the world outside the home, at about the age of five, he will in most societies perceive that men control resources and clearly occupy an enviable position. A secondary identification with the masculine role thus becomes superimposed on the female identification.'[16] If this insight is correct, it explains the ubiquitous presence of abusive rituals and reprogramming routines in the recruitment of young men to both outlaw gangs and official armed forces. I would also add, however, that the institutions of masculinist culture are also very important in their own right, for they serve to cohere, condense and establish men's power as a dominant gender class as a material fact that commands enormous amounts of the social surplus as well as social approval.

Sport is the most widespread and inclusive male initiation institution of our age. For untold numbers of boys and young men, through the various stages of capitalism, sport has provided a network of social fathers and male role models, augmenting or replacing the remote familial father, creating alternative sites for emotional bonding and social mobility to the woman-dominated family . In this translocal and transnational brotherhood women are absent, negatively mirroring men's absence from the family of kin. Sport successfully provides both real associations for boys and men, and symbolic genealogies in which men can existentially locate themselves when all other anchors have been torn up by the relentless demands of capitalist mobility.

More than any church, sport has been the great cultural unifier, the ecumenical force and common language, the great narrative for men and boys about heroic masculinity and the superiority of men in the industrial and post-industrial age. Sport's apparently timeless secret lies in the organized practice of embodied, supra-linguistic physical rites in deracinated time and space. These constitute a symbolic language of meaning and loyalties; a language that brings together those who know how to speak it; a language that has been diffused by the mass media to every corner of the world. As pioneer Marxist sport sociologist Jean-Marie Brohm has written:

> . . . sport has powerfully contributed to a *cosmopolitan consciousness*; a consciousness of a sporting humanity, in which the referential criteria are the record and the champion. . . Across a sporting planet, records and champions constitute a kind of *symbol of universality*. Through sport, the planet unifies itself around the values of competition. [17]

Universality, yes: the brotherhood of 'healthy, active men', regardless of class or skin colour; but one that appropriates and incorporates particularity: the flavour and loyalties of neighbourhoods and towns and the special qualities of individuals. Fused together by sport, the painful contradictions among these levels in real life appear magically to dissolve in sport's fictive scenarios.

The power of these scenarios is based in the intense identification between supporter and athlete or team. This is the conduit through which vicarious participants (audiences) are linked to active practitioners (athletes). Boys from every social layer, every urban and rural culture develop it in childhood . 'You can change your job, you can change your wife, but you can't change your football team,' said Rick Parry, the chief executive officer of England's Premier Football League.[18] 'You can move from one end of the country to another, but you never, ever lose your allegiance to your first team. That's what English soccer is all about. It's about fierce loyalty, about dedication.' And – unspoken but so absolute as to be taken for granted – it is about those qualities *in the masculine mode.*

Sport has triumphed as a global culture because, since its birth in the nineteenth century, it has succeeded better than any other institution in filling the father gap. It has found a way to locate its practitioners in a male-defined and male-populated universe that is dynamic, like the constantly changing circumstances created by capitalist industrial growth. But at the same time it has provided – has itself become – a constant, even the *one* constant, in this ever-changing world where the requirements of manhood are so hard to fulfill. Sport locates its celebrants in a known symbolic universe of fathers (ancestors) and stable, patriarchal relational structures when real families, and real jobs, are in constant upheaval, even disintegration.

Around the referential criteria of men's records and male champions, sport has overtaken many of the previous functions of an established masculinist church: the moral instruction of children; the ritual differentiation of men and women; the worship by both of a common divinity forged in the masculine mode; the national and international experience of collective bonding around that divinity. Our stadiums are not only mass theatres of spectacular entertainments. They are also cathedrals of men's culture, where male athletes are demigods, the owners, officials and media the priesthood. Like organized religion, organized sport is both a horizontal international masculinist network of community-based associations, and a pyramidal power apparatus of enormous cultural influence.[19]

## MARKETING – AND SUBSIDIZING – HYPERMASCULINITY

The basic assumption that underlies the entire growth and practice of the twentieth century sport nexus was captured in the pithy words of an advertising poster for the sports network in 1987: 'ESPN delivers the male'. (The typical ESPN viewer is a male high school graduate somewhere between 35 and 49, with a household income of more than $60,000.[20]) Calculate the coverage of women's athletic events on television as compared to men's. The disproportion is enormous; and it represents an extreme distortion downward of women's real participation rates in physical activities generally and in competitive sport particularly. Above all, note that the people who more than any others represent heroism and valour in our culture – the most marketable attributes of all – are men. Jackie Joyner Kersee may be as talented and accomplished as Carl Lewis – but it doesn't make any real difference. Martina Navratilova or Monica Seles may have throngs of admirers, but they do not have the charismatic weight or the economic clout of a Muhammad Ali, a Michael Jordan or a Joe Montana. All this is sustained by my own survey of the pictures of women athletes in *Sports Illustrated* compared with the photos of male athletes in three selected years, undertaken to determine whether the visual signals about women and athleticism had changed quantitatively and qualitatively in 'America's sport bible' over a roughly thirty-year period marked by massive changes in actual gender relations – including a major increase in the active physicality of women, through sport and other forms of participation.[21]

PER CENT OF TOTAL IMAGERY OF WOMEN IN
*SPORTS ILLUSTRATED* 1970 – 1985 – 1993

| | 1970 | 1985 | 1993 |
|---|---|---|---|
| Athlete in her own right | 3.4 | 9.0 | 8.2 |
| *Disqualified athletes | 4.0 | 10.8 | 11.3 |
| Accompanied by male | 21.8 | 15.0 | 12.9 |
| Supporter | 24.0 | 24.7 | 25.0 |
| Spectator | 9.1 | 24.1 | 17.0 |
| Sex symbol | 8.7 | 14.0 | 24.7 |
| Other | 16.5 | 9.5 | 7.5 |

*Disqualified athletes refers to images of women athletes that *blatantly* disqualify their athletic competence (falling, crying etc.). With respect to the most important category – 'athlete-in-her-own-right' the recent figure is still clearly and consistently under 10 per cent.

Sport heroes are men *by definition*. Over the course of the twentieth century they have acted as audience magnets of unheralded power – drawing into their orbit billions of men, whose attention was thus made available for the commercial propaganda of industrial and finance capital and for military and para-military mobilization. The integral relationship between modern sport, masculinity and masculinism was actively cultivated by the popular press in the latter half of the nineteenth century and grew qualitatively more intimate in the 1890s, when the 'sport section' of the daily newspaper was introduced. Radio's love affair with sport originated as a way to recruit purchasers for radios, then audiences for sponsors. It expanded the reach of professional athletics into living rooms, kitchens and bedrooms in the twentieth century's inter-war period. With each relationship between sport and the new media came new forms of interlocking ownership among sport and media organizations. Media barons bought teams and stadiums whose events in turn sold their papers or radio broadcasts.[22]

But it was the marriage of demographic research with television advertising in the 1960s, and the birth of 'pyschodemographics' as an advertising tool in the 1970s, that increased by a quantum measure the ability of the mass media – especially television – to not only reach men, but also to extract their relatively plentiful dollars.[23] Using demographic and then psychological analysis, sponsors, owners and networks worked hand in hand to develop links between programming and advertising geared to group, sub-divide and exploit specific layers of viewers in targeted ways. The tools of 'psychodemographics' opened up the fears and desires of viewers to direct economic exploitation.[24] And as men were the relatively advantaged gender economically, they became the favoured audience for broadcasters and sponsors alike.

Thus the mature masculinist symbiosis of sport and the media typical of contemporary times came into being. Today, the interdependent relationships between the athletic, industrial and media sectors of this masculinist nexus are both broad and profound.[25] Total revenues generated by sport and sport-related activities of all types in Canada and the United States in 1989 (from the sales of tickets to the purchase of sports equipment) stood at more than $88.5 billion annually according to one estimate, and was projected to rise $160 billion by the turn of the century – at which point Canadian and American firms would be spending 13.8 billion dollars on advertising through sport alone, while globally sports advertising would reach $30 billion.[26] As none of these figures include salaries to public education and recreation personnel involved with sport, nor the huge infrastructural costs involved in sport-related public education and recreation systems, even this estimate of the 'sport economy' is only partial.

Clearly we are dealing with sums of money equivalent to the gross domestic products of small nations, or the budgets of large states, provinces and cities. For example, television rights for the National Football League alone, from 1990 to 1994, earned the NFL *$3.6 billion.* (That is equivalent to the entire budget for hospitals in Ontario, Canada's most populous province.) As a result of sport's dramatic profitability, huge transnational corporate sectors are now associated with and utilize sport to maximize their sales by reaching and influencing the richest audiences. Where once beverages (beer, soft drinks) and personal grooming were sports' main sponsors, now big-ticket items in hardware (cars, home office equipment, sound systems, etc.) and financial and communications services (credit cards, couriers, stock brokerages) are increasingly dominant in the sport nexus.

The industrial sector most closely associated practically and symbolically with the commercial performance of sport is the one that manufactures sport equipment. The number of elite professional athletes in the world is very small, speaking strictly of those who make a decent living as athletes. The trick is to use advertising linked to heroic spectacle – and in ways that blur their distinctions and create seamless webs between them – to motivate ordinary people to emulate athletes directly by buying sporting goods; and to worship them indirectly by buying fetish (novelty and fashion) items, and much larger commodities as well. And it seems that, indeed, nothing sells like the stuff that's peddled by big, strong, heroic champions – male, it goes without saying. Take for only one current example to what effect NBA superstar Shaquille O'Neal has been put. 'I take a stroll, attempting to count the stores in which one can purchase an item bearing the euphonious name of the seven-foot spokescenter,' Steve Rushin wrote in August 1994 in *Sports Illustrated*, in a story about his trip to the largest indoor shopping mall in the United States:

> ... An unmistakable size-20 Shaq shoe stands sentry in front of World Foot Locker. One cannot handle the autographed shoe, for it reposes under glass like the Star of India. What the shoe really is, is the star of Bethlehem, drawing Mall-walking magi into the store ... Sam Goody stocks the rap album Shaq Diesel ... At toy Works, I adore the Shaq action figures by Kenner. Shaq's film debut, *Blue Chips*, has come and gone at the movieplex. Shaq Attack! and Shaq Impaq beckon from bookstores. Shaq-signature basketballs line the shelves at Oshman's. Field of Dreams stocks wood-mounted photos of O'Neal: Shaq-on-a-Plaque. I stagger to the Coffee Beanery, Ltd., looking for Swiss Shaqolate Mocha, Vacuum-Shaq-Packed in a foil Shaq-Sack.[27]

The economics of the sport industry sector reflect, reinforce and exploit the differentials of gender. For example, according to Richard J. Barnett and John Cavanagh[28], Nike's shoe sales total over $2 billion per year in the United States alone; and total sales in 1994 were $4.73 billion. Between $500-$600 million comes just from basketball shoes sold through the Chicago Bull's superstar Michael Jordan. In 1993, Nike spent almost $90 million on advertising and marketing. Nike clothes and shoes are made mainly by women in non-union factories in Southeast Asia. Typically, a pair of shoes costs $5.60 to produce in Asia. This already includes a profit for the sub-contractors Nike uses. The same shoes are sold for over $100 in Canada and the U.S.. The workers who make Nike shoes and sew Nike clothes are paid about $1.35 per day, for an approximate annual wage of $500 for each woman and the family that depends on her earnings. Michael

Jordan's promotional fee from Nike, on the other hand, was $20 million dollars in 1993 – a fee that well exceeded the annual payroll of all the Indonesian factories making Nike shoes.

The marketing of sport and sport-related commodities is not a politically innocent venture, for through it fundamental messages are being diffused via masculinist conventions that link sport and the men who identify with it to much broader and more sinister ideologies and projects. Speaking of the surge of 'sport/war tropes' during and following the time of the war in the Persian Gulf in the United States, Sue Curry Jansen and Donald F. Sabo observe:

> The growing presence of sport programming in international communications media, including the increasing prominence of American professional team sports in European sport media, seems to indicate that sport/war tropes and scenarios, derived from the images and icons of U.S. history and popular culture, are becoming part of the semiological structure of the global 'war system'. Sport/war media framing devices, which were so widely used during the Persian Gulf War, appear to have tapped into and revitalized the deep structure of patriarchal meaning and values that have pervaded hierarchies of domination in all Western societies for millennia.[29]

For a long time, the vast public subsidy of privately-owned sport enterprises went unacknowledged and unquestioned, except by the smallest of minorities. 'Amid all sport's sponsors, the largest and oldest barely speaks its name,' noted *The Economist* in July 1992,[30] under a sub-head that read 'Thanks for the subsidy'. 'Greek cities supported the ancient Olympics; modern governments put billions into the infrastructure of sport, in schools, local playing fields and leisure centres. Less publicly, they also hand out taxpayer's millions to professional sport.'

The owners of professional sport – proprietors of teams, the international and national Olympic committees – are exquisitely aware of how important these billions are to their own prosperity and to the economic power they gain from such subsidies within municipal, state, provincial and even federal economies. The IOC's City Contract for awarding the Olympic Games, for example, holds not the IOC but the *host city* ultimately responsible for all the costs. The people of the province of Quebec are still paying for 'The Big Owe' as it is known locally, the stadium constructed for the 1976 Montreal games at a cost of billions of dollars, and hapless home to the Montreal Expos. Twenty years later, it is still leaching hundreds of millions of dollars in interest payments on its debt and for extensive repairs as it literally disintegrates piece by ill-constructed piece. The people of Ontario found themselves saddled with a $350 million dollar debt in 1990 as a result of Conservative and Liberal government commitments to the Toronto Sky Dome. (In 1986, at the same time as it announced the allocation of $300,000 to a campaign against violence against women, the Ontario government pledged $30 million to the dome. By 1989 it had given an additional $320 million, of which 150 million dollars was reclaimed by a social democratic government in 1993). Some cities are paying debts on empty stadiums because the resident teams picked up and left for more lucrative pastures. Out of the 94 stadiums used by professional football, baseball, hockey and basketball between 1953 and 1993 in the U.S. and Canada, 67 were publicly owned. As well, the more recent the construction, the greater the incidence of public ownership. There is a clear trend for the public to invest more, not less, in professional sport, despite the appearance of cutbacks in direct subsidy to Olympic, recreational and educational sport programmes.[31]

Yet today, in more than twenty cities across North America, owners of sport teams are threatening to move away if more public dollars are not invested in even more and larger facilities. It is almost bizarrely incongruous that in today's neo-conservative political climate, when the business class worships at the altar of the market and agitates so vociferously to deconstruct most forms of government, sport owners and multi-million dollar players have no shame or sense of contradiction in looking to the taxpayer to underwrite the major capital costs of professional sport. To them this is a legitimate expense, when health, welfare and education are not. In Cincinnati, local government found $540 million for stadium construction just after laying off 400 staff members from its schools. And the pattern is being repeated all over the continent.[32]

As difficult as figures on the extent of corporate sport may be to come by, it is almost impossible to assess the cost of the form of public subsidy to sport that takes place via its instruction in the public school and recreation systems. The purchase of equipment, the construction of facilities and the salaries of teachers and officials whose primary function is to teach sport (as the main form of physical education) are the principal categories of public expenditure on sport in these areas. This truly vast network of local and educational facilities and personnel where sport is practised underwrites the viability of commercial sport and is profoundly affected by its standards and icons. From its facilities emerge the few elite athletes who graduate from the local to the big leagues; *and* their devoted followers, the millions of fans who do not graduate with athletic honours but identify with and revere those who do. This is where masculinist ritual and veneration come together in childhood to produce the adult sporting male, organized and funded by the state.

## SPORT AND POLITICAL CHANGE

In North America we are living through a decade in which many of the quantitative acquisitions of the labour and social movements – affirmative action, environmental protection, abortion rights, childcare and welfare provisions and liberal/democratic commitment to universal education – are being rolled back with extraordinary rapidity by governments of the Right. The growing governmental power of the Right is linked to a broad revival of religious fundamentalism and violent right-wing movements. With the ascendance of anti-social impulses in the commanding structures of power, we are witnessing a crisis of pro-social programme and organization; and a massive growth in the economies and the spectacles of coercion, where men's relative power and privilege as a gender class are most directly embodied and institutionalized.

For example, according to Statistics Canada, public expenditure in Canada in the past five years has increased by a whopping 35 per cent in the judicial-prison system while commensurate reductions to health, education and social services have taken place. In the U.S. the trend is even more pronounced. In the last ten years the state of California has poured 10 billion dollars into the prison system and is planning to pour a similar amount into its gulag in the next few years to accommodate the flood of new convicts being produced by the 'three-strikes-and-you're-out' law recently enacted.[33] The funds are coming from the same sources as the funding of stadiums – a full scale gutting of health and education budgets. (Affirmative action has been killed in California state universities, with the exception of . . . athletes). In August 1995, conservatives in the U.S. House of Representatives voted to cut $9 billion out of labour, education and health funding, while planning to vote the Pentagon $7 billion more than it asked for.

Right-wing minorities with political programmes based on authoritarian, anti-humane, anti-cooperative and anti-environmental impulses have created effective vehicles (including economic associations and political parties) to advance their interests; while moderately egalitarian majorities are faced with a crisis of political programme and political instruments. This is happening despite almost a century of consumer capitalism and its supposedly liberalizing ideological effects. Since we are in the midst of a long wave of capitalist contraction and upheaval that will not be cancelled out in the immediate future by the effects of electronic or biotechnological innovation, or by the new capitalist frontiers in Eastern Europe, Russia and China, this means that women and those many men who support their reproductive, social and economic rights, in North America and in all other places where pro-social politics are in retreat, face some perilous times. The Republican majority in the United States Senate and House of Representatives have views on gender relations no different in effect from the masculinism now being reasserted in Eastern Europe, Russia and the countries of the former Soviet Union; or demonstrated by the Chinese bureaucracy in their treatment of women at the recent United Nations Beijing Conference. The last Republican majority in both houses gave the United States McCarthyism, complete with its demonization of homosexuals, non-conforming women and the left. The present majority is virulently homophobic, and appears hell-bent on accelerating the feminization of poverty and pushing back women's reproductive rights as part of its larger socio-political project.

What I am suggesting here is that the masculinization of corporate culture – with sport as its leading legitimating institution – has nourished ideals of masculine and elite entitlement and gross inequality among all layers of the population; and that these are helpful to and being mobilized by regressive political movements. The provenance of the violence and inequality of men's culture generally and sport particularly lies primarily in sport's ritual connection to combat and war as a masculine sphere that is qualitatively differentiated from and valued over the feminine sphere. With a very few exceptions, organized death (the hunt and war) and their rituals – notably athletics – have been the exclusive spheres of men since gathering-hunting days. But war is not all that men have done or been; nor is the technologized Clausewitzian 'total war' of the twentieth century equivalent to an aboriginal hunt for food, or organized self-defence against aggressors. To the extent that hegemonic masculinity draws its ideals directly from a hyperaggressive and dominating warrior culture – the warrior culture of the great class-stratified 'civilizations' – and in turn validates such a culture, the hypermasculinity, or 'surplus aggressivity'[34], it models and creates will be itself anti-social: combative, competitive, and physically coercive. This suggests that changes in the gender conditioning of men and the institutions that achieve this conditioning are a precondition to lasting and meaningful changes in economics and politics.

The recent, hard-won formal right of women to participate in police and armed forces in many industrialized countries was undertaken to demonstrate that women are as capable of being warriors as men. However well individual women have succeeded – and there have been some spectacular successes – it has been a grudging, difficult process with disappointing results for those who saw major potential for gender equality in this strategy, and for the many of the extraordinary women who decided to prove their worth in warrior terms, even in the face of harassment and assault, as has been the case in the US armed forces. Women's formal right to inclusion has not changed their generally subordinate position within these hierarchies; nor much of the sexist treatment of women by men members; nor – and this is the superlatively important point – the nature and purpose of the hierarchies themselves. And so it is with women's situation in sport – a site where they too have sought inclusion on equal terms. We have yet to see qualitative transformations in men's sporting institutions, despite the extensive changes in family and kinship forms around them, and the significant incursion of accomplished women into their structures and organizations.

What this indicates is that the answers to dismantling the institutions of organized masculinist coercion – be they primarily symbolic like sport, or practical, like the military – can only come from strategies broader than the incremental inclusion of women within these structures. What is needed are strategies that affect the economic viability of these sectors and cause them, in Marx's formulation, to 'wither away'. And this in turn has a number of simultaneous and interdependent consequences. It means that social and political attention must be turned to changing the current arrangements in family organization, social parenting and identity formation that produce and idealize hypermasculinist norms and ideals across class and other cultural divisions. Central directions in social policy must be set and implemented, geared to help both sexes to compensate for the erosion of their time and resources within contracting capitalism in ways allow them to share reproductive work between them. Without such policies[35] that restore the father to childhood, we will not be able to diminish a key source of the feelings of violent instrumentality that sustain the athlete-warrior as the dominant icon of heroic masculinity and coercive privilege in our culture today.

The social willingness to redesign society along these lines is present, to more or less articulated degrees, among wide layers of the population in North America – a product of the felt need to find better ways of organizing family and sexual life under prevailing economic conditions. But that willingness is extremely difficult to develop or mobilize as long as the terms of public discourse and culture are so dominated by the norms, ideals and tropes of masculinist mass culture, including sport. For this reason, effecting deep changes in gender arrangements will also require effecting a number of other major changes to the political economy of gender relations, and sport in particular. Central to such an enterprise are changes in the ownership, control and content of the mass media of communications.

One of the most important staples of the mass media of communications in North America – particularly the U.S. – are genres of entertainment that present violent and anti-social spectacles of men's culture. Some of these are entirely fictive – such as police-dramas and men's action stories in television, films, novels, comic books and video games. Others present real battles with symbolic meaning – i.e. sport. In their 'official' political and moral rhetoric – viz. the O. J. Simpson coverage – media owners and editorial spokespersons disapprove of what these spectacles celebrate.[36] Yet funding for such spectacles increases year by year and decade by decade. As a result, one question that has become the subject of heated debate is: In presenting anti-social violence affirmatively, do the media *cause* violence? It would be accurate to answer no, not directly, the way mass unemployment, child abuse and transparent political tyranny do. Indirectly, however, it would be equally correct to argue that they do – through the enforcement of profound political ignorance and their cultural validation of coercion and greed in the service of commodity consumption.

The interior landscape of the contemporary psyche has been saturated with physical and discursive practices literally engineered to penetrate its conscious defences in the service of buying and selling. In North America especially, the mystified ideal of 'choice' – of car, of house, of body, of toothpaste, of children – has been the credo of the consumer age. But, as Marxist theoreticians have long pointed out,[37] real choice only exists in the presence of real options by those who are aware of the alternatives. The patent dysfunctionality of our political and economic systems demonstrates that we are suffering from a failure of the left and social movements to apprehend and make known real *political* choice. The consciousness wired for maximum consumer consumption is not the consciousness best wired for enlightened social action. If little in one's early cultural practice demonstrates social harmony, political responsiveness, positive action, respect and reciprocity, it will be difficult to envision – let alone implement – social choices that would lead to the realization of these principles in collective and individual life. Our collective ability to *imagine* actually finding alternative forms of economic and social organization is gravely threatened, as a multiplicity of media, old and new, continue to spew out endless bits of de-politicized information.

Among those who affirm the political importance of culture in affecting political life, there are many who belittle the importance of economic factors in shaping media culture. They would do well to re-examine their views in light of a number of recent corporate mega-mergers involving reconfiguring and monopolizing the underlying structures of media production and distribution on an unprecedented scale: Disney-ABC, CBS-Westinghouse, and the marriage of Sports Illustrated owners TIME-Warner with media maverick Ted Turner.[38] Even Turner, widely known for his 'rugged individualism' in corporate affairs, could no longer resist the dynamic toward cartelization and both vertical and horizontal integration on a global scale. On the other hand, those who dismiss or diminish the importance of gender culture to the dynamic and momentum of such corporate projects would do well to consider how large a role the products and the norms of hypermasculinity generally, and the revenues and conventions of sport particularly, play in the high-noon manoeuvrings of media capital and its new allies in the industrial and financial sectors. One must not neglect, especially now, either the centrality of sport-generated funds to media capital, or the formative nature of sport ritual and masculinism to media and corporate culture.[39] In sport the destructive effect of the concentration of the media in the hands of commercially driven and male-dominated elites has perhaps its best illustration.

If it is true that a significant part of the atavism of sport culture is due to its instrumental exploitation of men's gender anxiety by commercial and militarist interests, the question becomes: how to unravel the development of sport and physical culture from these imperatives. At present, emergent physical practices can be born; but they cannot flourish. The private, commercial ownership of sport and the mass media distorts communication and culture, and caricatures, omits or appropriates oppositional practices. But if we cannot democratize self-expression (including in our physical culture and its celebratory rituals), we cannot communicate our ideas without commercial mediation. This qualitatively inhibits our ability to learn from our experiences and forge common ideas and actions through our communications. Broadly speaking, then, we need to remove the huge, multi-layered public subsidies to sport in all their forms; and redeploy those resources in other, pro-social directions.

To achieve this, political action at the level of the state in at least three key ways is required. First, government must be made to change the practical and regulatory environment that sustains the current sport-media symbiosis. At the level of central governments, we need public policy that allows us to reclaim cultural space from its commercial – and athletic – inundation. After almost a century's experience with mass communications, and possessing a clear understanding of the patterns and outcomes of concentration (private and public) in the ownership of media, it is more than time to call for a major public rethinking of the criteria and objectives of broadcasting licenses, trust legislation and governmental regulatory bodies. It is time to rewrite the legislation regulating the airwaves and the ownership of other cultural industries and properties – including sport – in ways that reflect this new assessment. It is also time to demand that public broadcasting networks end their close relationships with commercial sport. It is time to increase, not decrease, public funds to cultural practitioners of all kinds to ensure that forms of extra-commercial speech can survive – indeed thrive. Without this, no emergent cultural development in physical culture can ever hope to challenge the dominance of masculinist corporate sport. Funding for the expansion of the non-commercial cultural realm, including physical culture, can come from increased taxes on those in the commercial sport nexus. Such taxes are more than fair, for they only seek to recover a part of the investment made in corporate sport by the community in the first instance.

Second, government should play a key role in disestablishing sport as the *official physical culture* of schools and public recreation systems. Educators and governments can work to devise policies to develop alternative experiences and alternative tastes in active physicality among children and youth by changing the place of sport in public educational and recreational systems. These systems are strategically important. They still exist in public, not commercial space, and are therefore more amenable to change by the direct action of parents, teachers, students and community users acting as motivated citizens, not commercial consumers. These systems are also the most important sites of sport and proto-sport socialization of children, creating the formative experiences that shape them for life. Changing the way physical culture is taught and practised in the public education and recreation systems is therefore one of the key priorities in effecting a change in sport specifically, and in gender culture as a whole.[40]

Finally, government must be brought to reduce all its expenditure on high performance sport radically downwards to reflect the actual contribution of such sport – negligible or negative – to the overall health and well-being of society. Governments claim to support high-performance sport, with its associated biomedical specializations and resulting athlete abuse, in the interests of advancing our capacities to achieve physical fitness and well-being. Meanwhile, in reality, the bodies of the majority of adults are trapped in life routines where adequate exercise and play – vital to stress release and therefore to immune and mental health – are impossible to come by. It will come as no surprise to socialists that poverty, not lack of access to an Olympic swimming pool, is the leading cause of ill health and the world's greatest killer according to the World Health Organization in a report it released in May, 1995.[41] The gaps between the rich and poor – including in gender terms – are widening, not closing; both within the industrialized countries and in the developing world. If physical activity is among the most important determinants of physical and mental health; and if access to it and practice of it are socio-economically and genderically differentiated; then the public policy conclusion must be to pursue strategies that make pleasurable, health promoting, recreational physical activity a reality for the majority of the population.

This goal, and not the subsidy of professional and high-performance sport, should be where we spend our public education, health, fitness and cultural dollars. It represents a real investment in population health; one that pays off both socially and economically. We do not need more high performance sport but the *real* opportunity to be active ourselves – to, literally, recreate ourselves. We do not need more steroids and betablockers. We need green spaces to play in, relations of harmony and inclusion among participants, and the social and economic wherewithal to enable people to take care of their health and physical needs.

The wealth/health equation has a distinctly gendered dimension with important consequences for overall population health. Not only are women more disadvantaged with respect to self-care and recreation by virtue of their poverty and longer hours of work as compared to men; their relative, indeed deteriorating poor health has a boomerang effect on the health of children and men – family members – throughout society. This points to the need to devote *extra* attention to the health of the majority of women, not less. We should be targeting women's physical health with social policies that make true accessibility to active physicality a social priority and meaningful reality. And we need government action to reallocate resources so as to realize reordered priorities.

Within high performance and competitive sport, however, even as we act to reverse current norms in public spending on recreation and fitness, we should also support efforts to combat the unhealthy consequences of gross biomechanical and pharmaceutical abuses and obsessive training practices and relationships that characterize athlete/coach/owner/government interactions. We need to act on these matters because it is in the image of drugged and obsessive athletes – 'winners' – that millions of young people commit serious harm to themselves, both physically and psychically. The drug culture and other training abuses in sport can be dramatically attenuated in short order if government develops the will to impose *systemic disincentives* for banned substances and practices, disincentives that target employers (including governments) rather than athletes.

At present employers want athletes whose performances are enhanced by banned practices, yet officially claim they are opposed to such practices and walk away scot-free when individual athletes are apprehended. Corporate sport reaps the benefits of athlete abuse but does not bear the economic or physical costs of transgression. Athletes on the other hand continue to be caught in a double bind, knowing that performance enhancing drugs are key factors – often *the* key factor – in their athletic careers.[42] If employers had to forfeit standing and money to meaningful degrees, they would stop requiring *de facto* athlete abuse. And this would help to provide less self-abusive models to the millions of young non-elite athletes who emulate the aesthetic ideals of high performance sport. Anorexia and bulimia are the two disorders that most speak to the physical mortification among girls and young women driven by idealized femininity, including the athletic kind. The masculine counterparts of this are steroid abuse (estimated to be a factor in the lives of perhaps a million young North American men) and bicep and calf implants among older 'baby-boom' men. As well, it is time to encode standards for youthful participation in sport that correspond in letter and spirit to child labour laws, and undermine the exploitation of young people via sport.

## CONCLUSION

Earlier in this essay, I described sport as a practice geared to address men's need for connection with other men – fathers, brothers, sons – and to their apparently profound need for the society of men. I suggested that sport was a cultural practice that grew vast by compensating for the loss of such company in early and middle childhood in industrial society; and by training good male workers, soldiers, managers and owners for life under capitalism. I described it as a ritual practice that brilliantly addresses, as well as grows out of, a 'crisis of masculinity', though not in pro-social or progressive ways.The selective reflection and celebration of masculinist and unequal relationships within sport and the media, and the exclusion of new and actual gender relationships from the symbolic field do not prevent the *economic* changes that have eroded the traditional gender division of labour and compelled a renegotiation of gender relations from occurring in daily life. But they do prevent new cultural ways of dealing with these changes from emerging and finding public validation. In this respect the culture of sport contradicts the economic times; it embodies a 'residual' gender ideology measured against actual life conditions. Seen through this lens, the domination of men's sport within the culture is a popular (mass) phenomenon, but not a democratic or pro-social one. This constitutes an excellent reason to seek to dismantle the grip sport now has on physical culture and the way it monopolizes media space and public attention.

Is there a crisis of masculinity today? Can men's gender distress be a direct, as well as indirect, factor in politics? And does it play a reactionary role? I think the answer to all three questions is yes. 'Thousands of men came early, anxious to get a good seat, waiting outside the stadium,' ran the lead sentence in a feature article in the *Toronto Star* late in September 1995.[43] The men it described were not waiting for a baseball or hockey game, however. They were waiting to attend a 20,000-strong meeting of 'Promise Keepers' – an evangelical Christian 'men-only group [that] fills [the] huge spiritual void', in the words of reporter Leslie Scrivener, a void left by 'poor relationships with their fathers and other men'. In the mass rallies, men pledge themselves to cherish and to 'serve' their wives and children, and to be good citizens in their communities. 'The movement seems to have touched a nerve among thousands of men feeling unsure of their roles as fathers and husbands in a time of dramatic social change,' Scrivener comments. One systems engineer manager – the typical member is white and middle class – felt 'an emptiness and need' that only men's company and collective solidarity could assuage. Combining evangelical religious techniques with the 'language of combat and sport', Promise Keepers has filled that manager's need and that of many hundreds of thousands of American and Canadian men. Promise Keepers began with a meeting of 4,200 men in a University of Colorado basketball arena in 1991 (its founder was the head coach of the university's football team); by 1995, it filled thirteen major U.S. stadiums and had an annual budget of $64 million.[44] There is a Promise Keepers industry of hard cover books, study guides, compact discs and cassettes of religious music, T-shirts, magazines and much, much more.

At the same time, Louis Farrakhan and the Nation of Islam lead a march on Washington by African-American men to 'atone' for their sins, and become good fathers and community members. Women are not welcome on the march, though some leading African American women activists gave the march their blessing. It is clear that Farrakhan, as well as Christian fundamentalists, intend to build their base and their agenda on the mobilization of men's gender anxiety. The messages of respect for women and commitment to children and community are important ones for men today, and clearly they are finding mass resonance. But the evangelical Christian or Islamic separatist traditional patriarchal gender frameworks to which these messages are being attached – via the hypermasculinist metaphors of war and athleticism as part of the ritual invocation – will most likely organize men who are in gender crisis in explicitly Right-wing ways. This may be unavoidable if there are no alternatives that speak to men's gender needs from a socialist articulation that is emotionally and spiritually attractive. At present the men's movement that has been informed by feminism and socialism – despite tremendously important contributions to scholarship, theory and education[45] – remains minoritarian; not least because socialism as a movement has not itself integrated an understanding of the importance of gender issues and gender culture into the way it wants to organize society.

There are many people who share the critique of sport I have advanced here, in more or less complete or articulate ways. They are reformers within athletic institutions; individuals and groups who have chosen other ways to be physically active; parents looking for different ways to give themselves and their children the skills and health that physical activity can uniquely confer. Socialists would do well to support them, and to challenge the hegemony of hypermasculinist sport culture in whatever ways they can. For until we pay much more attention to all our gendered institutions of ritual and parenting – in this case contemporary sport, social fatherhood and the remote father family system – we will continue to support inequality and domination in our midst even as we struggle to move beyond them.

NOTES

1. 'The O.J. Case: Further words of testimony', compilation of excerpts from the press, *The Globe and Mail,* October 7, 1995 (citing Rupert Cromwell of *The Independent,* London);. Cf. Barbara Ehrenreich, 'Media Matters', *The Nation,* November 6, 1995: 'Altogether, Nexis reports 24,142 newspaper articles mentioning O.J. in 1995, compared with 12, 175 containing the word 'racism, 7,688 touching on 'welfare reform' and a mere 1,592 on the subject of global warming.'
2. Howard Witt 'Churches and Comics' (Chicago Tribune Service) *Montreal Gazette,* October 2, 1995.

3. In July, 1995, *Sports Illustrated*, the 'bible of American sport', finally did a feature on sport and domestic violence. It acknowledged that serious wife abuse and date rape were proportionately more prevalent among athletes than among their non-athletic peers. William Mack and Lester Munson, 'Sport's Dirty Secret', *Sports Illustrated*, July 31, 1995, p. 67. The violence of athletes also shows up in higher rates of arrest of athletes for other kinds of assault and criminal behaviour. See Austin Murphy, 'Unsportsmanlike Conduct', *SI*, July 1, 1991.
4. I use the term 'masculinity' to refer to a general conception, understood by all of a society's members, whether in compliance or transgression, of what ideal manhood should be. The term 'masculinism' I use to describe the male-dominant gender order of our society. I prefer this term to 'patriarchy' because 'patriarchy' is used to connote a gender order in which men are dominant in general; and a very particular mode of production and family form. I prefer to keep patriarchy as a term to describe the latter; and to use masculinism as the generic term for all male-superior gender orders. Masculinism is able as a term to subsume a number of different forms of family, and includes all arrangements in which men are the dominant gender. Given that the role of the family father as such has been weakened by the disintegration of the family wage system since the second world war, the term is also helpful because it draws attention to the privileged place of men and the values associated with their qualities and roles in social and political institutions – rather than limiting the view to the power of biological and family fathers *per se*. For a more detailed explanation of my preferred terminology, see V. Burstyn, 'Masculine Dominance and the State', *Socialist Register*, London, Merlin Press, 1983.
5. For a full treatment of this thesis, see V. Burstyn, *The Rites of Men: Manhood, Politics and the Culture of Sport* (working title), University of Toronto Press, forthcoming.
6. There are too many important contributions on women and athletics to list here. For two recent collections of articles treating a wide variety of themes, see Susan Birell and Cheryl Cole, eds., *Women, Sport and Culture*, Human Kinetics, Champaign, Ill., 1994; and Margaret Costa and Sharon R. Guthrie, *Women and Sport: Interdisciplinary Perspectives*, Human Kinetics, Champaign, 1994. Cheryl Cole's 'Resisting the Canon: Feminist Cultural Studies and Technologies of the Body' marks a new stage in such scholarship, as sport is studied as an integrating force for women as well, not simply as an institution in which women should fight for inclusion. In dialogue with feminist studies on sport as a whole, see Michael A. Messner and Donald F. Sabo, *Sport, Men and the Gender Order*, Human Kinetics, Champaign, Ill., 1990; Brian Pronger *The Arena of Masculinity: Sports, Homosexuality, and the Meaning of Sex*, Toronto: Summerhill Press, 1990.
7. Christian Graf von Krockow as cited in J. M. Brohm, *Sociologie Politique du Sport*, Presses Universitaires de Nancy 1992, Nancy, p. 119.
8. I have chosen this term because while biological sex characteristics ('sex') and sexual desire ('sexuality') are both important, both are always shaped and constrained by the effect of gender ('role'). Therefore I use gender as the organizing principle of the reproductive order. I consider men and women to be members of two distinct and ranked gender classes. For a discussion of my reasons for this view, see V. Burstyn, 'Masculine Dominance and the State' *Socialist Register*, 1983. See Gayle Rubin's theorization of the 'sex-gender system' in 'The Traffic in Women', Rayna R. Reiter ed., *Toward an Anthropology of Women*, Monthly Review Press, New York 1975, pp. 157–210.
9. On the importance of childhood and gender for sport – and of sport for childhood and gender – see Michael Messner, 'Boyhood, Organized Sports and the Construction of Masculinities', *Journal of Contemporary Ethnography*, Vol. 18, No. 4, January 1990, pp. 416–444. Michael S. Clarkson has surveyed the nature of parental involvement in the formation of elite athletes in team and individual sports, contemporaneously and historically. See 'In praise of single mothers', *Toronto Star*, August 25, 1995. The article was

poorly named, since its focus was not primarily on the mothers of the 23 of the top 30 players in the NBA who grew up without their fathers, but rather on the players relationships with their absent fathers. This story represents just one section of his larger survey, in which the pattern of absent (usual) or authoritarian (minoritarian, but marked) father is replicated throughout all the major sports and their high-performance practitioners. In personal interviews, these players all talked about wanting either to please their absent fathers or to show them up, dominate or humiliate them via their athletic performances.

10. For a review of recent research findings on how the mind structures memory, feeling and ideation, see Joseph E. LeDoux, 'Emotion, Memory and the Brain', *Scientific American*, June 1994. For an assessment of the importance of sexuality in gender identity, see Ethel Spector Person, 'Sexuality as the Mainstay of Identity: Psychoanalytical Perspectives', *Signs*, Vol. 5, No. 4, 1980.
11. Carnes, Mark C., *Secret Ritual and Manhood in Victorian America*, Yale University Press, New Haven, 1989.
12. See Dorothy Dinnerstein, *The Mermaid And The Minotaur: Sexual Arrangements and Human Malaise*, London, Harper & Row, 1976; Nancy Chodorow, *The Reproduction Of Mothering: Psychoanalysis and The Sociology Of Gender*, University Of California Press, Berkeley, 1978; and Michael Kaufman, *Cracking The Armour: Power, Pain and the Life of Man*, Toronto, Penguin Books, 1993.
13. See Anthony Rotundo, 'Patriarchs and Participants: A Historical Perspective on Fatherhood in the United States', in M. Kaufman ed., *Beyond Patriarchy*, Oxford University Press, 1987. Also see Mark Carnes, *op cit*.
14. For an in-depth and cogent discussion of the role of men's cultural genres in all media in the development of ideals and behaviours of manhood around fictive ideals in U.S. culture, see James William Gibson's *Warrior Dreams: Violence and Manhood in Post-Vietnam America*, Hill and Wang, New York, 1994.
15. That there are also negative consequences for girls and women is also understood. The effect of parenting arrangements on women's gender-identity is the subject of a whole literature of its own.
16. Cited in Mark C. Carnes, 1989, *op. cit.*, p.106.
17. Jean-Marie Brohm, 1992, *op. cit.*, p. 126, (my translation, author's emphasis).
18. CBC *Sunday Morning* , Centrepoint ('World Cup 1994'), May 30, 1993.
19. Rejean Tremblay, a senior Montreal sports writer, observed to *Globe and Mail* reporter Kirk Makin in the middle of the 1994 Stanley Cup playoffs that 'many years ago people here were Catholics. Now they are Canadiens' fans. This is something unnatural. It goes much too far.' Sport psychologist Saul Miller told Makin about a 'revelation' he had one day at a Denver Broncos football game 'while 75,000 fans roared and the team romped under its 40 foot Bronco mascot.' Miller was on the field and 'looked up at this huge horse up there, painted orange. I swear it looked like the great god Ba'al or something. It was their tribe, and they chanted and sang.' Kirk Makin, 'The Peanuts and Beer on Canada's Spectator Sports', *Globe and Mail.* May 21, 1994.
20. William Oscar Johnson and John Walter, 'Every Day is Game Day', *Sports Illustrated,* Dec. 2, 1992.
21. Women's images in advertising averaged out at about 28% of total imagery (31%, 28.5% and 26%) and story illustration averaged out at about 12.5% (11%, 14% and 12%).
22. For a good overview of these developments, see Sut Jhally, 'The Spectacle of Accumulation: Material and Cultural Factors in the Evolution of the Sports/Media Complex', *The Insurgent Sociologist*, No. 12, Vol. 3, 1984.
23. For an analysis of men's relative economic privilege within changing family demographics in the post-war period, see Barbara Ehrenreich, *The Hearts of Men,* New York, Doubleday, 1983.
24. For a brilliant history and analysis of advertising's project of emotional manipulation, and the tools ('psychodemographics') developed to effect this, see Joyce Nelson, *The*

*Perfect Machine*, Between the Lines Press, Toronto 1987.

25. For some idea of the reach and extent of the sport nexus in 1992, see the survey, 'The Sports Business: Faster, Higher, Richer', *The Economist*, July 25, 1992, pp. 3–17.
26. Tom Fennell, D'Arcy Jenish, et al, 'The Riches of Sport' *Maclean's*, April 9, 1990, pp. 42–45.
27. Steve Rushin, 'The Megamall', *Sports Illustrated*, August, 1994.
28. Richard J. Barnett and John Cavanagh, *Global Dreams: Imperial Corporations and the New World Order*, New York/Toronto, Simon and Schuster, 1994. Total sales for Nike in 1994 – $4.73 billion, according to Christopher Hume, 'Nike Selling the Swoosh along with the Shoes', *Toronto Star*, October 28, 1994. For a grand overview of corporate-sport-governmental relationships in the Olympic sector, see Vyv Simson and Andrew Jennings, *The Lords of the Rings: Power, Money and Drugs in the Modern Olympics*, Stoddart, Toronto, 1992.
29. Sue Curry Jansen and Donald Sabo, 'The Sport/War Metaphor: Hegemonic Masculinity, the Persian Gulf War, and the New World Order,' *Sociology of Sport Journal*, Vol. 11, No 1 (March 1994).
30. *The Economist*, July 25, 1992.
31. Robert Baade and R. Dye, 'Sports Stadiums and Arena Development: A Critical Review' *Economic Development Quarterly*, 2 (3), 265–275. See also sport scholars David Whitson and Don McIntosh 'Becoming a World-Class City: Hallmark Events and Sports Franchises in the Growth Strategies of Western Canadian Cities' in *Sociology of Sport Journal* 10, 1993.
32. *The Economist*, September 9, 1995, p. 90.
33. Editorial, 'Budget Scandal', *The Nation*, August 28/September 4, 1995. Cf. Tom Hayden and Connie Rice 'California Cracks Its Mortarboards', *The Nation*, September 18, 1995; and Mike Davis, 'Hell Factories in the Field' and editorial 'The Prison Boom', *The Nation*, February 20, 1995, pp. 223, 229–237;
34. For a brilliant theorization of this idea, see Gad Horowitz, *Repression: Basic and Surplus Repression in Psychoanalytic Theory – Freud, Reich and Marcuse*, University of Toronto Press, Toronto, 1977.
35. So far, only Sweden has undertaken to legislate policy that enables men as well as women to become qualitatively more involved in childrearing. Other countries, however supportive of the 'family' also support the traditional gender division of labour.
36. Michael A. Messner and William R. Solomon, 'Outside the Frame: Newspaper Coverage of the Sugar Ray Leonard Wife Abuse Story', *Sociology of Sport Journal*, 10, 1993, pp. 119–134.
37. For a recent productive elucidation of Marxist cultural theory's general argument in this direction, see Judith Stamp comments on Adorno and Horkheimer in her's *Unthinking Modernity: Innis, McLuhan and the Frankfurt School* (Montreal and Kingston; McGill Queen's University Press, 1995) pp. 31, 35–39.
38. 'Ted turns over a new leaf' *Variety*, Sept. 25, 1995. Note the sport trope of the copy: 'The man who used to position himself as a moody loner was suddenly transmogrified into an ebullient 'team player''.
39. Michael Maccoby, *The Gamesman: The New Corporate Leaders*, Simon and Shuster, New York, 1976.
40. Recent curriculum changes at the University of Toronto School of Physical and Health Education provide one very concrete example of the way that physical activity can be re-thought and re-taught; and show what the preparation of a new kind of physical educator could be like. There are three key directions evident in these changes. The first accentuates the elements of pleasure and cooperation in physical activity, and minimizes pain and competition. The second validates both homosocial and heterosocial sport, with emphasis on women's vigorous physicality and men's access to non-sport physical disciplines. The third politicizes and makes cultural the way that the understanding of the

body and physical activity are taught. The University of Toronto's changes represent a balanced, integrated approach which it hopes will be carried out into the public systems by its graduates as they become educators themselves. Unfortunately, U. of T. is virtually *alone* among all North American schools in moving in this direction.

41. *Why are Some People Healthy and Others Not? The Determinants of the Health of the Population*, Aldine DeGruyter, New York, 1994; Cf. Editorial 'Elucidating the Relationships between Race, Socioeconomic Status, and Health', *American Journal of Public Health*, June 1994, Vol.. 84, No. 6, pp. 892–893.
42. For a political and economic history of the development of steroid use among Olympic and other professional athletes, and the specific conditions of Canadian Olympic sport at the time that Ben Johnson tested positive for steroids at the Seoul Olympic Games in 1988, see V. Burstyn, 'The Sporting Life' *Saturday Night*, March 1989.
43. This and the following quotes taken from Leslie Scrivener, 'In changing world, men flock to Jesus', *Toronto Star*, September 24, 1995.
44. Joan Breckenridge and Gay Abbate, 'Movement issues 'wakeup call' to Canadian men,' *The Globe and Mail*, September 25 1995.
45. And among these, a number – including Michael Messner, Donald Sabo, Bruce Kidd, R.W. Connell and Jim McKay – have made pioneering contributions in the field of sport studies.

I would like gratefully to acknowledge the supportive discussions and helpful criticisms of Geoffrey Smith, David Centon, Johnathan Burston, Lynn King and Leo Panitch.

# SOCIALIST HOPE IN THE SHADOW OF CATASTROPHE

Norman Geras

In his last book Ralph Miliband identifies as one of a number of crucial problems socialists need to address – problems putting in question the credibility of the socialist project itself – the massive evidence we have, particularly from the present century, of atrocious human cruelty, murderous division and conflict, the seeming aptitude of our species for large-scale organized blood-letting. The sceptical question as to whether with such 'human material' a radical re-ordering of society toward cooperative harmony and altruism is not merely a utopian illusion has, Miliband suggests, to be confronted seriously. He urges us, nevertheless, against the pessimistic answer to that question, judging it 'a counsel of despair to say ... that evil on a huge scale is part of the human condition, that its conquest is impossible'.[1] In this essay, written in tribute to a life's work of unwavering socialist advocacy and consistent, level-headed clarity, I support Miliband's general standpoint, but by way of examining more closely some of the assumptions about human nature that he reviews or himself deploys in articulating it.

The challenge posed by history, Miliband begins by saying, is to 'the fundamental optimism about human capabilities which pervades the socialist enterprise – a belief, inherited from the Enlightenment, in the infinite perfectibility of human beings'. I take this as one distinctive view of human nature and shall identify it for the time being as assumption (1). Having so expressed it, Miliband then goes on to put it, as he says, 'in more contemporary terms', as if only expressing the same thing in another way. In fact, however, he presents in the reformulation, or at least he licenses, a second, different view. For he speaks now just of 'the belief that human beings are perfectly capable of organizing themselves into cooperative, democratic, egalitarian and self-governing communities, in which all conflict would certainly not have been eliminated, but where it would become less and less frequent and acute.' I shall call this for now assumption (2), and I differentiate it from (1) on the grounds that where (1) asserts that human beings are perfectible, (2) requires no such ambitious claim. It requires only that, whatever imperfections human beings may have, these are not so great as to exclude the possibility of creating communities with the specified characteristics, communities of a socialist kind. And (2) even permits, via the reference to continuing although rarer and more moderate conflicts, the inference that there might be enduring human faults: tendencies perhaps to selfishness, to indifference toward the misfortunes of others, to undue pride or vanity, needless aggression or whatever else. Along with the run of better human qualities, such tendencies would also be, on this assumption, a permanent part of the constitution of humankind.

In any case, whether on the grounds of the more or of the less ambitious claim, because human beings are perfectible or because the weaknesses in their nature are not so vitiating as to be bound always to defeat the collective efforts conceivable from their virtues, 'socialism's essential point of departure', Miliband says, 'is – has to be – that there is no implacable curse which dooms humankind to perpetual division and strife.' By negating this last proposition we will get, of course, the source of the original sceptical question; we will get a view of human nature according to which there *is* such an implacable curse. Let us call this, then, assumption (3). It is the assumption, as we have already seen it expressed, 'that evil on a huge scale is part of the human condition'. It is the assumption that 'humanity . . . cannot escape from the slaughterhouse, and is doomed to add, generation upon generation to the end of time, to the catalogue of collective cruelty.' It is the assumption that, as to the many smaller-scale 'individual acts of cruelty perpetrated by men and women upon each other, or upon children, or for that matter upon animals', these too 'are to be explained by traits ineradicably embedded in human nature'.

One further passage will complete the set of views I want to distinguish from one another for consideration. Miliband for his part asserts that more plausible than this last pessimistic view is the idea that:

> such acts [of cruelty] . . . are mainly produced by the insecurities, frustrations, anxieties and alienations that form an intrinsic part of class societies based on domination and exploitation. The 'injuries of class', allied to injuries of race, gender, religion and many others, readily lend themselves to pathological and morbid deformations which deeply and adversely affect human relations. This can only be effectively tackled in societies where conditions are created which foster solidarity, cooperation, security and respect, and where these values are given substance by a variety of grassroots institutions in all areas of life. It is these conditions which socialism seeks to advance.

Now, I take the precaution of saying that, so far as Miliband's own intended meaning is concerned, his argument here, of a kind common in socialist and other radical discourses, probably does not yield a further and quite separate view of human nature. This argument is construable, in particular, as being consistent with assumption (2). For the notion we have seen to be contained in (2) that human beings are characterized by a combination of virtues and vices, or (otherwise expressed) that human nature embodies different and even opposed kinds of inner potentiality or tendency, is perfectly compatible with the idea that it is the social conditions in which people live that, loosely speaking, shape those people, bringing out some qualities, blocking or frustrating others, and so on. There are aspects of Miliband's text which indicate just such a line of thought. I shall come back to this.

I propose to wring another meaning from the passage just quoted all the same. This meaning is that the social conditions people inhabit do not merely bring out or frustrate, encourage or deform, the various qualities generally present within human beings; rather, they create them. Or, formulated differently: the social conditions, or relations or institutions, fully determine the traits borne by any given group of social agents. Human nature, in other words, is neither like this nor like that, for there is no human nature. There are just socially, culturally, historically produced specificities and differences. I call that assumption (4) and I permit myself forcibly to extract it from what Miliband says for two reasons. One is that it remains a standard position upon this general terrain of problems and so needs some consideration here. The other is that though Miliband's views do not, strictly speaking, entail it, there are nevertheless aspects of his text also – so I shall later argue – that evince a certain over-socializing or over-historicizing tendency on his part. It seems reasonable therefore as a procedure of discussion to include the limit position of this tendency for the sake of greater comprehensiveness.

I now collect up and re-order the four different views I have elicited, giving each one a brief and standardized formula.

From (3) → (a) Human nature is intrinsically evil.
From (1) → (b) Human nature is intrinsically good.
From (4) → (c) Human nature is intrinsically blank.
From (2) → (d) Human nature is intrinsically mixed.

This formulaic listing is for convenience only, and is consciously made at the cost of two over-simplifications which I at once try to undo.

The pessimistic assumption – (a) – need not require that people are by nature wholly, or even that they are all inordinately, evil. It could just take the form, and it is perhaps more likely to, that impulses towards evil are sufficiently strong and extensive in humankind that they can never be lastingly pacified, and must continue to produce horrors of one sort and another on both a small and a large scale. Equally, the optimistic assumption – (b) – that human beings are intrinsically good does not have to exclude that these beings are capable of nastiness, even nastiness of a serious kind. Indeed the derivation of assumption (b) from a formula of perfectibility implies that human beings precisely are so capable. It is just that, under (b), this capability is to be seen as less typical of, or less powerful within, the species, as adventitious and removable, as due possibly to the corrupting influence of bad circumstances or inadequate education; where the potentiality for good is more integral, more deeply laid. Both (a) and (b), in other words, can be construed in ways allowing that human nature is, as I have put it in formula (d), mixed. However, (a) and (b) take a position on the weight of, respectively, evil and good within the 'mixture', so as especially to insist on the long-range centrality of one of them. My simplified formula in each case merely accentuates the viewpoint in order to distinguish it sharply from (d), in which the balance between good and evil within humankind is left more open.

It is perhaps prudent also to point out that the view of human nature as expressed in (c), human nature as a blank, is not so much simplified in that formula as purified. By which I mean that this view is hardly ever held by anybody in pure form, but rather in conjunction with other propositions with which it is inconsistent. There is no good reason for taking it other than freed of the inconsistencies. In any event, (c) shares with (b) a belief that human evil is eradicable; but the belief is differently based in the two cases. Proponents of (b) think that evil is not intrinsic in human nature because good is; whereas proponents of (c) think that evil is not intrinsic in human nature because nothing is.

Finally (d), given what has already been said, is obviously to be entertained here in a form that makes it genuinely, and not only apparently, distinct from (a) and (b). This is to say that, with the balance between potentialities for good and potentialities for evil being taken as more open than in those formulas, neither kind of potentiality is held to bulk so large as to be overwhelming or to render the other, whether now or at any time, inconsequential or null. Base or egregious human impulses, under assumption (d), are not so all-consuming as to make pervasive and enormous evil forever inevitable, but nor are they so weak or insignificant that they might be conceived as entirely eliminable, as one day gone, as even now 'really' something else than they appear, not human impulses after all, but alienated, capitalist, class-oppressive or class-oppressed, patriarchal, corrupted ones. Conversely, benign and admirable tendencies, under assumption (d), are not so dominant as to make the possibility of serious human evil only a temporary, albeit long, historical phase which may one day pass, nor so feeble or so sparsely distributed as to make attempts to limit and counteract that baleful possibility a pointless quest. Both sorts of impulse or tendency are conceived under (d) as being permanent features of our nature, realities to be negotiated, lived with, if possible understood – and if possible tilted toward the more benign and admirable, and tilted as far that way as possible.

In completing my clarification of the four assumptions, I anticipate the argument that follows. The socialist enterprise, along with other ideas of radical human progress, generally presupposes, as Miliband says, rejecting assumption (a). I want to argue that seriously confronting even so – as he suggests we must – the sceptical question which is raised by the sponsors of assumption (a) amounts to this: that socialists henceforth should not allow themselves the easy convenience of assumption (b) or assumption (c). To adopt either of these is precisely not to take the mass of evidence to which Miliband alludes *seriously*. It is to make light of it. The hope of socialism has to be sustained on the basis of assumption (d). The goal of a much better and a more just society is to be fought for not because human beings are by nature overwhelmingly or essentially good, nor because they do not have an intrinsic nature; but because and in spite of the combination in their nature of bad impulses with good ones. Because of the bad impulses, this struggle is necessary. In spite of them, it is to be hoped, a socialist society may yet be possible.

Socialist advocacy is too often and too much informed by the kind of thinking I encapsulate in assumptions (b) and (c). Now, I repeat, the two assumptions are not the same in the way they ground an optimistic outlook: to the suggested permanence of great evil the first opposes the claim that there are deep, massively preponderant tendencies towards good inherent in humankind, whereas the second just opposes the notion of an infinite human plasticity. This difference is not immaterial. The first view has the significant advantage of being willing to deal in *some* conception of a common human nature, such as the second view for its part rejects. And I call this an advantage, because the claim that there is no human nature at all is at best a thoughtless exaggeration, one that it is impossible to uphold with any genuine lucidity of mind; which is why its advocates so freely propose or assume what they also deny, here say what they there take back, as the need of the moment may be. I have argued this case already at some length twice, once in relation to historicist and structuralist positions within Marxism, more lately in criticism of a 'post-modern' variant of the same thing. So I shall not go into it here again.[2]

I concentrate instead on what I perceive to be the shared weakness of viewpoints (b) and (c). This is their common unwillingness to accept, as significant realities in their own right with some independent explanatory weight in human affairs, dispositions in the make-up of human beings that are less than beneficent – whether of selfishness and envy, malicious glee, the enjoyment of power or advantage over others, a certain passion to exclude, cruelty, destructiveness, and a good number of other things. So far as some such dispositions may appear to leave a rather large mark on the historical record, these are always really (so the suggestion is) a product or expression of something *else*. Rendered in one conception overwhelmingly benign, and in the other entirely empty of fixed content, human nature does not autonomously contribute anything of its own to how things can go badly, the apparent human capacity for evil becoming mere epiphenomenon *par excellence*. Can this way of thinking withstand a sober look at how grim the historical record in fact is?

Let us now bring into relation with the more easily optimistic assumptions about human nature to be found in the arguments of many socialists, some views about it emerging from an experience *in* that record: of all the events of the twentieth century mentioned in the present connection by Ralph Miliband himself, the one that has perhaps done most to instil a general melancholy about future human possibilities. The Holocaust as I shall be referring to it here, some now well-known reservations about the term notwithstanding, has come to occupy a prominent place in contemporary consciousness. It has given rise to an extensive literature, coming from survivors, from historians and theologians, from most kinds of social scientist, from psychoanalysts, novelists, poets, dramatists, literary critics. But it has not left much of a mark, it has to be said, on the moral and political philosophy of socialism, and this reflects a broader state of affairs, in which the Holocaust has not figured very conspicuously amongst the concerns of moral or political philosophers in general.

It was a human catastrophe which may be thought, for all that, to pose some troubling questions for anyone committed to radical and progressive change, and it is certainly not a good reason for ignoring these questions that troubling is what they are. The words of the Polish sociologist Anna Pawelczynska, herself a former prisoner at Auschwitz, are to the point here:

> People living within the orbit of European civilization today defend themselves from the naturalistic eloquence of facts which have no analogy in their experience by a failure of the imagination . . . Such people, as members of that same human species to which the murderers and their victims belong, resist identifying with either murderer or victim . . . [They] protect their view of the world, their optimistic philosophy of life, from the consequences of understanding the concentration camp as a dimension of the evil man can do and of the depth of contempt to which he can sink.[3]

A socialist philosophy worthy of being taken seriously cannot afford such a 'protected' optimism, shut off against the brutal realities beyond just by virtue of declining to look at them.

In 'The Visit' by Tadeusz Borowski – a survivor of Auschwitz who transmuted his experiences there into a series of unflinching, terrible stories, before later taking his own life – the narrator details some of the wretched human sights he has witnessed in the camp, and goes on:

> And every one of the people who, because of eczema, phlegmon or typhoid fever, or simply because they were too emaciated, were taken to the gas chamber, begged the orderlies loading them into the crematorium trucks to remember what they saw. And to tell the truth about mankind to those who do not know it.[4]

Irene W., another survivor, speaking of how she has had over the years to attend to the needs of daily life without allowing her memories to overwhelm her and prevent her from functioning normally, reports:

> Yet it's always there; it's more a view of the world, a total world-view . . . of extreme pessimism, of sort of one feels . . . of really knowing the truth about people, human nature, about death, of really knowing the truth in a way that other people don't know it.[5]

The 'truth about mankind' and 'the truth about people, human nature' is what they call it; a truth, they both say, that others do not know. What is this truth?

There are doubtless different facets of it, but in the more theoretical literature on the Holocaust it looks, with some writers, rather like our assumption (a). Thus, according to the theologian Richard Rubenstein, 'just as depth psychology was able to expose the ineradicable dark side of human personality', so the world of the death camps has shown it to be 'an error to imagine that civilization and savage cruelty are antitheses . . . Mankind never emerged out of savagery into civilization'.[6] Another theologian, Arthur Cohen – for whom the Holocaust is *tremendum*, a kind of unfathomable abyss of evil, 'orgiastic celebration of death' – has written in like vein:

> Liberalism (and in its radicalization, Marxism) may well be the fallen messianism of the Jews, the familiar secular inversion of Jewish utopian hope, but liberalism is predicated upon assumptions regarding the nature of man and his educable potentiality which the *tremendum* destroyed . . . In the holocaust is a configuration of evil; it writes large what should have been recognized all along – that the oppository, destructive character of evil drains of credibility every notion of an ongoing teleology of the good that was required by the rational optimisms . . . of the nineteenth century.[7]

Something similar can be expressed more indirectly, and I take as a case of this one of the few well-known contemporary political philosophers to have addressed himself, albeit briefly, to the subject of the Holocaust, namely Robert Nozick. Nozick lists the multiple and wanton barbarities, to read the details of which, as he puts it, 'staggers and numbs the mind'. He goes on to suggest that the Holocaust is an event 'that radically and drastically alters the situation and status of humanity'. He explains the suggestion so:

> I do not claim to understand the full significance of this, but here is one piece, I think: It now would not be a *special* tragedy if humankind ended, if the human species were destroyed in atomic warfare or the earth passed through some cloud that made it impossible for the species to continue reproducing itself . . . Imagine beings from another galaxy looking at our history. It would not seem unfitting to them, I think, if that story came to an end, if the species they see with that history ended, destroying itself in nuclear warfare or otherwise failing to be able to continue.

Nozick, it is true, also qualifies his suggestion in a number of ways. He does not mean that human beings deserve this to happen; it would involve much suffering and individual loss; it would be wrong for anyone actually to bring it about. Nor does he overlook other, earlier cruelties and calamities. Perhaps it is just the case, he says, 'that the Holocaust *sealed* the situation, and made it patently clear'. He wonders, too, whether we might be able to redeem ourselves as a species, were people to begin to take the suffering of others upon themselves by suffering whenever they did. As it strikes me, however, the point here is that, despite these various qualifications, the judgement which they qualify already concludes a balance sheet between the actual past of humankind and its possible futures. If 'its loss would now be no *special* loss above and beyond the losses to the individuals involved', if humanity has forfeited 'its claim to continue', as Nozick thinks it has, and if this is so, the talk even of an effort of redemption notwithstanding, does that not amount to fixing the nature of the species by the enormities of evil in its past, to the discount of any better possible futures? More than by whatever good we might still hope to bring about, not to speak of the good already done, we are characterized by the atrocities and iniquities that have been perpetrated, in a judgement of metaphysical resignation and despair.[8]

Looking into the depths of the experience on which Nozick here reflects, it can be hard not to share something of the same mood. What Elie Wiesel has to say in a related connection is apposite. 'Examine them', he writes – with reference, this, to 'snapshots' of the Holocaust, photographs of murder in progress which we have by courtesy of the murderers themselves or of the numerous spectators to murder – 'and you will forget who you are ... Nothing will be important any more. You will have glimpsed an abyss you would rather not have uncovered. Too late.'[9] The person is perhaps unfortunate who does not know a like response to horrors of this magnitude. A mood of resignation or despair in the face of them is to be resisted, all the same, by those who can. We ought to resist the cosmic pessimism of Nozick's judgement; resist any unilateral definition of human nature in terms only or principally of its worst excesses; resist the identification we have seen made above, between the Nazi universe of death and *the* truth about humankind. So, anyway, I shall eventually get around to arguing.

We need, in resisting it, however, to respect what is *a* truth here and not just casually dismiss this as some would-be irrelevance to socialism and other utopian projects. I have in mind the sort of dismissal which is involved in claiming that an event like the Holocaust discloses nothing about the inner or natural propensities of human beings, because the behaviour patterns and personality traits it reveals to us are to be put down, either wholly or largely, to the historically determinate social and situational conditions of the event. Such a claim, it may even be thought, has a certain plausibility on account of the very extremity of the case. Why judge human nature, it could be asked, on the basis of conditions of life and death that were exceptional, on the basis of a hellish and in no way typical human situation?

An initial answer to this seemingly plausible question is that we are in possession of some considerable wisdom from and about that particular hell which emphasizes to us, warns us, that the actions, reactions, postures and personalities constitutive of it, exceptional and shocking in many ways as they obviously were, were also continuous with ones familiar in and to ordinary human beings in more ordinary circumstances. This was a world populated not by monsters and brutes – or not only by monsters and brutes, for in some necessary and still usable moral meaning there were more than enough of these – but by beings who were precisely human beings, with characteristics that are all too recognizable, human vices and weaknesses amongst them, common faults and frailties.

Most easily recognizable in that regard are the bystanders: those who, not directly active in the process of mass murder, did nothing to try to stop it either. These are the people who affect not to know, or who do not care to know and so do not find out; or who do know but do not care anyway, who are indifferent; or who are afraid, for themselves or for others, or who feel powerless; or who are weighed down, distracted or just occupied (as most of us) in pursuing the aims of their own lives. Such people formed the background to the tragedy of the European Jews and they continue everywhere to provide an enabling condition for other tragedies large and small, and for great but avoidable suffering. The ubiquity of the bystander surely testifies to a remarkable capacity in members of our species to live comfortably with the enormous sufferings of others.

It is not only the bystanders, however, who are recognizable here. It is also the perpetrators. The theme is a difficult one and must be treated with some care, since it comes otherwise to promote a glib and corrosive moral cynicism, actually encouraging what it purports only to observe. There is a need to understand; but without being too understanding. Yet the theme itself is inescapable. If amongst the perpetrators is to be found, as one would expect, an ample complement of sadists and thugs, there is now a large literature documenting for the more general run of them – that is, the camp personnel, the members of execution squads, the civilian users (which means users up) of slave labour, the planners and the bureaucrats and the doctors of death – that these bearers of Nazi genocide fell well within the range of psychological normality. They were not, for the most part, psychopaths. They were ordinary people.

And the same literature makes available to us a wide-ranging exploration of the mechanisms, psychological and social, by which such ordinary people could bring themselves, or be induced by others, to contribute their share to the evil. These mechanisms are many and I can only gesture towards them here: the fears and resentments focused on people who are different, and the feelings of self-enhancement or even elation at the disaster brought upon them; the thought of being authorized to act by a legitimate higher source, or the thought that this, one's own 'segment' of the overall process is only one of a very large number and not the decisive one morally speaking; the idea of its being an impersonal role, a job, and thus not due in any strong sense to the particular individual filling it; self-serving, careerist motives; a simple bending to social pressures, not wanting not to conform with the opinions of one's peers. And being implicated gradually, incrementally; accustoming oneself, as to anything in the way of a routine; for many, not being able to *see* what finally happens to the victims of the process; regarding them as insignificant morally; dehumanizing them, first in thought, then by social and symbolic practices, in the end by physically demeaning and brutalizing ones. By a combination of these means the line is crossed.[10]

It is as necessary to insist upon what is not being said here as to emphasize what is. This is not offered in that style of knowing and generally satisfied pessimism which assures us that deep down we are all so badly flawed as to become, just given the appropriate circumstances, instigators of or accomplices in any moral crime. It is not true. There are always those who refuse and those who resist. There are people who risk everything, and others who, though they cannot find the strength to do this, still do what they feel they can to oppose or mitigate the consequences of the crime in question. To explore the motivational pathways toward participation in or compliance with great iniquity is not to say that these must inevitably be taken. Nor is it to deny the reality of the choice there is, restricted or dangerous as it can sometimes be: the choice to act *against* the habits of thought and the impulses just rehearsed, upon other motives, for better reasons.

The point, therefore, is not a cynical, but it is a realist one. It is that even this (as it is sometimes said) utterly demonic of twentieth-century horrors was the work of human beings such as we are acquainted with. It was compounded of well-known sorts of prejudice, ambition, temptation, taste of power, evasion, moral failure. When they are not doing philosophy or talking theoretical politics, socialists and other radicals know as well as anyone the motivational range here, comprising, with all the admirable qualities and the excellences, also elements which are less than admirable, and indeed some of them downright repugnant. This range is simply part of the stuff of ordinary existence. It is a form of practical experience taken from every area of life: every family, circle of friends and acquaintances, every neighbourhood; every milieu, social stratum, vocation, organization. It is an experience – again, together with what is generous, loving, courageous and so on – of jealousies and vanities, petty unkindnesses and hatreds, wilful deceits, self-importance and self-promotion. It yields to us a knowledge complementary to the one we have from the Holocaust itself: a knowledge of the ordinary raw materials of great evil, those common vices and human failings which can become, in another setting or combination, suddenly exorbitant.

Lastly in this connection, there is the victim group to be considered as well. With a share of the same common vices and failings distributed unevenly across it, it too becomes stained by the crimes of the perpetrators. Another difficult theme. To write about this as it were from the outside, however carefully, runs the risk of appearing to proffer a judgement on others, of which everyone *from* the outside ought to be cautious. 'It is a judgement', as Primo Levi has put it, 'that we would like to entrust only to those who found themselves in similar circumstances, and had the possibility to test on themselves what it means to act in a state of coercion.'[11] I shall let Levi himself represent what is a rather more general message from survivors of the Nazi concentration and death camps.

In some reflections on what he has called the 'grey zone', Levi for his part firmly casts aside any levelling cynicism in this matter, writing:

> I do not know, and it does not much interest me to know, whether in my depths there lurks a murderer, but I do know that I was a guiltless victim and I was not a murderer . . . and that to confuse [the murderers] with their victims is a moral disease or an aesthetic affectation or a sinister sign of complicity . . .[12]

But Levi asserts, all the same, that '[i]t is naive, absurd, and historically false to believe that an infernal system such as National Socialism was, sanctifies its victims; on the contrary it degrades them'. The grey zone is one feature of what he has in mind. He refers by this to 'the space which separates (and not only in Nazi Lagers) the victims from the persecutors':

> Only a schematic rhetoric can claim that that space is empty: it never is; it is studded with obscene or pathetic figures (sometimes they possess both qualities simultaneously), whom it is indispensable to know if we want to know the human species, if we want to know how to defend our souls when a similar test should once more loom before us, or even if we only want to understand what takes place in a big industrial factory.[13]

The grey zone, Levi says, has 'ill-defined outlines which both separate and join the two camps of masters and servants'. If it is never empty, that is because 'in the Lager and outside, there exist grey, ambiguous persons ready to compromise.'[14]

It needs to be emphasized at this juncture that Primo Levi was not well disposed towards the too facile equation of the Nazi camps with other sites of hierarchical power: 'the comparison', he has said, 'arouses revulsion in us, those of us who have been "marked", "tattooed" . . . There's no gas chamber at Fiat.' The more notable therefore is his repeated allusion, in these reflections just quoted, to the existence of some similar elements 'in the Lager and outside'. The Nazi camps were not for him a microcosm or the mere 'condensation' of the world beyond them; but he was willing to describe them as being 'a distorting mirror' of that world nonetheless.[15]

It is a not uncommon observation amongst the survivors. Levi again: 'the prisoner who gets ahead on the backs of his comrades exists everywhere'. Hanna Levy-Hass (in a diary written while she was imprisoned at Belsen): 'I shall keep firmly in my mind everything that I have seen, everything that I have experienced and learnt, everything that human nature has revealed to me . . . I shall judge each man according to the way he has behaved, or could have behaved, in these conditions that surround us.' Viktor Frankl: 'Is it surprising that in those depths we again found only human qualities which in their very nature were a mixture of good and evil?' 'In the concentration camps . . . we watched and witnessed some of our comrades behave like swine while others behaved like saints. Man has both potentialities within himself . . .'[16]

On the basis of her conversations with survivors of the death camps, Gitta Sereny has spoken of the 'fatalistic lack of vehemence of those who have come to terms with the inevitability of human failings in everyone, themselves included'.[17] In the attitude she thereby identifies is joined an ancient, indeed a common sense knowledge with the wisdom brought back – and at what a cost – from the places of Nazi barbarity.

Now, a standard socialist, and more broadly progressive, riposte exists to being presented with considerations of this kind. It would disqualify them at a stroke from being accepted as genuine wisdom. Common sense, it is often said, is a form of ideology; and, likewise, so-called practical experience is a bounded experience only. Both are the product of particular social forms, historically specific worlds. As such, neither common sense nor practical experience can be a reliable guide to the patterns of behaviour we may expect with other social forms, in future possible worlds. Whether inside the camps or beyond them, what we have knowledge of are people who grew up in a deforming social environment. Even if it is the case that the Holocaust universe is recognizable as having been populated by ordinary human beings, these were human beings who had been moulded by capitalism, class, patriarchy and the rest, by gross inequalities and differentials in power, with the profoundly limiting and corrupting effects upon their attitudes that all that must entail. Anything vouchsafed to us, consequently, out of the experience of the Holocaust is relevant only for the type of society which gave birth to, or at least accommodated, it. It is not relevant to the prospects and character of a future society which has been radically transformed.

As much weight as is bound to be given to arguments of this general kind by those of us who entertain the possibility of progressive revolutionary change, in such blanket form they are inadequate – in face both of the terrible enormities and of the more run-of-the-mill individual failings they purport to respond to, and with which the human story is in fact so crowded. I shall now go on to offer three reasons why trying thus to 'neutralize' the negative features of this story, by just ascribing them to societal defects of a historically specific and remediable sort, is unconvincing. It is a poor basis for the hope of human progress.

First, one may bring to this domain an argument of Marxian pedigree but which ought to carry force also more widely, with anyone sceptical of grand projects of a speculative nature. This is the argument that the better society of the future is to be thought of, and fought for, as emerging out of real tendencies within the present, and not counterposed to the latter as a merely abstract ideal unanchored in existing empirical forces or in any proper grasp of them. That argument, much used (and not only by Marxists) in relation, for example, to what sort of political or economic goals are foreseeably feasible, and to the question of who are likely to be the agents for achieving them, is rather less often invoked by socialists in relation to the topic under discussion. When it comes to what kind of beings human beings are and might one day become, and more particularly to what limitations they have and how these might constrain the feasible shapes of an alternative future, it is not uncommon, then, for socialist advocacy to be couched in terms of a quite remarkable leap. This can take us from people as we know and have known them to beings wonderfully freed of the familiar human faults and vices, or saved at any rate from ever having to let these reveal their unpleasant outward effects; to people improved, in the well-known phrase, beyond recognition.

It seems, however, as appropriate to this area of reflection as to any other to hold that we have to start from where we are, therefore from the realities of human motivation, of moral weakness as much as moral strength, with which we are familiar, and not simply fly forward towards a speculative ideal. The least that one can say is that it ill befits socialists, whether of Marxist formation or of some other more or less realist cast of mind, to find easy refuge in such an insubstantial ideal.

But I want to take it further than this. For some will be tempted to minimize the weight of the point by treating it as a *merely* political one: intended, that is, to give some hope of proximate practical success, but having no deeper theoretical significance, no implication for the degree of changeability or fixedness in the human personality over the longer term. This temptation should be resisted. The point, I will maintain, does go deeper. It comes down to the need to show a proper – some would say materialist – regard for the continuities and the resistances of human history in the framing of any emancipatory project. This history certainly encompasses continuities as well as discontinuities, some of the continuities are long ones, and some of these long continuities are long precisely because they are due to nature, both external and human (a circumstance of which Marx, incidentally, was well aware, for all the emphasis he gave in his work to historical particularity and change).

Let us take a range of common human emotions, say, anger, desire, love, fear, pride, shame, melancholy, disgust; and some familiar dispositions too, say, submissiveness and dominance – whether in a sexual context or outside it – and community, spontaneity, constancy, self-regard. Like the more basic human needs and the most common human capacities, such emotions and dispositions plainly have a general, transhistorical basis. Whatever cultural variation their forms might display, it would not be plausible to propose that they are all wholly social constructs, and the idea of some future society in which they would be no more gives meaning, well and truly, to the phrase 'beyond recognition'. This is a world virtually unimaginable by us. It is hard to say whether it would be, for the new kind of 'people' within it, a utopia, but it scarcely looks desirable from here.

Let us now take in turn – and as is not the same thing – a range of some of the less attractive human qualities and tendencies: say (in a list loosely paralleling the one just given), hatred or vengefulness, greed, covetousness and envy, overbearing attachment, moral cowardice, vanity, self-abasement, destructiveness; and then servility, love of power, cruelty; and ethnic prejudice, lawlessness, fanaticism, uncaring privilege. We should like to believe in the possibility of a world with much less of this sort of thing, much less of it, especially, that is accorded public space and the means of advancement or growth through hierarchies of great privilege, sites of tyrannical power, bouts of collective violence, and so on. But how much more plausible or imaginable is a world, even, from which these uglier human attributes have disappeared? They seem generally to bear connections of one kind and another to the common emotions and dispositions by way of which I came to them: as exaggerated or aggravated forms of those, fixations of them, deteriorations, imbalances. It suggests that they too have, in some sort, a durable natural foundation, capable as they are of being brought out by a very wide variety of interpersonal circumstances and relationships – such as there is also bound always to be in any society of more or less equitably distributed freedoms. It seems more realistic to reckon that humankind will have to go on living with these less salutary human attributes in some proportion. If socialism, at any rate, will still be a society of human beings, much about them will be recognizably the same. We have nothing at present but the emptiest of speculations to tell us that the common faults and vices might disappear or all but disappear; that everything that is productive of grave mischief belongs with the discontinuities of history, with the societally generated, and nothing of it with our underlying human nature.

This brings me directly to the second of my three reasons. For there is in any case an odd feature, rarely remarked upon, of arguments of this sociologizing type which assert that nothing or very little is to be attributed to human nature. It is an assumption of, so to say, fixed explanatory quantity, such that the relation between (for short) sociological and naturalist explanation of human behaviour must vary inversely: if human behaviour has much to do with social conditions, it has little to do with natural traits; if very much, then very little; and so on. Or, expressed in qualitative terms, if the social is very important in explaining human behaviour, then human nature (if it is allowed that it exists at all) is very unimportant. This is not the only way of thinking about the issue, however, and it is not the most persuasive way. One might observe, instead, that whatever the explanatory weight here – and it is undeniably immense – of social structure and cultural mores, there is, as well, a weight that is due to our natural make-up and of its own considerable magnitude. There is, because as much as the particularities of society and culture may influence the forms of conduct and the run of inclinations and values within human populations, such particularities can only work, to put this baldly, on what it is *in* people to do or be. They can only work on the potentialities, and within certain limits, that are set by the nature of our species.

You can train a horse, and you can accustom a cat, to various things. But you cannot teach a horse to read or get a cat to live on vegetables, and you will not get either to be forever stationary, like an object. There are, by the same token, natural limits to what human beings can do and can sustain, and there are material needs, capacities and impulses which will find expression in one social form or another. Nothing about the rich diversity of social forms, or about the irrepressible freedom of the human will and creativity of the imagination, subtracts by so much as a single scintilla from the contribution to human affairs which is made by natural determinants of that kind.

I want to explore the relevance of this point to our subject by coming back to Ralph Miliband's reflections. There are aspects of these, I said earlier, that can be read as affirming a hope in progress on the basis of assumption (d): the assumption of a mixed human nature, with potentialities for both good and evil. I noted his formulation envisaging socialism together with some persisting, albeit very much diminished, human conflict. This formulation would allow the possibility of some continued wrong-doing also, though it does not itself necessarily entail it. In fact, Miliband writes in the same connection of a situation 'where collective and individual *misdeeds* can be turned into increasingly marginal phenomena'. And he writes, as well, of 'a context in which collective cruelty would be . . . made impossible by the resistance which it would evoke'.[18] Both anticipations suggest a continuing space, as this may be put, of potential evil.

For what has been pressed back to the margins of social life still has its place *at* the margins, and presumably therefore also its living sources; and we know well enough how the marginal can often find its way, whether creeping or irrupting, towards the centre. Likewise, a thing (collective cruelty) made impossible by the resistance 'it would evoke', sounds to have some impulses sustaining it still, to be a live capacity and not merely a historical memory of what was there once but is no longer, having been eradicated or smoothed away. I propose, in the light of these inferences, one kind of interpretation of the long passage I earlier quoted from Miliband, referring to 'conditions . . . which foster solidarity, cooperation, security and respect, and where these values are given substance by a variety of grassroots institutions in all areas of life'.[19] It is an interpretation in which the said conditions and institutions are conceived as being, at least in part, externally blocking or obstructing, and simultaneously accommodating and facilitating. That is to say, they put up barriers against certain types of human tendency or impulse, while at the same time leaving room to certain other types. Such a conception of them precisely concedes the existence of what I have just called a space of potential evil. It does so in the metaphor of blocking, which presupposes something there needing to be blocked, troublesome tendencies and impulses of a durable sort, not entirely removable by education, acculturation or whatever.

A competing conception would make the human person, or else the miscreant human person, more entirely the product of the conditions and institutions which envelope it. It is a conception of these conditions and institutions as 'possessing' the innermost core of the individual self, or as disfiguring it; so that, once given a good social environment, we would have only good individuals, without significant residue of ill-will or viciousness. Now, of course, any adequate notion of the person will need some pretty large element, as it were, of this latter kind of conception. For social structure and culture do certainly 'enter' the make-up of the person, shaping its very identity, as much as they can be thought of also as external barriers, or channels, against and along which the human-natural dispositions of individuals have to make their way. The overall balance of any viewpoint is therefore everything here. Some other aspects of Miliband's reflections than those I have focused upon so far situate him closer, I believe, to the extreme limit of this possessing or disfiguring conception of social conditions than is warranted.

One indication is his use of the metaphor of pathology. Adverting again to the long passage quoted towards the beginning of this essay, we find Miliband referring there to the 'injuries' of class, race, gender and religion – as though acts of cruelty or other misdeeds were the result of damage from without and not inner possibilities of the normal organism. Equally, his talk in the same place of 'pathological and morbid deformations' may evoke an image of diseases foreign to the healthy body, so of external provenance once more. It is true that in thus counterposing as he does explanation of cruelty in terms of the psychological byproducts of 'societies based on exploitation and domination' to explanation of it in terms of 'traits ineradicably embedded in human nature', Miliband speaks of cruelty as being produced 'mainly' by the former.[20] However – and it is the crux of the point being pursued – this is a unilateral and misleading formula. How does one adjudicate what is 'main' in this context? It might be replied that, since we can imagine other social conditions in which human beings would behave cruelly very much less than they do now or perhaps hardly at all, this suffices to validate the judgement that cruelty is principally due to adverse social conditions. But one could imagine, too, other *beings*: beings who, even in adverse conditions, would not be provoked to the amount and to the extremes of cruelty, oppression, venality, violence and so forth, of which human beings have shown themselves to be so richly capable. The point is that adverse social conditions have the effects that they do only upon a certain configuration of naturally delimited potentialities and dispositions; and, this being the case, those potentialities and dispositions merit the distinction, for their part also, of being accounted 'main'.

The issue may be further elucidated by considering another aspect of Miliband's argument. Self-consciously and explicitly, to 'the attribution of guilt to human nature' he opposes what he sees as 'the crucially significant fact that it was from above that have almost always come the initiation and the organization of mass killings'. The 'mass of "ordinary people"', he says, have seldom been responsible for the decisions producing wholesale slaughter. 'Most such collective actions have been initiated and organized by people of power in pursuit of whatever purposes and fantasies moved them.' Miliband does at once go on to qualify any too easy optimism over this fact by adding that ordinary people have nevertheless often enough acquiesced to, cheered on or participated in the episodes of blood-letting initiated by people of power.[21] But the qualification does not go far enough. For it needs to be stated clearly also that these people of power are not from elsewhere, they are from amongst us. They are members of our species, a species in which there have ever been candidates aplenty, not just for being acquiescent and obedient to the powerful, but for occupying places of power and privilege themselves. Human beings have shown themselves very available for this and rather good at it, and it is a vain recourse to believe that it has nothing whatever to do with their intrinsic nature that they have.

A would-be Marxist (or just sociological) argument generally comes in here to say that our nature is the effect of class, power, privilege and so on, and not any of these the effect of our nature. But a different Marxism (and sociology) is possible in response. It says that human beings would not have been open, open so long and so geographically universally – and not only open, but so *very* available – to the class option of social organization and the benefits of power and privilege, if these things did not meet any impulse in their make-up. Why have they not, unanimously or in large enough numbers to be effective, simply refused the chance of enjoying huge power or advantage over others – as being intolerable to them, humanly unliveable? It is as if a single individual, having been presented over a lifetime with many opportunities to behave badly, and having taken them, betraying people, profiting unjustly at their expense, openly harming them, losing no sleep over any of it, were then to plead that this reflected nothing at all about his inner character, but was the result of external circumstances only. How widely would he be believed? Even allowing for there having been other, neglected possibilities in his nature which could have produced a different kind of life, one would be unwise to let them obscure the traits of character which he had actually seen fit to give free rein.

By way of another observation on this ill-doing individual, I come now to the third reason for thinking it unconvincing to try to ascribe all bad features of the human story to the influence of defective but remediable social conditions. There is a charitable impulse that explains why we are often reluctant to see wickedness as in a person's character. We give her the benefit of her moral freedom: that she might be able, even with a record behind her of misdeeds, to prevail over whatever it was that led her to them, by making different and better choices from now on. Envisaging this possibility, we treat the ill of which we know she has been capable as being something extraneous to her actual character, in a sort of wager that she may prove it to be so. The strong desire evident in progressive political discourses and the social sciences and humanities more generally – and formalized earlier in what I designated assumptions (b) and (c) – to deny any malignity intrinsic to human nature itself might perhaps be seen, then, as a methodological generalization of this generous impulse. It represents a wager on the good character of humanity within the more favourable enveloping conditions and institutions of a future utopia.

There is no question but that this does describe something of the nature of the socialist hypothesis, taken *by and large*. Unless, in a different institutional and cultural setting, humankind in its generality can prove itself of very much better character (to speak in such terms) than it has shown itself hitherto, the hope of socialism would have to be reckoned a delusion. Taken, however, as anything more than this broad expectation of improvement, taken as the hope of a world all but free from significant human nastiness, the suggestion is self-defeating. For if it is asked in the spirit of this suggestion why people enfolded, raised, in good and supportive conditions, and leading lives as unthreatened by the more frightening or debilitating of social ills as can be envisaged, and reinforced in all their attitudes by cultures of a humane and tolerant kind, why they still might, some of them, find it in themselves to perpetrate continued mischiefs – the simple answer to this question is that they might because they can. Like the opportunity of better patterns of behaviour, the mischiefs are just a possible product of their freedom.

It is, indeed, an anomaly of one common way of thinking about a socialist future to see this future as populated by beings with a freedom enormously expanded and enhanced, and simultaneously to envisage those beings as so much the creatures of their now benign social conditions that they could not be the authors of any evil choice. They could be. It is an implication of their freedom, *ex hypothesi* greater than ever before, that they would not be exhaustively delimited by the conditions that surround them. And this is more especially the case when one considers, as I have already in passing invited readers to do, what the range and variety of interpersonal relationships must continue to be. Of mothers and fathers to children, brothers to sisters, lovers to each other and to possible or actual other lovers; of friends, neighbours, collaborators, colleagues, workmates, passing strangers and acquaintances of every degree; of carers to cared for, doctors to patients, public officers to members of the public; of the bold to the cautious, the orderly to the chaotic, the exuberant to the pensive or the weary; of those agreeing to those dissenting, 'insiders' to 'outsiders'; and then with a multitude of differences within every imaginable category – it would be an endlessly shifting picture of human contacts and situations. Within this multiplicity of forms, a freedom of putatively unprecedented scope renders the image of the socialist person as mere benign 'effect' (effect, that is, of *generally* benign circumstances) an unpersuasive one.

A shadow stretches across the vision at the heart of the socialist project. It reaches there from what may seem to be the remotest distance, from the very depths of the concentrationary universe. Socialism is often thought of as a world of almost infinite potentiality. With good reason is it, since who could now foresee or estimate the further wealth of creativity that would be opened up by extending to everyone on the planet the chances of even a moderately secure existence. If that wealth could be but glimpsed, it would astonish any person living. We touch here on an idea of unlimited human possibility. Over and again, however, those who have survived incarceration at Auschwitz and the other sites of Nazi murder and enslavement articulate something learned there in exactly such terms. 'Normal men do not know', David Rousset has written, 'that everything is possible. Even if the evidence forces their intelligence to admit it, their muscles do not believe it. The concentrationees do know . . .' Livia E. Bitton Jackson has written, similarly, of the time 'before [she] knew that there are no limits to human cruelty'. And Charlotte Delbo also: 'Did you know that suffering is limitless/that horror cannot be circumscribed'. And Primo Levi: 'I know that in the Lager, and more generally on the human stage, everything happens . . .' And Elie Wiesel: 'Evil, more than good, suggests infinity.'[22]

Can it be an accident how many who say this present it, confidently but not in accents of dogmatism, with that lack of vehemence referred to by Gitta Sereny, in the mode of what is *known*? They tell in any event of a particle which the vision of socialism shares with the experience of the Holocaust. It is, to be sure, a 'small' particle only, since we compare here a hope of the best for humankind with the very worst, the most infernal product of the human spirit. But small as it is, it is highly fertile: the capacity for imagination and choice, for reaching beyond the given, whether time, circumstance or boundary. It may be a mistake to expect that great evil could not continue to threaten once there was no longer any great (social) cause of it. It could come, like acts of great goodness, like any masterpiece, from a concatenation of small causes magnified or transmuted in the medium of the imagination and the will.

* * * * *

It has become a common theme in discussion of the Holocaust that this tragedy now puts in serious question what have been, over the last two centuries, some cherished assumptions of Western civilization and modernity. As Henry Friedlander has written, 'Since the eighteenth century we have largely accepted the ideas of the Enlightenment, including the idea of progress . . . [A] serious consideration of the Holocaust would necessitate a re-evaluation.' Or as it has been expressed more recently by another writer, 'Auschwitz decisively closed the Enlightenment era of faith in the coordinated growth of reason, moral betterment, and happiness.'[23] I conclude the present essay by agreeing that some re-evaluation in this matter is indeed called for and faith in human progress not appropriate; but by arguing that *hope* in human progress, and more particularly in the possibility of socialism, is tenable and necessary nevertheless, and the alternative to this hope extremely unappealing.

In so far as they were haunted by assumptions of teleology, inevitability, perfection or paradise, the notions of progress that have characterized socialist and, more generally, democratic and radical political traditions certainly need to be moderated. There is no necessity at all of steady forward movement without possibility of regression and catastrophe, and even 'modest' utopia, never mind perfection or paradise, is not only not the pre-written truth or destiny of humankind, it is not even its prevailing tendency. All it is (we have to hope) is one of its possibilities, and this forever shadowed from within by other darker possibilities. Democrats, liberals and socialists of the last century would not have anticipated the horrifying and, as it has now proved, endless killing grounds of this one. That in itself is testimony to what their shared ideas about progress lacked, the shadow of potential disaster, the threat of forms of evil which challenge the best resources of our understanding.

Neither as beckoning truth or end-point nor as linear, uninterrupted forward advance should we think about human progress today. We have to think about it simply as an enduring battle – an open process – to try to create societies from which the gravest social and political evils familiar to us have been removed; and to try to prevent, drive back or put right, as the case may be, any resurgence of these evils where or once they have been removed, any fresh emergence of unmerited inequalities and privileges, all episodes of persecution, sporadic or not so sporadic injustices, tyrannies large and small, crimes by some persons against others, hitherto unrecognized forms of wrong. We would do well to substitute for every image of progress as a course being travelled, a road, a journey, or as an unfolding, a line of development, the spirit of it being rather a struggle without end[24] – which is what it is for all practical purposes anyway.

In the light of what has gone before here, I think we would do well also to substitute a working hypothesis of, precisely, modest or minimum utopia for all visions more ambitious, whether an end to alienation, unpoliced social harmony, the elimination of serious wrong-doing, the absence of new political menaces or of old but renewable ones. By modest or minimum utopia I mean a form of society which could generally provide for its members the material and social bases of a tolerably contented existence or, as I have already put this, from which the gravest social and political evils familiar to us have been removed. The point of this substitution is not, as such, to reject more ambitious visions: universal and all-round individual development, perpetual peace, ubiquitous altruism, and so on. It is only to highlight the following: we do not need to know – and in fact we do not know – that any of these visions is a real possibility for humankind in order to know that it is a matter or crying need that certain ills, for their part all too well-known, should be finally remedied if *this* at least is possible.

We surely require no ideal of perfection, near perfection or even breathtaking excellence – and whether as an outward state of affairs or as the inner character of the human being – to recognize the need for radical institutional change. It is enough that without such change relations of injustice, sometimes terrible injustice, and conditions of life of a wretched and awful kind, are allowed to persist. Let these be attended to and the more maximalist dreams of socialist utopia may take care of themselves. Or they may not. Or they may await another day. It is of less moment. I have myself offered a speculation as to the likely creative consequences of extending to everyone on the planet just a moderately secure existence. The case for doing this, however, is quite strong enough irrespective of what may be thought of the strength of the speculation.

I support, then, a limited notion of progress and of socialist utopia. Two other points need, briefly, to be made about this. First, limited, modest or minimal as the proposed conception is, it is not to be confused with the idea that the objectives in view are attainable through merely small modifications to the prevailing economic and social order, the order of world capitalism. The conception is modest or minimal only vis-à-vis some of those more far-reaching aspirations typically associated with notions of utopia. Vis-à-vis the world we actually inhabit, the programme of providing everyone with the material and social bases of a tolerably contented existence, of trying to get rid of the gravest social and political evils familiar to us, remains revolutionary through and through. It is incompatible with the extremes of wealth and need, the patterns of effort and reward, the structures of economic power and social powerlessness, which capitalism goes on reproducing.

It is the more necessary, perhaps, to insist on this first point in view of the second one here: which is that it follows from the argument I have put forward above about the 'mixed' potentialities in human nature that a limited socialist utopia would have to be limited as well in the specific sense of being a *liberal* political order. Opposing the idea of perfectibility or intrinsic goodness, accepting the threat of evil as a permanent human possibility, we cannot entertain any confidence in some would-be universal benevolence and harmony, or in the prospect of an end to the rule of law. On the contrary, in the light of what human beings can do and have done to one another, we have every reason to want to continue setting limits around the more harmful and menacing types of human potentiality. All the paraphernalia of the rule of law – of secure, enforceable individual rights, democratically based legislation, checks on power, independent judicial processes, the means of redressing injustice, the means of defending the polity and the community against attack, and so on – follow. The realm of freedom is restricted, then, not only on account of the unpassable boundaries of the realm of material necessity. It is restricted also on account of another, inner limitation; one that we have, by now, more than enough grounds for not taking too lightly.

Still, when all this has been said, we cannot give up on socialist utopian hope and on the hope of progress. To advise resigned acceptance of the world as it is – life-and-death inequalities, universal exploitation, widespread political oppression, festering communal hatreds, genocide, recurring war – as well as being, as Miliband says, 'a counsel of despair', is to eschew a naive, optimistic teleology, only to speak the script of another, grimmer one. It is to risk making oneself, in a certain manner, the willing voice of ugly moral forces.

Some sense of situational perspective may not come amiss here. Even in the depths, in the most notorious of the humanly-created hells of our century, there were many who did not give up hope. Plenty of others did, of course, and they cannot be blamed for it (as sometimes unfortunately they have been, in more and less round about ways). But many did not. It is a theme, with its own important place in the literature of the Holocaust, that I will not go into here other than to say that these many fought as they could to survive, and to preserve what they could of dignity and value in conditions of the most appalling barbarity.[25] What part do the better situated have to make themselves the sponsors of discourses of human defeat?

If continued hope in the better possibilities of human nature can come, as it sometimes did 'down there', from an extra piece of bread, a small gratuitous act of kindness or solidarity, the recollection of a few words of poetry, then who can now say what might reasonably be hoped for if the great social and institutional causes of inequity and suffering, the great economic barriers to a more fulfilling existence for millions of people, could be levelled or lowered? To be sure, caution is today in order on the question of whether and how that objective can be achieved, as on the question of just what we could expect from its achievement in the way of the 'moral betterment' of individuals. It is every bit as much the case, however, that nobody can claim to *know*, with any degree of certainty, either that it could not be achieved, or that its effects of moral betterment would be negligible.

This cannot be known from where we stand. It is a speculation as empty as any more utopian. Although for obvious reasons not the focus of this essay, the fact is that the human record is replete also with acts of moral heroism and moral excellence, and with ordinary, unspectacular day-to-day decency. Countless human beings live their whole lives long without killing or maiming or torturing or otherwise severely harming their fellow beings. Mutual human sympathy and beneficence run both deep and wide. What the future balance might be between these better tendencies and the worse ones, in conditions putatively more encouraging to the former, cannot confidently be known. Given this, to add one's voice, whatever influence it may carry, to the chorus disparaging ideas of progress just contributes some small further weight to the many obstacles to progress, helping by a little more to ensure that it is not only not inevitable, but is, even as a possibility, more distant and more difficult.

To teach, for example, that Auschwitz gives us the truth about human nature – not merely a truth, the truth – simply serves to strengthen what truth it, unhappily, does have. At the limit the Holocaust then becomes, more than a tragic, ghastly event with its own historicity and conditions, the symbol of inexorable human *fate*, in a reversal of the very idea of progress. Humanity's accumulating crimes live on, not, and as they ought to, as a memory of the evil men and women can do, of what has to be guarded against, fought. They live on, in the minds of all those who succumb to learning this as 'the truth', in the shape of the thought that such is what we are and have to be. This is an option, it has to be said, that is not only not appealing. It is repellent. We cannot give up on utopian hope or socialism. We cannot give up on progress. They are not *less* apt in light of what we know about the bad side of human nature. They are more necessary.

For one other thing may be added finally. To accept the world as it (more or less) is, is to help to prolong a state of grave danger. This world, accommodating and countenancing too much of what ought not to be tolerated – plain, persistent injustice, stark, avoidable human suffering – is a world very receptive to present and future atrocity, a world overpopulated with bystanders. It is one in which the idea is harder and harder to resist that just anything at all may be done to people while others look on; and there be no consequence. As long as the situation lasts, it degrades the moral culture of the planet. It poisons the conscience of humankind.

NOTES

1. The arguments reported here and in the paragraphs immediately following are from Ralph Miliband, *Socialism for a Sceptical Age*, Cambridge 1994, pp. 58–62. They are to be found also in an excerpt from the book, published as 'The Plausibility of Socialism', *New Left Review* 206, July/August 1994, at pp. 5–8.
2. See my *Marx and Human Nature: Refutation of a Legend*, London 1983 (reprinted 1994), and *Solidarity in the Conversation of Humankind: The Ungroundable Liberalism of Richard Rorty*, London 1995, especially chapter 2.
3. Anna Pawelczynska, *Values and Violence in Auschwitz*, Berkeley 1979, p. 4.
4. Tadeusz Borowski, *This Way for the Gas, Ladies and Gentlemen*, London 1976, p. 175.
5. Cited in Lawrence Langer, *Holocaust Testimonies*, New Haven 1991, p. 59.
6. Richard L. Rubenstein, *The Cunning of History: The Holocaust and the American Future*, New York 1987, p. 92 (italics removed).
7. Arthur A. Cohen, *The Tremendum: A Theological Interpretation of the Holocaust*, New York 1993, pp. 15–21, 46–7. For an account of Cohen, see Dan Cohn-Sherbok, *Holocaust Theology*, London 1989, pp. 68–79.
8. Robert Nozick, *The Examined Life*, New York 1989, pp. 236–42.
9. Elie Wiesel, *One Generation After*, New York 1970, p. 46.
10. The theses of Hannah Arendt (*Eichmann in Jerusalem*, London 1977) and, more lately, Zygmunt Bauman (*Modernity and the Holocaust*, Cambridge 1989) are widely known. See also in this connection: Gitta Sereny, *Into That Darkness*, London 1991; Christopher R. Browning, *Ordinary Men*, New York 1993; John Sabini and Maury Silver, 'On Destroying the Innocent with a Clear Conscience', in Joel Dimsdale, ed., *Survivors, Victims and Perpetrators*, Washington 1980, pp. 329–58 (and reprinted in their *Moralities of Everyday Life*, Oxford 1982, pp. 55–87); Herbert Kelman, 'Violence without Moral Restraint', *Journal of Social Issues* 29/4 (1973), pp. 25–61; and Henri Zukier, 'The Twisted Road to Genocide: On the Psychological Development of Evil During the Holocaust', *Social Research* 61 (1994), pp. 423–55.
11. Primo Levi, *The Drowned and the Saved*, London 1989, pp. 28–9.
12. Ibid., pp. 32–3.
13. Ibid., pp. 25–6.
14. Ibid., pp. 27, 33.
15. See Ferdinando Camon, *Conversations with Primo Levi*, Marlboro (Vermont) 1989, pp.

19–20.

16. Ibid., p. 20; Hanna Levy-Hass, *Inside Belsen*, Brighton 1982, p. 41; Viktor E. Frankl, *Man's Search for Meaning*, London 1987, pp. 87, 136.
17. Sereny, *Into That Darkness*, p. 208.
18. *Socialism for a Sceptical Age*, p. 61 (and *New Left Review* 206, p. 7). Emphasis added.
19. Ibid. – and see above.
20. Ibid.
21. Ibid., p. 60 (and *New Left Review* 206, p. 6).
22. David Rousset, *The Other Kingdom*, New York 1947, p. 168; Livia E. Bitton Jackson, *Elli: Coming of Age in the Holocaust*, London 1984, p. 120; Charlotte Delbo, *Auschwitz and After*, New Haven and London 1995, p. 11; Primo Levi, *The Drowned and the Saved*, p. 33; Elie Wiesel, *One Generation After*, p. 47.
23. Henry Friedlander, 'Postscript: Toward a Methodology of Teaching about the Holocaust', in Henry Friedlander and Sybil Milton, eds., *The Holocaust: Ideology, Bureaucracy, and Genocide*, New York 1980, p. 324; and Henri Zukier, 'The Twisted Road to Genocide', p. 424.
24. Cf. Primo Levi, *The Drowned and the Saved*, p. 27 – notwithstanding the 'sociological pessimism' there registered.
25. Outstanding in this connection is Terrence Des Pres, *The Survivor*, New York 1976.

# ARE THERE LEFT ALTERNATIVES? A DISCUSSION FROM LATIN AMERICA

Carlos M. Vilas

## A DISORIENTED LEFT

Any discussion of the Latin American left and its capacity to bring about alternatives to the existing capitalist order should first address the ambiguity that surrounds the very term 'left'. From one point of view this is a positive thing, testimony to the fact that particular organizations, ideological affiliations or international policy options no longer enjoy a monopoly of 'the left'. At the same time, however, it suggests a need for some necessary clarification, so that it is clear what we are talking about. In this latter sense, in what follows I understand 'left' to simply refer to that broad range of collective actors (parties, fronts, alliances etc.) who consider themselves as belonging to that part of the political spectrum. This does not eliminate the ambiguity that surrounds the term left, but I hope it will provide a framework for this discussion.

In fact the objective situation of the Latin American left is itself ambiguous. It performs a relatively important role in the institutional political life in several countries (such as Brazil, Uruguay, El Salvador, Venezuela, Nicaragua, Mexico, Argentina), as recent elections have shown; yet it has still not been able to move beyond parliamentary minorities and control of some areas of local government – that is, areas of Latin American politics that have been traditionally weak in relation to the centralization of power in the executive. Despite the critique of strong presidential regimes that has been developed in some academic circles in the United States, and echoed by their colleagues south of the Rio Bravo,[1] it remains the case that the most important political decisions, in actual facts as well in legal provisions, are made by the executive.

It is clear, however, that this new configuration of the electoral map is leading the left to pay closer attention to institutional areas which it had regarded until recently as of only secondary importance. The expansion of the institutional horizons of the political left is taking place along with increasing involvement of social actors in local and sectorial issues. This coincidence of perspective could have a significant impact on the ability of the left to create a solid electoral base. In any event, it has to be acknowledged that the left option is still much more notorious in the social sphere than within the framework of institutional politics. Left wing political parties are facing hardships in mobilising that majority of the electorate whose living standards are currently in steady decline. While recognising the electoral advances that have been made, it is also obvious that a large proportion of the electorate who belong to the popular classes and the petty bourgeoisie still do not see the left as an electoral option. In this sense the link between social dissatisfaction and electoral preference has been broken.

The institutional involvement of left wing parties and political organizations has been accompanied by a smoothing in their programmes and proposals. The Latin American left has entered the electoral process with uneven results; however that involvement has not led to the formulation of political strategies offering alternatives to the current state of things. Their energies are devoted to criticising the prevailing macroeconomic order and the policies to implement it, and any proposals for change tend characteristically to be sectoral and local in their concerns. There are differences between one case and another, of course. In Argentina the Frente Grande – a political coalition gathering several progressive tendencies which left Carlos Menem's governing Partido Justicialista (PJ) due to the neoliberal policies being implemented – is placing the emphasis on exposing the corruption, fraud and authoritarianism of the political regime; demands for openness and public morality were central to its 1995 electoral campaign, while its critique of economic policy was not accompanied by any meaningful alternative proposal. In Venezuela, Causa R is in a similar position. The Brazilian Workers Party (PT) and the Frente Amplio in Uruguay, on the other hand, did show themselves willing and able to offer proposals rooted in an alternative socio-economic framework. In Mexico the Partido de la Revolution Democratica (PRD) has focussed on the question of democracy, but seems less forceful when it comes to economic strategy. In El Salvador, the FMLN is still involved in the specificities of the post-war setting – most of all, the full accomplishment of the peace accords; in Nicaragua, by contrast, the tension between the struggle to defend what remains of the revolutionary achievements of the past decade, and the consolidation of constitutional democracy, has produced a split in the FSLN. With very few exceptions, the Chilean left has opted to follow in the wake of Christian Democracy in administering a political system that still retains many of the features that date back to the military dictatorship of Augusto Pinochet.

So what proposals for global, structural change there are, are sporadic. The Latin American left appears motivated by the need to adapt to the new scenario emerging out of recent global and regional political changes – the end of the cycle of the Central American revolutions, the crisis of Cuban socialism, the acceleration of global financial integration, the end of the cold war system – rather than by its overall transformation. In fact, the changes in that scenario are leading the left to modify its own ideological orientations, programmes, organizational structures and range of action.

This is an issue of central importance for the discussion of alternatives to the present neoliberal capitalist order and its negative impact on the perspectives for development and social progress in Latin America, and indeed the future of the democratic process itself. Political options do not arise in a vacuum; they are always proposed by collective actors claiming to represent the objectives, needs, interests and aspirations of given groups and social classes. A group of intellectuals may offer an alternative project that is technically viable and theoretically consistent, but it can only be politically effective when it is taken up by people. This does not in itself guarantee its viability, still less its success – but without it there is not even prospect of victory. And given that the relation between the intellectuals (in the Gramscian sense) and the popular classes is never direct or immediate, the discussion should also address the question of the organizational mediations that will translate the intellectual blueprint into a political proposal for social change.

To what extent or in what senses are we witnessing to a new situation, and to what extent or sense are we facing a renewal or updating of the dilemmas and conflicts that the Latin American left has been debating since its very beginnings? Are we facing something quite new, or rather the recomposition of a political scene which, notwithstanding what is new about it, seems very like the traditional panorama of Latin America? The next section will address these issues; section II will then consider the transformations of the socio-economic structure of Latin America and their impact on the redefinitions of the left. The third section examines some of the tensions that have arisen between the contents and achievements of the proposals of the left, and the institutional framework of representative democracy – the case of the EZLN in Chiapas providing a particularly graphic illustration of these tensions. Finally, section IV offers some thoughts on the spaces within the existing structures and institutions to which the left apparently has access. I would like to stress that the purpose of this piece is to identify a problematic, rather than to discuss all its contents and projections.[2]

## I. RUPTURES AND CONTINUITIES

Any discussion of the current situation of the Latin American left involves, to a greater or lesser degree, an implicit comparison with the past. Whereas in previous times the left attempted to confront and eventually overcome capitalism and build some sort of socialist alternative, today it merely tends to graft sectoral reforms, focusing more on neoliberalism as a particular variant of capitalism than on capitalism as an overall socioeconomic and political structure. So it seems appropriate to begin by considering whether all those projects which were presented or considered as alternatives to capitalism, were in fact alternatives – independently of their capacity to inspire great struggles or high levels of popular mobilisation.

It can be asserted without risking revisionism that most of Latin American left-wing organizations, parties, fronts etc, including the majority of those calling themselves socialist or communist, in fact stood for approaches and policies for reform, however wide-ranging the modifications they proposed.[3] The characterization of these organizations and regimes as 'of a socialist orientation' arose out of the discourse of the protagonists themselves, from their positioning with regard to the international political conflict – their antagonism to the United States and their support of the Soviet Union – as well from the fear and ideological rigidity of their adversaries, as much as a reflection of the content of their projects for confronting, reforming or replacing the capitalist system. From the triumph of the Cuban Revolution onwards, the radicalism of anticapitalist perspectives tended to be assessed in relation to one specific type of political action – the armed struggle. Throughout the period of the Cold War, however, the focus and political assessments on domestic actors were severely overdetermined by the development of the bipolar conflict.[4] A circumstance that confirms the peripheral character of Latin America in relation to the capitalist system, and the determining influence of its central actors over the processes and initiatives that develop in peripheral, semi-sovereign countries.

The profound political and socio-economic transformations demanded by the Central American revolutions – and which in the case of Nicaragua were carried out in the early years of Sandinismo – had a clearly popular, democratic and anti-imperialist character, but not necessarily an anti-capitalist one.[5] This is not to diminish in any way the heroism of the revolutionaries nor the importance of these revolutions; but it does express clearly the correlations and coalitions of forces that have driven these processes forward. Even where some variant of socialism did figure in the initial revolutionary project, the intention became ensnared in the dynamics of subsequent political conflicts. In Cuba's case, the revolutionary design followed the inverse course; a revolution that initially presented itself as a popular and democratic movement for national liberation became socialist as a result of its very dynamics and of the decisions made by the revolutionaries in the context of their defensive confrontation with United States aggression. In other words, socialism was the result of a political practice articulated to a particular configuration of the international system, rather than the result of a preexisting ideological blueprint.[6] In turn, U.S intervention crushed Popular Unity in Chile (1970–73) and the New Jewel experiment in Grenada (1979–83) at such an early stage that we cannot offer anything more than general hypotheses on how these processes might have evolved.

Furthermore, from the late 1940s on, with a few and outstanding exceptions such as in Chile, Uruguay or Peru, Socialist and Communist parties have lost gound in Latin America's popular classes. The political identity and loyalty of rural and urban workers, as well as large sectors of the petty bourgeoisie, became tied to the parties and organizations of a populist, Social-Christian, or nationalist appeal, much more than to Marxist or Maxist-Leninist organizations. This poses a complex political problem, of course; for the hypothetical actors of left politics did not feel themselves to be addressed by the conventional socialist or communist parties. In fact this is not the correct way to pose the problem; such a formulation should begin by asking which left it was to which the working masses were indifferent, or perhaps even hostile. In other words, the approach should take as its starting point the specificity of the social formations on the periphery of the capitalist world, a question that inspired a number of important debates within the Comintern. However the Latin American left has been reluctant to consider this problematic, possibly because it might have led to a serious questioning of its own perspectives.[7] The question arose again in the context of the Central American revolutions, although, due to the particular characteristics of those processes and that scenario, the discussion developed with very little reference to that held in the Comintern.[8]

To sum up, then, as far as this first point is concerned, the situation is not entirely new. Only in a few exceptional cases was the Latin American left systematically anti-capitalist, even if it did opt for radical methods and strategies of struggle. The reason for it is to be found, as suggested earlier, in the specificity of capitalist development in the region and the identity of the actors whose interests, demands and expectations provided the foundation of the projects for change. And here, as in so many things, the analyst must take care not be be taken in by the discourse of the actors.

## II. CHANGES IN THE SOCIOECONOMIC STRUCTURE

Acknowledging that the present situation of the left has antecedents is not tantamount as saying that we are dealing with a linear process. The development of sectoral perspectives and piecemeal proposals for change and adaptation has occurred within a context of structural transformations, cultural changes and institutional modifications, set in the framework of a redefinition of the international arena.

The crisis of the eighties and the response to it from the Latin American governments has produced profound changes in labour markets, deepened social inequality and impoverished large segments of the working classes and the middle sectors. These were manifestations of the impact of technological change and global capitalist restructuring on Latin America; state intervention reinforced its negative impact on some groups and classes, forcing them to carry the burden of adjustment. Taken together these changes and policies foster even deeper differentiations within the popular classes. In the context of shrinking formal employment and downgrading of both working conditions and wage levels, some small sections of workers have been able to improve their relative position in terms of wages and living standards, while the majority has been left out. This differentiation has had an impact on the traditional forms of trade union militancy too. On the one hand, the overall fall in the number of jobs and in formal employment has reduced the level of union affiliation, to which the processes of flexible accumulation has also contributed. On the other hand, the growth in informal employment has meant that increasing numbers of workers find themselves outside the reaches of trade unions. Finally, a growing participation of middle class elements in the leadership of trade unions introduces additional imbalances between the union rank-and-file and their leaders.[9]

This aspect of the current problematic marks a difference from past situations. The proletariat has never constituted a numerical majority among the popular classes as a whole. The industrial proletariat in particular, which is central to the thinking of the socialist and communist left, has usually been a relative minority among the urban labouring classes, which encompass large numbers of self-employed, unpaid family workers, seasonal labourers and the like, which are either not involved in wage labour, or are only in an intermittent manner. However, from its earliest times the working class movement attempted to represent the working class as a whole – including both proletarianized and not yet or not fully proletarianized workers. Moreover, the proletarianization of the labour force – in the sense that it became wage-earning and not solely in terms of its disengagement from a source of reproduction – was a goal of both the trade unions and the left. This goal derived from the understanding of the dynamics of capitalism and on its objective tendencies of development, which were supposed to lead to an increasing conversion of non-wage into wage labour.

What we are now witnessing is a process of proletarianization that divorces growing numbers of the working population from their conditions of reproduction, together with expelling them from the formal labour market, de-waging them and as a result weakening the extent to which feelings of collective identity are a shared reference point. This is an aspect that did not enter into the left's calculations, since its magnitude and its relation to the processes of accumulation go far beyond any discussion about a 'reserve labour army'. In some sense the past ability of the labour movement to represent the broad spectrum of the popular classes was based on capitalism's tendency to integrate the labour force into the production process in the interests of capital. Today the prevailing tendency is towards the accumulation of capital combined with social exclusion. The unemployed are no longer a reserve army of anything, and the concept of marginality, questioned and questionable in the sixties, has now gained legitimacy.

*Classes and subjects*

This is the context in which we have to address the issue of the apparent dissolution of classes into a broad spectrum of subjects and actors who would constitute themselves outside and independent of any stable collective articulation to the processes of accumulation. From this perspective growing internal differentiation of the traditional social base of the Latin American left (waged workers, professional middle sectors, technicians, small businessmen etc.) is also expressed through the emergence of a broad spectrum of 'new social subjects' whose ways of organization and demands relate only uneasily to the traditional organizations who were the focus of the politics of the left, namely parties and trade unions. The factors that define the identity of these new subjects and the issues around which they organize – e.g. gender, ethnicity, sexual preferences – are articulated in a complex and often tense way with class criteria. These actors and movements do have class references, insofar as they express, and act within, a framework of poverty, oppression and exploitation; yet in no sense can they be reduced to a crude class determination.[10]

In its most extreme manifestations the current theoretical shift in the discussion of social mobilisation presents it as the sum of individual motivations and problems, so that the possibility of a collective recomposition remains always contingent and unstable. If the concept of 'worker' or 'peasant' assesses a substantive relationship to class, the concept 'subject' in most cases suggests transitory identifications deriving from conjunctural motivations – or at the very bottom motivations that arise less from objective situations than from the way particular subjects 'read' them.

Any meaningful discussion of this question should start by acknowledging that it refers to rather complex processes, embracing widely differing contents, outreaches and characteristics; and that it works in quite different ways and with quite different meanings for different social classes. The destructuring of the popular classes is not matched by any equivalent process among the ruling classes. The loss or transformation of identity among social actors is much more the experience of the poor than of the rich, of the workers rather than the capitalists, of trade unions more than enterprises. Structural changes are reducing the 'classical' proletariat, transforming what remains of it and driving the peasantry as a class to the very brink of extinction. Flexible accumulation calls for the drastic reduction of labour costs as a condition of the recovery of business profits. This economic condition demands certain political conditions too – the destructuring of the labour force into a sum of differentiated subjects or actors separated one from the other. While the concept of class implies a hypothesis of shared interests and a relatively clear consequent direction of collective activity, one individual is much like any other (with the result that the distinction between classes loses all meaning), or alternatively is so different from every other individual that any class-based grouping also becomes a mere fiction.

The destructuring of the working class, the peasantry and other actors in the world of labour has its counterpoint in the strengthening of the organizations and strategies of the capitalist class, increasingly supported by the state, the mass media and the international financial agencies. This forces us to develop an approach accounting for these changes, but obviously it is not enough in itself to invalidate the heuristic potential of the concept of class.[11]

The new plurality of social actors and the specificity of their agendas evolved mostly independently of parties and trade unions – which has to do with a number of intervening factors. First among them is the context of authoritarianism and dictatorship which took shape in Latin America from the 1960s onwards and persisted well into the 1980s. Throughout those more than two decades the parties that mobilized popular and middle sector votes and demands were persecuted, banned and driven underground; their leaders and rank and file experienced violent persecution, harsh repression or were forced into exile. The history of human rights violations and of state terrorism is to a great extent the history of the repression against the members and sympathisers of these organizations, and indeed of anyone who had anything to do with them.

In the past these parties had taken on many of the demands that later would be raised by the 'new movements' – such as housing, access to basic services, nutrition, the political rights of women etc – while usually subordinating the specific demands of each sector to the political perspectives of the party, where these actors and their demands came to lose their specificity. The 'indigenous question' was reduced to a matter of land as land was reduced to a means of production; the question of the social condition of women was addressed from the point of view of the labour market, or of the right to vote, not in terms of gender. Together with other factors, the elimination of parties and trade unions from the public arena, or at least the limits imposed on them, opened a space where these as well other more traditional demands – such as local or community-based issues – could be openly expressed and sometimes did not have to confront authoritarian or repressive responses.

This is not the time or the place to draw up a balance sheet of advantages or disadvantages of one or other kind of relationship. It is appropriate, however, to point out that as a result of these quite different origins and paths of development, the relationship between social movements and political parties has become one of the most complex issues, as well as one of the most conflictive, that the Latin American left has had to face. It is no accident that the most successful expression of the Latin American left – the Brazilian Workers' Party (PT) – is also the one where the relationship between the social actors (trade union movement, community organizations, women's movements, and Christian Base Communities) and the party is, relatively speaking, fluent and without severe conflicts. At the other extreme, the Mexican PRD, Causa R in Venezuela or the Frente Grande in Argentina all point to the travails of both sets of actors in the search for forms of agreement and coordination. The recently founded Democratic Front for a New Guatemala (Frente Democratico Nueva Guatemala), if it manages to overcome the inevitable initial difficulties, could become a successful example of how social organizations have given birth to a political organization that will fight in the electoral sphere.[12]

In every case political questions are posed which, notwithstanding their links to the theoretical issues raised above, do require a differentiated approach. For here, specific as well as conjunctural circumstances bear a heavy burden, often to the point of determining the success or failure of a particular experiment.

## III. PROPOSALS FOR CHANGE AND INSTITUTIONAL FRAMEWORKS

Do on-going changes in the institutional setting, with a relative consolidation of the mechanisms of electoral representation, play any role in the left's programmatic redefinitions, or are they rather the result of transformations in the international arena? Is there a reformist or even a conservative tendency in the institutional setting of representative democracy which might lead the left wing parties to soften their programmatic demands and converge on the centre?

The articulation of programmes and strategies was vigorously discussed by the First and Second Internationals. In those instances two principal questions occupied the centre of the debate: 1) is it possible for a proletarian party to achieve control of the bourgeois state apparatus appealing to that state's apparatuses to that end? 2) If the answer is yes, is it possible to transform the bourguois state while preserving those same institutions?[13] Although Latin American Socialist and Communist parties opted at an early stage for the electoral road, the issue was confronted in a concrete expression for the first time in 1970, when the Chilean Popular Unity won the elections and Salvador Allende became President. However, this was the last time the issue was debated. The tragic end of the Popular Unity government through a military coup encouraged and supported by the U.S. government proved that, in that conjuncture, those who had responded negatively to those earlier questions were correct; there was no institutional road to radical change. The Chilean experience did have an influence on the revolutionary organizations of Central America – a region where concern for legal institutions was conspicuously foreign to the political performance of the ruling classes.

Furthermore, the breakdown of the evolutionary road in Chile reinforced the identification of the political programme of the left with the means to achieve it. This confusion of levels and dimensions, which as a matter of fact began to take place after the triumph of the Cuban Revolution, became more obvious in the Central American case. In some sense the left reproduced, with its own ideological imprint, the Schumpeterian reductionism with regard to democratic regimes. According to Joseph Schumpeter, democracy points to a set of electoral procedures (disregarding such fundamental questions as the balance between or independence of the different branches of government, the accountability of civil servants, the rule of law etc.), while for a great deal of the Latin American left the radicalism of proposals for change should be evaluated first and foremost by reference to the means chosen to achieve them. The armed road, whose purpose was to undermine the state apparatus and deliver a series of insurrectionary situations, was considered the identity card of a revolutionary perspective; in a similar vein the 'institutional road' to the global transformation of the capitalist system was rejected almost by definition. Put this way, the question of which road to follow took precedence over the question of the substantive content of proposals for change, in a markedly voluntaristic framework.

These elements make still sharper the contrast with the current situation, when the issue of the articulation of programmes and methods has disappeared from the agenda. The generalization of electoral processes and the much-debated assessment of the Central American revolutionary experiments have led to the reverse position from that assumed in the face of the Chilean conjuncture of 1970. It is now explicitly accepted that for the left there is no alternative to the electoral road. At the same time it is generally accepted that the proposals for change have to be moderated in order not to threaten the stability and consolidation of the democratic regimes. The issue of the relation between the project and the methods or ways to achieve it has now reentered the debate through the literature, largely vulgar in character, about governability. What is at issue here is to avoid overburdening the state apparatus, thus ensuring it will not overheat or seize up, while preventing panicking or excessively threatening the actors situated on the right of the political spectrum.[14]

The theoretical and practical complexity of the issues involved in the debate about means and contents was overcome by the simplicity of the slogan 'Don't make waves'. At bottom it suggests an acknowledgement that the negative response to the questions posed a century ago was and remains the correct one, with the difference that today that conclusion, far from leading to a creative search for alternatives, has the effect of blocking such a search and limiting the content and perspectives of any project for change to what is acceptable within the institutional layout of the political system – i.e. within the current balance of power. Thus, just when the discourse of the autonomy of the political system in relation to its structural base becomes broadly accepted, the existence of that system is linked to or identified with the preservation of a given structural configuration – the actually existing capitalist system in a given country – and subsequently with a specific class domination.

In a particularly graphic and poignant way, the split of the FMLN in El Salvador into two different organizations points to the complex nature of the issue in both its theoretical and operative projections.[15] While internal strategic, methodological as well as operative differences existed within the FMLN from its very inception in 1980, they deepened during the peace negotiations and surfaced after the January 1992 accords with the right-wing ARENA's (Nationalist Republican Alliance) Salvadorean government. Under the leadership of Joaquin Villalobos, the ERP renamed itself as 'Expresion Renovadora del Pueblo' thus wiping out any reference to revolution while keeping the original accronym. After several open confrontations with the leadership of FMLN – including accusing them of 'ideologism', militarism and destabilization of the post-war political process – ERP together with RN formally abandoned the FMLN. In addition to the former Social Democratic MNR (Movimiento Nacionalista Revolucionario, by then a minor political party which keeps its affiliation to the Socialist International) the former guerrillas opted to build the new Partido Democrático (Democratic Party, PD). In May 1995 PD submitted a 'San Andrés Pact' to other political parties and the government. Focusing on economic policy issues, the Pact reproduces the on-going government's programme of macro-economic adjustment and was repudiated by the entire opposition. The Pact was eventually signed by its proponents together with ARENA and the government, thus projecting the image of an appendicular adherence of former guerrillas to the political leadership of El Salvador's right wing hard-liners.[16] The three organizations which remained as FMLN decided to dissolve themselves in order to transform the Frente into a political party made up of internal tendencies – much as Mexico's PRD or Brazil's PT. Yet the priority attention paid to the still unaccomplished socioeconomic and human rights commitments of the Peace Accords in order to have the government honouring them – such as land distribution and effective dismantling of death squads – puts FMLN in a defensive stance vis-á-vis the government, ARENA and former leftists' claims to look forward and leave the past behind.

*The social and the political*

This abandonment or postponement of global proposals for change fosters the development of a disjunction between social protest and political behaviour that has been going on in several countries. Downgrading living standards of broad layers of low income and middle classes – expressed for example in massive impoverishment, social marginalization, growing inequality, unemployment, personal insecurity – has not resulted so far in any shift of that population towards political options involving electoral opposition to incumbent governments. When they enter the voting booth the poor and those who are growing poorer tend in general terms to avoid the most radical options – even those sectors of the population who had turned to radical political options in the previous decade. Take for example the reelection of Alberto Fujimori in Peru and Carlos Menem in Argentina; the majority vote for Fernando H. Cardoso rather than Lula in Brazil; the steady growth of the conservative PAN (National Action Party) in Mexico while the PRD (Revolutionary Democratic Party) experiences a number of electoral setbacks; the electoral triumph of ARENA in the municipal districts where the FMLN guerrillas had gathered consistent popular support during the revolutionary war. So the hypothesis that a sharp and general deterioration in the conditions of life of the people will necessarily lead people to move to the left of the political spectrum has proved problematic once again.[17] It would appear that after a cycle of military dictatorships, revolutions, wars, counterinsurgency and crisis, Latin American politics is resuming its more traditional profile: conservative domination resting on the electoral acquiescence of the dominated.

While avoiding excessive generalizations, it can be suggested that we are facing a shift in the political mood of segments of the Latin American working classes who in the recent past were willing to support, and even bring about, proposals for quite profound social and political change; or who at the very least had participated in important mobilizations supporting democratization, movements which implicitly or explicitly embraced projects of far reaching social transformation. The return to electoral democracy that is going on unevenly across the continent, and which in a real sense is an outcome of those mass movements, has nevertheless shaped a scenario in which the options for social transformation and the perspectives of the left are either severely diluted or quite simply absent. The social deterioration that has occurred in the course of the last decade within the framework of institutionalised democracy has provoked often very violent protests and no less intense repression in return – yet there is still no sign that social frustration and protests are likely to be transformed into political opposition. The reorientation of the left towards sectoral isues has contributed to keep people's dissatisfaction within the borders of the social realm.

There is a reciprocal causal relationship between these two aspects. On the one hand, changes in the international scene and in domestic life (political, socio-economic,institutional and cultural) have produced in the organizations of the left a disorientation and a search for new directions, inhibiting or at best postponing the formulation of integral alternative proposals at the very moment when such proposals would be most timely. On the other hand, the absence of alternative proposals reinforces the demobilization of people who are suffering as a result of the current situation and underlines their lack of confidence that they will find in politics any solution to their setbacks. The electoral support for characters such as Fujimori and Menem, therefore, can be understood as evidence that people are seeking an alternative to the lack of change and to the elegant and increasingly incomprehensible rhetoric of most conventional political actors. The room filled by these neo-populist neoliberal political caudillos is to a large degree the room the left has been unable to fill, or whence it was ousted by repression.[18] It is precisely at this level that the biggest political failure of the Latin American left becomes apparent – its inability to define a discourse or a solid and stable relationship with the oppressed, the impoverished and those exploited by the capitalist system.

Amid ruptures, reciprocal challenges and guilty self-justifications, some of the parties in Chile, Mexico, Nicaragua, El Salvador, Argentina, the Dominican Republic, Guatemala, Colombia who would describe themselves as left-wing, or reformist at the very least, are accepting the concept of democracy suggested by liberal political theorists in the U.S. (e.g. Schumpeter, Dahl) and Europe (e.g. Bobbio). Here politics is robbed of any potential for progressive change while restricted to a range of institutional or formal practices – so it should come as no surprise that the people treat it with distrust and seek other ways to express their protests. Nor should we be surprised that people opt for authoritarian leaders and highly personalized options when so many actors on the left display intent on demonstrating that there are no possible alternatives and that the hypothesis of global change is utopian and impractical and should be abandoned. Simultaneously concepts like 'people', 'working class', 'popular classes', which expressed and mobilized the social and political identity of the exploited and the oppressed, have been emptied of their traditional meanings – an expression of the crisis of social and political identities in broad sectors of the population. The popular identity, which in the political history of Latin America opened the way to citizenship for workers, women and indigenous peoples, is now substituted by the marginalization of the people and their replacement by a citizenry of isolated individuals whose reciprocal alienation is reinforced through the institutional reproduction of the social exclusion of most of the population.

### *Chiapas and the Left: a failure to connect*

The uprising of the EZLN (Ejercito Zapatista de Liberacion Nacional – Zapatista National Liberation Army) in Chiapas brings a particularly dramatic example of the uneasy relations between social and political actors, between social conflicts and political strategies. The entire Mexican political spectrum was taken by surprise by the Zapatistas, and the initial responses of support or condemnation should be understood as a function of that surprise rather than a result of reflection. Both political parties and the government had dismissed without a second thought the possibility that such a thing could happen in the Mexico of globalization and NAFTA, or in the post USSR's withering away era.[19] The PRD in particular, despite the state repression of its members and persistent denunciations of electoral fraud, insisted on the institutional road as the only way to achieve democracy and social change in Mexico; at the same time Carlos Salinas de Gortari was pronouncing the end of the Mexican Revolution from the Presidential chair. The Chiapas uprising, therefore, arrived for most people like a thunderclap on a sunny day.

Militarily, Chiapas was a noteworthy operation in armed propaganda. The successful seizing of five medium-sized towns, the combats during the first week, the subsequent orderly withdrawal, together with a most efficient resort to mass media, placed the rebels at the centre of national and international political life. Weapons were instrumental in turning world attention to Chiapas and the EZLN, much more than means to seize state or even local power, nor were they ever intended to be – the armed confrontations ceased after a fortnight. The communiqués through which the EZLN made itself known summarised the claims of the Mexican left – the illigitimate nature of Carlos Salinas de Gortari's government; the repressive stance of the Mexican state; PRI's (Partido Revolucionario Institucional – Institutional Revolutionary Party, the main government party) authoritarianism and corruption – as well as its demands for agrarian reform, popular structural changes, historical rights for indigenous communities, sweeping democratization, competitive and clear elections. The synthesis of denunciations and demands was placed in a symbolic framework which referred to an uninterrupted popular and national liberation revolution (e.g. the appeal to the national popular hero Emiliano Zapata) relying on the armed struggle.

It is not yet clear what it was that proved too much for the Mexican political left to accept; whether it was the fact that their demands had been presented in a format emphasising their confrontational potential, or whether it was the appeal to a symbolism and a method that the left had largely given up in the process of seeking acceptance as an actor by the system (of which, however, it remained critical). In this sense it is striking that most appeals issued during those early months by subcomandante Marcos were directed to 'civil society' rather than to the left-wing parties.[20] A wide range of social organizations inserted themselves into the vacuum that opened up between the guerrillas and the parties; they forced the government of Carlos Salinas to order a ceasefire and stop the bombing, and in February 1995 they were able to stop a new government offensive.

The activism of the social organizations contrasts with the ambiguities of the PRD, which criticized the EZLN for its recourse to arms, but was not in a position to accept the legitimacy in certain conjunctures, of this form of political struggle. Despite the fact that it was the most severe critic, and the most visible victim, of the fraudulent and authoritarian Mexican political regime, the PRD could not bring itself to admit that in certain extreme situations, the right to resist oppression by whatever means people felt to be most effective is a right in itself – a right whose acceptance goes back to both Greek classical political philosophy and medieval Christian political theology. In a country with a tradition of political violence like Mexico's, the question of violence was buried in a stream of rhetoric and in the unconditional defence of the actually existing legal system.

The trip of Cuauhtemoc Cardenas – PRD's presidential candidate – to the Lacandon jungle on the eve of the elections of August 1994 proved to be a disaster. The EZLN misinterpreted Cardenas' initiative as a cynical move to gain votes; as a result subcomandante Marcos made a public criticism of the lack of democracy and centralization of power within the PRD which was widely disseminated by those media that supported the government. In a society like Mexico, where authoritarianism is also part of the political culture of the popular classes, the image of a Presidential candidate taking verbal abuse from an anonymous masked man could not have been more negative. The electoral consequences of these and other failures were clearly seen in August 1994. The PRD did not incorporate the EZLN's demands into its national electoral platform – they were left as a matter for local political campaigning. Yet the PRI won Chiapas again, and the complaints of electoral fraud did not succeed in getting the elections annulled. After a few months the 'rebel government' of the PRD candidate for Chiapas' governor – a well respected social activist – dissolved into nothing; in these circumstances the central government decided to remove the PRI governor and appoint an interim government which included one of the principal intellectual supporters of the EZLN rising. Moreover, when new local elections were held on November 12, 1995, Subcommander Marcos called for electoral abstention and plainly disengaged the EZLN from any formal or informal association to PRD. His appeal prevented victories of the PRD's candidates – which, according to PRD sources, had been nominated by grass-roots and Mayan village organizations – and, on the contrary, objectively led to PRI's triumph even in districts under Zapatista control.

The failure to find common ground between Zapatistas, PRD and the smaller organizations of the political left occurred in a context in which the government and the PRI have access to resources which enable them to encourage divisions and combine negotiation with threats. In fact, the situation affords the government additional room for manoeuvre. Two years on, the EZLN has been limited to a local force and seems to be losing the political initiative. Its expectation that similar upheavals would show up in other parts of Mexico suffering as much or even more poverty and exploitation as Chiapas proved astray – nothing of that kind occurred even where there were large concentrations of indigenous people. The support of 'civil society' has proved to be disorganized and it is now declining, amidst economic crisis and political scandals featured by members of the Salinas de Gortari's family. The absence of a common ground for both left-of-centre political parties and Chiapas' rebels has prevented thus far the emergence of an integrated social/political left. Finally, after two years marked by neither military actions nor other spectacular events, the EZLN and Marcos are slowly disappearing from the headlines of newspapers and from prime time television news.

In a setting where the return to arms is no longer an option for either side – because of shortages of weapons and internal divisions within the EZLN on the one hand, and the national and international political pressure on the government as well as differences of opinion within the army, on the other – the plebiscite of August 1995, which produced a majority of votes supporting EZLN's conversion into a 'political force' (sic), could provide the EZLN with both an opportunity for an honourable exit and a threat with having to face up to its disappearance as a political actor even on a local level. The first would allow the guerrillas to present the laying down of their arms as a democratic recognition of the will of 'civil society'. The second, because the EZLN cannot individually aspire to becoming anything more than a local political party, losing its national presence and even having to compete with national political parties within Chiapas itself – unless some sort of coalition could be built. And furthermore, since Mexican electoral law forbids building local political parties, the observance of the democratic mandate of 'civil society' would drive the Zapatistas to enter very long and complex constitutional negotiations.

Meanwhile, time is working against the rebels. Their social base, even within the indigenous communities, is being eroded by the lack of supplies, the difficulties of communication, and fatigue. The contrast between the steady flow of food and supplies sent by the government to communities outside the EZLN 'liberated zone' and the situation within the zone, is enormous. The Mexican government is investing huge sums from its own resources in Chiapas, in addition to a $450 million loan from the World Bank. More government money has gone into Chiapas in the last two years than in the previous two centuries. In this financial sense the armed propaganda operation of January 1994 was also success, although for the moment their beneficiaries are the communities that did not answer the Zapatista call.

At the same time, the willingness of the Mexican government to include in its negotiations with the EZLN the question of indigenous communities throughout Mexico, and not just in Chiapas, offers the indigenous commanders (the 'Revolutionary Clandestine Committee') the chance to become spokespersons on behalf of all the indigenous peoples, including those who have not been part of the conflict, or do not live in Chiapas; indeed they can become the legitimate, perhaps the exclusive interlocutors of government on these issues. But this opportunity would mean the disengagement of the demands of the indigenous peoples from the overall political project within which the original Zapatista pronouncements had articulated them. In this sense there could emerge a difference of perspectives and perceptions between the indigenous leaders of the EZLN and the mestizo military commanders, with Marcos outstanding among them. In fact, as government-EZLN talks proceed, there is an evident protagonism of indigenous Zapatista commanders which contrasts with Marcos' former visibility.

The present position of the Zapatista uprising (for we cannot yet talk of a final outcome) reveals the effect of a combination of the negotiating experience of the Mexican government and the failures of the left to seize the moment. Ideologically disarmed, the political left was not up to the challenge presented to it by Zapatismo, and this opened a space for manoeuvre for the clientilistic and cooptative methods characteristic of the Mexican political tradition – where government is master. It may be argued that, in all, the Mexican political left read the EZLN in a non-political way, or out from a power perspective. It is difficult to avoid the impression that the left paid more attention to the symbolism of Zapatismo – the romantic mystery of the masked commanders, the literary strength of Marcos' writings, the reassessment of Emiliano Zapata, the risk or promise of heroic deaths – than to the political project submitted to civil society and the left and democratic parties, chief among them the PRD.

## IV. CONCLUDING REMARKS: THE POSSIBLE AND THE DESIRABLE

It is an empirical fact that the majority of organizational expressions of the political left in Latin America have postponed or rejected the formulation of proposals for a global alternative to capitalism. Given that that is the case, there is wide room for them to consolidate their position in the political system and even to lay the ground for further major advances both in terms of electoral support and of formulating more far-reaching alternatives. The actually existing capitalisms in Latin America have a series of exposed surfaces on which the left can write its critical proposals even without going so far as to criticise capitalism as a global system. When somewhere between two-fifths and three-quarters of the population live in poverty – and between a third and a half of them in extreme poverty – it does not require a great leap of imagination to see that there are enormous objective possibilities for the development of democratic and popular political perspectives. The effective occupation and expansion of these political spaces by the left might in fact provide a starting point for a strategy for gradual social change.

In this sense and within these limits, electoral processes and experiences of municipal or regional control are particularly relevant. At a time when large segments of the popular classes are distrustful of politics and politicians, local and regional administrations could prove to people that the left not only claims to be better, but actually is better. At the same time political power at these levels could provide the left with experience in dealing with matters which it has traditionally disregarded as irrelevant – such as facing concrete problems; the need to bring about effective and appropriate answers to them; budget management, among others. This is particularly relevant at a time when many people place greater emphasis on the management of local resources and on solving municipal-level problems than on national politics. It may also be that the presence of the left in these areas could have the important result of enhancing the reach of local administrations, taking advantage of the current emphasis by multilateral financial agencies on administrative decentralization and community participation. In this sense, this type of experience could help the parties and other organizations of the left to develop political responses to the problems they face, as opposed to the strong academic or ideological biases which has characterised many of its arguments and much of its language until now.

However, if the left aspires to something else than the local management of macroeconomic policies defined elsewhere it must be capable of articulating these local and regional levels with national politics. Poverty, social marginalization, insecurity, external debt, financial speculation, the reactivation of industry, democratization... all these issues inescapably call for an involvement at the national level, if there is to be the slightest hope of having even a minimal impact on them. In a context in which there is no global critique of capitalism, and in which furthermore the continued existence of representative democracy is taken as a point of absolute principle, it is nevertheless possible to overcome its limitations by articulating it with the many and varied forms of participatory democracy. In this sense, too, the experiences of local and provincial government in Brazil, Uruguay, Venezuela, Mexico among others provide some successful examples.

The combination of experiences of popular participation with the institutional procedures of representative democracy can also lead to a reelaboration of the concept and the practice of citizenship on the basis of the initiatives and interests of the popular classes, going beyond the distorting and limiting effect of the individualism through which citizenship is conceptualized in capitalist ideology. A reelaboration of citizenship which emphasises that part of its meaning which arises from social struggles for a decent life and for the collective design of a shared destiny. That is, a citizenship in which the exercise of individual rights is rooted in and enriched by the day to day practice of collective action. At bottom it is a question of recreating the concept of citizenship – just as the ruling class does it although from and in its self-interest, when calling for the collective exercise of their civil rights through corporate business pressures, manipulation of the mass media, mobilisation of government agencies and multilateral financial institutions, much more than through the exercise of the conventional principle of 'one person one vote'. From the point of view of the popular classes, it is a matter of legitimating a concept of citizenship which embraces the experiences of progressive collective action and of its own labour, settlers', women's, indigenous', or any other, organizations. In this sense, representative democracy would come to mean continuity and not rupture with the history of struggle and bargaining forged by the popular classes.

Tentatively then, and without being ingenuous, my hypothesis is that the current situation offers interesting possibilities to a left that is prepared to take them on board. Systems of representative democracy should not be seen as obstacles to projects for overall transformation; after all, the recent democratization of Latin America is, in the first instance, the result of the mobilizations, the struggles and the sacrifices of popular organizations and the organizations of the left. It could be argued that this was not the democracy that they fought for, but without popular involvement and the participation of the left, not even this would have been achieved. On the other hand, the attempts to develop along a revolutionary path have not been able to offer, thus far, very much more successful results. It is important, therefore, that we avoid fetishizing formal institutions and procedures – either from a positive or a negative stance.

Representative democracy is much more than the restricted – and often fraudulent and corrupt – versions 'actually existing' in several countries in our region. To accept the rules of the democratic game in these circumstances may mean doing democracy the greatest disservice, or at the very least accepting the blackmail of those who use the forms of democracy to reproduce the domination of minorities and further pervert the living standards of the popular majorities. Yet the refusal to participate in this farce does not automatically imply a turn to violent confrontation. A creative politics must be capable of finding or inventing effective ways of getting through these questions.

Once again the Latin American left must face the challenge of endowing democratic institutions with a real capacity to social transformation from the perspective of the popular classes. That is, to assess and strengthen the value of democracy without legitimating capitalism or abandoning the project for global socialist transformation. This involves searching and striving for sectoral or everyday improvements while focusing on the overall capitalist system as the very enemy to confront. When things are seen in historical perspective, we have to acknowledge that the difficulties we face today are neither greater nor less than those we have had to overcome in the past – but they are different. If the Latin American left was able in the violent, repressive and fraudulent contexts of the recent past to build a bridge of communication and representation to broad sectors of the popular classes, it would be foolish to suggest that in the present context, when possibilities are opening up within the institutional make-up, the enterprise is bound to fail. The efficacy of the Latin American left in building a solid popular base has always been founded on people's hopes rather than on their fears or just their needs. However, when odds look so deceitful, hopes have to be nurtured and raised by political education and commitment. Or, as Oliver Crommwell allegedly put it: 'Trust in God, and keep your powder dry'.

*Translation by Mike Gonzalez*

NOTES

1. For example Juan J. Linz and Arturo Valenzuela (eds): *The Failure of Presidential Democracy* (Johns Hopkins University Press, Baltimore,1994).

2. This piece continues from some of the author's previous writings: 'Is socialism still an alternative for the third world?' in W.K.Tabb (ed): *The future of socialism: perspectives from the left* (Monthly Review Press, New York, 1990) pp.205–218; 'What future for socialism?' in *NACLA Report on the Americas* XXV (5): May 1992: pp.13–16; 'After the Revolution: democratization and social change in Central America' in Shafik Jorge Handal and Carlos M. Vilas: *The socialist option in Central America: two reassessments* (Monthly Review, New York,1993) pp.79–143. For reasons of brevity the term 'Latin America' also includes the Caribbean.
3. See for example the compilation of source materials in Michel Lowy (ed): *Marxism in Latin America from 1909 to the present* (Humanities Press, New Jersey,1992) and Barry Carr and Steve Ellner (eds): *The Latin American left: from the fall of Allende to perestroika* (Westview Press, Boulder Co,1993).
4. Carlos M. Vilas 'Imperfect competition: the superpowers in Latin America' in John Weeks (ed) *Beyond superpower rivalry: Latin America and the third world* (New York University Press, New York, 1991) pp.83–93.
5. See Carlos M. Vilas: *The Sandinista Revolution: national liberation and social transformation in Central America* (Monthly Review Press, New York,1986); 'Nicaragua: a revolution that fell from the grace of the people' in *The Socialist Register 1991* (Merlin Press, London,1991) pp.302–321; *Between earthquakes and volcanoes: market,state and revolutions in Central America* (Monthly Review Press, New York,1995) – particularly chapter 5.
6. Carlos M. Vilas: *Transicion desde el subdesarrollo* (Nueva Sociedad, Caracas, 1989) pp.93–101.
7. However see Ernesto Giudice: *Imperialismo y liberacion nacional* (Granica, Buenos Aires, 1974) first published in 1940; also Cesar Germana: 'La polemica Haya de la Torre-Maritegui' in *Analisis* (Lima) 2–3 (April 1977) pp.143–181; Manuel Caballero: *Latin America and the Comintern 1919–1943* (Cambridge University Press, New York, 1986).
8. See for example Orlando Nunez Soto: 'La tercera fuerza social en los movimientos de liberacion nacional' in *Estudios Sociales Centroamericanos* 27 (1980) pp.141–157; and 'La ideologia como fuerza material y la juventud como fuerza ideologica'in J. Wheelock et al: *Estado y clases sociales en Nicaragua* (ANICS/CIERA, Managua,1982) pp.125–147; Carlos M. Vilas *The Sandinista Revolution* chap 3; 'Popular insurgency and social revolution in Central America' in *Latin American Perspectives* 56 (Winter 1988) pp.55–77; *Transicion desde el subdesarrollo* pp.49–74. It has also to be recalled that in the aftermath of the Cuban revolution and the Sino-Soviet controversy, several Communist parties experienced internal splits – as in Venezuela, Peru, Argentina, Brazil – which additionaly weakened their political hold.
9. Almost 60% of the delegates to the 1994 Congress of the Brazilian CUT were university graduates – in a country with 32 million illiterates: Iram Jacome Rodrigues: 'The CUT: new unionism at a crossroads' *NACLA REPORT ON THE AMERICAS* XXVII (6), May-June 1995, pp.3–34. In Argentina several trade unions participated in the privatization of state enterprises in their respective sectors (electricity, oil, maritime transport, commerce), thus becoming employers of their own members. The issue has provoked intense debates in Nicaragua on the privatization of state enterprises on behalf of their workers. See Carlos M. Vilas 'Farewell to the working class? Latin American workers after crisis and neoliberal reforms' in Sandor Halebsky and Richard Harris (eds): *Capital, power and inequality in Latin America* (Westview Press, Boulder, 1995) pp. 137–163.
10. Carlos M. Vilas 'Actores, sujetos, movimientos: Donde quedaron las clases?' in *Sociologica* 28, May-August 1995 pp.61–89.
11. It is a tragic irony that while the ruling classes remain firmly attached to the traditional motto 'divide et impera' (divide and conquer) in their relation to the working and popular classes, the so-called post-modern left has abandoned any meaningful concern for collective organization and struggles. A post-marxist left becomes fascinated with what

it considered to be a more sophisticated approach to social dynamics – as reduced to inter-individual contingent articulations – while the ruling classes indulge in what were once considered to be the simplistic views of Marxism – e.g. the actual manipulation of state power as a private tool for exploitation and domination.

12. FDNG represents the first attempt at a broad-based 'social-political left' and to unite Mayan and workers' and peasants' organizations since CUC (Comite de Unidad Campesina) fell victim to repression in the 1980s. Unlike CUC, FDNG also embraces human rights organizations and presented its own candidates in the November 1995 elections. On this occasion, and in spite of an aggressive institutional setting which included some fraudulent manipulations, FDNG collected about 8 percent of the overall turnout, thus appointing 6–7 reppresentatives to the Guatemalan parliament – all of them front-line union, human rights and indigenous organizations' activists, including several well-known women activists.
13. See a summary of the debate in Arghiri Emmanuel: 'The state in the transitional period', in *New Left Review*, 113–114 (Jan-April 1979) pp. 111–131.
14. The issue was initially posed by Michael Crozier et al in *The crisis of democracy* (New York University Press, New York, 1975) and then taken up again in the literature on transitions to democracy – e.g. Guillermo O'Donnell and Phillipe Schmitter, *Transitions from authoritarian rule: tentative conclusions about uncertain democracies* (Johns Hopkins University Press, Baltimore, 1986) esp. pp.13–14; Adam Przeworski, 'Democracy as a Contingent Outcome of Social Conflicts', in Jon Elster & Rune Slagstad (eds) *Constitutionalism and Democracy*. (Cambridge, Cambridge University Press, 1988) pp. 59–80.
15. FMLN (Frente Farabundo Marti para la Liberacion Nacional) was made up of five politico-military organizations: FPL (Fuerzas Populares de Liberacion, the largest one), the Salvadorean Communist Party (PCS), Ejercito Revolucionario del Pueblo (Revolutionary's People Army, ERP), Resistencia Nacional (RN), and the Central American Workers' Revolutionary Party (PRTC).
16. See the text of the Pact in *El Diario de Hoy* (San Salvador), 31 May 1995. Interestingly enough, the adherence of former leftists to this particular version of consensual politics has not been coupled by their right-wing partners: ARENA keeps on publicly honouring the memory of the late Roberto D'Abuisson (a founder of both ARENA and death squads, and according to the UN's Truth Commission the intellectual author of the massive killing of six Jesuit priests and two female university workers in November 1989) while its 'Principles, Goals and By-laws' remain committed 'To defend our Western traditions from the ideological assault as well the permanent aggression from international communism' as the party's primary goal.
17. See Vilas *Between earthquakes and volcanoes*, cit. chapt. 1.
18. See in this respect Carlos M. Vilas: 'Entre la democracia y el neoliberalismo: los caudillos políticos de la posmodernidad' in *Socialismo y Participacion*, 69, November 1994.
19. The belief that the time for armed struggle was definitively over for the left is also one of the central assumptions Jorge Castañeda's much publicized book *Utopia Unarmed.The Latin American Left After the Cold War*. (New York, Alfred Knopf, 1993).
20. *Shadows of Tender Fury. The Letters and Communiques of Subcomandante Marcos and the Zapatista Army of National Liberation*. (New York, Monthly Review Press, 1995).

# SOCIALISTS, SOCIAL MOVEMENTS AND THE LABOUR PARTY: A REPLY TO HILARY WAINWRIGHT

Barry Winter

In assessing the prospects for an independent socialist party in Britain in the 1995 *Socialist Register* [1], Hilary Wainwright draws on her long and extensive experience of left politics. She has set herself an exacting task: to update Ralph Miliband's review of the progress made in creating a new political formation between 1956 and 1976.[2] He envisaged a left-wing party 'able to attract a substantial measure of support and hold out genuine promise of further growth', but he concluded that after twenty years there was still nothing to show for it.

In contrast, Hilary examines the last two decades and claims that the prospects for a new party are now promising. To support this, she cites four 'very different' political developments which she thinks will combine to make this a possibility. These are the recent changes in the Labour Party and their effects on the Labour left; the rise of 'new' social movements and their new methods of organising; the collapse of the Soviet bloc and the opportunities this creates for libertarian socialists; and the increasingly international nature of politics and culture. I want to review these changes and question Hilary's reading of them: partly because I think that she makes too much of some of them; and partly because she neglects developments which, if taken into account, suggest something rather different. For these reasons, I find her often-repeated attempts to conjure up a new party unpersuasive.

My counter argument rests on the open acknowledgement that the socialist movement is in crisis – and insists that this crisis is as severe for those outside the Labour Party as it is for those who belong to it.[3] Although the humanitarian case for socialism is stronger than ever and even though opportunities are emerging, the dramatic demise of Communism and the more prosaic decline of social democracy have seriously damaged the whole of the left. This is true whether we agreed with either of these dominant traditions or whether our political lives have been spent contesting some of the harm that they have done.

We also have to face the hard truth that most people in our society are deeply hostile to what they see as politics. They are suspicious of people who peddle political ideas of whatever kind. Social and political conservatism and, in some cases, far more reactionary ideas prevail. This 'conservative culture', which inhibits any attempt to radically transform society, is partly produced by capitalist social relations. Unfortunately, social democracy and Communism have also reinforced social conservatism. In their different ways, they have helped to undermine the basis for socialism, in spite of the glaring social inequalities that exist. As a result, the political gap between radical socialists and the rest of society has become wider and deeper. For the vast majority of people, socialists are generally seen as having little or no relevance to the way that they experience or understand the world in which they live.

Sadly, sections of the radical left have contributed to this process of political isolation. Some groups mirror the worst features of the communist tradition; and some appear as archaic or simply odd. Many generate suspicion and disbelief among the relatively few people who come across them, repelling more support than they attract. Their appeal, such as it is, is often limited to idealistic but politically inexperienced young people, most of whom end up either drifting away or being driven away.

After some minimal progress, the Labour left today is also in a parlous state. Whether led by idiosyncratic parliamentarians, budding careerists or grass roots activists demanding democracy in one breath and denying it in the next, this left has an unfortunate record.[4] Some might go so far as to describe it as tragic. By opposing one-member-one-vote, for example, the Bennite left lost the moral high ground in battling with Labour right-wingers.[5]Many lived on the illusion that the denial of socialism by Labour leaders prevented a landslide of popular electoral support for a socialist programme. At times, futile battles were fought. Not only was the Benn-Heffer challenge for the party leadership in 1988 doomed to a massive defeat, but it exposed the Labour left as a marginal political force. [6] It has not recovered from these blows and this has helped its opponents to strengthen their grip on the party.

Some may argue that this portrayal of the current state of the left in Britain is very negative. If so, my defence rests on the need to be brutally honest. Too often, socialists have overdosed on false optimism and this has lured them into defeat and disillusionment. We simply cannot afford to keep repeating such mistakes. I also believe that, in some respects, my remarks echo Ralph Miliband's 1976 essay in which he surveys and dismisses the organised left and calls for a new political formation. It is when he completely rejects the Labour Party that I part company with him.

If we begin by acknowledging the political marginality of the left – and then try to understand its causes – this raises questions which Hilary does not seem to confront. Few reasons are offered to explain why, after forty years, those who shared Ralph's desire to set up an independent left still have so little to show for it.[7] More importantly, she does not review the progress of those on the left who saw a way forward through the Labour Party, or provide a clear analysis of its practice.[8] Such an analysis would benefit from not automatically assuming that the Labour Party is impervious to change, since this forecloses the debate before it starts.

While recognising the enormous difficulties which they faced, I believe that it is vital to examine the political perspectives of those who led, or who influenced, the Labour left. I think these perspectives were seriously flawed and resulted in the adoption of strategies and tactics which contributed to defeat. In particular, they seriously overestimated what could be achieved in the short term and underestimated the adverse political climate in which they were operating. Putting it bluntly, these lefts failed to recognise how they were losing support in the labour movement, and they neglected – or they were naive about – how the rest of society saw them and the Labour Party. It did not have to be like that. There were positive, political alternatives open to the left as some of us struggled to argue amidst the clamour (and sometimes amidst the abuse).[9] Unfortunately, angered by the intense hostility coming from the parliamentary party and their allies in the media, few on the Labour left were prepared to listen. Many fondly imagined that victory was within their grasp.

We can learn from this history. The interests of left unity should not be used to suppress dissenting voices; this type of unity impairs the clarity of analysis needed to underpin a socialist agenda and it is likely to prove self-defeating. So where does this take us? After all that has happened in recent decades, I want to suggest that in recognising the political gap between socialists and the rest of society the left is, in effect, starting again. We can, however, ask ourselves some crucial questions. Is it possible to create a left which has the potential to connect politically with the majority of people? In particular can we reach those people who have humanitarian concerns about what is taking place in society? Where will we find them and what will we say to them?

I think it is possible to develop this kind of left but it will take time. To gain a hearing, it needs to be a left located in the political mainstream. In this way, we can begin to make links and to gain support from people: some of whom will be found in the Labour Party where membership is currently rising, some of whom will be active in progressive social movements and far more, I suspect, will be involved in neither. The latter are more inaccessible but we must seek a variety of ways to reach them. We are dealing with heterogeneous constituencies which suggests that we should use all available forums for communication, both institutional and open, and employ suitable humility in analysis and strategy to people's real hopes and concerns. Voluntary isolation has no place in a new, assertive practice.

*The Changing Labour Party*

Hilary Wainwright offers a different focus. She considers that developments in the Labour Party will assist in the creation of her new political formation. She says that, under Tony Blair's leadership, the party has undergone some 'profound changes' because of its more explicit commitment to market-led economics and its lesser commitment to public expenditure and intervention. As a result, she notes that there is a growing discontent among party members, not restricted to the left, which will show itself should Labour win office. In her view, progress has also been made because the Labour left has learned to avoid 'beguiling short cuts' to socialism through taking control of the party's hollow structures. It is a more self-confident left than its predecessors, she claims, lacking illusions about its prospects, no longer believing that with a little more effort the party can be won to socialism.

While I hope that she is right about the Labour left no longer being tempted by apparent short cuts, I think the political scene looks rather different. It is more like a battlefield after a major defeat. The Labour left has been scattered. Some have deserted the field, others have changed 'sides', some are in a state of shock, others are polishing their bayonets, some are regrouping and many are nursing their wounds. If what remains of the left now lack illusions it may be because they also lack any clear idea of what can be done. Most are not battle-hardened soldiers preparing for the next sortie but people in considerable disarray. Hardly a cause for great optimism, I would suspect. In fact, the sizeable, self-confident Labour left that Hilary thinks already exists has still to be built.

The case for building and revitalising the Labour left rests on an argument about the continuing importance of the Labour Party in the foreseeable future. Many doubt the value of this kind of endeavour. Hilary stresses that in his 1976 essay Ralph describes Labour as being 'irretrievably tied' to reproducing capitalism. She reminds us that he claimed that it is a deeply and widely held illusion that the party can become an instrument for socialism, an illusion which holds the Labour left in 'permanent subordination'. While it is not entirely clear how far Hilary subscribes to these views, her longstanding desire for a new party – and the fact that she quotes Ralph without qualifying or questioning his remarks – suggests a close affinity with them.

In any case, I think that Ralph's approach to the Labour Party in the 1976 essay – a view which many on the left continue to uphold – was misguided. Not that I wish to make the counter claim and argue that Labour will be the agency for socialism. This only repeats a similar kind of error. Instead, I want to argue that social democratic parties are significant because they connect with what most people see as politics – in spite of the widespread cynicism about politics. In this optic, Labour is important because it may come to hold power. If we as socialists do not relate our politics to the Labour Party then in the public's view we hardly relate to the world at all. Perhaps Ralph had something like this in mind when he writes in his final work, *Socialism for a Sceptical Age*, that the radical left's best hope in the 'relevant future' lies in strengthening the left in social democratic parties.

To put it polemically, are we trying to relate to the mass of the population, via the Labour Party, or to the movements on the 'fringe'? The answer is that we need to do both but that means both. It is not enough to go where we think the radical action is. Instead of looking to the radical fringe as the solution to the conservative core, we must focus on the core itself. We have to begin to reach out to people who hold socially conservative views, intermixed as they may be with all sorts of other ideas. This takes us back to the Labour Party because most people in the party are not radically different from those in the wider society. If we can learn to communicate with the former then we are on the way to connecting with some of the latter and vice versa.

To argue for Labour's centrality does not mean holding any illusions about its record in office. There are many accounts which show that in a crisis Labour governments abandon their initial good intentions. Trapped by their lack of radicalism, they put the material interests of capital before those of labour. Indeed, the actions and arguments of the last Labour government helped prepare the ground for the subsequent swing to the right. The Labour Cabinet often reluctantly introduced measures which the Tories later took up with a vengeance. In this way, Labour acted as the political midwife of Thatcherism.[10] All this makes the debates in the Labour Party at such times even more important – and it will do so again. How that debate is conducted in the party, particularly how the Labour left conducts itself will be of considerable importance. What it says and does in the intervening period will also be crucial to the eventual outcome. From this perspective, those who simply anticipate the political fall-out that may result from such developments, hoping it will provide recruits to a new party, have vacated the political field.

We also have to be honest enough to recognise that Labour leaders generally reflect views that are closer to the party membership and to the wider society than ours. This means that we have to relate to the agenda which they set and respond in ways which are capable of winning a wider hearing. Labour lefts have often wrong-footed themselves by claiming that the party is being led, or misled, by a bunch of 'usurpers'.[11] This is a self-defeating illusion, implying that a change of personnel is really all that is needed: that if the present leadership can be replaced by some 'real' socialists, we will be on our way. While this argument has launched many a career in the labour movement, it conveniently ignores the real political processes at work, material pressures which have transformed generations of radical socialists into cautious reformers and which first need to be understood if we are to overcome them.

This brings us to the question of how to reconstruct a Labour left in the aftermath of the Bennite debacle and the rise of New Labour – and what the new formation should be like. As I have already argued, it will be a great help if it had a clear understanding of what went wrong and is willing to learn from these experiences. Having no illusions, something which Hilary values, simply is not enough. Claiming 'we was robbed' by out-of-touch party leaders will not do. Being oppositional is, and never was, enough. There are times when head-on confrontations are necessary and unavoidable. There are times when other, more subtle and strategic skills, are needed. There are also times when it is necessary to realise that the world has moved on, that we have to move with it or be left behind.

The bedrock of a future Labour left must be a clear commitment to genuine democracy and pluralism in its own practices, in the party and in the wider society. As I have already argued, this has not always been the case. The new Labour left must also learn how to connect with the rest of the party in a reasonable and tolerant manner. There have also been times in the recent past when this has not always been the case. It must be a left which is capable of winning respect and trust from people who do not agree with its ideas. Only then can it hope to secure their agreement in the longer term. It must be a left based on experience at the grass roots inside and outside the party, not one that is over-eager to play follow-my-parliamentary-leader yet again. In other words, New Labour needs a credible, new Labour left.

*Social Change and Social Movements*

It is not the Labour left which most appeals to Hilary, however, but the emergence of new social movements. For her, they provide the 'foundational change affecting prospects for a new political agency.' She acknowledges that these groups quickly wax and wane and that their significance is even now 'a little hazy'. She also records that they are fluid, diverse and highly localised and, while they have influenced the left, 'they are not entirely of the left.' Yet her enthusiasm for them is undimmed.

Before considering her reasons, a little more needs to be said about social movements. In the essay which precedes Hilary's, George Ross points out that those involved in such initiatives show a marked antipathy to the left because of the way that some lefts have treated them.[12] He adds that many 'are not socialist at all'. We can go further. In the essay which follows Hilary's, Frances Fox Piven is concerned about what she describes as 'the tide of identity politics'.[13] While she accepts that for some oppressed groups this has been a necessary development, she is also aware of the problems that it can create. She warns of the rise of 'hate-filled identity politics' which, she says, is partly the result of the massive dislocations of people set in motion by capitalist restructuring.

This means that we have to differentiate between the various social movements. On the one hand, some have made an invaluable, lively and creative contribution to radical politics, enlarging the meaning of politics itself – and Hilary has done much to make this known to a wider audience. On the other, there are social movements which presage a very dangerous future. Our reactions will range from welcoming some to resisting others, on the basis of their aims, methods and ethics. In Britain, we would oppose racially-motivated movements like the parents who withdrew their children from a Dewsbury school because of the preponderance of Muslim pupils. I would also want to resist separatist movements, like the campaign for single-sex education for Muslim girls. Even on 'our' side there are some that I prefer to keep at a critical distance. For example, some anti-racist groups show an enthusiasm for violence which I find deplorable.

If we take these comments as qualifying rather than questioning Hilary's enthusiasm for social movements, why does she place such faith in them? If I understand her correctly, it is not because they will give birth to a new political formation as such. Rather, it is because the socialist future is embedded in their practice in a very specific way. Unawares they are pioneering 'a new and distinctive political agency', as she puts it, in the way they organise, develop policies and mobilise new sources of power. Out of their practice will come forth a party, equipped with a political method fit for building socialism.

This strikes me as overloading them with too many expectations. Many radical movements may work in ways that empower the people involved and encourage participation. We may learn a lot from them. Organisations like CND have done this in the past without being harbingers of socialism or socialist practice. As Hilary says, some may even be models of social change that break with the mechanical ones found in some earlier socialist traditions. But there seems to be something of a gap between valuing current practices and seeing in this the makings of a new party.

My experience of recent social movements, particularly those opposing the Criminal Justice Bill, suggests a slightly less sanguine and less certain picture. This significant campaign brought together many young, unemployed people who showed great imagination and an energy which sometimes outran good organisation. They combined a sense of fun with a serious attack on the loss of civil liberties. They came into sharp conflict with the Socialist Workers Party which they felt was trying to turn its superior material resources to its own advantage. More significantly for my argument, the activists rarely managed to break out of their social ghetto and make wider connections.

This suggests a group of people who did the best they could in the circumstances. Likewise the motorway protestors and kindred campaigners have shown impressive skills and ingenuity. I have no wish to belittle their activities. Whenever people struggle some amazing things can happen. This has always been the case and there are numerous examples of what people can do when trying to take greater control of their lives, historically and contemporarily. All over the world, we can find people who are undertaking activities of this kind. Yes, in such actions we get a glimpse of a different future. Yes, it may be inspiring and a source of hope. It is only when Hilary suggests that in their methods they unwittingly prefigure her new political party that I begin to differ and when she later describes them as movements for 'socialist change' I feel that she goes too far.

*International Developments*

Another source of hope for a new party, Hilary claims, comes with the end of Communism. She says that the collapse of the Soviet Union has spelt the final crisis of an already confused and divided Communist Party in Britain. This has undermined attempts at social engineering from above and gives scope for the subordinate tradition of socialism from below. Exponents of the latter, she argues, have to face up to the realities of dealing with power. Again, this is only part of the picture. Arguably, what it also shows is that the widespread unease in our society about the Soviet Union, although fostered by right wing forces, was well founded. Most people became critical about the lack of democracy in the Eastern bloc and were repulsed by what they saw. They were largely unmoved by the arguments of pro-Soviet apologists. This healthy response has, nonetheless, left us with a legacy of suspicion about anything that smacks of socialism. To gain a hearing, we are going to have to prove that we are very different.

People are also aware that, as the commmand economy, Communism was an economic failure. This raises some tough questions about what an alternative socialist economy might look like and some equally tough questions about how we can begin to move in that direction. A heavy but exciting responsibility awaits us in working out a way towards a democratic economy. Until we do, we can hardly expect the wider society to pay us much attention. Until we have something better to offer, we cannot expect to make great progress. This is a debate which offers a lot of scope for dialogue between socialists both inside and outside the Labour Party.

Nothing in this process suggests to me that the end of Communism will necessarily lead towards the formation of a new socialist party, however. If anything, its collapse has done more to poison the public mind about socialism and has made many people less inclined to listen to us. It may have persuaded some people that attempting to radically change society only makes matters worse.

Hilary also argues that national sovereignty is being contested in ways that offer new openings for the left. That may be true, but she goes further. The prospects for direct political representation for her new socialist party have increased, she says, thanks to these internal and external challenges to the British state and the parties that cleave to it. Among the examples she gives are the pressure for electoral reform coming from Europe and the growing importance of the European Parliament which gives greater scope to its participants.

She sees these developments combining with a self-confident left's growing disillusionment with the Labour Party leading towards the founding of a new party. This disenchantment is true for those inside as well as outside the party, she says, and is partly due to the dropping of 'the party's founding socialist commitment'.[14] What we have here is speculation based on optimistic oversimplification. It is equally possible to suggest a more complex and potentially more dangerous picture. For example, electoral reform may happen. It may also give scope to forces on the right which may have a far greater potential for support than a politically isolated left. A swing to the right may be the outcome of the failure of a future Labour government. Therefore for Hilary to see in the developments simply the rise of a new socialist party could be to neglect the wider picture. For, even if it happens as she predicts, then the left could even be fighting for its political life.

But perhaps this argument takes us too far into the future. What I really wish to stress is that the gap between the left and the rest of society presents us with some immediate problems. What we do will help shape what happens and, right now, there is a pressing job to be done. It is imperative to build up the Labour left to meet these changed circumstances, as Ralph argues in his final work, It will be vital for that left to become politically credible in the wider society, in the labour movement and among progressive social movements. This must be based upon a widely-held recognition that what the left says and does is reasonable; that its political demands make sense; that it is not trying to cut corners or cheat in any way; and that it values and respects the work of independent political activists. Unless and until we begin to close the gap between socialists and the rest of society, then we cannot make very much of the opportunities which present themselves. Indeed, we may be at great risk.

Commitment to democracy will have to be a vital part of any reasonable left's political agenda. It can provide the basis for a broad appeal in a diverse and divided society. Who knows, it may even help us to focus on the main enemy, which is not the Labour Party leadership, but the undemocratic class of owners and controllers of capital who run our society, regardless of who is in government. This is the greatest challenge we face – to make our socialism relevant and coherent wherever we operate. This, I would suggest, is much more important and far more pressing than investing our hopes in the formation of a new political party.

*Postscript: the Socialist Labour Party*

'I believe that the case for a Socialist Labour Party is now overwhelming.'[15] With this ringing declaration, Arthur Scargill, the miners' leader, made known his intention to establish a new political party. He wants it to contest every seat in the next general election. His initiative rests on the claim that the changes to Clause Four of Labour's constitution in 1995 are not only 'an unmitigated disaster' but are virtually irreversible. Labour, he says, is now almost indistinguishable from the Democratic Party in the US, the German Social Democrats and the Liberal Democrats in the UK.

Although there are some who welcome this clarion call, the general reaction from the left has ranged from indifference to hostility. Writing in *New Times*, the Democratic Left journal, Kevin Davey is scornful, describing the timing as 'absurd' given the prospects of a Labour election victory. On the support the group is attracting, he claims: 'Arthur's party is over before it has started.'[16] No Labour MP has signed up and the Socialist Campaign Group of MPs has given the new party the thumbs down, insisting that it is not the time to leave the Labour Party. As this essay shows I share this view, but what of those socialists who for years have been arguing for a new left? Is this what they had in mind when they claimed to see positive signs of the emergence of a left party to challenge Labour?

The answer is, apparently not. Hilary Wainwright has called for a far-reaching debate instead, making it plain that she intends to reject the Socialist Labour Party.[17] In view of her previous arguments this is interesting. She candidly admits that Arthur Scargill has put people like her on the spot, noting that for a decade she and others have worked together 'with the long term possibility of a new party *at the back of our minds*' (my italics), but without any sense of urgency. She also notes that it has been the subject of 'hundreds of speculative meanderings over a pint'. I would suggest that there has been a little more to it than that. In 1995, for example, I had the opportunity to hear Hilary address meetings on these issues twice in one week and her contribution to the *Socialist Register* of the same year on the same subject is the reason for this article.

She also warns that Scargill's party could damage the chances of making a more effective, electoral challenge to Labour in the future. It would be better to wait until conditions for a new alignment, based on the prospect of winning mass support, are far more promising. This will be when we have proportional representation and a major split in the Labour Party, she argues.

Thus, having talked up the prospects for a new party in her articles and in many speeches, she is now talking them down in response to one being established. The wishful thinking, which I questioned earlier, has been replaced by a greater realism about the conditions facing the left, but where does that leave the politics? Until the new party of the kind that she envisages can be born, it becomes something of waiting game – waiting for proportional representation and waiting for Labour leaders in government to generate a split in the Labour Party. It ends up in political limbo: rejecting my argument that socialism can be regenerated in and around the Labour Party and from the base upwards; and rejecting the formation of a new party because of the centrality of the Labour Party. This leaves Hilary looking for crumbs of political comfort and, in spite of the wealth of her experience, it robs her of relevance. At a time when there are many people wanting to find ways forward, the message is blurred. At best, it seems to be suggesting that they should keep busy in the hope that in some ill-defined way this will be useful when things change for the better.

If this is the case, then it will not do. Socialist politics desperately needs to have direction itself and to be able to suggest it to others. We have to be practical visionaries offering people ways to make progress. Prolonged ambivalence is no more help than absolute certainty. So while trying to understand the complexity of the world, we must also strive to make our ideas relevant. We have to devise a living politics that makes sense to people now and which encourages them to participate in the process. That, for me, means taking commitment to the Labour Party very seriously.

So while allowing for intellectual doubt, we also have to make a commitment: to engage with political agencies that offer the prospect of some advance. It is not possible to build anything solid from the sidelines. The results of such efforts may sometimes be interesting, even entertaining, but they will also be ephemeral. Once made, our political commitment must be genuine. Anything less may suggest hypocrisy and even dishonesty to the people with whom we wish to make links. Socialists always have to make hard choices. For, as others have said, we are forced to live in interesting times.

## NOTES

My thanks to several comrades and friends in the ILP who have commented on earlier drafts of this article, in particular Sarah Bracking, Phil Knowles, Vin McIntyre and Eric Preston. Not all of them will be impressed with the outcome.

The postscript on the Socialist Labour Party and the left was written later in response to Arthur Scargill's well-publicised proposals to set up a new party.

1. Hilary Wainwright, 'Once More Moving On: Social Movements, Political Representation and the Left', *Socialist Register, 1995*, London: Merlin Press, 1995
2. Ralph Miliband, 'Moving On', *Socialist Register, 1976*, London: Merlin Press, 1976. Several critical replies were published in *Socialist Register, 1977.*
3. I share this general perspective with members of Independent Labour Publications (ILP), formerly the Independent Labour Party (ILP). Founded in 1893, the ILP co-founded the Labour Party in 1900 and affiliated to it. The ILP left the Labour Party in 1932. after the debacle of the second minority Labour government. It returned to the Labour Party in 1975 as Independent Labour Publications, a radical publications and pressure group. For a short history of the ILP and an outline of the modern ILP, see Barry Winter, *The ILP, Past & Present*, Leeds: ILP, 1993
4. The fullest statement of the ILP's views on the Labour Party and the left in this period appears in Eric Preston, *Labour in Crisis*, Leeds: ILP, 1983. Together with the pamphlet, Eric Preston, *A Hitch Hikers Guide to the Labour Party*, Leeds: ILP, 1987, this contrasts with Hilary Wainwright, *Labour: A Tale of Two Parties*, London, Hogarth Press, 1987.
5. Interestingly, Peter Hain MP, who was a leading member of the Labour Coordinating Committee in its left-wing period, now acknowledges that it was a mistake to oppose one member, one vote.
6. The Socialist Society lent support to this venture through its involvement in the Socialist Movement which attracted relatively large crowds for a time but which lacked substance. For a critique of the Benn-Heffer campaign, see Eric Preston, 'The Charge of the Benn Brigade.' *ILP Magazine*, Leeds: ILP, summer 1988.
7. As Hilary puts it: 'It is tempting to think of this network of disparate activists as a party in waiting; in reality it is a coalition of the disenfranchised with as yet no very clear definition of its future.' *Socialist Register, 1995*, p.93.
8. Most accounts of this period are either journalistic or impressionistic. The most promising analysis is Leo Panitch, 'Socialist Renewal and the Labour Party', *Socialist Register, 1988*. Although this begins impressively, it eventually disappoints. The author seems to be trapped by his premise that Labour is 'incapable of transformation' which cuts short a detailed consideration of the left's strategy itself. Instead, we are presented with a view of the Labour Party which makes any efforts to change it futile from the outset. Can we really be so sure?
9. See Eric Preston. op cit.
10. Op cit.
11. For an example of this approach in relation to the Kinnock leadership see Eric Heffer, *Labour's Future: Socialist or SDP Mark 2?*, London: Verso. 1986.
12. George Ross, 'Saying No to Capitalism at the Millenium', *Socialist Register, 1995*, London: Merlin Press, 1995
13. Frances Fox Piven, 'Globalizing Capitalism and the Rise of Identity Politics', *Socialist Register, 1995*, London: Merlin Press, 1995
14. In fact, when the Labour Party was founded in 1900, as the Labour Representation Committee, it did not have a socialist commitment. To ensure trade union leaders' support for the new party, its aims were restricted to securing political representation for labour. It was 18 years later, at the end of the first world war and after the Russian revolution, that the party adopted its formal commitment to common ownership, the famous Clause Four. This was replaced at the 1995 party conference after Tony Blair's successful campaign to persuade party members that the text should be modernised. The new clause begins by describing Labour as a democratic socialist party.
15. Arthur Scargill, Future Strategy for the Left: A discussion paper on the consequences of the Labour Party Special Conference, April 1995, and the Labour Annual Conference, October 1995
16. Kevin Davey, 'From King Coal to Clown Prince', *New Times*, 25 November 1995
17. Hilary Wainwright, 'Not Yet, Arthur', *New Statesman & Society*, 24 November 1995

# BUILDING NEW PARTIES FOR A DIFFERENT KIND OF SOCIALISM: A RESPONSE

Hilary Wainwright

Barry Winter and I share a common starting point: a common concern with how the left can connect and communicate with the majority of people.

He believes that the most effective strategy for socialists to reach the people is primarily through the Labour Party and through building the left within it. This conclusion rests on the idea that the left will not get a hearing unless it is positioned in 'the political mainstream' – and he tends to see such a location as being the Labour Party. Political activity outside the Labour party, he describes, though not totally dismissively, as 'the fringe'.

His argument also depends on the idea that, after all, most of the people in the Labour Party are pretty representative of the wider population and if we can communicate effectively inside the party we are 'on the way to connecting' with this wider population. He believes that failures of the Labour left to achieve this wider influence are a result of major tactical blunders and anti-democratic behaviour rather than due to deeper limits on change built into the Party's institutions – which in turn, I will argue, shape, though not justify, some of the Labour left's undoubted mistakes.

I believe, by contrast, that the left's position inside the Labour Party has changed from being the opportunity it arguably was in the past into an imprisonment, which actually distorts and constrains the left's ability to convince the people of the relevance of radical socialist politics. The implication of my argument is that any section of the left which restricts its political location to the Labour Party and refuses seriously to consider the prospect of a party to the left of Labour, isolates itself from the people. It will make *itself* marginal, 'on the fringe' of political debate. My case is that in the long or even medium run, the most effective way for the radical left in the UK to engage with the political mainstream, as in most other West European countries, is with a political voice to the left of social democracy. This is not to say that working through such a party is an exclusive option; there would still be a significant left working mainly within the Labour party as, for example, in Denmark, Germany, Norway, Holland and Spain where there is a significant social democratic left, strengthened by the existence of a political competitor to social democracy's left. (Incidentally, Ralph Miliband explicitly assumes the influence of such radical sources of electoral as well as social pressure when he argues that the radical left's best medium term hope lies in strengthening the left in social democratic parties. He still held to his analysis of the limits of working from a permanently subordinate position within these parties).

This fundamental difference in strategy towards a shared goal influences our understandings of the importance of social movements, the political ramifications of the collapse of Soviet Communism, the decline of social democracy and the pressures of Europe and Scotland on Britain's unwritten constitution – the further points of disagreement itemised in Winter's critique. I will dwell first on the source of the strategic difference and secondly set out the case for seriously preparing for parties of the radical left which present an electoral challenge to Labour (I put it in the plural because such preparations for an electoral – as well as extra-parliamentary – coalition are already underway in Scotland).

In the Labour Party's early years, the structure of the party, based on trade union affiliations as well as the affiliation of political societies and parties did provide for the left a captive audience of politically alert listeners. There were several reasons for this, both to do with the character of trade unions in that period and the early structure of the trade union/ party alliance. First, trade union membership then was a much more conscious commitment, a commitment to collective resistance to the employers and more often than not, the state. Although one should be wary of generalising, it was a commitment against the grain of majority opinion, and often taken at some risk. As a result trade union branches and the structures built up from them, trades councils, district committees and so on, were generally lively and well-attended, real live centres of debate, discussion and action about the needs of working class people. This in turn influenced the character of union participation in the Labour Party, especially at a local level. After all, Trades Councils were 'Trades and Labour Councils' affiliated to the Labour Party. Left activists could with real justification assume that the trade union affiliates with whom they were working and arguing as they built the Labour Party were a live connection between socialists and the wider public.

In the last 60 years, changes in the character of the unions and in the structure of party–union relations have turned this captive activist audience into something nearer the dead souls of Tom Nairn's famous description of the block vote. Ironically, the very success of the Labour Representation Committee's original project, to establish the trade unions as a legitimate estate of the realm, weakened the role of Labour's union affiliates as a live connection between the left in the Labour Party and the public outside.

Moreover it made the block basis of affiliation and representation open to abuse, by left and right, since the union delegates casting votes in highly politicised discussions, were representing a membership which, except in rare periods of mass industrial action, or on issues directly affecting their interests, were politically apathetic.

Since the 1960s, ever since trade unions had the almost habitual, indeed with the check-off system, automatic, support of over 30% of the population rather than a small, class conscious minority, the left in the Labour Party has faced a serious dilemma: to win any serious influence in the Labour Part and to do so on a sustainable and democratic basis, the left had to convince a significant section of this mass trade union membership to support left socialist policies. Such a task itself requires a political party, with its own press, campaigns and education, able to reach beyond the full-time and lay officials representing the membership in the forums of the Party. In other words to move Labour to the left, the left needed their own organisation with equivalant functions – other than electoral – to a party.

In its heyday in the 1920s, this is what the Independent Labour was, a left party within the larger federated structure of the Labour Party. The Communist Party also tried to play this role, first by attempting to affiliate to the party then by acting in effect as the industrial wing of the Labour left. Apart from the limits of the Communist party as an advocate of democratic socialism, the Labour Party became increasingly centralised, losing many features of its genuinely federal political character, making any kind of dual membership or lasting alliance with another political party – even one which abstained from independent electoral activity – virtually impossible. One reaction to this and to Labour's dramatic turn to the right under Ramsey MacDonald, was a split in the ILP with an initially significant section leaving to form their own electoral party. At that stage, without a proportional electoral system and without any trade union support, such a move did not solve the dilemma (though those who tried to maintain the ILP's existence inside the party were no more able to overcome the dilemma than those outside).

There have been moments of course, when industrial and political developments have radicalised the mass of trade unionists, without the midwife of a socialist party. The mid-1970s, with the miners' strike bringing down Prime Minister Edward Heath was such a moment. This produced the move to the left in the trade unions which gave the Bennite left its hope of victory. But the ultimate defeat of Bennism illustrates the dilemma of the left described above. The 'Bennite' left did not have the sort of organisation – in effect a campaigning, educational political party – which could have worked at the base of the unions to build on the organic militancy of that period and turn it into a sustained shift in consciousness. They had an organisation that could lobby trade union representatives, at many different levels; but beyond activist newsletters, local rallies and conference fringe meetings, it could do little more. In tactical terms it was an impressive organisational effort. As such it was able to harvest the consequences of an earlier shift in consciousness but it could not sustain and deepen that radicalisation. All too often, as Winter implies, it accepted the undemocratic mechanisms of the block vote because they worked in the left's favour. On the other hand, there were occasions when the campaign for constitutional change and for Benn to be leader did open up debate in the unions to a remarkable degree. Where they were successful, however, they could not maintain the commitment. They often ended up controlling structures where there was no sustained base of support for their position. This is one factor behind the relative ease of Tony Blair's rout of the left.

Sometimes the left was able to use control of the institutions, however hollow their initial popular content, to built popular support. Ken Livingstone's radical but immensely popular GLC would be a case in point. But more often than not the necessity to defend or win control over structures in which political participation is low has tied up the energies of Labour left activists in inward-looking wrangles. Thus while there are many critical lessons to be drawn about the tactics of the Labour left in the 1980s, I would argue that what dragged them down was the structures they inhabited of which they were insufficiently critical.

The only solution to the left's dilemma within our present electoral and party system would be the possibility of dual membership of Labour as a coalition party, with other political parties of the left. The (unique) relationship between the ANC and the South African Communist Party illustrates the possibility; a relationship with many similarities to the ILP's relationship to the Labour Party in its early days. But even to make the comparison, highlights how radically the Labour Party has changed since the fluidity of those early years. The process of making itself electable on the terms set by the British establishment, has led the party to mirror the establishment's view of the left and treat it as an embarrassment, something to be hidden, camouflaged and otherwise side-lined. Frosts from the Cold War at different periods have stiffened this anti-pluralist ethic.

This ditching of pluralism for reasons of electoral expediency has become extreme in reaction to four successive defeats, all blamed to various degrees on the left. It is this which has created a felt need on the left for their own political voice.

My case for such an independent voice does not rest on optimism as Winter implies. On the contrary it is because of the serious difficulties facing the left that such a political initiative needs to be prepared, through careful negotiation. In particular, there is a growing awareness of the need to work now to prepare a positive focus for the disillusion that will set in under what we might as well call 'Blatcherism'. People remember that as disillusion set in under Callaghan and the first moves towards monetarism, there was an ominous growth in electoral support for the far right. Racism and xenophobia are now more firmly entrenched in the Conservative party than ever before, as indicated by the resignations and growing disaffection of its 'Christian democrats'. A left that simply continues with a 'business as usual' routine in the Labour Party, however hard-working, cannot create the confident alternative that will be necessary to prevent Portillo and his crew from sailing to power on the demoralisation created by Blair.

It is because this need for new directions – diffuse and inchoate though these presently may be – is widely felt that the basis for new political initiatives exists. My examples of a new confidence amongst some leading left MPs, for instance, were intended not to imply some revival of the Labour left but to illustrate how when some left MPs made common cause with campaigns outside the Labour Party and helped these movements gain a popular platform they had a real impact, bridging that chasm between socialists and the rest of society. This is leading to a detached co-habitation between many on the Labour left and the leadership of the party. They inhabit the same home but even more than before follow entirely different political lives.

Similarly my focus on recent progressive social movements was not driven by some naive presumption that they could give virgin birth to a new political party. It is rather that in their practice, influenced as it was and is, by the failure both of social democracy and Soviet communism, they have been testing out new methods of organising, new understandings of social change, and in particular the connections that link individual consciousness self-awareness, practical knowledge and skill to the collective capacity and the collective power to transform structures. A critical development of these insights needs to be central to the left's future initiatives if they are not to be dogged by past failures.

Barry Winter says that for me the past does not weigh heavily. In one sense that is true. But it is not because I have taken the social movement escapism pill. Rather it is because as someone who became a socialist in opposition to the actual experience of both Soviet Communism and social democracy, I have sought since their collapse and demise, to think through why and how the libertarian left with which I have identified is different. This does not mean that I now believe that the libertarian left, influenced as it is by involvement in social and radical trade union movements, has a clear programme and strategy. But it does mean I have a clear, methodological, as well as substantive sense of why the socialism for which, with many others, I am working, is different; why in a certain sense the past in so far as it is the past of regimes and governments that ruled in the name of socialism, is not my past.

In elaborating a different kind of socialism we need to learn from the past and especially to discover socialist traditions that have been suppressed and marginalised. But with perspectives clarified by an understanding of history and a knowledge of previously hidden continuities, a modern vision of socialism can best be made practical through focusing reflective attention, with an international lens, on present and future experiments in social co-operation, public ownership and democratic participation.

While Barry Winter may consider that I am cavalier towards the past, I find that for Barry the present does not sufficiently impinge. In particular the present state of decay of the British state and the pressures it is under from within – most notably Scotland, but also the implosion of the royal establishment, the revelations of the Scott inquiry, the rebellions of the young and poor whose city councils can no longer provide public services – and from without, the steady encroachment of European integration. Barry Winter rather begrudgingly admits that the unstoppable pressure for constitutional reform is likely to lead to electoral reform. This, he says, might give scope to the forces of the right. Indeed it might. In fact constitutional reform of itself is never automatically progressive. That is why the left needs to be well ahead of the process, not just predicting that change might happen and that the picture is complex and dangerous. We need to spell out what kind of electoral reform, what kind of bill of rights, what powers for local and regional government, what kind of republic. And knowing that electoral reform at Westminster is almost unavoidable as the pressure surrounds this archaic citadel on all sides, we need to prepare to make the most of it to give political expression to the millions of people who presently feel disenfranchised. If anything is going to play into the hands of the right, it is to imagine that the 'inside left' can change the Labour Party to provide an adequate voice for the generations of disaffected voters it has alienated in the past.

I detect in Barry Winter's writing an effort to maintain a taboo. A taboo on serious discussion of what is part of the political scene in virtually every West European political system: a party to the left of social democracy, trying with varying degrees of success to rethink socialism, but with a continuing commitment to a different economic and social system. In effect it is a taboo, prevalent in England at least, on openly imagining what possibilities might emerge under democratic constitutional arrangements – as if the left had some vested interest in the existing unwritten constitution and should not think beyond it.

At the end of 1995 Arthur Scargill had the confidence – born of frustration and a touch of arrogance perhaps – to break the taboo. Scargill's virtue is his ability to identify an injustice and insist publicly on action to right the wrong – whether the government's pit closure plans or the political injustice of the radical left's exclusion from political representation. His flaw, in my opinion, is his voluntaristic presumption that others might follow his lead despite the absence of the prior process of coalition building that could produce a more strategically effective initiative. It is up to others who share some elements of his long term goal to respond to his initiative and turn it into a far reaching debate that may well end up with outcomes different from that which Scargill presently proposes. At the time of writing it appears unlikely that this will be possible. It is likely that others on the left with different timetables and more inclusive ways of organising will need to pursue their own discussions (for instance left organisations from within the Green party, the Labour party, the Democratic Left and independent socialists in the Socialist Movement and Red-Green network are already engaged in a process of convergences).

The problem of left political representation which he addresses is too important to leave to Scargill. It is not just a crisis of representation for his particular brand of socialism but for all those – left greens, for example – who believe in a socialisation of wealth and a transformation rather than mere amelioration of capitalist political economy. Now that the Mandleson/Blair leadership is following to its practical conclusion the view that everything associated with the left's influence in the early 1980s has to be exorcised, it has become an urgent issue. Many long-term Labour activists have made the painful decision to leave the party: others have made the equally painful decision to hang on for the time being. Many politically active citizens are homeless or lodging in temporary accommodation.

But the silencing of the left is not just a matter of frustrated activists. A small, but significant number of voters also feel that their views no longer have a legitimate voice in the political system. It's not just the anecdotal evidence of local left activists who have told me about how they have been rung up by people who want details of Scargill's new party, or indeed of the reports from his office of hundreds of requests, especially from trade unionists, for party cards. Opinions polls show significant minorities with views on taxation, public spending, privatisation and public ownership to the left of New Labour's. There is also the question of the marginalisation of what Fenner Brockway called the 'outside left' for the wider political culture. The suppression of this left by the current Labour machine is an extreme response to the way in which the electoral system makes the floating voter the magnet to which the main parties are drawn. There is an inbuilt pressure on Labour to look over its right shoulder which can only be countered by pressures in the party bolstering up the left against short-term electoral imperatives – a diminishing possibility after four electoral defeats – or by an electoral competitor to labour's left, which is not a serious possibility until there is real momentum towards the introduction of a proportional electoral system.

As the transformation of Labour into a party of modern capitalist management proceeds apace, however, the refusal of many Labour Party socialists seriously to discuss even the long term prospects and conditions for a new party will become a seal on their own subordination. Their timidity in providing an intellectual and campaigning alternative focus – if not an electoral one – increases the humiliating phenomenon of grown men and women slavishly obeying a leader who is intellectually vacuous, however tactically brilliant he and his team may be.

The case for a left electoral challenge to Labour and hence for proportional representation is a perfectly respectable one which could quite legitimately be supported by people within the party. A left electoral challenge under a proportionate electoral system would overcome the bias towards the centre; it would provide both a left ally for and pressure on Labour in government – opening up, formalising and in effect making democratic the coalition that the labour movement claims to be. None of this case adds up to the kind of 'betrayal' of which some Labour socialists accuse anyone who advocates even serious debate about a left party.

Moreover, there are a variety of ways short of an electoral challenge to Labour, in which the left inside and outside the Party could work together campaigning and refining shared socialist policies in the build-up to the election and in opposition to many of the policies that a new Labour government will pursue. The exact timing of an electoral challenge could then be open, to wait for conditions in which such a challenge would gain mass support, rather than lost deposits.

But what are the conditions for left party, parties or an electoral alliance to come into being as an effective political force? The experience of northern Europe where left parties have between 8 and 18% of the vote points to two conditions: first the existence of a proportional electoral system and secondly the occurrence of a major split in a Communist or social democratic party or both. In New Zealand, working with the colonial legacy of a Westminster first-past-the-post system, a split from the Labour Party there in response to the Thatcherite economic policies pursued by a Labour government led to the creation of a new left breakaway led by Jim Anderton, which, in coalition with an already-established Green Party and radical Maori party, has proved not only a serious electoral challenge to Labour but also a decisive factor in overturning the electoral system. But the breakaway was equivalent to Tony Benn, Ken Livingstone and Peter Hain, if not Robin Cook and Michael Meacher, splitting from British Labour.

In Britain, the historical lack of a strong communist party, the demise of the Independent Labour Party and Labour's monopoly of labour-movement political representation – partly thanks to an electoral system designed to protect the establishment – has denied the left a base from which a challenge to Labour might grow organically. In this context, a few sustained campaigning movements, notably CND, have periodically acted as a convivial shelter for the politically homeless.

Discussion of the prospects for a new left party or electoral alliance in Britain needs to take account of very different national dynamics, especially in Scotland and England. In Scotland, as already mentioned, there is, in preparation for a Scottish parliament, work under way for a left electoral alliance. One of the possible components, Scottish Militant Labour, has already a small number of local government seats. The Scottish National Party is itself, on present policies, a left electoral challenge to Labour. In England, too, the emphasis has to be on preparations. After all, there is much to prepare for: the strong possibility of a real momentum towards electoral reform, assuming the Lib Dems are in a strong position after the election; the strong likelihood of policies proposed by a Labour government for which many left MPs will find it impossible to vote.

There are also many preparatory problems to consider – for example, problems of structure that determine how one approaches questions of programme and policy. Scargill's proposal extols the original constitution of Labour, with its coalition-like character. Moreover, he stresses that 'radical opposition in Britain is symbolised not by the Labour and trade union movement, but by the groupings such as those which defeated the poll tax, the anti-motorway and animal rights bodies, Greenpeace and other anti-nuclear campaigners, and those fighting against open-cast mining'. But the structure he proposes, 'a simple socialist constitution', does not allow for the diversity and flexibility that a coalition of left political organisations and a closer relation with these new movements would require.

Then there is the question of electoral intervention. If the preparations followed the Scottish model, then there could conceivably be a selective and realistic electoral intervention even at the next election. It could involve support for socialist Labour MPs, Green Party candidates and the left of Plaid Cymru in Wales, plus one or two high-profile challenges in safe Labour seats with leading New Labour MPs or safe Tory seats – if there are such things.

Finally, there is the question of policy. Again, given the fissiparous state of the left, it would be more realistic if the coalition of electoral-alliance model were followed and an agreed platform of economic, constitutional, social and international themes drawn up instead of a detailed party manifesto. A green socialist alliance of this kind would not be exclusively electoral. It would provide a platform and information exchange for the variety of trade union and green campaigns now emerging. Even during the election campaign, it could organise for policies and support for extra-parliamentary campaigns where it did not back a particular candidate.

A vacuum has been steadily opening up in British politics to which Scargill has now responded, without any of the political sensitivity needed effectively to begin to fill it. If the radically minded left inside the Labour Party is to help to renew the left, it will not suffice to scoff at the idea of a new left. The possibility is irreversibly on the agenda, the debate is about what kind, when, following what preparations, negotiations, period of non-party coalition. For this, the left in Britain needs to learn from the successes and failures of the radical left across the world. Just as the British establishment, Labour as well as Conservative, can no longer cling on to the political cosiness of a two party monopoly, so the British left can no longer plead 'British peculiarities' and retreat into inner Labour Party obscurity. It has to learn, drawing on international experiences, how to take its message to the people, independently, no longer under the cover of Labour.

## NOTES

1. See *Arguments For a New Left: Answering the Free Market Right*, Oxford: Blackwells, 1994.